Palgrave Studies in the History of Finance

The study of the history of financial institutions, markets, instruments and concepts is vital if we are to understand the role played by finance today. At the same time, the methodologies developed by finance academics can provide a new perspective for historical studies. Palgrave Studies in the History of Finance is a multi-disciplinary effort to emphasise the role played by finance in the past, and what lessons historical experiences have for us. It presents original research, in both authored monographs and edited collections, from historians, finance academics and economists, as well as financial practitioners.

More information about this series at
http://www.palgrave.com/gp/series/14583

Chris Briggs · Jaco Zuijderduijn
Editors

Land and Credit

Mortgages in the Medieval and Early Modern European Countryside

palgrave
macmillan

Editors
Chris Briggs
Selwyn College
Cambridge, UK

Jaco Zuijderduijn
Lund University
Lund, Sweden

Palgrave Studies in the History of Finance
ISBN 978-3-030-09763-9 ISBN 978-3-319-66209-1 (eBook)
https://doi.org/10.1007/978-3-319-66209-1

Printed on acid-free paper

This Palgrave Macmillan imprint is published by Springer Nature
The registered company is Springer International Publishing AG
The registered company address is: Gewerbestrasse 11, 6330 Cham, Switzerland

Acknowledgements

In July 2015, an international workshop on 'Mortgages in the European countryside, 1200–1700' was held at Selwyn College, Cambridge, in an effort to facilitate fresh scholarly discussion of an historically important yet somewhat neglected family of financial instruments: mortgages and annuities. The majority of the chapters in this book began life as papers presented at this lively meeting. Following the workshop, we were fortunate to secure further chapters from authors who had not presented on that occasion, namely Eline Van Onacker, Michael Schraer, and Giuseppe De Luca and Marcella Lorenzini. Furthermore, Craig Muldrew kindly agreed to attempt to draw out the common threads of the various contributions (as he had at the workshop) in an Afterword to the volume. We would like to thank the Economic History Society, the British Agricultural History Society, and the managers of the Ellen McArthur Fund (Faculty of History, University of Cambridge) for the financial support that made the workshop possible. We also wish to express our special thanks to Juliet Gayton for her help in organizing the workshop, and her wider input into this project. Finally, we thank the editorial team at Palgrave for their patience and support as we brought this volume to completion.

August 2017

Chris Briggs
Jaco Zuijderduijn

Contents

Editors and Contributors

About the Editors

Chris Briggs is a Senior Lecturer in the Faculty of History, University of Cambridge, a member of the Cambridge Group for the History of Population and Social Structure and a Fellow of Selwyn College, Cambridge. He is the author of *Credit and village society in fourteenth-century England* (2009) and of several articles and chapters on credit, law and living standards in the medieval rural world. He is co-editor of the journal *Continuity and Change.*

Jaco Zuijderduijn is Lecturer in the Department of Economic History, Lund University. He has published widely on financial history, including the monograph *Medieval capital markets. Markets for renten, state formation and private investment in Holland (1300–1550)* (2009). In addition, he has studied the household economy in the pre-modern era, focusing on how individuals used financial markets during the life cycle. This theme is also present in his most current research interest: ageing and retirement in pre-modern Europe.

Contributors

Elise M. Dermineur is an Associate Professor of history at Umeå University and a Pro Futura Scientia Fellow at the Swedish Collegium for Advanced Study in Uppsala. Dermineur's publications include articles in the *Journal of Social History*, *Journal of Interdisciplinary History*, *Traverse Revue d'Histoire—Zeitschrift für Geschichte*, and *Social Science History*, among others. In 2017, she published *Gender and Politics in Eighteenth-Century Sweden*, a political biography of the Swedish queen Lovisa Ulrika (1720–1782). She is currently editing a collection of essays on women and credit activities in preindustrial Europe (Brepols, 2018).

Giuseppe De Luca is Professor of economic history at the University of Milan, and holds a Ph.D. in economic and social history from the Bocconi University. He has been visiting professor in several Spanish universities and has recently devoted his research effort to the interplay between finance and economic growth, and to the evolution of infrastructure financing. He is co-editor with Youssef Cassis and Massimo Florio of *Infrastructure finance in Europe. Insights into the history of water, transport, and telecommunications* (Oxford University Press, 2016), and his other recent publications include 'Informal credit and economic modernization in Milan (1802–1840)' *Journal of European Economic History* (2013); 'Milanese finance, 1348–1700', in *Handbook of key global financial markets, institutions, and infrastructure* (2013); and 'Between theory and reality: economic crises and the historiography of early modern Europe', in *Merchants in time of crisis (16th to mid-19th Century)* (2015).

Nicolas De Vijlder is a Ph.D. student at Ghent University, where he was involved in a research project on the rural land market in the Southern Low Countries during the fifteenth and sixteenth centuries.

Juliet Gayton (Ph.D. University of Exeter, 2013) is an independent researcher specializing in the rural history of seventeenth-century England. She focusses on customary copyholders, their land tenures and transfer behaviour in the land market. This latter includes both permanent transfers of inheritance, sale/purchase, and *inter vivos* surrenders and Life exchanges and the temporary sub-letting of both land and dwellings. An important related aspect is the use of copyhold land in the borrowing and lending of mortgage loans with its implications for the rural credit market. Her work also involves examining the different patterns of activity between male and female copyholders.

Michael Limberger is Associate Professor at Ghent University. His research focusses on the economic and financial history of the Southern Low Countries during the late medieval and early modern periods.

Marcella Lorenzini is postdoctoral researcher at the University of Trento. She holds a Ph.D. in Business History from the University of Milan and is focusing on the dynamics of informal credit markets in early modern Europe. She is co-editor with D'Maris Coffman and Cinzia Lorandini of the volume, *Financing in Europe: Evolution, Coexistence and Complementarity of Lending Practices from the Middle Ages to Modern Times,* (Palgrave Studies in the History of Finance). Her latest publications include 'The credit market and notaries in Verona in the second half of the seventeenth century', *Journal of European Economic History* (2015) and 'Infrastructure financing in the early modern age. The beginning of a "Little Divergence"', in *Infrastructure finance in Europe. Insights into the history of water, transport, and telecommunications,* ed. Y. Cassis, G. De Luca and M. Florio (2016).

Craig Muldrew is a Professor in the Faculty of History, University of Cambridge and a specialist in in early modern economic and social history. He has published two monographs, *The economy of obligation* and *Food, energy and the creation of industriousness: work and material culture in agrarian England, 1550–1780.* He has also written articles in the field of legal history concerning debt litigation and its relationship to the nature of community, on the cultural nature of money and on wages in the early modern period. He is also interested in the importance of industrial growth in the early modern English economy and is engaged on a long-term project examining the development of the concept of self-control and its effect on the structure of community and on the creation of savings, as well as how local paper credit came to be trusted in eighteenth-century England.

Michael Schraer graduated from the University of Cambridge in 1976 with a Double First in Economics before embarking on a successful career as a government and corporate economist and, latterly, as a senior executive in corporate strategy, corporate finance and real estate management. In 2016, he obtained a Ph.D. from Cambridge entitled 'Real estate and the Jews of the crown of Aragon, 1150–1400'. He has also published 'Salamon Abnarrabi—a Jewish rentier in late fourteenth-century Zaragoza', *Journal of Medieval Iberian Studies* (2015). His research interests include the economics of medieval real estate, economic history of the medieval Iberian Jews and the anti-Jewish riots of 1391 in Castile and the crown of Aragon.

Eline Van Onacker is a postdoctoral research fellow (FWO Flanders) at the University of Antwerp. In her Ph.D. (soon to be published by Brepols as *Village elites and social structures in the fifteenth- and sixteenth-century Campine area*), she dealt with inequality and social stratification within a peasant region. Her current research focuses on how different types of communities and different social groups dealt with periods of grain crisis. Formal (poor relief) and more informal (land and credit markets, informal networks) mechanisms of redistribution and coping and access to food are at the core of her research.

D. P. Waddilove is the Newton Trust Research Fellow at St. Catharine's College, Cambridge. He is a legal historian of early modern England with special interest in development of financial law in the Court of Chancery. His Ph.D. dissertation, 'Mortgages in the early modern Court of Chancery' examined mortgages as an instrument of secured lending in the early modern period and explored the origins of equitable doctrines underpinning the law of mortgage in common-law states. He was both an undergraduate and Ph.D. student at St. John's College, Cambridge before beginning his Ph.D., he earned a master's degree from Yale University and a law degree from the University of Michigan and practised commercial litigation in the USA.

Imogen Wedd studied social sciences at the University of Sussex, followed by a postgraduate diploma in law (Common Professional Examination) and qualification as a Company Secretary. After bringing up her two children she worked as manager for law firms in the south and east of England for a number of years, before going back to study. In 2009, she completed a master's degree in history at the University of Cambridge and is now working towards a Ph.D.

Abbreviations

AHR	American Historical Review
C&C	Continuity and Change
EcHR	Economic History Review
JEH	Journal of Economic History
P&P	Past & Present
TNA	The National Archives, London

List of Figures

List of Tables

CHAPTER 1

Introduction: Mortgages and Annuities in Historical Perspective

Chris Briggs and Jaco Zuijderduijn

Mortgages were among the most important and widely used financial instruments in the pre-modern European countryside; offering land as a collateral for a loan was a technique used from the Mediterranean to the British Isles. Land was a popular form of collateral for loans because it cannot disappear, or be taken away or hidden from creditors (or: mortgagees), and is therefore generally regarded as a particularly strong security. Only land has this particular quality: all other assets can be destroyed or removed by debtors (or: mortgagors) trying to prevent creditors to recover losses. Similarly, persons acting as guarantors and sharing liability for a debt can become impoverished, run off or pass away.

No wonder then that land was already used as a security in Biblical times. The book of Nehemiah, written around 400 BCE, and describing events around 450 BCE, already mentions the mortgaging of land by

C. Briggs (✉)
University of Cambridge, Cambridge, UK
e-mail: cdb23@cam.ac.uk

J. Zuijderduijn
Lund University, Lund, Sweden
e-mail: cornelis_jaco.zuijderduijn@ekh.lu.se

C. Briggs and J. Zuijderduijn (eds.), *Land and Credit*,
Palgrave Studies in the History of Finance,
https://doi.org/10.1007/978-3-319-66209-1_1

peasants looking to cope with dearth. By doing this, the peasants managed to borrow, so they could buy food, but there was also a downside to the transaction, as the debtors lost their right to the land for as long as they did not repay their creditors. They complained: 'we are helpless because our fields and vineyards belong to others' (Nehemiah 5:3–4). Hearing of this, an angered Nehemiah then proceeded to speak to the creditors, telling them:

> please, give back to them this very day their fields, their vineyards, their olive groves and their houses, also the hundredth part of the money and of the grain, the new wine and the oil that you are exacting from them. (Nehemiah 5:11–12)

Apparently, as this chapter from the Book of Nehemiah shows, 2500 years ago creditors were willing to lend on collateral of land and this continued to be a preferred security ever since.

This volume is dedicated to the use of land as a collateral for loans. This topic is first of all important from a financial-historical point of view, as it deals with the question of how participants in exchange could secure transactions. A second reason to study mortgages is their role in economic and social change. The use of land as a collateral for loans has been linked to agricultural transitions that brought about the productivity improvements in the rural economy that are regarded as a prerequisite for sustained economic growth. The precise role of mortgage credit in this development is still unclear: did it allow enterprising peasants access to credit so they could invest and extend their landholdings? Or did it contribute to impoverished peasants eventually losing their land to their creditors—as apparently already happened in the time of Nehemiah?

The various chapters of this book all deal with the financial, economic and social aspects of mortgage credit in the pre-modern European countryside. They are all case studies into the actual use of land as collateral for loans, and the effects on economy and society. Such an approach is fruitful, as scholarship on the use and effects of mortgage credit is too often of a theoretical nature, assuming certain practices and their effects, rather than establishing these based on archival research. This empirical research has been ongoing for quite some time now, and some of the more recent results were, for instance, presented in a volume on rural credit edited by Schofield and Lambrecht (2009). Whereas these authors took an all-encompassing view that included the enormous number of 'small-scale credit agreements' of the pre-modern countryside (Schofield and Lambrecht 2009, p. 4), the present volume is focused on what one might call rural 'high finance': large loans on collateral of land. One of the main focal points is the development of mortgage contracts and mortgage law over time: the pre-modern European countryside was characterized by regional variety of mortgage contract types. As a result, conditions for lenders and borrowers were not the same everywhere, and large differences can be observed in the use of land to secure loans, as well as the use and socio-economic effects of mortgage credit. The contributions to this volume indicate a gradual convergence of mortgage contracts and mortgage law: initially, these provided much security to the lender, but over time there was a general development towards a more balanced 'mortgage system' that also looked after the interest of the borrower. It seems that this process of 'institutional change' was crucial for turning mortgage credit into a very popular credit instrument and that this was achieved in many European areas by the seventeenth century.

Rather than presenting a general overview of the historiography on mortgage credit—for this we refer to the excellent introduction to this topic by Lambrecht and Schofield (2009)—the introduction rather discusses the contract types used for mortgaging, the development of mortgage contracts and mortgage law, and their relation to economic growth and social developments. We begin with sketching the contract types available to those looking to use land to secure a loan.

1.1 Mortgage Contracts and Mortgage Law: Security, but for Whom?

Participants in many economic transactions deal with what Avner Greif called the 'fundamental problem of exchange': the risk that a counterparty does not live up to his or her obligations (Greif 2000). This problem occurs in any transaction where payment is postponed; to solve it—or at least minimize the risks involved—creditors are likely to demand securities from their debtors. Securities tend to come in many forms, ranging from informal arrangements, such as having witnesses to a transaction, to more formal arrangements, such as drawing up a legally binding contract. Usually, more valuable transactions require more formal securities: once a deal exceeds a certain value, the creditor is likely to demand stronger securities. On the one hand, this is because bigger loans can result in bigger losses, while on the other hand, it reflects the fact that bigger loans make cheating more attractive for the debtor: when the gains of cheating outweigh the damage of (for instance) reputation loss, informal securities no longer suffice, and creditors will demand formal securities, such as mortgages. Generally speaking, once loans exceed a certain threshold, it becomes worthwhile for creditors to demand a mortgage as a security. Michael Schraer's chapter in this volume, for instance, demonstrates that medieval Jewish moneylenders' mortgage-backed loans were substantially bigger than their other loans, suggesting a relation between loan size and the use of collateral as a security. Other case studies indicate that mortgages were not taken out for loans worth less than at least a month's wages; in fact, usually the principals easily exceeded several months' wages (Lambrecht 2009, p. 78, and the chapters below by Dermineur, Gayton, Van Onacker and Wedd).

Mortgage contracts differed: some provided creditors with strong securities, allowing them almost automatic compensation once the debtor failed to repay the loan, or failed to pay mortgage interest. Others allowed debtors more leeway and did not result in immediate expropriation as soon as a single payment was missed. In general, it seems there were four contract types available in pre-modern Europe. They differed in terms of possession—who was allowed to work the land that was put up as a security?—and ownership—who held legal title to the collateral? Figure 1.1 gives the main contract types, based on Goebel's (1961) reconstruction of securities of Roman law. Even though Roman law was not used everywhere in Europe, and the Latin terms mentioned in the scheme hardly ever emerge in the historical records, the figure does provide a general idea of the options available to creditors and debtors looking to use land to secure a transaction.

A first option—*mancipatio cum fiducia*—was to provide the creditor with relatively strong security, granting him or her both possession and ownership of the land until the debtor repays the principal. In contrast, another option was to provide the creditor with relatively little security, by using the *hypotheca* that only granted him or her 'a possessory interest in the property': until a judge allows the creditor to execute his or her claim to the collateral, the debtor retains both ownership and possession. In between these two extremes, we find the *pignus* that allowed the creditor possession of the collateral, and the *in iure cessio cum fiducia* (or *fiducia*) that allowed him or her the ownership while the debtor was allowed to continue in the possession of the collateral. In the European countryside

Mancipatio cum fiducia 'The debtor vests ownership and possession of the property in the creditor'	*In iure cessio cum fiducia* 'The debtor vests ownership in the creditor but retains possession of property by leave of the creditor'
Pignus 'The debtor retains ownership, but grants possession irrevocably to the creditor until repayment of the debt'	*Hypotheca* 'The debtor retains both ownership and possession of the property, but transfers to the creditor a possessory interest in the property'

Fig. 1.1 Real securities of Roman law
Source Goebel (1961, p. 29)

of the later Middle Ages and early modern period, we encounter contracts resembling the *pignus* (Ertl 2017, p. 15), and most of all the *fiducia* and *hypotheca*: contract types allowing the debtor to retain possession of the land for the duration of the mortgage contract were most usual.

An angered Nehemiah had to deal with debtors who had secured a loan by transferring ownership to their creditors, thus losing title to their lands, or so it seems at least. In theory, they could recover the land by repaying the debt plus possible interest—conditions similar to what later would be known as the *fiducia* of Roman law. This also was the usual type of contract used in Italy (De Luca and Lorenzini, this volume). And even though England did not have a Roman law tradition, using land as a collateral went along the same lines there as well (see the chapters here by Briggs, Gayton, Waddilove and Wedd). In Flanders, such contract types were common in the thirteenth century (Thoen and Soens 2009, p. 24) but seem to have been used less often in later centuries. Here, another contract type—the *hypotheca*—emerged and was generally used from the late Middle Ages onwards. It provided the creditor with a claim to the property, so that he or she could expropriate in case of default. The debtor retained ownership and possession for the duration of the contract, unless a judge intervened and ordered expropriation to compensate the creditor for default. Here, the position of the creditor was less strong, as expropriation required a court order; the debtor was in a better position, as he or she retained ownership until a judge ordered expropriation. This was the usual type of contract in the north-west of mainland Europe (see the chapters by Dermineur, Limberger and De Vijlder, Van Onacker and Zuijderduijn).

For creditors, the *fiducia* was the more attractive contract type; for debtors, this was the *hypotheca*. The former appears to have been available almost everywhere in the Middle Ages, whereas the latter only emerged in the course of the later Middle Ages, first in the north-west of Europe and the Iberian Peninsula, and later also in England and Italy. The general development of mortgage credit involved a move towards more debtor-friendly mortgage contract types. Schraer discusses how the introduction of the *censal*—which resembles the *hypotheca*—in late medieval Aragon gained so much popularity that it caused Jews—who usually used the *pignus* contract type—to lose ground. In Italy, a new contract type resembling the *hypotheca* was introduced towards the end of the sixteenth century, to protect the debtor: the chapter by De Luca and Lorenzini describes how the *census consignativus* improved the position of the debtor by no longer requiring a transfer of ownership of the collateral to the creditor. They explain how Pope Pius V created this financial instrument, issuing a Papal bull in 1569 that aimed to improve the position of debtors.

Apart from the introduction of new mortgage contracts, another option to make borrowing on collateral of land more debtor-friendly was to adjust mortgage law (Van Bochove et al. 2015). Such an adjustment helped to make mortgage credit much more popular in areas where the creditor-friendly *fiducia* was used as the standard contract type. In his chapter, Briggs demonstrates that in late medieval England initially land was hardly ever put up as a collateral because debtors believed the risk of losing the land too big. The pledging of land as collateral seems rather to have been done by debtors unable to raise money in any other way. The latter is also suggested in the chapter by Waddilove, who also explores the motivations behind adjustment of mortgage law. In England, this was done via the development of a legal doctrine known as the equity of redemption, which protected debtors against losing the land they had put up as collateral.

In general, it seems that mortgage law also developed from 'strict' to more 'relaxed', thus improving the position of the debtor by offering protection against all too easily conducted expropriation at the hands of their creditors. Zuijderduijn's chapter on Mijnsheerenland, Holland indicates that this protection came to a large extent from law courts' ability to rule over foreclosure: in sixteenth-century Holland judges decided whether this would be allowed or not, and in doing so, it appears they had ample methods available to postpone the debtor's loss of his or her land. In England from the seventeenth century onwards, the equity of redemption allowed judges to rule on foreclosure, thus ending the practice of 'automatic' forfeit as soon as the repayment deadline was missed. Creditors mostly seem to have agreed with this relaxation: Waddilove's chapter suggests that both creditors and debtors might have demanded a less strict mortgage law and that when Chancery formulated the equity of redemption, it merely followed an existing practice of allowing debtors more leeway.

Both with respect to mortgage instruments and mortgage law, general developments seem to have favoured the debtor. However, we should be careful not to interpret this as a linear and irreversible development: new social and economic realities, such as a redistribution of wealth from peasants towards commercial farmers and urban landholders, and the subsequent widening of the socio-economic distance between participants in exchange, may for instance have brought a demand for stronger securities among mortgagees. Thus, the expansion of mortgage markets from the village level, to the regional level, may have created incentives to (temporarily) improve the security of the creditors. This is the development described in Dermineur's chapter on eighteenth-century Delle, France, where debtors were forced to put up additional securities apart from land, to be able to secure loans with emerging urban creditors.

1.2 Mortgage Credit: Winners and Losers

Mortgage credit has been widely linked to productivity growth in agriculture during so-called transformations or transitions that increased productivity and are widely regarded as a prerequisite for economic growth (Timmer 1988). Such agricultural transitions involve either upscaling by creating larger units of arable land, or investments in agricultural techniques, or both. Mortgage credit has played an important role in debates about agricultural transitions: it may have allowed enterprising peasants to attract the funds required for either acquiring more land or investing in agricultural techniques, but may also have contributed to upscaling in a different way, through the expropriation of the land of smallholders at the hands of their creditors.

The latter was prominent in an older historiography that regarded smallholders as an obstruction to growth: peasants supposedly were unwilling to take risks and invest, and instead aimed at self-sufficiency, and did not achieve productivity growth (see the discussion of this literature in Hoffman 1996, pp. 16–17). But once peasants were replaced by large landowners who aimed at production for the market, and were willing and able to invest, productivity increased. Thus, peasant landholding is believed to have been reduced considerably in Holland before 1600, a development that has been linked to the large-scale urbanization of the Dutch Republic in the seventeenth century (De Vries 1974). In England, peasants lost ground in the eighteenth century, when smallholders gradually yielded to commercial farmers, who then proceeded to increase agricultural productivity (Mathias 1983). One reason why peasants could be removed from their land was expropriation at the hands of creditors of debtors unable to pay their debts or mortgage interest (see the literature mentioned in chapters by De Luca and Lorenzini, and Zuijderduijn, below).

A more recent historiography is more positive with regard to peasants' willingness and ability to increase productivity. For England, Allen (1991) demonstrated that the supposed link between the disappearance of smallholders, productivity growth and Industrial Revolution in England was unsubstantiated: productivity growth was largely realized by remaining smallholders—not by commercial farmers that emerged in the eighteenth century. Hoffman (1996) and Hoppenbrouwers (2001) made similar claims for the countryside of France and Holland. This view would suggest that peasants were willing and able to make investments in soil quality and drainage, buildings and tools.

How did a part of the smallholder population of the European countryside manage to make the investments associated with productivity gains? And how did another part lose its land to an emerging group of commercial farmers? The various chapters in this book provide valuable clues as to how mortgage credit fits into the history of agricultural transformation, social change and economic development. First of all, there is not much evidence for scores of destitute debtors putting up a mortgage just to make ends meet, and eventually facing expropriation. In regions where the creditor-friendly *fiducia* contract type prevailed, or mortgage law was still very strict, the number of mortgagors was quite modest, as becomes clear from the chapters by Briggs on medieval England, and De Luca and Lorenzini on Italy. Apparently, smallholders were well aware of the risks that mortgage lending under adverse conditions came with, and usually had ample resort to different techniques that allowed for the borrowing of smaller sums that could secure survival. That few took out a mortgage for such reasons is also indicated in Gayton's chapter on Hampshire, England: only a minority borrowed out of dire circumstances, usually pledging relatively small portions of their land as security, and borrowing relatively small sums of money.

All of this is not to say mortgagors did not lose any land: in sixteenth-century Mijnsheerenland, Holland, there were 1.3 foreclosures per 1000 inhabitants per annum—much more than today's average in the Netherlands (0.1 per 1000 inhabitants per annum) but much less than in the present-day USA (5.7) (Zuijderduijn, this volume). Apart from the question of whether this should be regarded as large-scale expropriation of peasants by wealthy creditors that drove Holland's sixteenth-century agricultural transition, or 'business as usual' in a society lacking insurance schemes and social security, it is important to point out that Mijnsheerenland's law court was very easy on the debtors, allowing them lengthy extensions to pay their dues. Those that lost their land had certainly not been 'tricked' into a financial transaction that inevitably led to expropriation. In her chapter on Kent, England, Wedd also points out that loss of property was not an unlikely outcome of mortgaging land and that this was so even after the equity of redemption had improved the position of debtors. It was not only peasants that were expropriated though, as gentry also failed to recover mortgaged land; in Kent, mortgage credit was not an instrument that merely transferred land from the poor to the wealthier.

By using land as a security, property owners could attract money and assets worth the equivalent of several months' income. What did they use this for? Gayton's chapter gives the reasons that peasants in Hampshire, England had for borrowing. She indicates that many peasants borrowed on collateral of land during economic upswings; they appear to have responded to business opportunities first and foremost, and not to economic hardship. Such business opportunities included investments in land and other assets: the mortgage was often used as a means to finalize a transfer of land or another type of real estate, refurbishing or building, and funding business ventures. A similar productive use of loans is suggested by De Luca and Lorenzini for seventeenth-century Italy. However, apart from such investment purposes, mortgages also served another important goal: arranging intergenerational transfers such as dowries and inheritances, as is also pointed out in Muldrew's Afterword to the volume. Where partible inheritance was practised, and children inherited equally, families risked ending up with numerous scattered landholdings. To prevent this from happening, heirs often decided to reorganize the inheritance, compensating some heirs with financial instruments in lieu of plots of land; an annuity on collateral of the land may have been a solution—a point also made by Limberger and De Vijlder in their chapter. In the end, mortgages were thus at the heart of local redistribution of land (Knibbe and Borghaerts 2017, p. 136; Ogilvie et al. 2012, pp. 35–36; Béaur 2009, pp. 156–159), by either facilitating its acquirement, making possible intergenerational transfers or causing expropriation, and as such, they contributed to changes in property structures.

Nearly all chapters report an increase in the use of mortgage credit over time. Reliable evidence of the number of transactions comes from the Low Countries, where loans on collateral of land were registered by local authorities. In their chapter, Limberger and De Vijlder show an absolute increase in the number of mortgages in the manor of Kruikenburg, near Brussels; the relative increase can be estimated as going from roughly five or six mortgages per 1000 inhabitants per annum in the fifteenth century, to about ten in the sixteenth century. By 1550, the level may even have been about twelve per 1000 inhabitants.[1] Van Onacker's chapter provides evidence of an increasing use of mortgage credit in villages in Brabant, going from less than five mortgages per 1000 inhabitants in the fifteenth century, to more than ten in the sixteenth century. Zuijderduijn's chapter reports ten mortgages per 1000 inhabitants in Mijnsheerenland, Holland, in the sixteenth century. To put this in perspective, the latter figure is not too far away from today's for the province of Zuid-Holland in which Mijnsheerenland lies, which is twenty mortgages per 1000 inhabitants per annum. This evidence indicates the strong development and liveliness of late medieval mortgage markets, especially considering these operated in the absence of mortgage credit banks, and relied on interpersonal credit entirely.

For mortgage markets to function in an effective way, a sufficient number of participants in exchange are required. Where a sufficient number of creditors and debtors are active, it can be said that mortgage markets are 'thicker' and therefore more effective: competition brings a reduction in price volatility, as well as information costs, since participants in exchange can easily compare interest rates. In 'thicker' mortgage markets, economies of scale also allow for the improvement of the institutional framework, such as the introduction of sophisticated land registries, which further contribute to low information costs (Van Zanden et al. 2012). These advantages disappear when the number of either creditors or debtors diminishes, and mortgage markets become 'thinner'.

The importance of a fairly equal land distribution for the functioning of mortgage markets is discussed in the chapter by Van Onacker. Where smallholding was widespread, such as in the Brabantine Campine area, 'thicker' mortgage markets allowed creditors and debtors to participate under relatively favourable conditions. Van Onacker's chapter points to a question that cannot be resolved yet: what happened when this social balance was disturbed? At least in some regions land was increasingly concentrated in the hands of a few wealthy local property owners and some absentee landholders, often living in nearby towns. This caused the number of participants in exchange to be reduced, and mortgage markets to become 'thinner', which in theory should have increased price volatility, and may also have had an adverse effect on the viability of mortgage market institutions. Under such circumstances, it is not unlikely that the position of smallholder-debtors deteriorated in particular, as there were fewer counterparties available, and also fewer counterparties among social equals. To what extent shifts in property structures could force debtors to agree to less favourable borrowing conditions is visible in Dermineur's chapter: to be able to contract loans with an emerging group of urban creditors, peasants in Delle, France, in the eighteenth century, had to offer extra securities. This suggests that as soon as mortgage markets expanded to include larger areas, and the physical and socio-economic distance between participants in exchange increased, adjustments to mortgage contracts and mortgage law might have been necessary. How exactly mortgage markets were adapted to new realities—either changes to local land distribution or the increased participation of non-resident creditors—is largely a question for future research, however.

Altogether the case studies in this volume suggest that the use of land as collateral for loans only began to increase once mortgage instruments and mortgage law developed to become more debtor-friendly. As long as debtors felt insecure about mortgage credit, fearing they stood a high risk of losing their land, only destitute peasants were willing to put up land as a collateral for a loan. Only a balanced mortgage system that secured both debtors and creditors could persuade a sizeable proportion of the rural population to begin to use land as a collateral for loans. And only then could mortgage credit make a substantial contribution to agricultural transitions. This observation should remind us that for economic transactions to emerge, both creditor and debtor should feel secure about a positive outcome. As a result, the long-run development of European mortgage systems may seem counterintuitive: for mortgage markets to take off, in many regions the security of creditors first had to be reduced, and the security of debtors had to be increased. In the words of Craig Muldrew in his Afterword to the volume, in this way it became possible 'to use the value of real estate to make capital markets and credit work'.

1.3 Beyond Europe: Mortgages and Development

In recent decades, the extent of early modern development in the northwest of Europe has been questioned from a global comparative perspective. Authors from the so-called California School claimed that China was as developed as England or the Dutch Republic before 1800 and that the Industrial Revolution and European expansion of the nineteenth century cannot be ascribed to the unique early modern development of these European countries. This debate on the 'Great divergence' may also raise questions about pre-modern mortgages and agricultural development outside of Europe. In this respect, Taisu Zhang's (2011–2012) article on mortgage law in pre-modern China is of particular interest. The author demonstrates that Chinese mortgage contracts resembled the *mancipatio cum fiducia* of Roman law: the creditor received landownership on condition that the debtor could retrieve this by repaying the principal. Furthermore, the creditor was granted possession of the land and kept the yield as a compensation for the money lent (2011, pp. 156–157). Mortgage law was also relatively relaxed from the perspective of the borrower, who could repay the principal and recover the land at any point in time. Zhang argues that as a result, few Chinese landowners were forced to alienate their land, causing small-scale agriculture to prevail. 'The "problem" with Chinese property norms', Zhang writes, 'was not that it was too rigid, but rather that it was too flexible and accommodating' towards individuals who had put up their land as a collateral for a loan. 'This may well have generated important benefits for social stability and cohesion, but, over the long run, did lead Chinese agriculture onto a fundamentally different path than English agriculture' (Zhang 2011–2012, 195–196).[2] In Zhang's view, China's agricultural sector thus failed to modernize because smallholders who put up their land as collateral for a loan could quite easily hold on to their right to redeem their land (even though they did not possess it for the duration of the 'loan'), whereas in England mortgage law led to peasant expropriation and the emergence of commercial farms.

Apart from the question of the precise economic and social consequences of a contract resembling the *mancipatio cum fiducia*—which was very common in China, but hardly found in late medieval and early modern Europe—and which requires further research, the present volume allows us to put Zhang's claim regarding the comparative development of China and England into perspective. Indeed, mortgage law in England initially was quite strict and carried a theoretical risk of expropriation, but this mostly scared property owners away from putting up land as collateral for a loan, as is demonstrated by Briggs's chapter. And even after mortgage law was relaxed with the equity of redemption around 1600, and the use of mortgage lending increased markedly in the seventeenth century, it seems this did not really result in large-scale expropriation. A longer time frame and broader comparative approach thus seem to indicate Zhang's explanation for China's agricultural development might require some refinement: although very valuable, Zhang's largely legal approach does not take into account the possibility that in spite of the presence of mortgage systems, only few people put up their land as collateral for a loan. Neither does it tell us all that much about the actual effects that mortgage credit had on agricultural development and property structures.

1.4 Contents of the Volume

Regardless of how mortgages were linked to agricultural transitions—whether by making investments possible, expropriating smallholders, or both at the same time—these effects are only likely to have manifested themselves where a sizable number of both creditors and debtors engaged in transactions, and 'thick' mortgage markets emerged. Such a situation required a balanced mortgage system, where mortgage contracts and mortgage law served the interests of both creditors *and* debtors. How such balanced mortgage systems emerged in pre-modern Europe, and what effects they had on social and economic developments, is the subject of the following chapters.

The book starts off with Briggs's chapter on the use of mortgage credit in medieval England. Using a sample of 56 manors, he addresses the question of the conditions under which land was used as collateral for loans, concluding that the mortgage was so unattractive for debtors that this financial instrument was hardly used. This was different in early modern, or at least seventeenth-century, England, as case studies by Gayton on Hampshire and Wedd on Kent indicate: by then, mortgage credit was widely used. Both suggest the equity of redemption allowed for a widespread use of this financial instrument. The next chapter by Waddilove reflects on the circumstances under which Chancery might have formulated the equity of redemption, suggesting demand from both creditors and debtors for a more relaxed mortgage law might have played an important role. The remainder of the chapters discuss land and credit in Continental Europe. Schraer discusses how Jewish moneylenders in medieval Aragon accepted various types of collateral for loans including land. De Luca and Lorenzini explain how a sixteenth-century Papal bull paved the way for a more widespread use of mortgage credit in large parts of Italy. The final four chapters provide case studies into mortgage credit in the north-west of Europe: Dermineur discusses developments in the use of collateral in Delle, France, and Van Onacker analyses the use of mortgage credit in the Campine area in present-day Belgium, while Limberger and De Vijlder do this for an area in the vicinity of Brussels. Zuijderduijn's contribution is concerned with mortgage law and the extent of expropriation in sixteenth-century Mijnsheerenland, Holland. In an Afterword, Muldrew offers a critical discussion of the various case studies and suggests lines for future research.

Notes

1. Calculated on the assumption of a fifteenth-century population of Kruikenburg of 1285 inhabitants and a sixteenth-century population of 1525 (De Vijlder 2013, p. 486).
2. In the section this quotation is taken from, Zhang calls debtors 'sellers', indicating the debtors had entered into a conditional sale.

Bibliography

Secondary Works

Allen, R.C., 1991. 'The two English agricultural revolutions, 1450–1850', in B.M.S. Campbell and M. Overton (eds.), *Land, Labour, and Livestock: Historical Studies in European Agricultural Productivity* (Manchester: Manchester University Press), pp. 236–254.

Béaur, G., 2009. 'Credit and land in eighteenth-century France', in P.R. Schofield and T. Lambrecht (eds.), *Credit and the Rural Economy in North Western Europe, c.1200–c.1850* (Turnhout: Brepols), pp. 153–167.

De Vijlder, N., 2013. 'De rurale grondmarkt in Zuid-Brabant (15de-16de eeuw): een braakliggend stuk prijzengeschiedenis', *Eigen Schoon en de Brabander*, pp. 477–500.

Ertl, T., 2017. 'Small landlords: Land transactions in and around Bozen (South Tirol) in the mid-thirteenth century', *Vierteljahrschrift für Sozial- und Wirtschaftsgeschichte*, vol. 104, pp. 7–28.

Goebel, R.J., 1961. 'Reconstructing the Roman law of real security', *Tulane Law Review*, vol. 36, pp. 29–66.

Greif, A., 2000. 'The fundamental problem of exchange: A research agenda in historical institutional analysis', *European Review of Economic History*, vol. 4, pp. 251–284.

Hoffman, P., 1996. *Growth in a Traditional Society: The French Countryside, 1450–1815* (Princeton: Princeton University Press).

Hoppenbrouwers, P.C.M., 2001. 'Mapping an unexplored field. The Brenner debate and the case of Holland', in P.C.M. Hoppenbrouwers and J.L. Van Zanden (eds.), *Peasants into farmers? The transformation of rural economy and society in the Low Countries (middle ages-19th century) in the light of the Brenner debate* (Turnhout: Brepols), pp. 41–66.

Knibbe, M., and P. Borghaerts, 2017. 'A capital market without banks: Lending and borrowing in Henneraarderadeel, Friesland, 1537–1555', in F. Ülgen (ed.) *Financial Development, Economic Crises and Emerging Market Economies* (Abingdon: Routledge), pp. 126–141.

Lambrecht, T., 2009. 'Rural credit and the market for annuities in eighteenth-century Flanders', in P.R. Schofield and T. Lambrecht (eds.), *Credit and the Rural Economy in North Western Europe, c.1200–c.1850* (Turnhout: Brepols), pp. 75–97.

Mathias, P., 1983. *The First Industrial Nation*, 2nd edn. (London: Methuen).

Ogilvie, S., M. Küpker and J. Maegraith, 2012. 'Household debt in early modern Germany: Evidence from personal inventories', *JEH*, vol. 72, pp. 134–167.

Schofield, P.R., and T. Lambrecht (eds.), 2009. *Credit and the Rural Economy in North Western Europe, c.1200–c.1850* (Turnhout: Brepols).

Thoen, E., and T. Soens, 2009. 'Credit in rural Flanders, c.1250–c.1600: Its variety and significance', in P.R. Schofield and T. Lambrecht (eds.), *Credit and the Rural Economy in North Western Europe, c.1200–c.1850* (Turnhout: Brepols), pp. 19–38.

Timmer, C.P., 1988. 'The agricultural transformation', in H. Chenery and T.N. Srinivasan (eds.), *Handbook of Development Economics, Volume 1* (Amsterdam: Elsevier Science), pp. 275–331.

Van Bochove, C., H. Deneweth, and J. Zuijderduijn, 2015. 'Real estate and mortgage finance in England and the Low Countries, 1300–1800', *C&C*, vol. 30, pp. 9–38.

Van Zanden, J.L., J. Zuijderduijn and T. De Moor, 2012. 'Small is beautiful: The efficiency of credit markets in late medieval Holland', *European Review of Economic History*, vol. 16, pp. 3–22.

Vries, J. de., 1974. *The Dutch Rural Economy in the Golden Age, 1500–1700* (New Haven: Yale University Press).

Zhang, T., 2011–2012. 'Property rights in land, agricultural capitalism, and the relative decline of pre-industrial China', *San Diego International Law Journal*, vol. 129, pp. 129–200.

CHAPTER 2

Mortgages and the English Peasantry c.1250–c.1350

Chris Briggs

2.1 Introduction

Mortgages and other transactions in which loans were secured on land were widespread throughout the medieval European countryside. Such transactions could potentially allow agriculturalists to access significant amounts of capital. This chapter will argue, however, that mortgages or equivalent instruments were less common among peasants in England in this period than they were in other parts of Western Europe. This is a feature that demands attention, as does its larger implication that medieval capital markets were comparatively underdeveloped in rural England.

An essential first step is to establish the basic categories of English peasant land. Broadly speaking, such land fell into two categories in this period. The first was freehold, the tenure of which was protected by the royal courts. Freehold land was conveyed by charter from one party to another, with minimal reference to lordly authority. The other category is customary land, the focus here. Customary land was servile or villein property, held by unfree tenants who typically owed labour services as

C. Briggs (✉)
University of Cambridge, Cambridge, UK
e-mail: cdb23@cam.ac.uk

C. Briggs and J. Zuijderduijn (eds.), *Land and Credit*,
Palgrave Studies in the History of Finance,
https://doi.org/10.1007/978-3-319-66209-1_2

well as cash rents for their properties, as well as a range of other obligations such as heriot (a servile death duty). Technically the possession of the landlord, customary land could only be conveyed from person A to person B in the landlord's court, the manor court, and possession of such land could only be granted by the lord.

The following entry, from the court records of the manor of Heacham (Norfolk) dated November 1317, is a typical example of the mortgage discussed here:

> Memorandum that Geoffrey Gosse and his wife Cecilia came into full court and pledged [*invadiaverunt*] to Peter Coubel 3½ rods[1] of land for a term of five years, for 10 shillings sterling which they received from the same Peter as a loan; the condition being that if the aforesaid Geoffrey and Cecilia fully pay the said 10 shillings at the end of the aforesaid five years then the aforesaid land shall revert to the aforesaid Geoffrey and Cecilia; but if at the end of the aforesaid five years the aforesaid Geoffrey and Cecilia fail to pay in whole or in part, then the aforesaid land shall remain to the aforesaid Peter and his heirs in perpetuity, without contradiction of any person. [*in margin of roll*:] Memorandum. [fine] 6 pence.[2]

This records a transaction in customary land between two village parties. The land is transferred from a mortgagor/borrower to a mortgagee/creditor, with conditions about what will happen to the land if repayment is or is not effected. The 'fine' paid reflects the fact that this transaction required the landlord's permission. Presumably, too, the fact that the instrument was registered in this way meant that it could be enforced in future if necessary, or disputes about it be more easily resolved, but this is an issue on which we have relatively little information.

In its form and provisions, this written contract is a 'classic' medieval mortgage. A key characteristic of the medieval mortgage is that the creditor would take the revenues from the land during the term as his interest. It is not explicitly stated in this example that should happen, but it seems very likely. Here, the borrowers had to pay the full principal (10*s*.) back at the end of the term, so there is no indication that the revenues would be used to pay off the principal (as they were in a *vifgage*). Some of the other transactions discussed below differed from this in their form and provisions. However, their essential purpose was the same. All recorded the transfer of the possession of a piece of real property (if not its ownership or title) from debtor to creditor in exchange for an advanced sum, with conditions relating to future payments. The purpose of each transaction was to secure a debt.

Such 'classic' mortgage contracts are encountered in many different medieval European contexts. Examples are known from at least the early eleventh century onwards in regions like Normandy and Flanders (Van Werveke 1968; Lewis 1979). In many of the best-documented examples, the lender was a monastery, and the borrower a financially embarrassed knight. However, the laity lent and borrowed on mortgages also. From the thirteenth century, not only social elites but also a wide spectrum of society, including peasants, was involved. Existing research suggests that for the rural people of the Low Countries, northern and southern France, Catalonia, Valencia and northern and central Italy, written credit instruments were much more common than was the case in England. This included the use of instruments which allowed credit to be secured on land, such as the mortgage itself, or the *rente* (known variously in different regions as *renten*, *rentes constituées*, *censal* and so on) (Briggs 2009a). In the *rente* contract, a 'lender' bought an annuity drawn on the property of the 'borrower'. Across Europe in general, the *rente* generally replaced the mortgage because the former avoided the charge of usury to which the latter was subject, and thus became acceptable to the church authorities, mainly because the lender could not *demand* that the principal be redeemed (Schnapper 1957). A turning point in the church's prohibition of the mortgage was the Council of Tours (1163) at which Pope Alexander III banned clergy from creating mortgages. Later rulings extended the same ban to the laity. However, observers agree that the mortgage did not entirely disappear and that mortgage and *rente* coexisted across Europe between the thirteenth and fifteenth centuries. Mortgage and *rente* performed similar functions, since in both instruments land or buildings served as collateral for a loan. Like the mortgage, the *rente* offered security to a lender because the property on which the *rente* was charged could, in theory at least, be seized in case of default (Duby 1968, pp. 254–257; Ertl 2017; Gaulin and Menant 1998, pp. 40–45; Gilomen 1998, pp. 120–121; Herlihy 1965, pp. 239–241; Renault 2011, p. 129; for the rough equivalence of mortgages and *rentes*, see for example Brennan 2006, p. 177; Rosenthal 1993, p. 132; Van Werveke 1968, p. 164; Van Bochove et al. 2015).

Work on medieval English peasant society, however, suggests mortgages of customary land like the example quoted above are rare. Nor does the *rente* contract or anything equivalent appear to have existed in

English rural society. A form of annuity was used in England in the thirteenth century by Jewish lenders, the 'fee rent'. However, this Jewish instrument was formally banned in 1269 and had little impact on rural society (Richardson 1960, pp. 102–106). Historians who have studied land transactions in manorial court rolls have identified and discussed relatively few conditional transfers connected to credit of any kind. This is especially true of the period before the Black Death, my focus here (Schofield 2004). In the fifteenth century, such mortgages are somewhat more common (Briggs 2009a; Mate 1993, pp. 60, 65). Court rolls of the pre-plague period of course supply many thousands of examples of *post-mortem* and *inter vivos* transfers of customary land, and temporary leases of customary land from peasant tenant to subtenant, all of which are testimony to the active market in customary land of the thirteenth and fourteenth centuries, which has been extensively studied. Yet very few of them take the form of conditional transfers explicitly connected with credit. So, the Heacham entry cited above is something one very rarely encounters in the court rolls.

In the case of customary land, we can be fairly confident in dismissing the possibility that many such instruments were created but are not recorded. Mortgages were conveyances, and all conveyances of customary land had to be performed in the manor court and enrolled in its records. A fine had to be paid for any such conveyance. Individuals who sought to pledge customary land outside the manor court, or tried to pledge it secretly by charter, were very likely to be punished and to have their attempted transactions deemed invalid. In the court rolls of Heacham, two entries of the year 1315 order the seizure into the lord's possession of two pieces of land each of which had been gaged without lord's licence some 18 years earlier.[3] Similarly, an entry dated 1344 in the court rolls of the manor of Horsham St. Faith, near Norwich, records the case of a man (John Crombe) who had tried to convey one rod (¼ acre) of customary meadowland by charter to a citizen of Norwich (called Edmund Cosyn), almost certainly as security for a loan. The transfer was deemed invalid, and Cosyn was forced to return the acre of meadow to the landlord. The inference that the initial transfer was intended as security is based on the fact that the entry recording the seizure of the land is accompanied by an acknowledgement of a debt (a 'recognizance') of 10*s*. owed by Crombe to Cosyn.[4]

Overall, when one looks at the currently available evidence concerning the mortgaging of English peasant land, or the broader pledging of such land as security for debts, there is little solid evidence for the practice.

A preliminary investigation has also been made of mortgages (by charter) of freehold peasant land. Those, too, seem rare, at least to judge by the survival of mortgage and related defeasance deeds as a proportion of the larger corpus of peasant freehold charters from this period (Briggs 2009b).[5]

The evidence on the employment of real property as collateral would thus seem to fit a larger view of medieval rural credit England which sees it as a system based largely on oral, unregistered transactions in which personal pledges, rather than landholdings, were the main security or guarantee of repayment for a creditor. The information about this credit market comes from manor court litigation about unpaid debts, most of which were contracted orally. Such a world of informal, largely oral, unsecured, short-term credit contrasts with the situation in other parts of Continental Europe at the same period.

What is the significance of an investigation of this contrast between England and the Continent in the use of the mortgage and its equivalents? If a peasant could offer land as security, then a creditor might offer a bigger loan over a longer term than where there was no collateral. If holders of customary land did not use this property to secure credit—thereby realizing the value of that property—then this could have had a negative effect on access to capital and levels of investment and welfare. This question of the ability of poor people to exploit their assets has been called the 'de Soto problem', in reference to the influential Peruvian economist Hernando de Soto (De Soto 2000; Van Zanden et al. 2012; Besley et al. 2012; see also Bogart and Richardson 2009). To solve the 'de Soto problem', it is not enough for poor borrowers to be in de facto possession of assets such as land. They need to be able to prove their exclusive rights to these assets through legally recognized registration and enforcement systems. If the supposed contrast between England and the Continent in the use of mortgages and their equivalents suggested by existing research is supported by a fuller investigation, one possible interpretation of this would be that medieval England achieved much less success in solving the 'de Soto problem' than certain areas of Continental Europe did in the same period. In particular, it has recently been argued that Holland had stronger property rights in land than other areas (including England), which in turn encouraged various kinds of loan that were secured on real property. Thus, it is argued, *capital markets* emerged early in Holland—i.e. based on long-term credit, involving large, formal cash loans. This was one of the reasons for Holland's precocious economic development, starting in the late medieval period (Van Zanden et al. 2012).

The first aim of this chapter is to ask whether it is true that mortgages of customary land were equally rare everywhere in England, between c.1250 and 1350. A systematic search for mortgages across space has not been previously attempted. If there were some locations where mortgages were more evident and numerous than others, why was this? After confirming the overall rarity of mortgages of customary land, the chapter's second aim is to investigate the possible reasons for this feature. The final aim of the study is to assess the implications of the rarity of mortgages for the impact and importance of rural capital markets in England in this period.

2.2 A Wider Search for Mortgages

An ongoing research project entitled 'Private law and medieval village society' has studied the rolls of manor courts in two groups of five counties, an 'eastern' and a 'western' group (Fig. 2.1).[6] The project's main focus is civil litigation in manor courts. The project team sampled the records of the courts of over 100 different manors to find the most revealing lawsuits relating to the manorial law of contract. The mortgage was not a primary focus of this work, yet a by-product of the research was the collection of evidence on mortgages of peasant land. Entries recording mortgage contracts (note that these entries record the creation of mortgages, and not litigation) were searched for and extracted simultaneously with the litigation material from among the very diverse recorded business of the medieval manor court ('mortgage' is used here to mean any form of conditional transfer of land made in exchange for a sum of money, occasionally described explicitly as a mortgage). This chapter draws most heavily on the records of the 44 'eastern manors', all of which have been searched for mortgages. A systematic search for mortgages was also undertaken for 12 'western manors' selected from a total of approximately 60 sets of manorial records studied in the larger project. The 12 were chosen mainly because they offer relatively lengthy and unbroken runs of court records. In both regions, the manors studied represent a mixture of ecclesiastical and lay ownership (Table 2.1; Figs. 2.2 and 2.3). As indicated above, mortgages and other conditional transfers are unusual and stand out from the typical run of court roll entries. It is hard to miss even isolated examples when trawling the rolls, and certainly not a cluster of them.

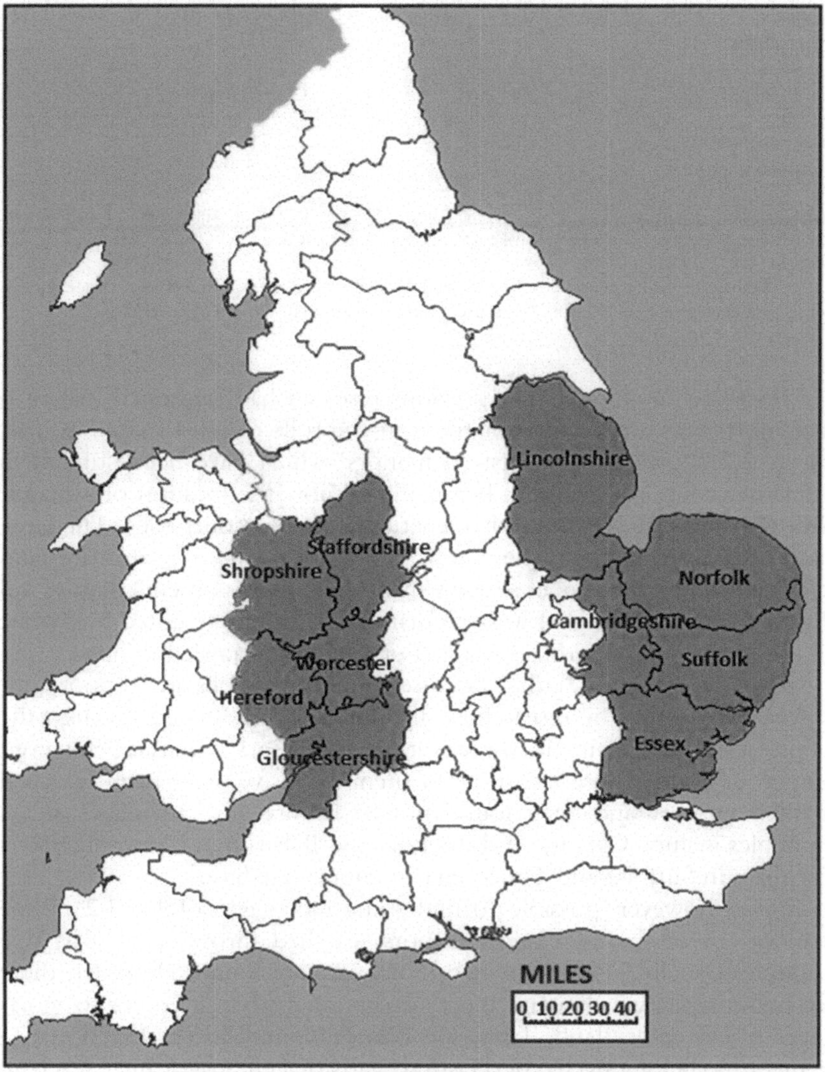

Fig. 2.1 'Private law and medieval village society' project: 'western' and 'eastern' counties investigated

Table 2.1 Type of landlord in manor court roll series used in search for mortgages

	Lay lord	*Church lord*	*Total*
Eastern manors	24	20	44
Western manors	7	5	12

Note The western court record series searched were: Alrewas, Bagots Bromley, Bockleton, Farewell, Halesowen, Longdon, Ombersley, Stoke Prior, Thornbury, Ruyton XI Towns, Whitchurch and Worfield

Source Database of manor court record series studied in the 'Private law and medieval village society' project, full details available at http://www.geog.cam.ac.uk/research/projects/privatelaw/

This search confirms what previous research had suggested, which is that mortgages are simply not there in the rolls of most manor courts. Figure 2.2 shows the 44 'eastern manors' which have been studied in the larger court roll project. The markers show the location of a manor with the start date of its surviving series of manor court rolls. The large circles represent manors where at least one mortgage of customary land has been found. The small squares mean 'mortgages absent'. Figure 2.3 shows the same for the 12 western manors. It should be noted that while all the surviving court rolls for a manor have been trawled in most cases, in some they have not, either because some of the rolls are in poor condition, or because the researchers did not have time to go through the whole series and maintain the coverage of manors required. However, numerous court roll series, some of them extensive, have been searched in their entirety and been found not to feature any mortgages at all. Examples include Oakington, Littleport and Balsham in Cambridgeshire; Fornham in Suffolk; and Thornbury in Gloucestershire.

It was, however, possible to find some mortgages (Table 2.2). Nine manors out of the 44 eastern manors searched throw up at least one example. Usually, just one or two mortgages are found. However, there are two manors which stand out as exceptional when it comes to mortgages of customary land. These are East Hanningfield (Essex), a manor at this time belonging to the Hastings earls of Pembroke, and Heacham (Norfolk), a manor of Lewes Priory, Sussex.[7] At East Hanningfield, the surviving court rolls start relatively late (1331) and there are not many court sessions with records surviving between that date and our end-date of 1350. However, eight mortgages have been identified. At Heacham, in a period of just 12 years (1315–1327), 21 conditional transfers of

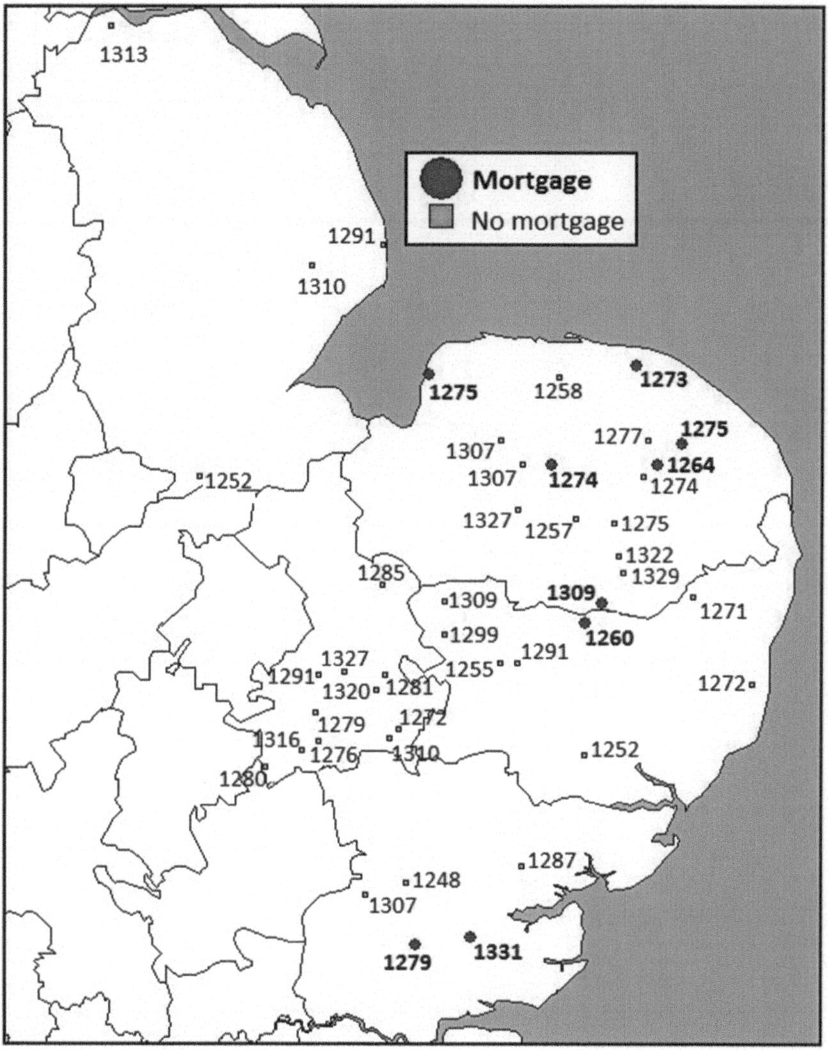

Fig. 2.2 Eastern manors with court rolls searched for mortgages of customary land

Note Dates indicate start dates of manor court roll series

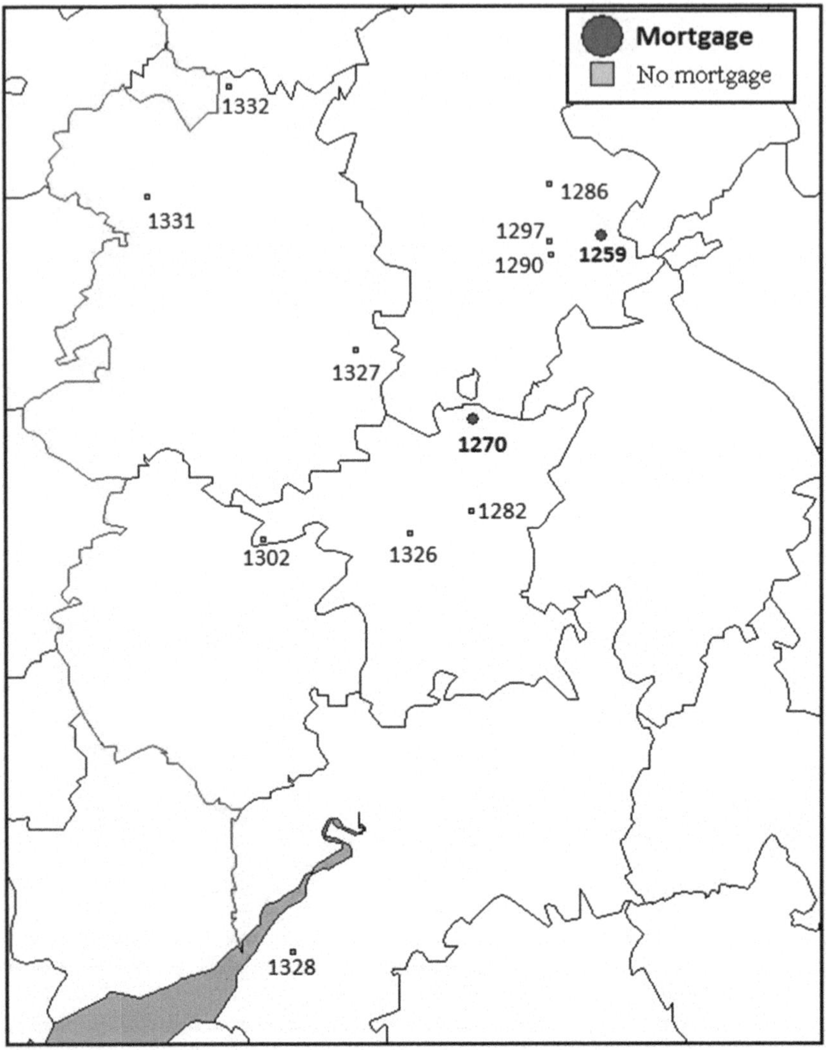

Fig. 2.3 Western manors with court rolls searched for mortgages of customary land

Note Dates indicate start dates of manor court roll series

Table 2.2 Manors where at least one mortgage is identified

Manor	*Years searched*	*No. mortgages*
Eastern region		
Bressingham, Norf.	1309–1322	1
Coltishall, Norf.	1275–1350	1
East Beckham, Norf.	1273–1345	2
East Hanningfield, Essex	1331–1350	8
Gressenhall, Norf.	1273–1350 (select yrs)	1
Heacham, Norf.	1275–1327	21 + 7 gages of standing crop
Horsham St. Faith, Norf.	1265–1272, 1275–1290, 1309–1327	1
Ingatestone, Essex	1279–1347	1
Redgrave, Suff.	1260–1273, 1340–1349	1
Western region		
Alrewas, Staffs.	1259–1273, 1286–1288, 1315–1316, 1327–1350	40
Halesowen, Worcestershire	1270–1282, 1336–1348	1

Source Bressingham: Norfolk Record Office [NRO], WAR 1–11; Coltishall: Cambridge, King's College Archive Centre, COL/360–365; East Beckham: NRO, WKC 2/49–53; East Hanningfield: Essex Record Office [ERO], D/DP M 832; Gressenhall: NRO, ING 2–21; Heacham: NRO, Le Strange DA1–DA9; Horsham St. Faith: NRO, NRS 19495–19500, 19505; Ingatestone: ERO, D/DP M 1–11, 13–17; Redgrave: University of Chicago Library, Bacon MSS 1–2, 19; Alrewas: Staffordshire Record Office, D(W)0/3/1–37, Landor (1907, 1910); Halesowen: Birmingham City Archives, 346201–346212, 346278–346320

customary property were recorded. There were also seven transfers of rights to standing crops, such as hemp or rye. In these latter arrangements, if the debt was not repaid, the creditor enjoyed the right to keep the crop or crops. In these two manors, in contrast to most places studied, mortgages and conditional transfers of tenant land seem to have been a relatively common element of court business. Both courts use unusual vocabulary in recording these transactions, such as the verbs for pledging land (*invadiauit* and *inpignorauit*). Such verbs are rarely found in English manorial records, being much more typical of continental Roman law sources (e.g. Gay 1983, p. 194).

The court rolls of the 'western manors' tell a similar story. For 10 out of the 12 manors, not a single mortgage can be located in the surviving records. However, one western manor, Alrewas in Staffordshire, features an exceptional number of mortgages of tenant land in its records, and in this respect, it resembles Heacham and Hanningfield. The Alrewas rolls covering the years 1327–1349 yield some 40 mortgages.[8] Overall, the pattern seems the same in both east and west: one or two manors with lots of mortgages, and a majority with very few or none.

Why were mortgages common at Heacham, Hanningfield and Alrewas but rare or non-existent elsewhere? There are several possible reasons. It could be that specific individuals had particular knowledge or experience of these instruments, and popularized their use locally. The transactions did not all involve distinct persons. Eight of the 28 transactions at Heacham, including the one cited at the start of this chapter, involved Geoffrey Gosse as mortgagor/debtor. Geoffrey appears in the rolls more generally as a prolific debtor and player in the land market, and not necessarily a poor or marginal man in local society (Beauroy 1995, pp. 69–70). At Alrewas, 12 out of the 40 mortgages involved one William le Forestere as lender. If such individuals had a penchant for the use of mortgages, then this could explain their popularity in particular locations.

Another hypothesis concerning the concentration of mortgages in particular places concerns the geography of peasant customary landholding, as well as the restrictions over the size and structure of and traffic in those peasant holdings, features which themselves reflected a complex mix of factors such as settlement geography, patterns of lordship, and the relative importance of freeholders. It has often been observed that in midland England, customary holdings at this date were relatively likely to be preserved in standard units, such as virgates of around 30 acres, and that the splitting up of such units for exchange tended to be prohibited either explicitly or (more often) implicitly by seigniorial authorities, or by the community. By contrast, in East Anglia—that is, in Norfolk, Suffolk and Essex in particular—many studies show the fragmentation of standard holdings into small parcels by c.1300 and reveal a relatively light seigniorial touch when it comes to the traffic in customary land, or even the seigniorial encouragement of such traffic (Whittle 1998, pp. 49–53). There are exceptions to this necessarily simplified contrast between the midlands and eastern regions with respect to customary landholding, yet it is an important issue to consider in connection with the prevalence of mortgages.

If one wanted to mortgage land to raise credit, one would not necessarily wish to pledge one's entire holding (virgate, half virgate, etc.).

Anyone who did so, and then defaulted on the loan, ran the risk of losing an entire holding permanently. Also, it would have made no sense to transfer a complete holding to a creditor on a conditional basis. This would leave the debtor out of possession and thus with no income from which to repay the debt. However, if a potential borrower lived within a manorial regime in which it was permitted to break off a small portion of a larger holding to sell or, in this case, mortgage, then this might have been a more attractive option. One factor, therefore, that may have been conducive to the development of the mortgage, is a high degree of fragmentation of unfree holdings and a minimal restriction on fragmentation.

It is noticeable from Fig. 2.2 that the manors on which mortgages have been found are generally towards the east of the region. There are no such manors west of the Wash. All nine manors with mortgages are in Norfolk or Essex, apart from Redgrave, Suffolk, which is on the Norfolk border and is the archetype of the manor with an intensive land market and fragmented holdings (Smith 1984). There are no examples in Cambridgeshire, West Suffolk or Lincolnshire. Cambridgeshire court rolls have been studied particularly closely, and an example of a mortgage of customary land from this county has yet to be found (for similar results relating to Wisbech, Cambridgeshire, see Parkin 1998, pp. 214–218).

If one examines more closely the court rolls of the two eastern manors in which mortgages of customary land were unusually common—East Hanningfield and Heacham—one finds that they display characteristic features of East Anglian customary landholding: no obvious standard holdings; ample smallholdings; and no obvious restriction on the movement in small parcels of land that probably represent a portion of an individual's entire holding.

At East Hanningfield, the holdings transferred *inter vivos*, or made vacant on the death of a tenant, came in a variety of shapes and sizes. None is referred to by a term for a standard holding, such as 'virgate'. There are holdings expressed in numbers of 'ware acres' (or 'war acres') (*akerwar'*), in numbers of 'day works' of land (*daywercas*), or simply in terms of acres and rods of unspecified 'land'.[9] There is to be sure a hint of there being standard holdings of 'ware acres', as holdings of 5 and 15 'ware acres' are mentioned quite regularly. Interestingly, the mortgages themselves tend not to tell one what category of land is involved in the transaction. The only mortgage that does so involves the pledging of 'two ware acres within a certain croft'.[10] In general, the land pledged in mortgages is in the form of relatively small parcels or units, such as a croft, or three rods of meadow.

At Heacham, the records provide an even greater impression of the presence of a classic 'East Anglian' customary landholding regime. There is evidence of an active land market in the very high numbers of fines paid for licences to transfer customary land via a surrender by the seller 'to the use of' (*ad opus*) a buyer, who was then admitted. Some of the parcels involved were tiny. In 1314, for example, there was a surrender and admission *ad opus* to a plot described as just 14 feet by 8 feet in area.[11] There are also reports of people making sales without a licence, and also temporary demises (sublettings) of customary land. There was a great deal of scope for dispute about who had title to which portion of customary land, as one would expect where traffic was so intense. The landholdings of individuals at death could be very small. For example, in a court held in December 1322, one John Skule was reported as holding 3 ½ rods from the lord at death, paying a heriot of 6d.[12] The amounts mortgaged are also small, being a few acres or rods. Of the mortgages in acres and rods, the smallest at Heacham in this period is a half of one rod.[13]

At first glance, it appears as if the Alrewas holding structure was dominated by standard holdings, such as virgates and half-virgates, which is what one might expect for this area of the country. Out of 70 customary tenants in Alrewas itself listed on a rental (list of tenants) with custumal (description of customs and services) dated 1341, 51 were either virgaters or half-virgaters (Birrell and Hutchinson 2004). This Alrewas virgate was probably 30 acres in extent (Graham 1994, p. 9). However, the rental gives a misleading impression of the reality of landholding structure. The court rolls provide plenty of evidence of a traffic in small parcels of land after 1327, including single rods and selions (common field strips) (Graham 1994, p. 13). Similarly, the mortgages were secured by small plots, often of less than an acre. As at Heacham and Hanningfield, the de facto fragmentation of holdings at Alrewas was probably a stimulus for the mortgage market.

There are a number of potential reasons why mortgages gained some popularity as a form of land transfer in particular manors. One potentially significant consideration, however, is the character of the customary landholding regime in the locality concerned. From the point of view of mortgagors/borrowers, it made most sense to be able to pledge a small portion of a larger holding. At Heacham and Alrewas especially, but also at East Hanningfield, there was a situation of fragmented customary holdings in which this factor was potentially important. Elsewhere, the standard holding was more common. This was the case, for example, in much of Cambridgeshire, where some locations such as the manors of Crowland Abbey, or those of the Ely bishopric, in effect formed part of a 'midland' customary landholding system based on standard holdings (Briggs 2009a). It is therefore perhaps not surprising that mortgages of customary land have not been traced for that county. Some locations had a number of characteristics which in combination could potentially encourage the employment of mortgages. At Alrewas, for instance, the low cash rents paid by customary tenants to the lord were perhaps additionally significant. The 1341 rental is careful to state the ancient customary rent of two shillings per virgate. Modern commentators agree that this is very low. It could well be that it simply made economic sense for Alrewas customary tenants to mortgage parts of their holdings to secure relatively large loans. Because their outgoings on rent were so low, the mortgagors could afford to pay off the loans.

Yet, even though mortgages became quite common in some places, it is still necessary to recognize that explicit evidence of the use of customary property to secure credit is rare in this period. Fewer than 100 contracts have been identified in a search of the records of hundreds of manor court sessions (Table 2.2). Although many locations in East Anglia and beyond presumably enjoyed characteristics such as fragmented holdings and active land markets that may on the face of it have been conducive to the pledging of land as collateral, mortgages were clearly rare in general. What factors account for this?

2.3 Why Were Mortgages Rare Overall?

Drawing on existing studies, one can suggest three particularly important explanations for the rarity of mortgages and other forms of conditional transfer of customary land: their potentially usurious character; the weakness of property rights in land; and the unattractiveness to borrowers of the terms of mortgages. In this section, we consider these explanations using the evidence from East Hanningfield, Heacham and Alrewas.

2.3.1 *Usury*

Medieval canon lawyers regarded the kind of mortgage arrangement with which this chapter is concerned as an infringement of the church's law against usury, referring to it as a form of 'cloaked usury' (McLaughlin 1939; Haren 2000). As noted, church councils banned mortgages in which the income from the pledged land was not deducted from the principal sum loaned. In the case of Heacham and Hanningfield, the court roll entries do not make it explicit that the mortgagee would draw the revenues from the land during the term, but it seems highly likely that this occurred. Several Alrewas entries, indeed, do strongly suggest that the creditor took the fruits of the land during the term and perhaps cultivated it himself. In these mortgages, the contract specifies that if the land was sown or 'composted' at the point of debt repayment, the creditor 'shall have his crop and his "up worthyng", or the price of the same, by judgement of neighbours'.[14] The phrase 'up worthyng' is obscure, but it seems to refer to the costs of cultivation, for which the creditor should be compensated if the land was redeemed before the crop was harvested.

In England, church courts concerned themselves with prosecutions of usury in which the accused party had been involved in mortgage lending (Helmholz 1986). Did peasant creditors avoid the creation and enrolment of formal mortgages because they feared prosecution for usury in the church courts?

This is possible in principle, but more work is needed to shed greater light on this idea, and in particular, its implication that English church authorities were more inclined to prosecute usurious practices than their counterparts in Continental Europe where, as noted, mortgages were apparently more prevalent. One would need to investigate the frequency with which usury prosecutions involving mortgages took place in ecclesiastical courts, and also to check the exact type of transactions that were deemed reprehensible. We should also remember that manor courts in this period had the power to deal with breaches of the usury ban, and occasionally did so. There have been no instances found in the manorial records searched of complaint against conditional transfers on the grounds that they were usurious. Three of the Alrewas mortgages were made in favour of a chaplain, Thomas Faleyn (for this man and his financial dealings, see also Swanson 1993). The Hanningfield rolls also record a transaction of six acres pledged in 1341 to Richard the rector of East

Hanningfield by William Atte Heg, for a loan of 60 shillings. Such clerics might be thought especially susceptible to accusations of usury arising from such arrangements.

Most importantly, if usury had been a widespread concern, this would be another reason to expect the general adoption of the *rente* device in an English agrarian setting, which does not appear to have happened.

2.3.2 *Property Rights*

Holders of villein or customary land did not enjoy exclusive or absolute property rights over their land. Title remained with the landlord, a fact that was reflected in the fines for seigniorial permission for any transfer of such land to a third party. It is possible that the minimal use of customary real property to secure credit flowed from the fact that borrowers did not fully 'own' their land in a meaningful sense.

Seigniorial permission was required to secure a valid pledge of customary land in exchange for credit, presumably because this was a transaction in which the future title to the land might shift to a different person. This is reflected in the fine paid for the enrolment of the mortgage. At East Hanningfield, this requirement for seigniorial permission was made explicit by the wording of several of the mortgages, which begin by stating that '[the mortgagor] *by lord's licence* has pledged [*inpignorauit*]', and so on. Also, at Heacham and Alrewas, it is stated that the pledging of the mortgaged land was made *in plena curia*, i.e. 'in full court', again stressing that this was all done publicly and with the knowledge of the lord's officials. If a lord effectively needed to be asked permission to validate a conditional transfer, this raises the possibility that in some manors that permission was refused, leading to the non-employment of mortgages by tenants. Unfortunately, little evidence has been found thus far in the court rolls to either support or refute this possibility. It has to be asked however, what incentive lords or their officials would have had to object to conditional transfers, if they were informed of and approved of the identity of the transferee.

Probably, more important was the attitude of the creditor/mortgagee. We have very little information from the court rolls concerning the property rights of mortgagees in conditionally pledged customary land, which is in itself no doubt a reflection of the rarity of mortgages of this kind of property (Poos and Bonfield 1998). However, one may wonder whether a potential creditor would want to take on, at least potentially, customary land that did not carry exclusive property rights. Would a pledge of a customary acre constitute effective security for a lender, given that in theory, the lord at any stage could evict a holder—including a mortgagee—and take the holding back into his possession? One must add to this the fact that the systems of written property registration in existence in this society would have made it very difficult for a potential creditor to access reliable information about the specific rights and obligations attached to particular plots of customary land offered as collateral in the first place.

A connected argument is that a freeholder creditor might not wish to take permanent possession of customary land because it carried servile obligations, including labour services. To investigate this further, one would need to undertake a close examination of the personal status of all the mortgagees in the transactions identified, which would be a difficult task with an uncertain outcome. It is interesting, at least, to note that the two most important mortgagees at East Hanningfield, in terms of the number of transactions, were both villeins. These men, John de Chetwode and William Chaynel, are near the top of a list of 56 customary tenants swearing fealty at the first court of Agnes, Countess of Pembroke, in early 1349. This evidence perhaps points to the likelihood that many of the lenders/mortgagees who used customary land as collateral came from within the villein tenant community.

The case of Alrewas is particularly important for the issue of peasant property rights and mortgages. A distinctive feature of Alrewas is that it was an 'ancient demesne' manor, that is, it was in the hands of the king at the time of the Norman Conquest, as Domesday Book confirms. The manor was granted to its lords, the Somerville family, by King John in 1204. Freeholders—tenants and free sokemen—were present among the manorial tenants in our period. However, the largest group of tenants (109) was described in 1341 very deliberately as 'customary tenants of base tenure, who in domesday are called villeins'. These were not full-blown serfs or villeins with the full range of disabilities that implies. Instead, like other tenants of ancient demesne manors, they were privileged customary tenants, halfway between freemen and villeins proper. They did owe unfree obligations such as heriot and merchet (a marriage fine), but very light labour services (Birrell and Hutchinson 2004). Twelve of the 21 mortgagors recorded at Alrewas can be found on the 1341 list of customary tenants. Thus while we have been justified in treating the Alrewas mortgages thus far as transactions in customary land, it must be recognized that this was a distinctive type of customary land. It could therefore be that mortgages were common at Alrewas because the customary tenants enjoyed stronger property rights than their counterparts on manors that were not ancient demesne. However, neither Heacham nor Hanningfield was an ancient demesne manor, though mortgages were evident there, and the rolls of other ancient demesne manors examined for this chapter do not feature mortgages, such as those of Worfield (Shropshire). Thus, the evidence concerning ancient demesne supports the view that the nature of property rights is not the primary explanation for the overall rarity of mortgages of customary land. That view is supported by the finding, mentioned earlier, that mortgages of freehold land—a type of land which enjoyed relatively strong property rights—do not seem to have been any more common among the peasantry than mortgages of customary land (Briggs 2009b).

2.3.3 Were the Mortgage Terms Too Disadvantageous to Borrower/Mortgagor?

In the mortgages which took the 'classic' form outlined via the example at the start of this chapter, the terms must have looked strict from the borrower's point of view. A specific day at the end of the term was set for the payment. If that term was not met, and if default occurred either 'in whole or in part', then the land would be forfeit to the creditor and his heirs for ever. In principle, even if a person paid all the debt apart from one penny, he could lose his land in perpetuity. We know that foreclosure did happen; in one Heacham example, there is an addition to the original court roll entry, in which a debtor came into court and renounced to the creditor any claim he had in land mortgaged some two years earlier.[15] With such penalties, it is perhaps not surprising that most would-be borrowers did not take the risk. If we follow this line of argument, it is the strictness of the terms of the medieval mortgage which offers the most convincing explanation for the rarity of mortgages of customary land in this period. For some historians, indeed, the evidence presented here would fit comfortably within a wider picture in which mortgages remained generally unattractive and exceptional in form and provisions prior to the emergence of the doctrine of the equity of redemption in the seventeenth century (Allen 1992; Baker 2002).

It is thus significant to note that while most of the mortgages examined provided for this strict form of foreclosure, not all did so

Table 2.3 Types of conditional land transfer on three manors

	(A) Total transactions	*Transactions in (A) with provision for permanent forfeiture*	*Transactions in (A) where mortgagee held property until repayment*	*Others*
E. Hanningfield	8	3	3	2
Heacham	21	15	2	4
Alrewas	40	13	24	3
Total	69	31	29	9

Note Heacham excludes conditional transfers of standing crops
Source see Table 2.2

(Table 2.3). A number of arrangements which vary in their details stated essentially that the pledged land should be held by the creditor until repayment and made no provision for its permanent loss. A typical example of this, from Alrewas, records that:

> Walter de Orby came into full court and pledged [*impignorauit*] to John le Baxtere one acre of land lying in Tounfeld upon le Sevenacres next to the land of John Franceis. To have and to hold to the same John and his heirs and assigns until the aforesaid Walter or his heirs or assigns shall fully pay in one day to the same John his heirs or assigns twenty shillings of silver. And when the said Walter his heirs or assigns shall have fully paid the said money, then they shall recover the said acre of land.[16]

Such arrangements made sense, especially to the debtor, since he avoided permanent loss of his property. Furthermore, if the debtor completely failed to repay, the creditor would eventually recover the principal out of the profits from the land, albeit with some delay. This arrangement was probably also less open to the charge of usury than the contract which allowed for foreclosure. In fact, this agreement is in essence very similar to a continental annuity or *rente* agreement, with provision for redemption.

The evidence from the three manors offers other interesting variants on the 'classic' mortgage form, which together provide reminders that conditional transfers were flexible, could be shaped by negotiation between the parties and did not always need to involve outright loss of the pledged land in the case of non-payment. Diversity was especially marked at Alrewas, where just 13 contracts out of the total of 40 provided for permanent forfeiture, only 10 of which took the classic mortgage format. Parties did not necessarily restrict themselves to a single type of contract. Yet despite this potential for flexibility in the use of customary property to secure loans, such arrangements remained rare across the country as a whole.

2.4 Did the Scarcity of the Mortgage Have a Negative Impact on the Rural Credit Market?

An initial area to focus on here is the fact that the mortgaging of land allowed the borrower access to a loan in cash. In the generality of credit revealed by manorial debt litigation, most of which was agreed orally, and of course unsecured, loans of cash were quite rare. On average, in the debt litigation data, only about five per cent of debts expressed in money are explicitly described as resulting from unpaid loans. Much more common than the cash loan was sales credit, particularly debts outstanding from the sale of commodities with a deferred payment (Briggs 2009a). A loan of cash was a potentially much more powerful form in which to receive credit as it gave greater flexibility to the borrower.

It should also be noted that the average size of the debts revealed by manorial debt litigation was quite small. The median debt in the records of five fourteenth-century courts was about three shillings, equivalent to about 12 days' wages for a carpenter in the 1340s. Debts over 20*s* in value were rare, never really composing more than about five per cent of all debts where the value of the debt is given. The same data suggest that well over half of all debts were 5*s* or below in value (Briggs 2009a, Table 2.5). The mortgage loans from the three manors provide a marked contrast to this (Table 2.4). There are 34 legible loans in the mortgages from Hanningfield and Heacham. They range from 4*s* to 13 marks sterling (£8 13s 4d). However, only five of these 34 mortgage

Table 2.4 Size of mortgage loans on three manors

	A. Total loans	*Loans in col. A > 19s. 11d.*	*Loans in col. A > 39s. 11d.*
E. Hanningfield	8	5	4
Heacham	26	13	4
Alrewas	39	11	4
Total	74	29	12

Note includes conditional transfers of standing crops. Two Heacham loans and one Alrewas loan are illegible.
Source see Table 2.2

loans were in the sub-10*s*. bracket, and 18 were in fact sums of 20s. or above. At Alrewas, mortgage loans ranged from 4*s* to 42*s*, and 15 out of 39 legible debts were for 20*s* or more. Thus, it appears that those who mortgaged their lands could gain access to much larger quantities of credit than those engaged in the more usual oral, unsecured transactions. Those who borrowed on mortgages appear also to have had greater access to long-term credit. The unsecured informal credit revealed by debt litigation was typically extended for terms of about six months (Briggs 2009a). In contrast, an analysis of the 35 mortgages from the three manors which allow a term in months to be calculated shows that the median loan term was four years, that in 11 loans, the term was more than five years, and that only seven had terms under 12 months. Moreover, as already noted, some mortgages had no specified repayment date but could be repaid at any time. These are important points to bear in mind in assessing the rarity of mortgage lending.

On the other hand, one should not lose sight of the fact that even in places where there is no evidence of mortgage-based lending, rural credit markets developed and prospered in the early fourteenth century. At Littleport in Cambridgeshire, for example, some 530 debt cases were initiated in the manor court between 1316 and 1327, a total of disputed unpaid debts which represented a much larger total of credit relationships. The records of the 10 western manors that failed to produce a single example of a mortgage all nevertheless contain significant quantities of interpersonal debt litigation, which is testimony to a lively credit market. Largely oral credit transactions were arranged with the use of personal sureties, or pledges, who offered themselves to guarantee the repayment of the debt in the event of the default of the principal debtor. In the manor court, debts could be recovered from a principal debtor or a pledge through seizure of the movable property of the borrower or his pledge. Even where real estate was not offered as collateral, it was possible for creditors to gain some confidence that they were protected from risk in the event of default by a borrower (Briggs 2009a).

One must ask whether the functions performed by the mortgage were achieved in the medieval English village by means of other devices, with the result that the rarity of formal mortgages mattered little for the rural economy. One possibility is that someone in possession of land but in need of cash might simply have sold a portion of his or her holding outright and then replaced it later with a purchase on the market, rather than arrange a mortgage. Such an arrangement would not in any case have been all that different in its effects from a mortgage of the 'classic' kind, in which possession was conveyed to a mortgagee who received the profits of the land during the term. Furthermore, a landholder might have been able to raise more funds through an outright sale than with a mortgage, though we have seen that mortgagors did receive substantial loans. However, the main disadvantage of such a permanent sale was the outright loss of legal title to the land that had been sold, whereas during the term of a mortgage, the mortgagor did retain some rights to the mortgaged land. Furthermore, selling land to raise funds with a view to replacing that land later on involved risks connected to the future availability and price of land on the market.

Alternatively, the peasant in need of capital could simply have leased out a portion of his or her holding. Several commentators have raised the possibility that the temporary leases of land from peasant tenant to subtenant, which are frequently recorded in court rolls, may have been connected with credit (Briggs 2009a). These leases are quite distinct in the record from the formal mortgages discussed to this point. They consist simply of a note that a lessor had been granted seigniorial permission to demise land to a lessee for a term of years, or number of crops. In theory, the transaction underlying such entries could have been one in which a peasant borrower leased part of his land in exchange for a loan, with the loan being repaid in whole or in part out of the proceeds of the leased land during the term of the lease. Such an arrangement would have had a good deal in common with the mortgages under consideration in this chapter (for the lease as functionally similar to the mortgage, see Allen 1992). However, there seems to be little evidence to support the idea that this is what was going on in most leases. The suggestion is discouraged by an analysis of the parties to such leases. Crucially, too, the brief entries which record the leases provide no concrete reference to any lump sum advanced to the lessor at the start of the lease. It is highly likely, of course, that the leasing or sub-leasing of land represented a source of income to the lessor, since the lessee must certainly have paid rent, even though this is not recorded. Yet, it is hard to see the inter-peasant lease of customary land that is common in manorial court records of this period as functionally equivalent to the mortgage proper (Briggs 2009a).

2.5 Conclusion

The lending of money on mortgages was potentially important in the medieval countryside. A mortgage allowed a landholding peasant to tap the value of his property and gain access to capital which could be used for a variety of investment purposes, such as expanding livestock and landholdings. The mortgages examined here typically involved relatively large and long-term loans. We have found that some customary tenants in some locations did mortgage their lands and that the reasons for this localized popularity were probably complex. It seems likely that local variation in the tenurial character of customary landholding, especially with regard to the issue of fragmentation of standard holdings, meant that the use of customary mortgages was more attractive in some places that in others. Overall, however, the research presented here confirms that in England in the early fourteenth century, the use of real estate to secure credit seems to have been exceptional by comparison with other parts of Western Europe in the Middle Ages.[17] When it comes to explaining this rarity of the use of customary land as collateral, it is probably too simplistic to claim that it was due solely to the impact of the servile tenure of such land, and the restricted property rights that implied. There is, for instance, no explicit evidence that lords banned their customary tenants from mortgaging their holdings. It is possible that some creditors preferred not to take customary land as collateral because of its unfree character, or because of fears of arbitrary eviction, but this is largely speculation.

In pointing to the strict and potentially unattractive character of the terms and conditions of the standard medieval mortgage, this study supports the conclusions of earlier work which has commented on the rarity of English mortgages before the seventeenth century. Borrowers may have been unwilling to enter into agreements in which they risked losing their land if they found themselves unable to pay. It is useful to reiterate that the rarity of peasant mortgaging was not a feature restricted to the customary sector; there has yet to be convincing evidence brought forward to show that the freehold mortgage was very widely used. Mortgaging in general, rather than mortgaging of customary land only, seems to have been exceptional at this time. Since the standard form of mortgage was common to both freehold and customary sectors, it seems likely that it was the terms and conditions of the mortgage and the state of mortgage law that was unattractive to lenders and borrowers. In the localities studied in this chapter, parties often developed alternative and more flexible forms of mortgage which were not as strict as the standard form, in the sense that they did not stipulate the permanent loss of land to the mortgagee. These more flexible arrangements may have been attractive to creditors too. Some of these contracts were similar in essentials to the *rente* contracts that became so widespread in different parts of Continental Europe. It remains puzzling that such agreements did not gain a wider popularity in England.

Assessing the absence or extreme rarity of a historical phenomenon or institution, in this case the medieval peasant mortgage, is always difficult. We have considered the possibility that the mortgage was not widely used because it was not in great demand, since other village transactions performed an equivalent economic function. The evidence to support such a position is not strong. Yet, the question of demand for mortgages is worthy of more general consideration. This chapter has treated the rarity of peasant mortgages mainly from the point of view of institutional constraints on the supply of mortgage loans. Yet, it is also worth noting the possibility that demand for large-scale, long-term capital was relatively muted among English villagers and that this may form part of the explanation for the rarity of peasant mortgages of both free and customary lands in this period. Whatever the case, the relatively low level of mortgage lending appears to be consistent with the absence of what one might call a rural *capital* market proper in England before the Black Death, that is, one which involved the mobilization of large sums of money. As we have noted, however, it did not prevent the emergence in many localities of informal, oral *credit* markets, based on unsecured transactions, which were lively and well-developed by the European standards of the time.

Notes

1. A rod is ¼ acre, or 0.6 hectares.
2. Norwich, Norfolk Record Office [hereafter NRO], Le Strange DA8 (21 November 1317).
3. NRO, Le Strange DA7 (4 August 1315). The heirs of the mortgagee appear to be in at least partial possession of these lands.
4. NRO, NRS 12475.
5. See also the limited space dedicated to the use of land as collateral in a recent major study of charters: Kaye (2009).

6. Funded by Arts and Humanities Research Council 2006–2009, Ref. AH/D502713/1. The principal investigators were Professors Richard Smith (Cambridge) and Phillipp Schofield (Aberystwyth). The eastern counties: Norfolk, Suffolk, Cambridgeshire, Lincolnshire and Essex; western counties: Staffordshire, Shropshire, Worcestershire, Herefordshire and Gloucestershire.
7. Chelmsford, Essex Record Office [hereafter ERO], D/DP M 832; NRO, Le Strange DA1–DA9.
8. Stafford, Staffordshire Record Office [hereafter SRO], D(W)0/3/1–37; TNA, SC 2/202/206 (rolls of 1286–1288). The earliest Alrewas rolls (SRO, D(W)0/3/1–7) are printed in Landor (1907, 1910).
9. For 'ware acres', see Horrox (1994, p. 287). Two late thirteenth-century charters in the Essex Record Office convey 'day works' of land at East Hanningfield: ERO, D/Day T2/9; D/Day T2/11.
10. ERO, D/DP M 832 (17 March 1343).
11. NRO, Le Strange DA7 (July 1314).
12. NRO, Le Strange DA8 (10 December 1322).
13. NRO, Le Strange DA7 (29 January 1317).
14. E.g. SRO, D(W)0/3/26 (12 May 1341).
15. NRO, Le Strange DA 8; the renunciation of claim was made at a court session held 3 February 1323.
16. SRO, D(W)0/3/30 (14 February 1344).
17. And perhaps even by comparison with other parts of the British Isles: one function of the Welsh *prid*, or gage of land, was as security for credit: see Smith (1976).

Acknowledgements I am grateful to Matt Tompkins, who collected much of the data discussed here; to Jean Birrell for advice on the Alrewas court rolls; and to the late J. M. Beauroy for discussion of medieval Heacham. Jaco Zuijderduijn, Michael Schraer and participants in a number of seminars and conferences between 2013 and 2016 provided useful comments; all errors are my own.

References

Primary Sources

Birrell, J., and D. Hutchinson (eds.), 2004. 'An Alrewas rental of 1341', *Collections for a History of Staffordshire*, 4th Ser., vol. 20, pp. 59–82.

Landor, W.N. (ed.), 1907. 'The Alrewas court rolls of 1259–61', *Collections for a History of Staffordshire*, New Ser., vol. 10, Pt. 1, pp. 245–293.

Landor, W.N. (ed.), 1910. 'Alrewas court rolls 1268–1269 and 1272–1273', *Collections for a History of Staffordshire*, 3rd Ser., pp. 87–137.

Poos, L.R., and L. Bonfield (eds.), 1998. *Select Cases in Manorial Courts 1250–1550. Property and Family Law* (London: Selden Society, vol. 114).

Secondary Works

Allen, R.C., 1992. *Enclosure and the Yeoman. The Agricultural Development of the South Midlands 1450–1850* (Oxford: Oxford University Press).

Baker, J.H., 2002. *An Introduction to English Legal History*, 4th edn (London: Butterworths).

Beauroy, J.M., 1995. 'Structure sociale et espace seigneurial en Norfolk, c.1270–1330', Unpublished study.

Besley, T., K.B. Burchardi, and M. Ghatak, 2012. 'Incentives and the De Soto effect', *Quarterly Journal of Economics*, vol. 127, pp. 237–282.

Bogart, D., and G. Richardson, 2009. 'Making property productive: Reorganizing rights to real and equitable estates in Britain, 1660–1830', *European Review of Economic History*, vol. 13, pp. 3–30.

Brennan, T., 2006. 'Peasants and debt in eighteenth-century Champagne', *Journal of Interdisciplinary History*, vol. 37, pp. 175–200.

Briggs, C., 2009a. *Credit and Village Society in Fourteenth-Century England* (Oxford: Oxford University Press).

Briggs, C., 2009b. 'Credit and the freehold land market in England, c.1200–c.1350: Possibilities and problems for research', in P.R. Schofield and T. Lambrecht (eds.), *Credit and the Rural Economy in North Western Europe, c.1200–c.1850* (Turnhout: Brepols), pp. 109–28.

De Soto, H., 2000. *The Mystery of Capital. Why Capitalism Triumphs in the West and Fails Everywhere Else* (London: Black Swan).

Duby, G., 1968. *Rural Economy and Country Life in the Medieval West* (London: Edward Arnold).

Ertl, T., 2017. 'Small landlords: Land transactions in and around Bozen (South Tirol) in the mid-thirteenth century', *Vierteljahrschrift für Sozial- und Wirtschaftsgeschichte*, vol. 104, pp. 7–28.

Gaulin, J.-L., and F. Menant, 1998. 'Crédit rural et endettement paysan dans l'Italie communale', in M. Berthe (ed.), *Endettement paysan et credit rural dans L'Europe medievale et moderne* (Toulouse: Presses Universitaires du Mirail), pp. 35–67.

Gay, J., 1983. 'Recherches sur le gage immobilier. Le mort-gage dans le Comté de Bourgogne (XIIe-XIVe siècles)', *Mémoires de la Société pour l'histoire du droit et des institutions des anciens pays bourguignons, comtois et romands*, vol. 38, pp. 185–254.

Gilomen, H.-J., 1998. 'L'endettement paysan et la question du crédit dans les pays d'Empire au Moyen Âge', in M. Berthe (ed.), *Endettement paysan et credit rural dans L'Europe medievale et moderne* (Toulouse: Presses Universitaires du Mirail), pp. 99–137.

Graham, H., 1994. 'A Social and Economic Study of the Late Medieval Peasantry: Alrewas, Staffordshire, in the Fourteenth Century', Unpublished PhD thesis, University of Birmingham.

Haren, M., 2000. *Sin and Society in Fourteenth-Century England: A Study of the* Memoriale Presbiterorum (Oxford: Oxford University Press).

Helmholz, R.H., 1986. 'Usury and the English Church Courts', *Speculum*, vol. 61, pp. 364–380.

Herlihy, D., 1965. 'Population, plague and social change in rural Pistoia, 1201–1430', *EcHR*, vol. 18, pp. 225–244.

Horrox, R., 1994. *The Black Death* (Manchester: Manchester University Press).

Kaye, J.M., 2009. *Medieval English Conveyances* (Cambridge: Cambridge University Press).

Lewis, P.A., 1979. 'Mortgages in the Bordelais and Bazadais', *Viator*, vol. 10, pp. 23–38.

Mate, M., 1993. 'The East Sussex land market and agrarian class structure in the late middle ages', *P&P*, vol. 139, pp. 46–65.

McLaughlin, T.P., 1939. 'The teaching of the canonists on usury (XII, XIII and XIV centuries)', *Mediaeval Studies*, vol. 1, pp. 81–147.

Parkin, K., 1998. 'Courts and the Community: Reconstructing the Fourteenth-Century Peasant Society of Wisbech Hundred, Cambridgeshire, from Manor Court Rolls', Unpublished PhD thesis, University of Leicester.

Renault, L., 2011. 'Tabellions et crédit dans les campagnes normandes au XVe siècle: quelques hypothèses', in M. Arnoux and O. Guyotjeannin (eds.), *Tabellions et tabellionages de la France médiévale et moderne* (Paris: École des Chartes), pp. 121–143.

Richardson, H.G., 1960. *The English Jewry Under Angevin Kings* (London: Methuen).

Rosenthal, J.-L., 1993. 'Credit markets and economic change in southeastern France 1630–1788', *Explorations in Economic History*, vol. 30, pp. 129–157.

Schnapper, B., 1957. *Les rentes au XVIe siècle. Histoire d'un instrument de crédit* (Paris: S.E.V.P.E.N).

Schofield, P., 2004. 'Credit and the peasant land market in the medieval English countryside', in S. Cavaciocchi (ed.), *Il mercato della terra secc. XIII-XVIII. Atti delle 'Trentacinquesima Settimana di Studi' 5-9 Maggio 2003* (Florence: Le Monnier), pp. 785–796.

Schofield, P.R., and T. Lambrecht (eds.), 2009. *Credit and the Rural Economy in North Western Europe, c.1200–c.1850* (Turnhout: Brepols).

Smith, L.B., 1976. 'The gage and the land market in late medieval Wales', *EcHR*, vol. 29, pp. 537–550.

Smith, R.M., 1984. 'Families and their land in an area of partible inheritance: Redgrave, Suffolk, 1260–1320', in R.M. Smith (ed.), *Land, Kinship and Life-cycle* (Cambridge: Cambridge University Press), pp. 135–196.

Swanson, R., 1993. 'Clergy and manorial society in late medieval Staffordshire', *Staffordshire Studies*, vol. 5, pp. 13–34.

Van Bochove, C., H. Deneweth, and J. Zuijderduijn, 2015. 'Real estate and mortgage finance in England and the Low Countries, 1300–1800', *C&C*, vol. 30, pp. 9–38.

Van Werveke, H., 1968. 'Le mort-gage et son rôle économique en Flandre et en Lotharingie', in H. Van Werveke, *Miscellanea Mediaevalia: verspreide opstellen over economische en sociale geschiedenis van de middeleeuwen* (Ghent: E. Story-Scientia), pp. 159–190.

Van Zanden, J.L., J. Zuijderduijn, and T. De Moor, 2012. 'Small is beautiful: The efficiency of credit markets in late medieval Holland', *European Review of Economic History*, vol. 16, pp. 3–22.

Whittle, J., 1998. 'Individualism and the family-land bond: A reassessment of land transfer patterns among the English peasantry *c.*1270–1580', *P&P*, vol. 160, pp. 25–63.

CHAPTER 3

Mortgages Raised by Rural English Copyhold Tenants 1605–1735

Juliet Gayton

3.1 Introduction

The credit market in seventeenth-century England used a variety of instruments, ranging from informal pawns, trade credits and arrears to formal bonds, bills and mortgages (Holderness 1976; Spicksley 2008). A significant boost to both borrowing and lending had been given by changes in the usury laws at the end of the sixteenth century, which permitted some interest to be charged in certain circumstances.[1] At the same time, most activity, in rural areas at least, was restricted to interpersonal borrowing and lending because formal financial institutions had not yet been established (Muldrew 1998). In this overall context, there was a considerable increase after 1600 in the use of instruments such as mortgages where interest payments could be obtained. Lambrecht and others have demonstrated that annuities were popular in the Low Countries from earlier times, partly because they conveniently circumvented the usury laws by being classified as a sale (Lambrecht 2009). However, annuities do not seem to have been used in England in the

J. Gayton
Independent Researcher, University of Exeter, Exeter, UK

C. Briggs and J. Zuijderduijn (eds.), *Land and Credit*,
Palgrave Studies in the History of Finance,
https://doi.org/10.1007/978-3-319-66209-1_3

same way, and most of the occasional annuities found by this author were set up within the family via legacies in wills and were not part of the wider credit market. The mortgage seems to have been the preferred English instrument where land was used as security.[2]

Different groups within English society used mortgages in slightly different ways, and this chapter examines one subset of English villagers in the long seventeenth century. They were the copyholders, who, between the fifteenth and nineteenth centuries, were often the most numerous landholders to be found in rural areas. However, apart from an analysis of mortgage numbers found in north Yorkshire (French and Hoyle 1999), they have only been given a passing mention in previous research. The nature and scale of copyholder mortgages are therefore overdue for examination.

In order to raise a mortgage loan, a prospective borrower required sufficient access to, and rights of tenure to, land which could be offered as collateral. The nature of their tenure is therefore relevant to explore briefly at the outset. In early modern England, there were three major types of land tenure: freehold, leasehold and copyhold (including a version of the latter termed 'tenant right' found in northern England).[3] Freehold and leasehold still exist, but copyhold died out during the nineteenth century and was formally abolished in the 1920s. Copyhold tenure was based upon the manor, and holding rights were 'according to the custom of the manor'. Details of customs and transfers of holdings were recorded in the manorial court rolls. Hence, the term 'copyhold', as entitlement, was confirmed by *copy* of the relevant roll. The lord of the manor actually owned the land, and so copyholders were termed 'tenants' and paid a modest rent. They had formally to surrender or inherit copyholdings via the lord in his manorial court and paid him extra fines and heriots on such occasions. In principle, the lord could decide to whom to regrant the premises, but by the seventeenth century, this had become formulaic, and the copyholds could be inherited, bought and sold through the court without interference from the lord unless a transgression had occurred to provoke a forfeit.

The two principal types were 'copyhold of inheritance' and 'copyhold for lives' which had different securities of tenure. Copyhold of inheritance in which one tenant held the land was very secure and almost freehold and could be bought and sold or used as collateral for a loan. However, lives copyhold had two, or often three, persons with rights to a holding and could not be easily bought or sold. This meant that only copyholders of inheritance could use their property as security for a mortgage, as it had to be available for forfeit or sale if the loan could not be repaid (this finding was initially noted in Gayton 2013). The precise numbers and distribution of the two types of copyhold are uncertain, but a number of authors have concluded that inheritance copyholds predominated in the eastern part of England, while lives were more common in the west and south–west (Tawney 1912, p. 34; Allen 1992, App. 1, French and Hoyle 2007, p. xv). In the southern county of Hampshire where this study was based, both types coexisted and seem to have developed according to seigneurial choice rather than geography. The bishop of Winchester's manors had mainly inheritance tenure; those of the dean and chapter of Winchester had mostly lives; and Winchester College had both.

The mechanism for agreeing a mortgage with a copyholder of inheritance was the conditional surrender. The borrower tenants surrendered their land via the lord in the manorial court *on condition* that if they paid their lenders certain specified sums of money on or before identified dates, then the surrenders would be declared void. In the interim, the borrowing tenants retained occupation and use of the land, and at the end of the agreed term, the 'satisfaction' of the lender with the borrower's completed repayments was entered into the court rolls.[4] However, in the case of a delay in payments, or of disputes (of which there were remarkably few), the matter was raised at the manorial court and recorded, and the parties asked to sort it out. Leeway was given for a while, but if this was not successful, then the premises were forfeited to the lender at the next court. If the borrower merely died during the term, then the heir to the premises became responsible for repayment. However, no evidence has been found that these mortgages could otherwise be reassigned or sold on to others.

The source documentation for these copyholder mortgages is the individual manorial court rolls. Although historians have long mined these records for a variety of purposes, they have been overlooked as a resource for mortgage records. Those previously studying mortgages in England in the early modern period have focused on probate or litigation records, or the movement of title deeds involving freeholders (e.g. Muldrew 1998; Holderness 1976).[5] Unfortunately, as has been observed, the survival of long runs of manorial court rolls is patchy and fragmented (Van Bavel et al. 2012, pp. 354–355). Some of the most suitable records are therefore those from the large ecclesiastical and college estates which retained a corporate lordship over many centuries and have well-preserved records. The research results presented in this chapter are drawn from the records of three Hampshire manors with copyhold of inheritance tenure: Meonstoke owned by Winchester College; Crawley owned by the bishop of Winchester; and Hinton Ampner owned by the dean and chapter of Winchester.[6] Although these manors lie within a small area of southern England, there is no reason to suppose that the behaviour of the tenants on these estates was significantly different from those in other parts of the country. The results should be applicable to copyholders of inheritance elsewhere.

It is important to note that because these mortgage contracts were recorded in the court rolls at the time of first agreement, they therefore provide a register of *all* mortgages, and so they facilitate a full range of analysis to be carried out. This is in contrast to studies which have had to rely on probate or litigation records, as those did not usually include copyholders, and were in any event only a snapshot at the time of death, and/or where mortgages had ended in dispute. Muldrew, for instance, found that a mere four out of 1352 probate accounts for Hampshire contained a mortgage (Muldrew 1998, p. 105). A partial and misleading picture may therefore have been given, which may have led to a tendency for the historiography of mortgages to suggest that they were mainly used in times of crisis. Another similar advantage of copyholder mortgages was noted by Tawney who commented that 'copyholds were transferred publicly in the court of the manor, so that encumbrances on them could not be concealed' (Tawney 1941, p. 20). In other words, the manorial court acted as a form of land registry so that potential purchasers of copyhold property could find out if a mortgage was outstanding, whereas this was not possible with freeholder mortgages as there was no centralised or public open recording of them.[7]

Finally, the fact that this study is focused on the seventeenth century is important. This author has found no evidence of mortgages amongst English copyholders before the reform of the usury laws in the late sixteenth century (statute of 1571 but not confirmed until 1598). These allowed, for the first time, interest on loans to be charged up to a specified ceiling (initially 10%). So from 1598 onwards, the ability legally to charge interest seems to have produced a flowering of mortgage activity. It cannot be coincidental that the bishop of Winchester found it necessary to set up special separate mortgage surrender registers for his copyhold of inheritance tenants from 1598.[8] It is, however, possible that copyholders used mortgages before this date, but if so they have yet to be identified. Before 1571/1598, they would either have agreed loans without any interest or may have used covert means to effect them such as actual sale and resale. However, long and detailed searching through manorial records would be needed to identify them.

3.2 Dimensions of the Mortgage Borrowing

The analysis of copyholder mortgages was carried out for Meonstoke between 1606 and 1735 during which time 334 mortgages were agreed. The data for Crawley (73) and Hinton Ampner (22) was restricted to the period 1640–1705 and all three manors then gave an overall total of 429 in the analysis. However, not all information was available under every category analysed. Occasionally, mortgage entries contained gaps, such as imprecise terms, interest rates absent, or details of the lender. So, the total number of mortgages included in the following discussion of results varies slightly between topics.

The pattern of the volume of activity per decade as measured by the number of new mortgages taken out by copyhold tenants is illustrated in Fig. 3.1. It shows a gradual rise during the century from 1606 when the first mortgage was recorded. There was then an interruption during the civil war and Commonwealth period (1644–1660); a peak during the 1670s and 1680s; and a decline towards the end of the century, with a small upturn towards 1735. This latter could have been due to a lessening of need; or of the availability of other types of loans as economic

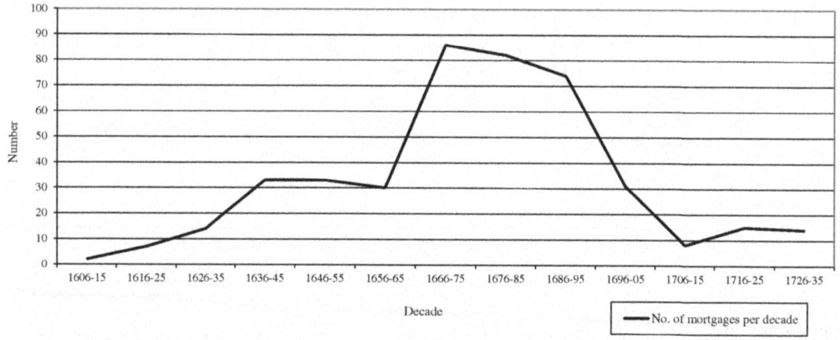

Fig. 3.1 The number of mortgages per decade 1606–1735
Sources Mortgage surrenders in manorial court rolls: WC Court Books 23047–23058 (Meonstoke and Vernham Dean court rolls); HRO, 11M59/E1/139/3–143/1 (Crawley court rolls); HRO, DC/J5/47–72 & DC/J11/1 (Hinton Ampner court rolls)

circumstances changed; or differences in control by the manorial lords and a more laissez-faire attitude with under-recording. It could also be a sign that new sources of institutional credit were becoming available, so that mortgages as an instrument may have become less attractive. If data becomes available in future from other regions of England, it would be useful to compare and see whether the above pattern is reflected elsewhere. The only other presently available study—of Slaidburn in Yorkshire—provides broadly similar results, but with a larger peak during the 1620s and 1630s than in the above; the same dip after the civil war; a peak (but a much smaller one) during the 1670s and a similar decline to the end of the century (French and Hoyle 1999, pp. 356–357).

Another factor underlying the trends might have been agricultural prices, particularly as many borrowers were farmers, so the main purpose might have been to deal with annual fluctuations in harvest and seasonal cash flows. To test this, local wheat prices were calculated from Winchester College lease income records in which part payment was made in grain.[9] Figure 3.2 then charts the total acreage under mortgage in any given year for two of the manors together with the wheat price in nearby Winchester.

A statistical correlation test showed there to be no correlation between the acreage used or amount borrowed and wheat prices.

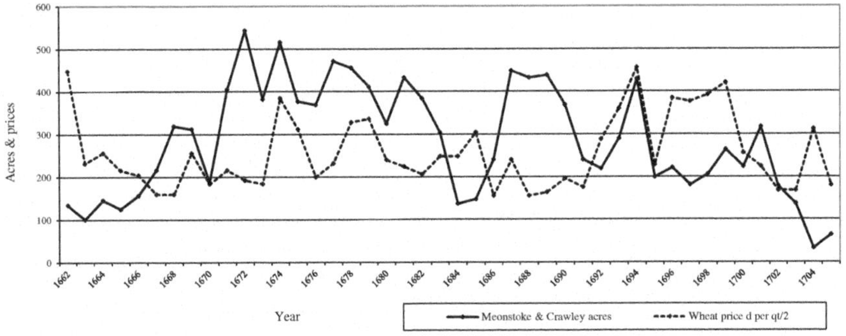

Fig. 3.2 Total acres under mortgage in any one year compared with wheat prices 1662–1705

Note Wheat prices are given in pence (d.) per quarter but divided by two to make scaling comparative

Sources Manorial court records as before (see n.6) for Meonstoke and Crawley only, with Woodmancott grain prices from WC Court Books 23047–23058

The tests were repeated using wheat prices slipped back by a year to allow for a possible time lag between price rises or falls and a mortgage response to these. However, there remained a complete lack of correlation, except briefly in the early 1690s which are a known national crisis period. The results for malt and oats prices were the same.

The conclusion is that crisis situations in agriculture are not indicated as a primary driver for these rural copyhold mortgages in the seventeenth century. This fits with Muldrew's findings when he compared litigation levels relating to credit with movements in grain prices and concluded that they were not strongly related (Muldrew 1998, pp. 228–229 and Figs. 8.7 and 8.8). However, he was not studying groups of borrowers who were chiefly farmers, as in this study; so the parallel nature of the results is interesting. It may be an indicator that mortgages were not being primarily being used to bolster farming activities, or it may merely reflect that a mortgage loan over several years may have been too long and inflexible as an instrument for covering seasonal agricultural fluctuations.

Interest rates are normally of relevance in credit studies, but there was little ability to vary them as the rates were preset by the national laws relating to usury. The Acts of 1571 and 1598 set a rate of 10%, and this was reduced in 1624 to 8%, followed by a drop to 6% in 1650 which was confirmed at the restoration after 1660. A further drop to 5% occurred in 1713. A full analysis of all the mortgages in the study showed that these rates were almost universally adhered to, and Fig. 3.3 shows the mean rates charged for Meonstoke.

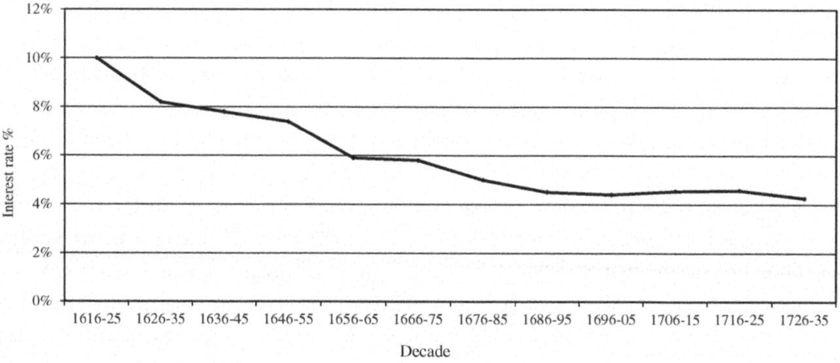

Fig. 3.3 Mean interest rates charged per decade in Meonstoke 1606–1735
Sources Mortgage surrenders in Meonstoke manorial court rolls as before (see n.6)

In consequence of the proscribed rates, no correlation was found in this study between changes in interest rates and patterns of mortgage borrowing. Interest rates show a stepped linear decline while mortgage borrowing shows many peaks and troughs. This suggests that although rates must have been a factor in determining whether a tenant could afford a mortgage or not, or how attractive lending was, there was little or no competition in rates. The study of interest rates alone does not therefore inform aspects of the lending market for these mortgages.

The 429 mortgages were borrowed by a total of 139 different copyholders in the three manors, of whom 14% were women.[10] Of this total, about 47% borrowed only once; a further 23% twice; and another 21.8% raised three or four mortgages. The remaining percentage raised more than four mortgages. So the great majority of borrowers did not use many mortgages, which suggests that their need was relatively short term. An analysis of the proportion of all copyhold tenants who had a mortgage in term in any particular year showed that it varied between a minimum of 6% in low years and up to 24% in the peak mortgage years of the 1670s identified earlier (Gayton 2013). One quarter of tenants using their property for a mortgage at any one time seems to indicate a significant level of participation in the credit market using this instrument.

The amount of capital raised in the principal in each individual mortgage was analysed to gain an understanding of how much was being borrowed and its range. Similarly, the length of term agreed for the mortgages was examined to assess whether the credit sought was short or long. Table 3.1 summarises the results.

Almost a third of the mortgages were below £50, and more than 80% of them were for sums below £200. Only 6% were for £300 and above. Some tenants took out several mortgages at once against different parts of their holdings, so that their combined borrowing total was more than the individual sums shown. The implication is that the maximum size of the principal was probably restricted by what lenders would risk, rather than what borrowers wanted. Up to a £200 or £300 maximum seems to have been the normal limit for any one mortgage. Even if £200 was a normal maximum, this was still a considerable sum of money in the seventeenth century and must have been significantly more than most other forms of borrowing could provide at that time. The ability to raise such sums using their land as collateral, must have made mortgages a primary credit instrument for copyholders.

Table 3.1 Summary of amounts borrowed and length of term used for mortgages

Manor:	*Crawley*	*H. Ampner*	*Meonstoke*	*Totals*	*% of Total*
Amount					
£500+	–	1	4	5	1
£400–£500	–	1	4	5	1
£300–<£400	4	1	11	16	4
£200–<£300	5	4	44	53	12
£100–<£200	25	6	86	117	27
£50–<£100	20	4	70	94	22
<£50	19	5	112	136	32
Total Nos.	73	22	331	426	
Term in years					
>7	–	2	3	5	1
6–7	4	–	5	9	2
5–<6	5	–	6	11	3
4–<5	8	1	9	18	4
3–<4	22	5	123	150	35
2–<3	13	5	81	99	23
1–<2	18	4	83	105	25
<1	3	4	22	29	7
Total Nos.	73	21	332	426	

Note In the top half of the table, three values were not known and thus omitted for Meonstoke; in the bottom half of the table, one value in Hinton Ampner and one in Meonstoke were unknown and omitted

Sources Manorial court records as before (see n.6)

It was possible to divide the amount borrowed by the acreage used as collateral to arrive at an indication of property and land values at the time. The results have not been tabulated here, but inevitably varied by the type of property being mortgaged. A small cottage could raise between £20 and £40; land only could raise between £4 and £9 per acre; and land with a dwelling between £4 and £10 per acre. The differences in mean rate per acre for land differed between the manors with the rate for Meonstoke emerging as more than twice that for Crawley and at least a third more than in Hinton Ampner. (The results for Crawley are more in keeping with Slaidburn which varied between £3.30 and £4.10 per acre for this period; see French and Hoyle 1999.) This may have been due to the relatively poor nature of Crawley land with its thin chalky soils. On the other hand, Meonstoke and Hinton Ampner were enclosed by this period, whereas some of Crawley was still in open fields. Enclosed land would fetch a higher price. The rates per acre used by Cromwell's Parliamentary Survey officials in 1649 were at least double for enclosed closes when compared with open-field plots.[11] This theory of differential land valuation in mortgages is supported by French and Hoyle's findings in Slaidburn where old enclosed land commanded a higher price per acre than those with new improvements (French and Hoyle 1999, p. 369).

The length of term agreed for the mortgages was fairly short. The large majority (90%) were for less than 4 years—with the most popular (35%) being for 3 years. This is far shorter than some freeholder mortgages which were separately discovered in title deeds, wherein some were for as long as 200 years and were reassigned and sold on in the manner of long leases.[12] Where a series of mortgages were raised, it was found that there was a pattern whereby many of the short—under one year—terms were agreed as a first 'starter' mortgage and then renewed for a longer term later when perhaps the borrower and lender had assessed each other for risk. It was also quite common to roll over one loan into a subsequent one, but not often with the same lender. It is not clear whether this was because the borrower could not pay and took a new mortgage to pay off the previous, or whether most lenders only wished to risk a loan for a short period. Whatever the reasons, the overwhelmingly short-term nature of these copyholder mortgages is a defining feature of them.

Rates of defaulting on mortgages were high during the medieval period. Whittle found, for example, that out of a total of 17 mortgages at Hevingham Bishops in Norfolk between the years 1444 and 1558, only three were successfully repaid (Whittle 2000, pp. 117–118 and 171). Such patterns elsewhere have led Tawney and others to conclude that the mortgage was chiefly an instrument used in crisis (Tawney 1925, Introduction; Tawney 1926, pp. 43–44). The copyholder mortgages in this study did not follow this pattern. Of the 429 mortgages studied, only 16, or 3.7%, ended in forfeiture. Of these, almost one-third (five) were because either borrower or lender died during the term and the heirs lost track of commitments. Another third (five) were during the civil war 1644–1648 period during which Hampshire was deeply affected and either borrowers or lenders died or were displaced. So this leaves six, or only 1.4%, which were straightforward forfeitures. There were, however, cases where the borrower sold the property near the end of the term, which suggests that they may have done so in order to repay the loan and avoid forfeiture. Others may have merely renewed a mortgage in order to pay off the debt if they could not repay, but it was not possible to distinguish these from genuine remortgages and ongoing investment rollovers. Whichever way the analysis was carried out, the percentage which ended in forfeiture or sale was at maximum about 20%. This was much lower than Whittle's proportion, and the 'at least one third' rate found by French and Hoyle (1999, p. 374). It suggests that even if in the medieval period mortgages were most often used in situations of personal financial crisis, that most of the copyholders in the seventeenth century were not using them in these circumstances. In order to explore this further, the data was analysed to assess what the motivations for borrowing may have been.

3.3 Profiles of the Copyhold Borrowers and Their Possible Motivation for Using Mortgages

It is not easy to assess the reasons why someone borrowed using land as collateral, and particularly so in rural areas where borrowers were not clearly engaged in commercial activity like urban merchants. However, their motivation is an important factor in any attempt to understand the credit market. This author had the advantage of an earlier detailed study of all copyhold tenants and their land transactions—both permanent and temporary—in the manors between 1645 and 1705 (Gayton 2013). The analysis of the court roll entries enabled a detailed profile to be made of both the copyholders and their various landholdings over a 60-year period. Far more background information than usual was therefore available about those who chose to raise mortgages. It was known, for example, when a copyholder acquired their holdings; if they sold portions or bought more; when they had died; or when marriages had been made. Any ongoing financial difficulties were often implied, and court roll comments about occupation could augment the picture. Furthermore, the landholding sizes were known and could be plotted to see how much of it was used in mortgages. The size of the landholding was also an indicator of relative wealth.[13] An informed guess could then be made, using all these details, about the reasons for borrowing.

The profiles thus constructed and compared showed that copyholders who borrowed using mortgages came from all holding size categories and that the use of mortgages was not restricted to a particular group of larger or more wealthy tenants. Some held and mortgaged merely a cottage, while others mortgaged many acres of land. Some included dwellings in their collateral and some did not. As they did not actually hand over their mortgaged property to the lender, it may not have mattered precisely which parts of their holding they chose to use, but there was always the risk that it might be forfeited, so that a careful choice would usually need to be made. The amount of land needed to raise a specific amount was related to its potential value as explained previously.

The following categories of motivation were identified:

- *Purchase*: this was suggested if the mortgage followed immediately after the purchase of a new property.
- *Refurbishment or building*: was indicated if a tenant had applied for a licence to pull down a dilapidated property; was admitted to a property which had previously been criticised at court for being in poor repair; if the tenant had recently built a new cottage; or if an elderly tenant had lingered on and failed to upkeep the premises.
- *Business and/or investment*: was suggested if the tenant was a merchant and/or not resident in the manor. If the tenant lived in the manor, then a long series of mortgages with no apparent difficulty paying them off also suggested investment.
- *Marriage portions or provision for children*: this occurred where a mortgage could be linked to a marriage settlement, or if it was clear that provision was being made *inter vivos* for a child (most usually a child who was not the customary heir).
- *Legacies and inherited debts*: this was suggested where an heir was left with a burden of legacies and or debt, including a mortgage, after a death. (Information in this category was augmented by wills.)[14]
- *Financial difficulties*: the indicators for this included a pattern of mortgages taken out on ever-increasing proportions of the holding, which culminated either in forfeiture of the premises or the sale of the premises, apparently to pay off the mortgages. There was often a late and rapid switching between mortgage lenders in an attempt to find someone who would risk a loan.
- *Not known*: used where no category could be assigned. Many of these were borrowers at the beginning or end of the study period where the previous or later history of their activity was truncated.

Inevitably, some of these categories overlap. For example, those burdened with legacies and inherited debt clearly also had financial difficulties. The division of category was based chiefly upon the cause of the difficulty. Similarly, some parents, such as William Wyatt whose story follows shortly below, appear to have been investing in order to provide for extra children who were not the customary heir. Their mortgages might also be classed as 'marriage or children'. The decision was taken to include very long-term—twenty years or so—credit activity as 'investment', and the 'marriage or child' category was used for those immediately following a marriage settlement or a legacy for child provision.

The restriction of the analysis to the period 1645–1705 when background information was available involved a subset of the overall study amounting to 347 mortgages taken out by 103 individuals.[15] Table 3.2 then summarises both the mortgages and the borrower by category of 'reasons', showing the results by manor in both number and percentage. Figure 3.4 charts the mortgages by category and by decade to show their patterns through the second half of the seventeenth century. An additional analysis not tabulated here was carried out during earlier research to compare the profile of the borrowers with the mean tenant profile in the manors (Gayton 2013, Appendix Table 8.1). Some of those findings are included in what follows as they show which section of the tenantry was most active in the various categories.

Table 3.2 and Figure 3.4 show that mortgages raised to assist with a property purchase were fairly evenly spread across every decade. They were the motivation for a mean of 9% of all mortgages, but 19% of the borrowers. The difference was because borrowers only used one or two mortgages in a series for this activity. The funds raised were presumably used to cover the immediate fine, purchase price and capital costs. The background study showed that the group of copyholders owning 25–50 acres were those most likely to borrow for this purpose and that two-thirds of the amounts borrowed were under £100. So mortgage raising to support property purchase was a short-term activity of modest monetary amounts, used by middle-ranking copyholders.

Loans to rebuild or refurbish property involved five per cent of mortgages and seven per cent of borrowers and generally required two or three mortgages in series. These borrowers were overwhelmingly from the lower landowning groups holding less than 10 acres, and nearly three quarters of the loans were for less than £100. It is perhaps not surprising that the poorer copyholders were refurbishing cottages rather than purchasing new, or that they needed a longer period of loans with which to accomplish it and complete repayment.

Mortgages associated with business or investment activity peaked sharply during the two decades 1666–1675 and 1676–1685. This pattern may be partly due to the activities of two or three long-term

Table 3.2 Mortgages categorized by apparent reasons for borrowing: 1645–1705

Category of Borrowing		*Purchase*	*Refurbish or build*	*Investment or business*	*Legacy or Inher. debt*	*Marriage or child*	*Financial Diffs.*	*Not known*	*Totals*
Mortgages									
Meonstoke	*No.*	23	12	66	41	10	57	46	255
	%	*9*	*5*	*26*	*16*	*4*	*22*	*18*	
Crawley	*No.*	7	4	12	5	6	22	17	73
	%	*10*	*5*	*16*	*7*	*8*	*30*	*23*	
H. Ampner	*No.*	1	1	5	4	1	5	2	19
	%	*5*	*5*	*26*	*21*	*5*	*26*	*11*	
Totals	*No.*	31	17	83	50	17	84	65	347
	%	*9*	*5*	*24*	*14*	*5*	*24*	*19*	
Borrowers									
Meonstoke	*No.*	13	4	9	11	4	5	17	63
	%	*21*	*6*	*14*	*17*	*6*	*8*	*27*	
Crawley	*No.*	6	2	4	4	3	5	4	28
	%	*21*	*7*	*14*	*14*	*11*	*18*	*14*	
H. Ampner	*No.*	1	1	2	4	1	2	1	12
	%	*8*	*8*	*17*	*33*	*8*	*17*	*8*	
Totals	*No.*	20	7	15	19	8	12	22	103
	%	*19*	*7*	*15*	*18*	*8*	*12*	*21*	
Av. no. morts per borrower		1.6	2.4	5.5	2.6	2.1	7.0	3.0	

Note For details of categories, see text
Sources Manorial court records as before (see n.6)

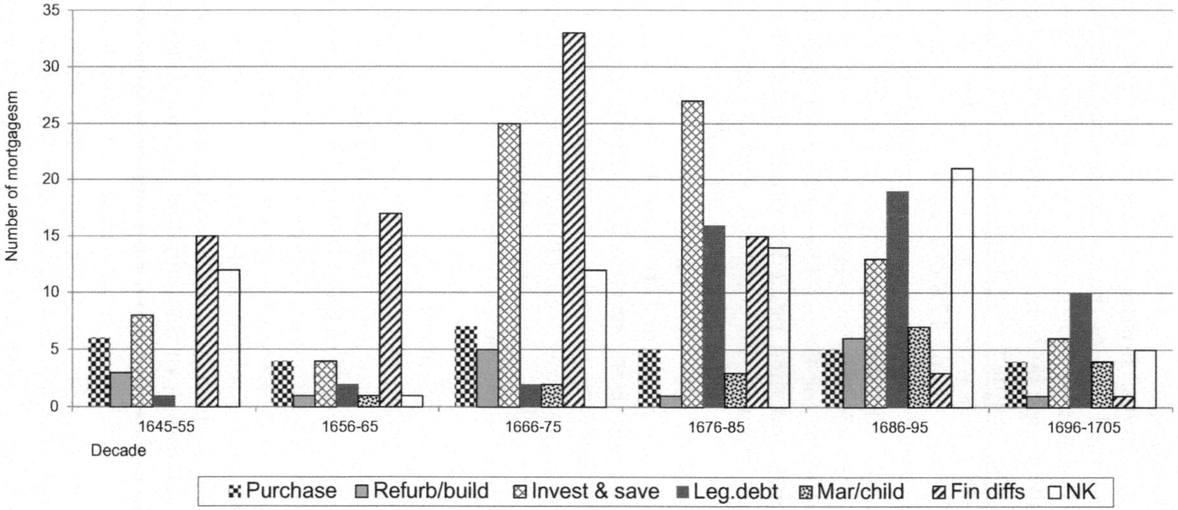

Fig. 3.4 The number of mortgages by reasons for mortgage and decade, 1645–1705
Note For details of the reasons categories, see text
Sources see n.6

investing copyholders in Meonstoke, or it may be a reflection of wider, better economic circumstances after the restoration followed by a well-known decline to the 1690s. Borrowers in this category formed 15% of the borrowers, but used 24% of the mortgages because they used an average of between five and six mortgages in series. Theirs was a longer-term activity, and all groups by holding size participated. However, as might be expected, the wealthier copyholders and those who were merchants in nearby small towns were over-represented, and they borrowed the highest sums of money. Some 42% of their loans were for more than £200—a figure more than twice that of any other category.

The need to obtain credit for the payment of legacies and debt, and provision for marriage and children were linked because they were all chiefly aimed at providing for family. The pattern through time shows that they began slowly and then peaked strongly during the last three decades from 1676 onwards. So although the categories combined accounted for one quarter of the borrowers and 19% of the mortgages, by the decade 1686–1695 they were the largest category. This was not because more people died or married. It seems to have reflected changes in behaviour, whereby during the seventeenth century, more parents left monetary legacies to children, particularly to daughters, as Spicksley has shown (2008). Heirs and widows were charged with dispensing legacies to them when they reached 21 years of age. It was also a time when far more marriage settlements by the copyholders began to appear in the court rolls, and the separate land-transfer study showed that conditional surrenders of land requiring maintenance, payment or marriage settlements were more common from the 1680s onwards (Gayton 2013, Sect. 5.8.3, p. 136). These may have reflected national developments in the strict marriage settlement (Erickson 1990). The majority of individuals in both categories came from the groups of copyholders who owned more than 25 acres of land. The main differences were that whereas the majority (63%) of marriage-related mortgages involved the raising of between £100 and £300, the legacy repayments' needs were mostly (also 63%) under £100. The former of these fits with the apparent 'going rate' for a marriage portion of £150–£200 for the middling sorts of copyholders at this time. The legacies were more varied, but some were intended to provide marriage portions so they were also at the £200 level.

Financial difficulties of a general nature were identified for a quarter (24%) of all mortgages, but only 12% of borrowers. This pattern was chiefly due to the activities of two particular tenants in Meonstoke who had very long-term difficulties and borrowed a total of 50 mortgages between them. The mortgages in this category were spread across the decades but, in contrast to other categories, were highest in the first four and then declined in the two decades at the end of the century. This is perhaps surprising when the 1690s are known to have been a period of national economic downturn. It would be interesting, if any future further research is carried out elsewhere in England, to see whether this pattern is repeated. It may reflect the turmoil of the civil war which raged particularly in Hampshire and the subsequent uncertainties of the restoration period of the 1660s. The borrowers in this category were mainly the 25 to 50 acre holders, which correlates well with the more general land-transfer pattern of the period where the middle-sized farmers were being squeezed out. Writers such as Tawney and Allen often identified this group as experiencing the most pressure as agrarian capitalism developed (Tawney 1912; Allen 1992). They borrowed a high mean of seven mortgages each, which suggests that the financial difficulties extended over at least a decade in many cases. The point made earlier is reinforced; that tenants in medium-term trouble tended to use mortgages to support a gradual decline in their financial circumstances over time. A sudden and dramatic crisis would have required the property to be sold, rather than raising a mortgage.

Finally, the 'Not Known' category contained 21% of total borrowers and 19% of the mortgages. They were chiefly either from Crawley where the bishop's records provided little background or in Meonstoke where the problem of truncated information, mentioned earlier, arose. The reason why tenants fell into the 'Not Known' category was therefore connected chiefly with difficult documentary sources, rather than correlating with specific motivations. They were probably spread across the other motivation categories.

The results of this analysis shed light upon the broad range of motivation of copyhold borrowers and how and when they participated in the credit market using mortgages. If one regards purchase, refurbishment, investment and marriage/children provision as positive needs for loans, then half of all borrowers (49%) and 43% of all mortgages were associated with such needs. This is in contrast to the 30% of borrowers and 38% of mortgages which appear to have been used to bolster failing finances or to deal with burdensome inherited finances and legacies. The pattern that has emerged is thus different from that in the historiography referred to in this chapter's introduction, with its focus on crisis needs. A few specific case studies will further illustrate the range of apparent motivation behind mortgage borrowing.

3.4 Borrower Case Studies

3.4.1 *John Moore: Purchase and Refurbishment*

John Moore was a typical example of a small copyholder needing money to purchase and refurbish a dwelling. He bought a 'cottage with curtilage and garden' in 1688 whose annual rent was 6d.[16] The court rolls do not record the purchase price paid by the vendor (just the fine and heriot associated), but the rate for a cottage at the time was between £20 and £40. The condition of this particular cottage was probably very poor. The previous owner had died in possession in 1671, and no heir came forward to claim entitlement until 1687. After almost 20 years of abandonment, the property may have become a ruin. In any event, Moore purchased it from the heir and immediately took out a mortgage on the premises for £25 at 5% for one year from John Hatch of Meonstoke; a farmer in the same village. The mortgage was repaid and then renewed in 1690 for £30; again in 1692 for £26; and then finally in 1695 for three years for £26—all at 5% interest and from the same lender. The mortgages then cease and were paid off. Moore continued to live in the dwelling until 1727 when he surrendered it to his son. It is significant that from 1692 the description of the dwelling changes from 'cottage' to 'house', suggesting that Moore had indulged in a significant rebuild. The modest-sized mortgages therefore seem to represent the cost of purchase, refurbishment and building.

3.4.2 *William Wyatt: Regular Borrowing for Investment*

William Wyatt was a long-term borrower for investment purposes over several decades. In 1645, he had inherited the largest copyholding of 142 acres in Meonstoke and had recently married. In 1647, after the birth of his first son William junior, he took out a 21-year licence to sublet 77 of his acres, leaving 65 acres to farm himself. He then embarked on a regular series of mortgages over a period of twenty years using parts of his 65 acres. From the early 1650s he used 29 acres with a dwelling to borrow between £150 and £200 at 6% interest from a series of different wealthy farmers in neighbouring villages. He always repaid them, and this pattern was for investment, not one of rolling over a debt he could not pay by remortgaging. The income from his subletting would have been more than sufficient to pay the interest, quite apart from his farming activities.

In 1667, two things occurred: his sublease finished and his son William junior reached the age of 21 years. Father William promptly surrendered 52 of his acres to his son and trained him in using mortgages to support his farming. Meanwhile, he continued to mortgage his own remaining land as before until he died in 1676. He had another son to provide for—the customary heir who was his youngest son, Thomas Wyatt.[17] It seems clear that William senior engaged in a long-term investment plan using subletting and mortgaging in tandem in order to be able to be fair to his two sons and provide almost equally for them both. The pattern of his borrowing was flat and regular over a 25-year period while they were growing up. Unfortunately, he died during the term of his last mortgages, and his son Thomas was not so skilful, as is discussed below.

3.4.3 *Thomas Wyatt: Legacies and Inherited Debt*

Thomas Wyatt inherited his father William's 90 acres in 1676, which had two outstanding mortgages still in term. One was for £60 at 6% for two years from a Sarah Lambert, spinster in Winchester, and the other was for £100 at 6% from a Peter Hawkesworth in a nearby village. The first of these used 21 acres as collateral, and the latter 27 acres. It appears that Thomas Wyatt was burdened by the inheritance of mortgage debt, plus the fines, heriots and admittance fees due upon his father's decease. Perhaps, also, as he was younger, his father had not had time to train him in the way that he had done for the older son, or perhaps Thomas did not intend to farm and was of different character.

In any event, Thomas immediately mortgaged his entire 90-acre inheritance, split between portions offered as security for five separate mortgages from five different lenders for £50, £60 and three at £100—totalling £410, all at 5% interest. This was considerably in excess of the total outstanding debts on his father's estate. He was clearly in difficulties, and only three years later in 1679, he sold 55 acres to Malarchy Horner—a draper in Bishop's Waltham. The mortgages were then repaid, and Thomas embarked on a series of much smaller mortgages using his remaining land whose purpose seems to have been regular investment.

3.4.4 *John Collins: Financial Difficulties*

John Collins received 89.5 acres in Meonstoke from his widowed mother Alice in 1651 and soon began using part of his land as security for mortgage loans.[18] Initially, between 1653 and 1660, he raised a series of 5 mortgages using a 37-acre close as collateral. All the mortgages were provided by William Smith of neighbouring Soberton at an interest rate of 6%. The principal sum agreed varied between £60 and £200 and suggests that Collins was in turn able to repay parts of a loan, but then needed more, and may have had financial difficulties.

By the middle 1660s, John increased his borrowing using a series of thirteen short-term one- or two-year mortgages ranging between £50 and £160 at a time; all with 6% interest; and using between 5 and 30 acres for each. He acquired a wide variety of providers all living in local villages. In any one year, between 56 and 93% of his land was under mortgage, and the cumulative total principal capital raised rose quickly to a peak of £630 in 1672. In 1674, he placed most of the pieces together in one mortgage on 80 acres which raised £600 from Robert Sharrock of the local town of Bishop's Waltham for six months. John then took three more short-term mortgages for a year producing another cumulative peak of £600 borrowed in 1677, before suddenly selling everything in 1678. Creditors were paid off, but at a price to his heirs. He had to bring his three sons to court to renounce any future claims by them upon the property.[19]

In fact, John Collins had found a way out, albeit one that involved disinheriting his sons in the process. He married Joanna Budd later in 1678 who was a wealthy widow with 117 acres of her own in neighbouring Exton. This manor had lives copyhold, so John could not try to use her land in mortgaging, and she firmly kept her own children in the lives.

3.5 The Mortgage Lenders

The mortgage lenders formed the other part of the credit relationship. They were always named in the court roll records because the conditional surrender was a form of contract. Sometimes, just a name was given, and on other occasions, the occupation and location of residence were added. The place of repayment of instalments was often recorded as 'at the house of x' where x was the lender, so that the location of their residence was known. Otherwise, there was less information about the lenders than was provided by the background study of the borrowers.

An initial analysis of the lenders showed that there were 230 different individuals who provided the 429 loans, or a mean of 1.9 mortgages each. This latter figure suggests at the outset that lending was a widespread activity using only a few mortgages from any particular lender. The number of times that a lender provided a loan is summarised in Table 3.3.

The table shows that at least two-thirds of all mortgages were lent by an individual who only lent once. And only 12% lent four or more times.

Table 3.3 The number of times that a lender agreed a mortgage to a copyhold borrower, 1606–1735

		Number of times an individual lent a mortgage						*Total no. lenders*	*Total morts.*	*Mean no. per lender*
		One	*Two*	*Three*	*Four*	*Five*	*>Five*			
Manor										
Crawley	No.	23	4	3	3	–	3	36	73	2.0
	%	*64*	*11*	*8*	*8*	–	*8*			
H. Ampner	No.	16	3	–	–	–	–	19	22	1.2
	%	*84*	*16*	–	–	–	–			
Meonstoke	No.	113	29	10	7	7	9	175	334	1.9
	%	*65*	*17*	*6*	*4*	*4*	*5*			
Totals	No.	152	36	13	10	7	12	230	429	1.9
	%	*66*	*16*	*6*	*4*	*3*	*5*			

Source Manorial court records of mortgages as before (see n.6)

A subanalysis not tabulated, demonstrated that of these latter multiple lenders, almost half made all their loans to one borrower. However, they were unusual. Most lenders seem to have been one-offs.

The analysis can only provide a snapshot of lenders who loaned to copyhold borrowers in the manors of study. It is therefore possible that apparently one-off lenders were in fact making more mortgage loans in other manors elsewhere. To assess this likelihood, the names of lenders in each of the manors of study were compared with each other to see if they reappeared. They did not, so a sampled check was then made in the bishopric mortgage surrender books covering twenty manors in Hampshire outside the study area. Two or three names such as Henry Crowcher, gent., of Droxford did appear in a few other manors, but the overall pattern was that there was no notable group of lenders who were active widely in Hampshire and in an apparently professional capacity. Most lenders were individuals making one or a few loans. The conclusion is that this is not a pattern of professional moneylenders, lawyers or other credit-related occupations. Rather, it suggests a considerable degree of individual arrangements between borrowers and lenders to suit the occasion and demonstrates the interpersonal lending which dominated throughout the century.

An idea of who the lenders were was obtained by examining their occupations and apparent status. These could only be identified with certainty for half (116) of the lenders, but there is no reason to suppose that

Table 3.4 The occupation or status group of 116 mortgage lenders to copyholders

	One-off loan	*2 or 3 loan*	*≥4 loan*	*Totals*		*Males Only %*
				No.	*%*	
Occupation or status						
Trader	11	5	4	20	17.2	28.2
Yeoman	10	5	10	25	21.6	35.2
Husbandman	3	4		7	6.0	9.9
Lawyer/Cleric	2	1	1	4	3.4	5.6
College/Cathedral staff	5	1	1	7	6.0	9.9
Gent.	5	2	1	8	6.9	11.3
Widow	17		2	19	16.4	
Spinster	22	3	1	26	22.4	
Totals	75	21	20	116		
%	*64.7*	*18.1*	*17.2*			

Note The category 'Trader' comprised individuals from the following occupations: tailor, blacksmith, shoemaker and clothier (three of each); girdler, maltster, miller, apothecary, combmaker; papermaker, innkeeper, carpenter; shoemaker and butcher (one of each)
Sources Mortgages in manorial court rolls as before (see n.6)

the unknown half were substantially different. However, the widows and spinsters are over-represented because they could always be identified. Table 3.4 therefore summarises the findings and shows the males-only percentages separately to indicate the contrasts with the overall results that feature the skew resulting from the over-representation of females.

Muldrew discovered that credit relationships occurred 'all over the social scale' (Muldrew 1998, p. 97), and Table 3.4 confirms this, although there is a great concentration in the middling levels of occupation and status. In other words, most of the lenders matched most of the borrowers in status, so this is not a pattern of wealthy aristocracy or urban investors offering loans to lesser folk. By far the largest group were farmers, either yeomen or husbandmen, followed by small traders and women—particularly spinsters. Representation from the other groups was much lower in number with 'professional' men constituting below six per cent and anyone suffixing 'gent.' to his name a maximum of around 11%. Finally, a group of between 6% and 10% were identifiable as close relations of the lords of the manor (or chiefly the stewards of the manors). In terms of multiple or single lending, the yeomen strikingly provided the majority of the multiple lending and therefore seem to have been most interested in

Table 3.5 The amounts in £ provided in a loan by occupational group of lender

Amount of loan	*<£50*	*£50–<£100*	*£100–<£200*	*£200–<£300*	*£300–<£400*	*£400+*	*Totals*
Occup/status							
Trader	3	4	7	5	1		20
Yeoman	5	5	3	11		1	25
Husbandman	5	1	1				7
Lawyer/ Cleric	1		1	1		1	4
Lord's staff		2	2		3		7
Gent.	1	2	1	1	1	2	8
Widow	8	2	5	1	2	1	19
Spinster	4	9	9	3		1	26
Totals	27	25	29	22	7	6	116
%	*23.3*	*21.6*	*25.0*	*19.0*	*6.0*	*5.2*	

Note If a lender made more than one loan, then the highest loan is used here
Sources Manorial court records of mortgages as before (see n.6)

longer-term investment. Conversely, the widows and spinsters formed the majority of the one-off and shorter-term lending.

The lender groups were then examined to see whether certain occupations lent greater or smaller amounts of money and whether different occupational groups predominated in certain decades during the study period (this latter not tabulated). Table 3.5 shows the lending by the maximum amount lent in any one mortgage if an individual made more than one loan.

All groups lent across the spectrum of amounts, except the husbandmen of whom 85% lent amounts below £100 and the wealthier yeomen of whom 50% lent equal to, or more than, £200. Widows most frequently lent smaller amounts, whereas more spinsters lent between £50 and £200. Otherwise, one 'gent.' lent a mortgage for £40 and one spinster lent £400, so there was great diversity. These overall patterns did not change through time, with the exception of female lenders, who were only active during the second half of the seventeenth century as previously explained. Otherwise, there was no discernible increase in the maximum amounts lent over time after the first two decades. The upper limit of £300 remained throughout the period. As borrowers did sometimes make multiple agreements in order to borrow higher total combined amounts, this upper limit seems to have been set by the lenders.

Clearly, the ability to lend depended upon the possession of funds with which to do so. The origin of funds was difficult to establish unless a probate account was found that specifically identified legacies which seemed to tie into the amounts subsequently invested. It was found that almost all the female lenders had acquired their funds from inheritance. The traders mostly appeared to be in business and may have had surplus, and similarly the farmers. However, a proportion of these had also received legacies too. Their motive in lending, apart from the obvious one of increasing their capital, was probably varied, but again difficult to determine from the documentary sources available. The separate study of female lenders showed that the majority were saving for marriage portions (spinsters) or needing to use a legacy for the raising of children (widows) (Gayton 2018). The traders and farmers may have been supporting their businesses, whereas the lord's staff appear to have been helping out otherwise well-known and respected tenants who were in difficult circumstances.

If a prudent prospective lender had capital available, they would then need to make a decision about how to invest it to provide a good return. In seventeenth-century England, the range of choice of instrument has already been outlined in the introduction. Informal arrangements were possible, and formal methods were available in the form of bonds, bills and mortgages. There were no financial institutions such as banks. Muldrew found evidence in probate accounts of the use of bonds and bills in seventeenth-century Hampshire, but these could be expensive to draw up using lawyers, and in the case of default, an expensive court case might be needed to recoup the loan (Muldrew 2012, p. 21). Investing in a copyhold mortgage would therefore seem to have been an ideal instrument for a lender with up to about £300 who wanted a return over a period of a few years, rather than days or weeks. A few freeholder mortgages were found by the present author in Hampshire title deeds which had loans of above £1000 and terms of several hundred years and were assigned and sold on. Copyholder mortgages never followed this pattern. They were short term and were not assigned to others. Also, as previously mentioned, the freeholder mortgages were not centrally recorded and could therefore be concealed, whereas the copyhold mortgage had a manorial court record and one for which the lender had not had to pay legal fees. Furthermore, the rate of interest was statute-determined and redress in the manor court if a default occurred would have avoided the need and expense of suing. The copyholder mortgage must therefore have seemed attractive, cheap to arrange and secure. The fact that a mortgage was secured by land may give the impression that the lenders had land-grabbing in mind. However, in the very rare cases when a borrower defaulted, on no occasion did the lender take and use the land. If it was forfeit to them, as in some cases where the borrower had died during the term, then the lenders sold the premises to pay off the money and did not take on the tenancy. It appears that building up land holdings was not their motive.

3.6 Relationships Between Borrower and Lender

The borrowers and lenders have so far been considered separately, but the question of how they were introduced to each other and how they may have related to each other is an important aspect of the credit market to consider. The manorial courts' system for copyholder mortgages did not require the use of other external agents or intermediaries such as professional moneylenders, lawyers or the equivalent of Continental *notaires*, and indeed, there is no evidence of their use. There may well have been known individuals to whom borrowers and lenders turned, such as village officials, or neighbours and distant relations. Such people would have had wide personal networks, an opinion which could be trusted and who became known for these abilities. It may have been that the estate stewards acted as intermediaries, as they were in a similar position to the village clerks discussed by Lambrecht. They recorded all land transactions and would have known all the tenant borrowers well and probably some of the lenders too (Lambrecht 2009, p. 90 et seq.). However, there is so far no documentary evidence about this.

If professional agents were not involved, then it was essential for each side to be able to assess the trustworthiness and risk of the venture. Muldrew has commented that as credit networks became more complicated, and more obligations were broken, it became increasingly important to make judgements about each other's honesty (Muldrew 2012, p. 21). In the centuries before computerised credit ratings, local knowledge and networks would have been essential to assess risk. Two aspects of the relationship between lenders and borrowers in this study were therefore investigated to see if light could be shed upon the issue—the distance between them and the nature of the possible social ties.

The location of residence of the lender was known from the court rolls for the majority (384) of the mortgages. It was then possible to plot the distance by road or track between the manor of the borrower and the lender. Table 3.6 summarises the findings.

The analysis shows that 20% of mortgages were acquired from lenders who resided in villages in which their borrowers' mortgaged land was also

Table 3.6 The distance of the residence of the lender from the borrower's manor in miles, against the amount loaned for a mortgage

	In vill	*>0–5 m*	*>5–10 m*	*>10–15 m*	*>15–30 m*	*Outside Hampshire*	*Total morts*
Max. amount lent per mortgage in £							
£500+	–	1	–	1	1	1	4
£400–<£500	–	4	–	–	–	–	4
£300–<£400	–	7	8	1	2	1	19
£200–<£300	3	25	14	2	1	2	48
£100–<£200	14	55	32	5	1	7	114
£50–£99	27	26	23	5	2	2	87
<£50	34	51	19	5	–	2	112
Totals	78	169	96	19	7	15	384
%	*20*	*44*	*25*	*5*	*2*	*4*	

Note The location of the lender was not clear for 65 of the mortgages, hence the lower total
Source Manorial court records of mortgages as before (see n.6)

situated, and 44% from lenders in adjoining manors up to 5 miles away. A further 25% of lenders lived in places between 5 and 10 miles away, and 7% lived more than 10 miles away but still in the same county of Hampshire. In fact, the lenders who lived outside Hampshire were all former children of the village who had moved after apprenticeships or marriage, so they would still have had the contacts locally to assess risk. The overall pattern is definitely not one of wealthy London traders investing in the countryside, but rather that lenders lived close to borrowers and were mostly located in nearby villages or market towns. This would have made the time, effort and costs of agreeing and making payments easier and more convenient, and doubtless also reflected the importance of the ability to obtain local knowledge about potential borrowers or lenders. The result accords with French and Hoyle's findings for Slaidburn in Yorkshire where they found that until the 1730s, mortgage lending was 'essentially local' (French and Hoyle 1999, p. 372).

Trust and risk assessment might also be reflected in the extent to which kin or other relationships may have existed between borrowers and lenders. The court roll records of conditional mortgage surrenders do occasionally include reference to a relationship. In other cases, wills or genealogical information such as baptism and marriage records could augment the information. Lenders bearing the same surnames as known

Table 3.7 Relationship ties between lenders and borrowers 1606–1735

Relationship ties		*Known kin*	*In vill or strong vill ties*	*Same vill surname*	*Link to lords*	*No ties known*	*Total lenders*
Manor							
Crawley	*No.*	5	9	2	2	18	36
	%	*14*	*25*	*5.5*	*5.5*	*50*	
H. Ampner	*No.*	4	3	2	1	9	19
	%	*21*	*16*	*11*	*5*	*47*	
Meonstoke	*No.*	14	69	18	7	67	175
	%	*8*	*39.4*	*10.3*	*4*	*38.3*	
Totals		23	81	22	10	94	230
%		*10*	*35*	*10*	*4*	*41*	

Sources Manorial court records of mortgages as before (see n.6)

manorial tenants suggest, but do not prove, that there was probably a kin connection, and finally, there were lenders connected to the lords—the college or cathedral staff and stewards. These would have had access to information about the borrower and be able to judge their need and trustworthiness. The relationship information could therefore be estimated, and the analysis is summarised in Table 3.7.

The largest group with a mean of 41% of lenders fell into the 'no specific ties known' category and may indeed have had no close connections. At the other end of the spectrum, only a mean of 10% of lenders were known kin of the borrower. (Hinton Ampner had a higher percentage as it had some brother/sister loans.) This suggests that either lending within close family was not popular, or perhaps even frowned upon, or that intra-family lending was usually done privately and would not, therefore, appear in formal contracts. A further 40% of lenders in Meonstoke, and up to 25% in the other villages, had known strong village ties with borrowers, being either current or previous inhabitants or known distant relatives of these inhabitants. The high figure in Meonstoke may relate to its position in the Meon Valley which was a tight valley community, whereas the other two manors lie higher on the chalklands and were more isolated. A small group of about 10% of lenders did not live close or have known ties, but they bore a surname found in the borrower's manor. It may be supposed that they were perhaps distant kin who would have family in the village to help to assess risk.

The data shows that the wide variety of lenders lived very locally to their borrowers and that there were often strong kin and village ties between them. This suggests, but does not prove, that many of the introductions will have been made privately and informally. A few lender case studies follow to illustrate how these worked in practice, and the case of Abigail Rothwell and John Godwin is particularly instructive.

3.7 Lender Case Studies

3.7.1 Abigail Rothwell Widow: Lender of £260 to John Godwin of Crawley

In 1686, Abigail Rothwell widow of Warnford lent £260 to John Godwin of Crawley at 5% interest over 6 years.[20] Warnford is a village some 20 miles distant from Crawley; there had never been any Rothwell families in Crawley; and so there were no obvious geographical or kin connections between them. A lender such as Abigail would therefore normally have appeared in the 'no ties known' column of lenders in Table 3.7 in terms of relationship ties.

However, a will was found for Abigail's husband John Rothwell, a yeoman farmer who died the year before. His inventory totalled £560, and he left the sum of £300 to his wife 'in full satisfaction of her jointure made to me before our marriage'.[21] So this was presumably the source of her funds for lending. The date of their marriage is not known, but a son John was baptised in March 1686, after his father's death. So a plausible assumption is that Abigail might need to invest funds for her growing son in addition to any of her own needs. Hence, the use of almost all her £300 in a mortgage loan to gain maximum interest, and the offering of a longer than usual loan term of six years.

In John Rothwell's will, he appointed overseers, one of whom was a William Godwin of Seavington. The latter was a wealthy leaseholder farmer living near Warnford, and as overseer, he would have known all Abigail's financial circumstances. However, William Godwin's family roots were in Crawley, and he had himself been lending a series of mortgages there to a Will Stevens. He made six loans to Stevens until the last one agreed in 1682, which was for £260 at 6% for 1.5 years. It became clear that Stevens would never be able to repay the ever-increasing sums, and so in 1685, William Godwin went with him to the manorial court and they jointly sold the property to a Crawley purchaser named

John Godwin, who happened to be either the nephew or first cousin of William Godwin.[22] John may not have been able to afford the purchase in the short term, so he needed a mortgage to provide the funds. It seems reasonable to suppose that William Godwin wanted his money back and that by introducing his relative who would purchase the land, to a friend's widow with the funds, then he was solving several problems at once. The figure of £260 is common to both loans.

So the personal interconnection between borrower and lender is revealed. The source of Abigail's funding was her legacy equivalent to her original jointure; her purpose in lending probably to support a young child and provide for their futures. The intermediary was her husband's overseer, who himself needed to recoup mortgages lent in Crawley; and in so doing encouraged his close relative John Godwin to purchase the premises and in turn to borrow to do so.

3.7.2 *Susanna Mitchell, Spinster of Hinton Ampner: Lender to Her Brother*

Elizabeth Mitchell, widow, of Hinton Ampner was buried in May 1641 and left a will in which she left legacies to four daughters.[23] She nominated one of these, Susanna, as her executrix. The will does not mention her son Richard or a copyhold of about 37 acres because he had already inherited it after his father had died, and she had merely enjoyed widows' rights to it during her lifetime.

In October 1641, Richard obtained a mortgage loan of £85 from his sister Susanna, at the statutory 8% interest rate over a period of two years. He used 32 acres or 86% of his landholding as surety. The timing suggests that Susanna had acquired her funds to lend from her mother's legacy, but Richard's reasons for borrowing are not clear. In the event, he died in early 1643 before the mortgage had been repaid. His widow then sold the 37 acres to pay his debts—including the mortgage from his sister. This suggests that Richard had financial difficulties.

This example of sibling lending seems to show a wish by a trusted daughter to have a formal contract of loan with a probably less trustworthy brother. The fact that the mother made her executrix of her will rather than Richard suggests that she could not rely upon him to manage her affairs. Susanna may therefore have been reluctant to give him an informal loan which was merely verbally agreed, so she used a formal mortgage contract to regain her funds if he defaulted or—as happened—that he died.

3.7.3 *Simon Hatch, Yeoman of Droxford: Lender to Three Meonstoke Borrowers*

The village of Droxford lies a few miles further down the Meon valley from Meonstoke. Many of its families were connected by marriage, and inhabitants of Droxford formed the largest single location for mortgage lenders to Meonstoke's borrowers. Their geographical proximity and kinship ties must have made it easy to assess the creditworthiness and risk associated with potential borrowers.

An example was the Hatch family, several of whom lent to Meonstoke borrowers. By the time of the hearth tax in 1665, Simon Hatch was reasonably wealthy as he occupied a sizeable four-hearth chargeable dwelling (Hughes and White 1992, p. 17). He subsequently rose to the position of reeve for Droxford, so he became a reliable senior local figure with wide networks of knowledge about local inhabitants. In 1676, Simon Hatch lent £120 to Peter Hatch of Meonstoke, who was a relative.[24] Peter offered 21 acres of land as security for the loan which had a term of three years at 5%. Unfortunately, he died before the end of the term, but the loan was paid off by his heir. In 1678, Simon Hatch then switched lending to John Richards of Meonstoke, to whom he lent £80 at 5% for a term of only one year. Finally, he made a loan in 1679 to Thomas Wyatt described earlier. One hundred pounds was lent at 5% for three years on 12 acres of land.

Simon Hatch lent sums between £80 and £120, and the security involved was always land without dwellings. Perhaps if a borrower had defaulted, then Hatch could have used the land himself for farming, but he did not want to risk acquiring an extra dwelling. His purpose in investing at this time is not certain, but two of his daughters Beatrice and Ellen married shortly after his death in the early 1680s. Their portions may have been one reason behind his need for income. (His son Simon junr. inherited his land and dwelling, so the daughters would have needed separate provision.)

3.8 Conclusions

This study has provided a window on a particular sector of the seventeenth-century credit market which has not been investigated in detail before. Copyholder mortgages agreed via conditional surrenders in the manor courts rarely appear in litigation or probate records and have therefore often been hidden from view. However provided the tenure was one of copyhold of inheritance, then it has been demonstrated that tenants were able to use their landholdings as security for a loan and that they did so in large numbers. At the same time, the provision of a written accessible record of the contracts in the manorial court made them secure and attractive to lenders, and legal fees were absent or minimal. Redress in the manorial court in the case of default was also less expensive or complex than suing in other courts. There was therefore evident enthusiasm amongst both borrowers and lenders to engage in mortgages, and a significant sector of the rural credit market has been revealed.

Borrowers came from all levels in village society ranging from a small cottage dweller to a yeoman with a hundred acres. The amount borrowed in individual mortgages varied between £7 and £500, but the great majority were under £200—a level seemingly set by the lenders. This represented a substantial sum of money in the seventeenth century and was more than could be raised by rural tenants by most other methods at the time. The preferred term of three years was longer than a pawn but nowhere near as long as some freeholder mortgages agreed for hundreds of years. The motivation for borrowing was shown to be split between the positive needs of purchase, building, investment and provision for family, and the more negative aims of coping with burdens of inherited legacies and debt and financial difficulties from other sources.

However, the copyholder mortgage was not used as an instrument for sudden crisis situations. The term of years for a mortgage precluded a very swift solution. The sale of the property would have been a crisis response. Defaulting rates were very low so whereas Tawney and other authors observing the late medieval period thought that the mortgage was an instrument for crisis borrowing, this hypothesis has been disproved for the copyholder mortgages of the seventeenth century.

Meanwhile, the lenders have been shown to have been mainly from the middling levels in society of farmers and local traders, augmented later in the century by an increasing number of women. Lenders consisted of a large number of individuals making only one or two loans, and the aristocracy and legal professionals were only occasionally involved. There was no need for the participation of external professional moneylenders or official agents as the manorial court administered copyholder mortgages, and there was no large-scale urban involvement in the provision of loans. This credit market was interpersonal and locally based in the rural areas. Borrower and lender usually lived within ten to fifteen miles of each other, and lenders had close village ties with that of the borrower but were not usually close kin. The primary objective was of short to medium investment for a few years, and the motive was to make capital work and grow. Lenders were not interested in using mortgage loans to grab land, as has sometimes been previously thought.

As copyhold was a very widespread customary tenure in the early modern period, the results found here should be reflected in the rural credit market elsewhere in England where copyhold of inheritance prevailed. Further research may confirm or amend the findings. In particular, the seventeenth century showed a flowering of this copyholder mortgage activity after the reform of the usury laws, and was interpersonal in nature in century before banks had been established. It would be interesting to know whether the pattern found here changed during the eighteenth century and if there was any impact upon it from the development of alternative and institutional sources of lending and investment.

Notes

1. Usury Acts: 13 Eliz. 1, c. 8 & 31 Eliz. 1, c. 18.
2. The term 'land' will be used throughout to include rural dwellings as well as land.
3. Kent had gavelkind tenure, referred to in the chapter in this volume by Imogen Wedd.
4. The ability to retain use of the land by the borrower was facilitated by the development of the equity of redemption from the mid-sixteenth century.
5. Copyhold mortgages do not normally appear in probate or litigation records as inheritance of them was customary rather than by will, and most disputes were dealt with in the manor court.
6. Original manorial record sources: Winchester College (hereafter WC) archives: Court Book series Numbers 23047–23058 (includes Meonstoke court rolls 1600–1735); Bishopric (B) manorial rolls series in Hampshire Record Office, Winchester (HRO), 11M59/E1/125/3 to 11M59/E1/143/1 (Crawley); Cathedral archives, now in HRO, series DC/J5/47–72, and DC/J11/1 (includes Hinton Ampner court rolls).
7. In the same article, Tawney noted that in 1611, a patent was granted for the establishment of a public office whose responsibility would cover the recording of (freeholder) transactions, but the ultimate fate of this is not clear.
8. Bishopric mortgage surrender books: HRO, 11M59/C7/1 et seq. The number of mortgages recorded amongst 20 of the bishops' manors quickly rose from a mere 8 per annum in 1604 to 50 p.a. in 1617/18 and up to 78 p.a. in 1623/4.
9. WC lease books containing corn rent income. Books 22716–22718, 23053–23055; item 22272; item 23170a; books 26105–26106; 26536–26537 (Lease income annual summaries for the manors of Vernham Dean and Woodmancott.)

10. Women formed about 25% of the tenantry, so they borrowed mortgages proportionately less than the men. Further exploration of these women's participation in mortgages will be found in a separate study (Gayton 2018).
11. The parliamentary surveys were carried out of estates confiscated for resale after the civil war. The dean and chapter estates surveys used in this chapter are now in HRO, DC/J10/2/1–2.
12. It is of course possible that those are merely the ones which have survived because it was necessary to retain and keep them over several generations.
13. The use of landholding size as an indicator of relative wealth needs caveats. It gives a misleading impression for those who were artisans and not farmers, when their 'wealth' did not derive from land. It also only measures the amount of land held by copyholders in the villages of study, whereas in reality, they may have had multiple holdings in different neighbouring manors which would add up to a larger actual personal estate.
14. Probate records were used from the Winchester Bishopric, Archdeaconry and Peculiar wills series held in the HRO, plus Prerogative Court of Canterbury (PCC) Wills in TNA. (All inhabitants in these ecclesiastically owned manors had their wills proved in the PCC during the Commonwealth period 1649–1660 whatever their status, as the church courts had been abolished.)
15. There were five individuals who borrowed for separate reasons with a gap of more than 10 years between them. They have been counted as two different individual borrowers with their different motives.
16. WC Court Book 23056, p. 63d.
17. Meonstoke manor had the custom of Borough English: inheritance by the youngest son.
18. WC Court Book 23055, p. 115d.
19. WC Court Book 23053, p. 172d.
20. HRO, 11M59/E1/129/2, p. 14d.
21. HRO, 1685A/081: will and inventory of John Rothwell.
22. HRO, 11M59/E1/128/10, p. 64.
23. HRO, 1641B/35: will and inventory of Elizabeth Mitchell.
24. WC Court Book 23055, p. 132.

References

Primary Sources

Hughes, E., and P. White (eds.), 1992. *The Hampshire Hearth Tax Assessment, 1665* (Winchester: Hampshire Record Series, vol. 11).
Tawney, R.H. (ed.), 1925. *A Discourse Upon Usury by Thomas Wilson DCL, 1572* (New York: Harcourt Brace and Co.).

Secondary Works

Allen, R.C., 1992. *Enclosure and the Yeoman. The Agricultural Development of the South Midlands 1450–1850* (Oxford: Oxford University Press).

Erickson, A.L., 1990. 'Common law versus common practice: The use of marriage settlements in early modern England', *EcHR*, vol. 43, pp. 21–31.

French, H.R., and R.W. Hoyle, 1999. 'The land market of a Pennine manor: Slaidburn, 1650–1780', *C&C*, vol. 14, pp. 349–383.

French, H.R., and R.W. Hoyle, 2007. *The Character of English Rural Society. Earls Colne, 1550–1750* (Manchester: Manchester University Press).

Gayton, J.D., 2013. 'Tenants, Tenures and Transfers: the Landholding Experience of Rural Customary Tenants in some Hampshire Downland Manors, 1645 to 1705', Unpublished PhD thesis, University of Exeter.

Gayton, J.D., 2018. 'Women's participation in rural copyhold mortgages in seventeenth-century England', in E. Dermineur (ed.), *Women and Credit in Pre-industrial Europe* (Turnhout: Brepols) (forthcoming).

Holderness, B.A., 1976. 'Credit in English rural society before the nineteenth century with special reference to the period 1650–1720', *Agricultural History Review*, vol. 24, pp. 97–109.

Lambrecht, T., 2009. 'Rural credit and the market for annuities in eighteenth-century Flanders', in P.R. Schofield and T. Lambrecht (eds.), *Credit and the Rural Economy in North Western Europe, c.1200–c.1850* (Turnhout: Brepols), pp. 75–97.

Muldrew, C., 1998. *The Economy of Obligation: The Culture of Credit and Social Relations in Early Modern England* (Basingstoke: Palgrave).

Muldrew, C., 2012. 'Debt, credit and poverty in early modern England', in R. Brubaker, R.R. Lawless and C.J. Tabb (eds.), *A Debtor World: Interdisciplinary Perspectives on Debt* (Oxford: Oxford University Press), pp. 9–32.

Spicksley, J.M., 2008. 'Usury legislation, cash and credit: The development of the female investor in the late Tudor and Stuart periods', *EcHR*, vol. 61, pp. 277–301.

Tawney, R.H., 1912. *The Agrarian Problem in the Sixteenth Century* (New York and London: Harper and Row).

Tawney, R.H., 1926. *Religion and the Rise of Capitalism* (London: Murray).

Tawney, R.H., 1941. 'The rise of the gentry: 1558–1640', *EcHR*, vol. 11, pp. 1–38.

Van Bavel, B.J.P., J. Dijkman, E. Kuijpers, and J. Zuijderduijn, 2012. 'The organisation of markets as a key factor in the rise of Holland from the fourteenth to the sixteenth century: A test case for an institutional approach', *C&C*, vol. 27, pp. 347–378.

Whittle, J., 2000. *The Development of Agrarian Capitalism: Land and Labour in Norfolk 1440–1580* (Oxford: Oxford University Press).

CHAPTER 4

Mortgages and the Kentish Yeoman in the Seventeenth Century

Imogen Wedd

4.1 Introduction

During the sixteenth century in England, opponents of 'usury' warned of social and moral decline if borrowing at interest was liberalised. The story of John Reddich of Kent, haberdasher and serial borrower, fits this negative view. It was guaranteeing a friend's debt which led him to make his first mortgage (or so he said). Thereafter, he entered a spiral of debt, mortgage and remortgage which quickly led to the downfall of his family. Married in 1675 to Margaret Jemmett of Edenbridge in Kent, he would have had a good portion (dowry) with her, but the successive deaths of her grandfather, father, two brothers and five sisters led to her inheriting her family's entire estate, built up over at least three generations and worth a capital sum of £9790 in 1680.[1] John was now styled 'gentleman' and was to be found with other gentry taking part in the Kent county administration (Cockburn 1980). Perhaps this went to his head; perhaps in addition to his guarantee he made rash investments; perhaps he was involved, like Daniel Defoe, in state insurance or

I. Wedd (✉)
University of Cambridge, Cambridge, UK
e-mail: iw232@cam.ac.uk

C. Briggs and J. Zuijderduijn (eds.), *Land and Credit*,
Palgrave Studies in the History of Finance,
https://doi.org/10.1007/978-3-319-66209-1_4

speculative trade ventures, but whatever the cause within fifteen years of the marriage the property had been lost (Quilter 2004, pp. 53–73). Margaret's mother, Timothea Jemmett, found her jointure estate mortgaged; her goods distrained for her son-in-law's debts and after being bought in for her by a friend distrained again. The eventual purchaser of the bulk of the lands, the neighbouring landowner Henry Streatfeild of High Street House, took counsel's opinion on the conveyance, but still found that at least one property had a second mortgage on it which he had to settle, and another mortgaged property resulted in a lawsuit.[2] In 1714, John and Margaret's surviving son, Richard Reddich, serving with the army in Flanders where he was shortly to be killed, made his will, leaving the small estate which his grandmother had salvaged for him in trust to pay an income to his mother, on the condition it would 'not be under the power and controll or be subject to any debt of any present or future husband of hers' and then after her death to pay the income to his father on condition he 'shall not make any sale Mortgage assignment conveyance of anticipation thereof or of any part thereof nor intent or attempt soe to do'; John's son clearly thought him a profligate.[3]

Yet, this moral tale is an extreme case; one can question how typical this is as a picture of mortgage debt in a community of small landowners in the period. We know that mortgage finance was available to the aristocracy and upper gentry, but we still know rather less about the mortgage market in rural areas and among the 'middling sort' in this critical period. J.E. Kew's study of Devonshire, which covers the mid-sixteenth century, is a notable exception but is fifty years old (Stone 1965; Melton 1986; Kew 1967, pp. 165–179). Medievalists and early modernists have established the importance of credit and creditworthiness in the economic system of England, and the importance of long-term credit for financing trade, industry and agrarian development (Matthew 2009; Muldrew 2001; Holderness 1976). Perhaps, like Kew, we no longer perceive the mortgage as the 'desperate expedient' and last resort described by Hugh Trevor-Roper, but there is still more to learn about its frequency, use and impact among rural agriculturalists (Trevor-Roper 1951 pp. 279–298). How easy was it for yeomen and gentry to raise capital? Were they operating in the same market as the aristocracy? Is it true, as has been suggested, that mortgage finance became more accessible in the second half of the seventeenth century, and if so can we draw conclusions about the reasons for this, and the role of legal changes? What was the social and economic impact?

If there is one part of England which should be capable of providing an answer to these questions, with plentiful examples of the yeoman or small agriculturalist, it is the Weald of Kent, part of the well-watered lowland basin which stretches across the south-east corner of England. The term 'Kentish yeoman' is not just descriptive, but it has connotations of prosperity and freedom which would have been recognisable to contemporaries:

> A knight of Cales, a gentleman of Wales,
> A Laird of the north country,
> A Yeoman of Kent with his yearly rent
> Could buy them out, all three. (Grose 1787)

Such prosperity can be accounted for by, among other things, the rise of London and the demand for food, access to fuel and water, the cloth and iron industries, early enclosure and favourable conditions of tenure, but for such opportunities to be exploited there must have been access to capital. The sixteenth and seventeenth centuries saw the introduction of new crops such as apples, cherries and hops, for which the county later became famous, but which are capital intensive and require time to mature. Here the prevailing system of land tenure was 'gavelkind', particular to the county of Kent, and characterised by freedom of disposition and partition among male heirs. This was in contrast to customary or copyhold tenure and with primogeniture (inheritance by the eldest son) which was the common law of England. This Kentish peculiarity ensured that land ownership was widely spread and that land could be freely sold or mortgaged, subject to the rights of widows and heirs (Robinson 1741; Lambarde 1576).

The examples in this chapter come from one administrative unit, the Hundred of Somerden, made up of the large central parish of Chiddingstone, and part or all of Brasted, Cowden, Edenbridge, Hever, Leigh and Penshurst. They make up all the surviving mortgage deeds which could be retrieved and put into context. Ideal as Kent may be for looking at yeomen, the disadvantage, as Michael Zell has pointed out, is that with so much freehold land, manorial records are patchy and wholly inadequate as a systematic source of information for analysis of property (Zell 1994, pp. 11–16). This is particularly true of the Weald, originally an area of 'dens' (woodland pasture) dependent on upland manors on the North Downs; permanent settlement was piecemeal and late; the name Somerden, for instance, is descriptive. Some properties seem never to have been within a manor; by the seventeenth century, landowners were buying themselves out of manorial dues, and the patchwork of scattered manors and frequent changes of ownership result in poor record survival. We are therefore heavily dependent on title deeds; these, too, raise issues of survival, but where a good set of records exists it is possible to put together a substantial and revealing history of a property.

4.2 The Nature of the Market

To explain the rapid increase in mortgages in the sixteenth and seventeenth centuries, historians have tended to look either to changes in the law or to changes in customary land tenure (Jones 1989 pp. 6–8). Three particular developments in the law are highlighted: changing attitudes to interest after the Usury Act of 1571, the development of 'equitable' remedies, particularly for the borrower, in the courts after 1625 and from 1675, and refinements in conveyancing instruments after the Statute of Uses and the Statute of Enrolments in 1536. The changes in customary tenure can largely be discounted as an explanation in this part of Kent, since all the mortgagors (borrowers) were freeholders, the majority holders in gavelkind which subsisted from pre-conquest times until 1926. If the rural mortgage market had followed the pattern described by Jones and others, one would expect step changes in the volume of transactions, an important role for semi-professional lenders in providing finance and for intermediaries in creating a market, and a commercialisation of terms and conditions. But was this the case?

For the Hundred of Somerden in the period 1550–1700, there survive 98 mortgages of sufficient quality to be analysed and contextualised, 95 mortgaging existing property and 3 purchasing on instalments.[4] To put this in perspective, there are just over four hundred properties, ranging from a field to a manor, where a record can be reconstructed for the period; from the surviving evidence, only a minority of these seem never to have had a mortgage on any part of them. This implies relative ease in obtaining capital, but for analysis of the timing, development and outcomes we have to look more closely at the individuals involved, and in particular at their wealth, status and position in society. Of the 95 mortgages on existing property, 23 are those of mortgagors (borrowers) who describe themselves as 'yeoman', 22 as 'gentleman', 21 are tradesmen, 17 are titled aristocracy or esquires, and the remaining 12 are city merchants, husbandmen or women; the three purchase mortgages are by a butterman, a yeoman and a clothier.

Although the status of titled people is clear, and 'esquires' can be defined narrowly as aristocracy below the level of knight, there has always been heart-searching about the use of the terms 'gentleman' and 'yeoman'. Strictly defined, 'gentlemen' were those granted that status by the College of Heralds, but as Wrightson suggests, the significant factors in practice were 'the recognition accorded to wealth, life-style and the exercise of authority'; they included clergymen and lawyers who were thought to be entitled by office to gentry status (Wrightson 1982, p. 24). The word 'yeoman' probably originates in the Saxon 'yemen' implying a free man which, however true for Kent, was out of date by the sixteenth century. Grose's explication is as follows:

> A Yeoman was an independent man, somewhat less than a Gentleman (a term formerly not so liberally dealt out as at present.) A yeoman occupied his own land, killed his own mutton, and wore the fleeces of his own sheep, spun in his house. The yeomanry of Kent were famous for their riches. This class of people is now entirely extinct, the title of Gentleman being almost as universally claimed in England as in Wales. (Grose 1787, p. 214)

I quail at the task of attempting to discover if my sample of landowners killed their own mutton. Perhaps more manageably, the yeoman is sometimes identified with the 'forty-shilling freeholder', the lowest level of society permitted the vote after 1430, but the problems of establishing how much property a man held, and at what point in his life we are to make that judgement, are insuperable (see the Freeholders Act (8 Hen. VI, c. 7), quoted by Seymour 1915). For my purposes, lenders and borrowers are analysed by how the parties describe themselves. This is a poor indicator of wealth; as William Lambarde pointed out, a Kentish yeoman often had no ambition to obtain a coat of arms for himself, despite prosperity which would have supported that status (Lambarde 1576, pp. 7–8). As Wrightson says, what is significant is how men perceived themselves and how their peers saw them (Wrightson 1982).

4.2.1 *Growth of the Market*

In the mid-sixteenth century, the usury laws were liberalised and charging interest became more socially acceptable. After the Usury Act of 1571, it was never again made illegal (within statutory limits), but the position of the mortgagor remained vulnerable (Tawney 1925). Since the fifteenth century, remedies had been provided by the equity courts (those with a jurisdiction to correct injustice caused by the strict interpretation of the common law), in cases where the mortgagor had defaulted on repayment but where the strict interpretation of the common law resulted in manifest unfairness or hardship (Simpson 1986, p. 243; Baker 2002; Turner 1931).

The traditional explanation for the step change in the market cites the case of *Emmanuel College v. Evans* in 1626 as marking the point when the courts broke out from the hardship condition; although the validity of this case as a precedent has been questioned, it is undisputed that the mortgagor gradually acquired a general equitable right to redeem even after default, matched by the right of foreclosure of the mortgagee (lender) represented in 1629 by *How v. Vigures* (Turner 1931, p. 27; Simpson 1986, p. 244; 1. Ch. Rep. 18, 1. Ch. Rep. 32, quoted by Simpson; Waddilove 2014). There were attempts to limit this right of redemption, but it became entrenched under the chancellorship of Lord Nottingham from 1675; the equitable right to redeem now became property in its own right, the 'Equity of Redemption', and could even be bought and sold; Brian Simpson dates this latter development from the eighteenth century, quoting *Casborne v. Scarfe* (1738) (Simpson 1986, p. 245). Thereafter, says Simpson, mortgages of land were treated simply as security for a debt, and 'in no branch of the law was the sanctity of the agreement less regarded'. The mortgagee could sell his interest, but subject to the mortgagor's right of redemption; the value of this right meant that it was often stated in the mortgage deed (Simpson 1986, p. 246). To sum up, the expansion has been attributed to two major legal developments, one in the 1620s and 1630s, and one in the 1670s and 1680s.

At first sight, the data from south-west Kent appears to support this traditional model, showing no particular increase after the Usury Act of 1571, but two step changes, the first in the 1630s and the second in the 1680s. Figure 4.1, analysed by date, shows all mortgages, including first mortgages, remortgages (where the borrower takes out a new loan, repaying the first), assignments (where the existing loan is transferred

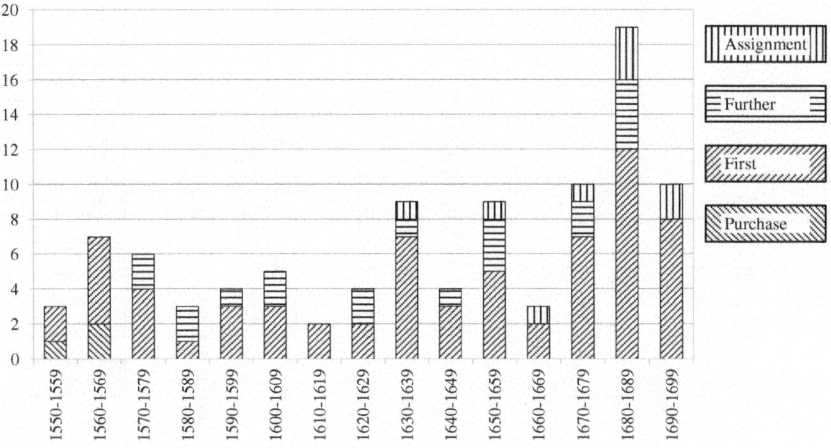

Fig. 4.1 Number of mortgages by type, 1550–1699
Sources See n.4

from one lender to another, the borrower being only indirectly involved) and purchases on instalments. Detailed discussion of the *term* of a mortgage is left until later, but if we separate out first mortgages from remortgages and assignments, the changes are less marked but still apply. The fact that a mortgagor has to remortgage may say as much about the lender as it does the borrower; one lender may be content to keep receiving interest for ten years or more, while another may require his money after two. Overall, however, additional borrowing and extensions of time may be more dependent on economic conditions than changes in law and the consequent availability of finance, so the distinction is worth making.

The results of a simple count of mortgages can be skewed by a handful of serial borrowers like John Reddich, so Fig. 4.2 shows the data for individual mortgagors only, dating borrowers by their first mortgage and ignoring for the moment the purchase mortgages. The ninety-five mortgages involved only 52 borrowers, of whom 34 borrowed once and the remaining 18 more than once. Although 70% of the mortgages occurred after the mid-point of 1625, the changes in volume at certain dates are somewhat different. There is still an increase in the 1630s, but it is notable that the 1560s also mark a relative high point. The numbers are of course small; the most that we can say is that mortgages in this sample drop back between 1570 and 1629 to rise again in the 1630s and again

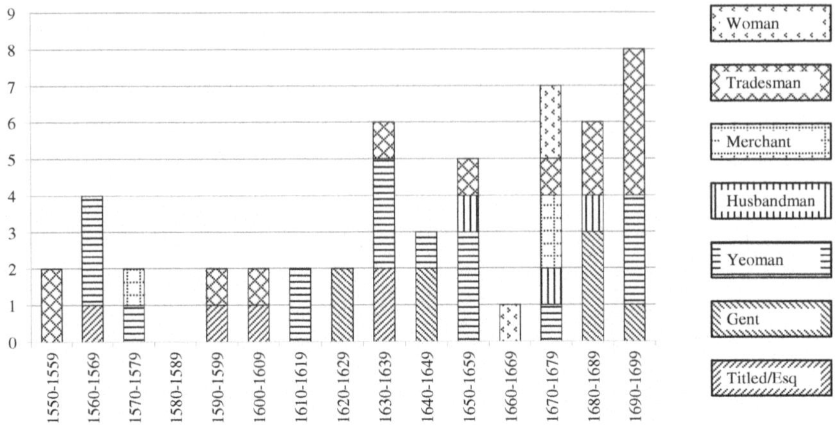

Fig. 4.2 Number of individual mortgagors in various categories, 1550–1699
Sources See n.4

in the 1670s, but the increase at the end of the seventeenth century is far less dramatic and perhaps more susceptible to economic explanations. There is no evidence of an immediate increase after the Usury Act of 1571; indeed, it is followed by a low point in this data set.

4.2.2 Borrowers and Lenders

R. H. Tawney suggested that in the sixteenth century lending was a bye-employment among merchants, but by the early seventeenth century professional financiers were emerging from among the scriveners and later the goldsmiths, in what was the beginning of a market infrastructure (Tawney 1925, p. 89). John Reddich's first mortgagee in 1681 was the London scrivener, William Warne, who lent him £800 on Stanfords End Farm in Edenbridge. Subsequent lenders were more varied: in 1683, George Arnold, esquire of London, lent him £2000 on Merchants Farm in Crowhurst; one year on, Henry Wade, vintner of London, lent him £600 on Polefields and Ware Lands; in 1686, John Peachey of London, who was his tailor, bought for £150 an annuity secured on Beechenwood. Then, in 1687, William Chapman of West Malling in Kent lent £250 on Beechenwood and Glathredge in Cowden, John Peachey's mortgage was extended, and Merchants Farm remortgaged to

William Killingworth, serjeant-at-law. In the same year, Beechenwood, Glathredge, Polefields and Ware Lands, with the addition of Liveroxhill, were remortgaged to Henry Streatfeild, also a lawyer but a long-standing local landowner and parish gentleman. Finally, in 1688, the outstanding mortgages were assigned, two to Henry Streatfeild and one to George Hooper, the scrivener, of Tonbridge.[5]

The impression this gives of gentry borrowing large sums in the London market is deceptive. Norman Jones described how the 1570/1 Royal Commission on usury in the south-west found several instances of professional lenders, viewed with much suspicion, but he suggested that the norm was something more local, and this is entirely in keeping with the Somerden results (Jones 1989, p. 72). Typical are the loans, yeoman to yeoman, made by John Ashdowne of Buckhurst of £20 on part of Crippenden in Cowden to his neighbour George Wickenden, and of £120 on Geers in Chiddingstone made in 1610 to Matthew Tye, or indeed the loan of £20 made in 1649 by the mercer Edward Everest to yeoman Richard Beecher on Stony Croft at Chested Green in Penshurst.[6] Figures 4.2 and 4.3 show lenders and borrowers broken down by status and date. Yeomen as mortgagors seem to have been borrowing, either under financial pressure or raising capital to invest in new opportunities, in the 1560s, 1630s, 1650s and 1690s. By comparison,

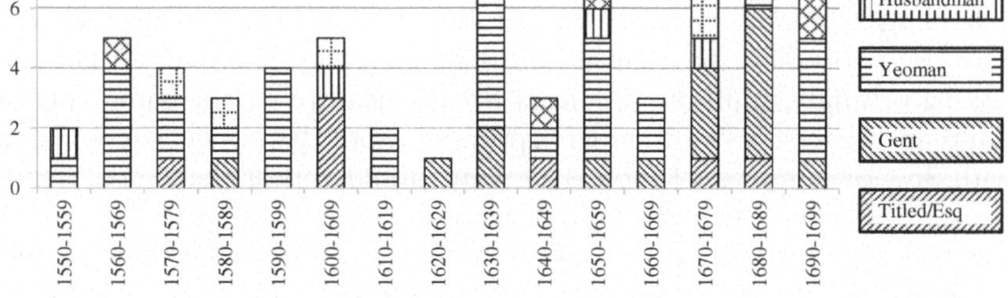

Fig. 4.3 Number of individual mortgagees in various categories, 1550–1699
Sources See n.4

gentry borrowers seem to have been borrowing most in the 1640s and 1680s, and those most conspicuous after 1670 seem to be the tradesmen; 60% of their mortgages date from after 1675, and in this twenty-five-year period, they represent 50% of the borrowers.

Matched with 52 borrowers are 77 lenders (new lenders picking up, of course, some of the remortgages and assignments), as shown in Fig. 4.3. Now it is clear that whereas yeomen represent 35% of borrowers during the period as a whole, they make up 43% of lenders, and the decades when they were borrowing most, they were also lending most, and not just to their peers. As a class, they were net lenders, but less so than the gentry who represented 13% of borrowers but 24% of lenders. The net losers were the tradesmen who represent 28% of borrowers but only 15% of lenders, borrowing greatly more often than they lent, and it would appear that they were borrowing predominantly from yeomen, sometimes their own brothers or cousins. Tradesmen may have been increasing as a proportion of the population in the later period, but if so this is not reflected in their lending. It is interesting that a few husbandmen were among the borrowers and lenders; they came at the lowest end of the farming scale, usually tenant farmers with perhaps an acre or two of their own; in a sample of 520 male wills for this period leaving property in the Hundred of Somerden, they represent 9% of the identifiable occupations of will-makers over the whole period 1550–1700, and 13% of those whose occupations are identified in the burial registers of the two largest parishes in the 1680s and 1690s.[7]

Only one yeoman occurs as both lender and borrower. In 1683, Benjamin Wakelin, who had recently inherited half the goods of his father, a successful butcher, lent to a neighbour £30 which was not repaid and was assigned to another lender two years later. Ten years on it appears that Benjamin had less surplus cash; in 1693, he mortgaged a field in Chiddingstone Town left him in his father's will and sold another; two years after that he sold his remaining inheritance.[8] Perhaps less surprisingly, multiple creditors do not feature in the same way as multiple debtors; 13% of lenders appeared more than once as compared with 35% of borrowers (Table 4.1). If it should appear that 'serial' lenders are under-represented simply because they are ranging further afield, this would be partially correct. Clearly, all the borrowers are local while some of the lenders are not, but the data shows that the mortgage market is actually surprisingly local overall.

Table 4.1 Multiple lending and borrowing

	Borrower	*%*	*Mortgages*	*%*	*Lender*	*%*	*Mortgages*	*%*
1 mortgage	34	*65*	34	*36*	67	*87*	67	*71*
2 mortgages	10	*19*	20	*21*	6	*8*	12	*13*
3 mortgages	3	*6*	9	*9*	1	*1*	3	*3*
4 mortgages	3	*6*	12	*13*	2	*3*	8	*8*
5+ mortgages	2	*4*	20	*21*	1	*1*	5	*5*
	52	*100*	95	*100*	77	*100*	95	*100*

Source See n.4

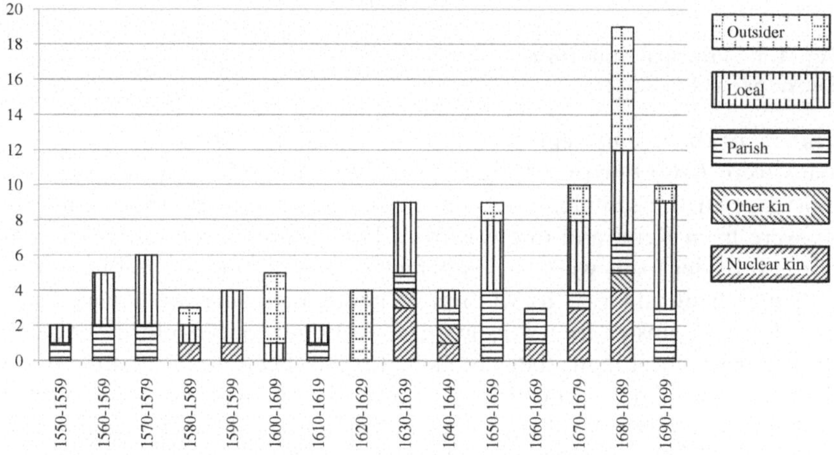

Fig. 4.4 Relation of mortgagee to mortgagor, 1550–1699
Sources See n.4

Figure 4.4 shows the relationship between lender and borrower, including all first mortgages, remortgages and assignments. The lenders have been divided into nuclear kin (mother, father, brother, sister, son, daughter, stepson and stepdaughter); other kin (in-laws, aunts, uncles and cousins); those who live in the same parish; those who are local, defined as coming from an adjacent parish (often in the latter case they will, of course, live in closer proximity to each other than those in the same parish), and outsiders. It appears that in rural society the outsider as lender is in a minority; the majority of lenders were kinsmen and local men. Unsurprisingly, perhaps, outsiders tended to be the larger

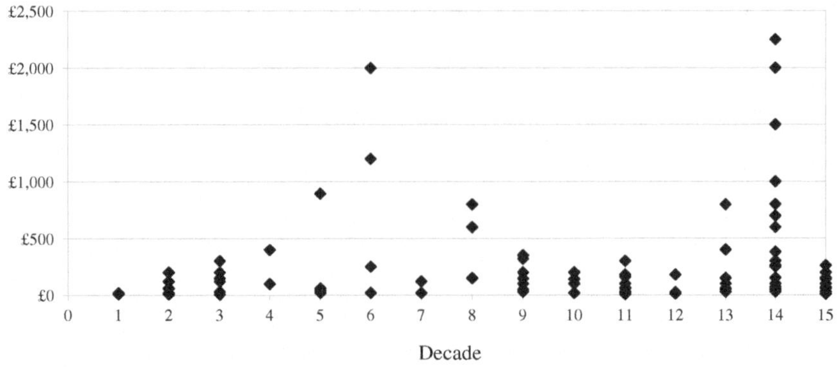

Fig. 4.5 Principal sums (in £)
Sources See n.4

lenders: of the twenty represented, nine lent over £500 and of these four loans were £1000 or over.[9] Figure 4.5 shows the principal sum for each mortgage in the sample. Thirteen of the outsiders were from London, six were from Kent, and one was from Hampshire. Seventy-five per cent of the outsider loans were to aristocracy or gentry, one to a yeoman, one to a merchant and two to widows of gentlemen; one was a very small loan from a spinster to a wheelwright. Although one could describe all the gentry as local men, they are likely to have been more urban-centred than the rest of the population. In short, the yeoman mortgage market was almost entirely local; the implication is that sufficient money was available in this rural area to supply the demand for capital, except in the case of the very largest loans.

If only the largest loans were funded by outsiders, what was the most typical? Table 4.2 gives the smallest, largest and average loan divided into six twenty-five-year periods. The largest sum lent by a yeoman was £895 (by Richard Streatfeild the ironmaster whose sons described themselves as gentlemen), and £350 was the largest sum borrowed. These are significant sums; at the end of the sixteenth century, a farm called Lockskinners was sold with seventy-three acres for £440, and even the smallest loan of £7 represented four to five months' wages for a labourer in southern England at that time (Phelps-Brown and Hopkins 1955).[10]

Among the lenders are four men who can be identified as scriveners or lawyers, those often at the receiving end of much of the opprobrium relating to 'usury', but two of the four are local; the third is William

Table 4.2 Size of mortgage loans

	All mortgagors				*Yeomen borrowing*				*Yeomen lending*			
	Smallest	*Largest*	*Mean*	*No.*	*Smallest*	*Largest*	*Mean*	*No.*	*Smallest*	*Largest*	*Mean*	*No.*
1550–1574	£10	£300	£83	9	£10	£120	£53	4	£10	£300	£104	7
1576–1599	£7	£895	£182	11	£7	£7	£7	1	£7	£895	£187	6
1600–1624	£20	£2000	£602	6	£20	£120	£70	2	£20	£120	£70	2
1625–1649	£20	£600	£250	16	£20	£350	£133	6	£30	£350	£124	7
1650–1674	£8	£800	£149	17	£60	£300	£144	6	£8	£300	£96	7
1675–1699	£30	£2250	£402	34	£70	£260	£155	4	£30	£150	£80	6
Unknown/ annuity				2								1
				95				23				36

Source See n.4

Killingworth, serjeant-at-law. The fourth, William Warne, was described as a 'cunning scrivener' in the dispute over the security he took over the land of John Reddich, an example of this mistrust—comparable to mistrust of bankers post-2008, perhaps.[11] None of these four men was ultimately a purchaser of the property, so their loans were clearly for investment purposes only; none appears to have been unduly acquisitive. Of the remaining outsiders, only Abraham Jacob acquired the property on which he lent, Stanfords End in Edenbridge, bequeathing it in his will to his sons.[12] Abraham was originally from Cambridgeshire, made his money as purveyor of wine to the Royal Household and settled in Bromley by Bow, his son John becoming the first baronet of Bromley.[13] Twenty-seven years later, the property in Edenbridge was sold to Robert Jemmett, husband of the unfortunate Timothea.[14]

Among the yeoman lenders, there is perhaps stronger evidence of a desire to acquire. John Ashdowne acquired both the properties on which he lent money; he sold the tenement at Crippenden immediately to another neighbour; however, the other property, Geers, remained in the family for three generations. Indeed, the purchase of a mortgage was tantamount to acquiring an option to buy. The will in 1566 of John Buss, a tenant farmer, includes instructions for a mortgage he had bought, clearly hoping to obtain property of his own.[15] Another significant motive must have been security; in the days prior to deposit banking, it was probably unwise to leave large sums of money in a farmhouse which was likely at best to be occupied only by women during the day. Few probate inventories show significant cash; Henry Piggott of Withers, dying in June 1688, left goods worth £103, of which his 'purce and girdle & Ready money in his purce & wearing apparell of all sorts' came to only £3 10*s*., and this was relatively high, equivalent to the value of his eight young pigs, or his bed, chest, trunk and sword.[16]

Clearly, the example of John Reddich is far from the norm; like that of Kew on Devonshire, this study has been found that the typical lender is not from London but a local man, and generally of the same social class as the borrower (Kew 1967, p. 175). This is more remarkable for south-west Kent, within thirty miles of London, than it is for Devonshire. There were cattle markets in Sevenoaks and Tonbridge, but Borough Market in Southwark would have been used, particularly for hops and fruit. This would take the larger producers at least into wider society, and their tradesman brothers and cousins, and indeed they themselves, would often have been apprenticed in London. The implication is surely that neither lenders nor borrowers needed to move outside their known and trusted contacts.

4.2.3 *Intermediaries*

Such a very local market has something to say about the need for market makers. In his history of banking, R. D. Richards identifies four types of intermediary in the period before deposit banking: merchants, brokers, scriveners and goldsmiths, of whom scriveners have been considered to be the first to attain prominence (Richards 1929, p. 1; Coleman 1951, pp. 221–230). The conveyancer for John Reddich's first two loans was the scrivener William Warne; Charles Bostock, a scrivener of London, may have been the intermediary in four loans from Abraham Jacob of London to the Holmden family of Edenbridge who appear to have been strangers to one another. All the other identifiable conveyancers were local. Henry Streatfeild, lawyer and member of Clifford's Inn, was responsible for twelve mortgages between 1675 and 1700, but there were few yeomen among his clients. Nicholas Hooper, the Tonbridge scrivener, and his sons and grandsons were responsible for 10 mortgages between 1568 and 1698, five of them for a yeoman mortgagor; William Cowdrey made two in the 1560s, Richard Antrobus one in 1614, Thomas Streatfeild two in the 1690s and George Toller one in 1659. How far these men acted as go-betweens, putting lender in touch with borrower, is hard to say, but the fact that none dominates the local business suggests a limited role; there was no 'first port of call' for a loan.

One possible clue as to the intermediary's role is the place of payment. The vast majority of mortgage repayments were to be made at the house of the mortgagee, three were at the house of the mortgagor and two at the tenanted premises; many do not state a place. Four give the house of a third party whose relationship is not identified; two of John Reddich's loans were to be paid at the business premises of his brother in London. The church porch as a place of payment appears regularly in the period 1550–1599. From 1670 onwards, we do increasingly find that mortgages are to be repaid at the premises of a lawyer or scrivener, or his inn of court; only one of the latter applies to a yeoman mortgage, and that is where the lawyer concerned is acting as trustee.[17] The results presented here concur with the suggestion of Holderness that 'the country attorney ... seldom operated beyond the range of his own local knowledge and experience. ... It was only for the relatively few large "estate mortgages" that outside help was often required' (Holderness 1975, p. 110). Whether we can infer from this that the lawyer was playing an increasing role as introducer is another matter; certainly, we could not go so far as to conclude that intermediaries were developing the market. What the figures have shown, however, is that lender and borrower knew each other in the majority of cases, and therefore, it is probable they would have been able to locate each other by repute, or enquiry at the church or market.

4.3 Terms and Conditions

4.3.1 Interest

Although there is apparently little correlation between the liberalisation of usury and the increasing numbers of mortgages in this sample, one would expect to see a link between the rates charged and the maximum permitted rate (Tawney 1925, p. 20; Jones 1989, p. 6). It does not seem to be so, although the interest is seldom named and usually has to be back-calculated from the repayment schedule. (We may speculate on the reasons for this.) John Reddich paid 5 or 6% for his loans between 1681 and 1688 at a time when the statutory rate was 6%. There is no sign that local rates were in any way different from those in London. Looking at all first mortgages, the disconnect between the statutory rate and the rate charged is noticeable; although the statutory rate is seldom breached, most mortgagees ask for interest in the region of 5%. Figure 4.6 shows the periods (of variable length) during which a particular statutory interest rate applied, and the interest actually paid per year, based on simple interest. The rate seems to have been based on the expected return on land; John Habakkuk made this suggestion many years ago, so whereas a debt might be seen as a loan at interest, a financial transaction, the mortgage seems to have been seen as a transaction in land for which rent was required, perhaps reflecting the caution about charges of usury (Habakkuk 1952). Even in the 1680s there seems to be no evidence of commercial attitudes to risk; John Reddich's interest rates levelled down to 5% even when his mortgagees knew of his difficulties.

Three mortgages with a premium date from the period when interest was illegal, and two are above the statutory rate. Of these, four are based on payment of an annuity and two on rent, so evading the narrow definition of 'usury'. For example, in 1561, the yeoman Robert Seyliard lent £60 for six years and leased the property back to the mortgagor, Robert

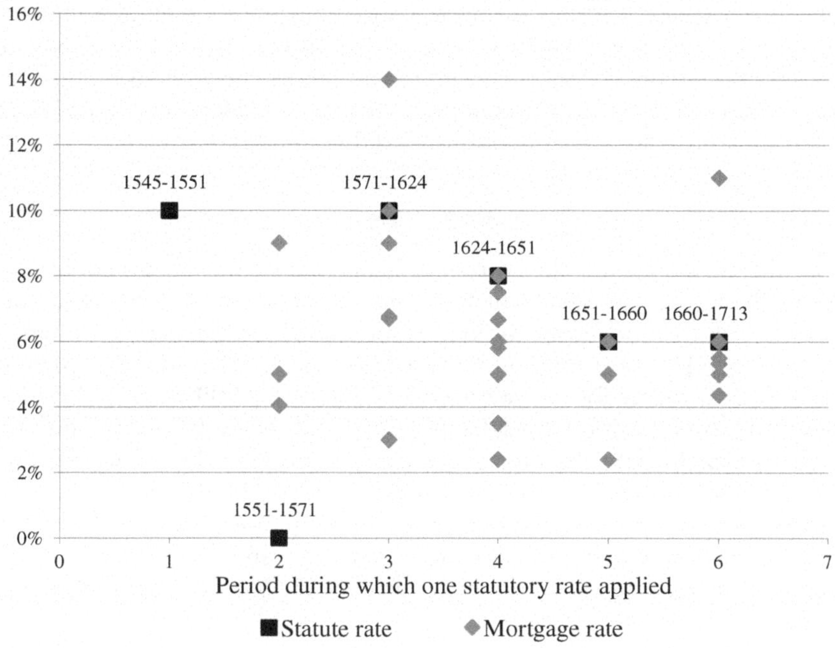

Fig. 4.6 Interest charged on individual mortgages
Sources See n.4

Fuller; the rental charged was one penny in the first year, ten shillings in the second year and thereafter £3 10*s*. a year.[18] There seems to have been an inbuilt incentive here for the mortgage to be repaid early, although it is possible that the money was to be used for a purpose which would generate income in the later years. In fact, the mortgage probably ran for its full term, because in 1568 Robert Fuller and his son Robert entered into a recovery (a device to clear the title of encumbrances), before the property was used to secure a marriage settlement a year or so later.[19] To purchase a property and charge rent for it was not illegal, and the mortgagee here received an average return of 4% per annum; the arguments by those in favour of liberalisation against making a distinction between rents and interest were cogent. A similar arrangement was entered into in 1574, when the rent on a field valued at £10 was 20*s*. per annum (10%), and in 1610 where the details of the rent have not survived.[20] An annuity occurs in 1576 which presumably justified the very high rate of 14%. Once interest was legal, the most common situation was for it to be stated as part of the repayment without giving it a specific name or rate, although in several cases interest payments are recorded on the dorse of the deed. In eleven of the sixteen first mortgages in and before the year 1625, there is no mention of interest or premium; thereafter, it is identifiable in 85% of first mortgages. Sensitivity about usury did not end in 1571.

4.3.2 Term

The charts have shown the pattern of loans taken out, but this could disguise changes in duration which are significant if we are looking at the concept of the mortgage as long-term capital or estimating volumes of lending. The posthumous 1689 edition of Sir Orlando Bridgman's book of precedents for conveyancers has a lease for 500 years 'where the money is to be let for a considerable time' and where before the distant final repayment date the mortgagee can give six months' notice for the principal to be repaid (Bridgman 1689, p. 34). However, the typical term stated in the deeds was one year; half of all mortgages are for a year or less, only three being for more than ten years, and there is limited evidence of a trend towards longer terms over the period (see Table 4.3).

Table 4.3 Length of term of mortgages

	≤1 year	*2–5 years*	*6–10 years*	*>10 years*	*Lease/life*	*Not given*	*Total*
1550–1559	2		1				3
1560–1569	2	3	2				7
1570–1579	3	2		1			6
1580–1589		3					3
1590–1599	3	1					4
1600–1609	1	3			1		5
1610–1619	1	1					2
1620–1629	4						4
1630–1639	7	1				1	9
1640–1649	1	3					4
1650–1659	2	5	1			1	9
1660–1669		1	1			1	3
1670–1679	5	4	1				10
1680–1689	9	5		2	2	1	19
1690–1699	8	2					10
TOTAL	48	34	6	3	3	4	98

Source See n.4

However, it is clear that such a mortgage was not necessarily intended to be for just a year. Provided interest payments were made and the mortgagor and mortgagee were both happy, the loan could continue for many years, despite the borrower being technically in default of repayment of the principal. Even where the mortgagee wanted repayment, the mortgage could be assigned, as we have seen. For example, William Wakelin (brother of Benjamin) mortgaged a property in 1679, assigned in 1691 and again in 1699/1700; on the second assignment, his payments of interest over each year were recorded on the dorse of the deed. In the first year, he paid on time (January); he was two months late in year two (March) and seven months late in the third, fourth, fifth and sixth years (September—perhaps harvest time). In year seven, he sold, but by this time he had kept the mortgage going for twenty-eight years.[21]

It was where technical default had taken place that the current law could be important. If the principal was unpaid at the end of the mortgage term, at common law the estate passed to the mortgagee, but as the equity courts increasingly stepped in, an equitable estate emerged which remained with the mortgagor. From the 1630s onwards in particular, mortgages can be seen to run on long after common law forfeiture: Edmund Medhurst's mortgage to his kinsman Thomas Medhurst was taken out in 1630 for an ostensible term of one year; he remortgaged in 1650 when Thomas Medhurst died and still had some expectation of being allowed to redeem up to 1655.[22]

4.3.3 Possession

Provisions for possession were an indicator of the changes in the law. Before liberalisation of interest, the mortgaged land was typically handed over to the mortgagee so that he could be repaid from the rents and profits; by the end of the sixteenth century, it was usual for the mortgagor to remain in possession, and even if the mortgagee took possession after default, equity made him account for takings in excess of his principal and interest (Simpson 1986, p. 246). Only one mortgage in the Somerden sample specifically states that the mortgagee is to be in possession, and this is the case of two brothers where the mortgagor is the elder, managing the family estate.[23] In three more, all dating from the decade of the 1550s, although not specifically stated, the mortgagee seems to be in possession. In four, the mortgagor is left in possession by virtue of a lease back, and in the remainder, the mortgagor is clearly left in possession by specific covenant or by presumption. For such as John Reddich, resident on one of his wife's properties but with the remainder put out on lease, the question of possession was one of who was to receive the rent, but for yeomen like the Fullers and Wakelins, it was of who was to farm the land and take the profits. Again, my results are consistent with those of Kew; possession by the mortgagor is one of the hallmarks of the 'modern' mortgage after 1560 (Kew 1967, p. 167). It was unusual, too, for the full value of a property to be borrowed (two-thirds seem typical), so for the mortgagee to be in possession and potentially to retain it on default had been a cause of difficulty and injustice.

To sum up, although the mortgage market for yeomen was distinctively local, the terms and conditions were similar for all borrowers. Interest rates were related to expected return on land, and the ostensible term was short but from the mid-seventeenth century could be allowed to run on over many years with an expectation that the property could be redeemed. After 1560, the mortgagee generally remained in possession.

4.4 Conveyancing

4.4.1 *Type of Mortgage Conveyance*

Mortgage in Fee and Mortgage by Demise

The basis of all mortgages of freehold land was, in layman's terms, a transfer from the mortgagor to the mortgagee, with a condition or 'proviso' that if the mortgagor repaid his loan the property would be returned to him. Initially, this was a conveyance of the property, the freehold or 'fee simple', but during the seventeenth century a form developed based on a long lease, an incumbrance or burden on the land which would cease on repayment, with the freehold remaining with the borrower.

The form common in the early sixteenth century was a conveyance with a separate defeasance, but this was replaced during the period with a single deed. Writing in the nineteenth century, William Cruise said that the 'former practice' of putting the provisions for redemption into a separate deed, the defeasance, was discouraged by Lord Talbot and Lord Hardwicke, which dates the change to the early eighteenth century (Cruise 1835, vol. 2, ch. 15 § 11–20; Melton 1986, p. 140). The very problem which made this type of format dangerous and to be discouraged, the potential separation of the two parts, is compounded for us by the fact that once the property was conveyed back to the borrower there was little need to retain the defeasance. Title deed records are therefore not the ideal source for an estimate of their volume; however, it seems that in south-west Kent the abandonment of this early form dates from earlier than Cruise suggests. Such evidence as has been identified consists of conveyances back and forth between the same people in a short timescale. Before Beechenwood was sold to Timothea Jemmett's husband, Robert, in 1658, it was in the ownership of the Wickenden family, long-term residents of Cowden. Between 1600 and 1613, it passed from Thomas Wickenden to Robert Tichborne, a neighbouring owner, and back again, twice.[24] This surely indicates a mortgage where a separate defeasance has been lost, not the genuine sale and purchase of the property. Even these are not found after 1650.[25]

The form of mortgage which took over contained the conditions for redemption within a single deed. Generally speaking, the deed used existing forms, though with increasingly detailed covenants. The medieval feoffment (transfer of the 'fee' or feudal holding) continued, but after the Statute of Uses in 1536, which controlled the increasingly popular device of transferring a property to 'feoffees' (trustees) to hold it for the 'use' of the beneficiary, the bargain and sale emerged as the main conveyancing instrument, and the usual basis of the 'mortgage in fee'. The feoffment depended on *livery of seisin*, the formal and public transfer of possession on the land, for title to pass; the bargain and sale (the agreement to sell) was able to take effect without a formal conveyance after the Statute of Uses provided for the 'use' implied within the agreement to be executed, and the legal estate transferred to the beneficiary. Under the accompanying Statute of Enrolments, this occurred when the written bargain and sale was recorded in the rolls of one of the courts of record at Westminster or with the justices or *custos rotulorum* at county level, if this took place within six months. Enrolment was a practice which was already established but was adapted to ensure that this execution took place, perhaps partly to ensure visibility, but also to avoid the automatic execution of verbal or unclear agreements (Kaye 1988, pp. 617–636).

About the middle of the seventeenth century, however, a new form emerged: a long lease for, say, 500 years, with provision for the mortgagor to retain possession unless he defaulted in payment. This type seems to have come into popularity because a lease was a chattel interest (personal estate), at the disposal of a deceased mortgagee's administrators, as opposed to land which descended to the heir, and it was, of course, the administrators who would have received the money had the debt been paid. It appears to have declined in popularity at a later date because of the technical difficulty that the 'reversion' of the fee simple (the right to the property after the end of the lease) remained with the mortgagor even if he defaulted (Simpson 1986, pp. 243, 248; Baker 2002, p. 312). A purchaser of a property mortgaged by long lease needed to purchase the reversion.

An anonymous precedent book, *The Compleat Clerk and Scriveners Guide* of 1655, places the mortgage in fee in prime place (Anon. 1655). Bridgman's precedent book, thirty years later, includes among the dozen or so mortgages only one, all the remainder being long leases (Bridgman 1689). However, the mortgage in fee remained popular among yeomen in Kent into the 1680s; overall, it is the most common instrument between 1550 and 1650, whether expressed as a feoffment or bargain and sale. The earliest in my sample is 1556 and the latest 1683, and although there are slight variations in detail, the basic form remains the same. The first mortgage by long lease occurs in 1655; between then and the end of the century, they outnumber the mortgages in fee two to one, but do not totally replace them. In addition to being chattels, another advantage was their exemption from manorial dues. Richard Stevens of Princkham in Chiddingstone caused his heirs problems when he took a conveyance of the farm in 1680 by long lease, with the intention of avoiding the payment of a heriot, then later changed his mind and took a conveyance by bargain and sale; a dispute arose as to the nature of the heirs' interest in the property.[26]

In fact, if a will was made, the testator could make provision to pass the land itself to his executors, in trust to pay his legacies. This example comes from the will of a meticulous man, Thomas Streatfeild, in 1627:

> Whereas heretofore I have lent unto Nicholas Fletcher of Shorehame in the countie of Kent yeom[an] the some of fortie pounds for the securitie whereof he hath made over unto me all his lands in Ottford my will is that if the said Nicholas Fletcher paie the money menc[i]oned in the said deed to my Executrix or Executor betweene this and the birth of our Lord god now next comeing after the date of this my will That then the livery and seizin hereupon had & executed and all conveyances hereupon made shalbe utterly voide to all intents & purposes but if default of payment bee

> made of the said money by the said Nicholas Fletcher or his assignes thenn I give and bequeathe the said Lands to my Executrix or Executor and their heires which of them shall take the execution of this my will upon them towards the payment of my debts & legacies and the p[er]formance of this my will.[27]

Other Types of Mortgage Deed

There are other types of mortgage arrangement; one was the grant of an annuity such as John Reddich made to John Peachey; these form about 10% of the sample, predominantly in the period before 1600. The mortgagee here was in fact purchasing a form of pension, with no intention that the principal should be repaid as a lump sum, but it was as much a way of raising capital as a mortgage in fee or by demise. John Reddich's grants to John Peachey are short leases, 21 and 31 years respectively, in which the annuitant paid a capital sum and the mortgagor paid a yearly sum, in this case for three lives (those of John Peachey's mother, his wife and himself) with the annuity reducing as each life ended.[28] Three mortgages involved the conveyance of the fee simple to feoffees; one involved a secret trust and two catered for alternative outcomes.[29] One of these is a lease and release between the vendor and purchaser; in general, however, the lease and release form which became popular for conveyancing a sale was not used for mortgages, although the release was used to transfer the equitable estate. Cruise and others suggest that Equity would even permit an 'equitable mortgage' where there was no deed at all, where the borrower deposited the title deeds with the lender; it is hard to see how these could ever be identified in the records (Cruise 1835, vol. 2, Title 15, § 11–20). Finally, and the form we would most recognise today, was the purchase of a property with payment in instalments: there are three examples, two at the very beginning of the period and a third occurs later in the seventeenth century but is a transaction between a son and his mother, so perhaps atypical.[30] Such different forms were in part a response to differing circumstances, but in the case of annuities in particular there appears to be a development over time, and the need in earlier periods to be cautious about offending the laws and norms relating to usury.

Remortgages and Assignments

Twenty mortgages in the sample come into the category of remortgage, to which the mortgagor was a direct party. Remortgages sometimes incorporated a further loan or further land, or were required after the death of one of the parties; one consisted of the sale by the original mortgagee of the legal estate, recognising the reversion to the mortgagor. Even where there was no further advance, they generally rolled up any unpaid interest into the new principal, the one circumstance where 'interest on interest' was permitted. There are nine assignments; in these, the mortgagor was an incidental party. Bridgman gives four assignment precedents, confirming their ubiquity (Bridgman 1689). Although the mortgagor was not a direct party, all include him, indicating that he has consented (whether he really had the power to dissent is another matter). In addition to the nine direct assignments of an existing loan, there are seven sale assignments accompanying the purchase of mortgaged property by a third party; these are not included in the sample examined in this chapter.

4.4.2 Enrolment and Registration

Although technically a bargain and sale was required to be enrolled, the inadequacies of this system are patent. (The 'lease and release' form of conveyance avoided the requirement, so registration would at all times have been partial.) It would have been the task of the conveyancer to check the rolls for former mortgages, but these could be enrolled in any of the courts of record at Westminster or at county level, so how far this was a practical task for a rural attorney is questionable; Melton suggests that part of the value of the London scrivener and proto-banker Sir Robert Clayton was access to the rolls (Melton 1986, pp. 137–142). Only the 'original' copy of the indenture was endorsed; the 'counterpart' was not, so estimating the degree of compliance is difficult. However, the deficiencies of the system are evident from the fact that the purchaser of John Reddich's estate, Henry Streatfeild, himself a lawyer and member of Clifford's Inn, had difficulties with two former mortgagees. It was a common cause of litigation.

Certain conclusions can be drawn for the yeoman mortgage market: after 1560, no mortgages of the conveyance and separate defeasance survive, and the possibility of them goes no further than 1650. The mortgage in fee dominated conveyancing up to the 1650s; thereafter, the mortgage by demise took over though did not totally supplant it. There were other types for other situations, including those involving feoffees, an annuity, or the purchase of a property in instalments. Remortgages and assignments were commonplace. The lack of any system of registration left the mortgagee rather vulnerable; he could and did fall foul of other encumbrances.

4.5 Outcomes

4.5.1 Forfeiture, Foreclosure and Sale

John Reddich had, by 1687, mortgaged and remortgaged all his and his wife's estate. Early in 1688, Stanfords End, Glathredge, Liveroxhill, Beechenwood, Polefields and Upper Ware Lands were sold to Henry Streatfeild for £3680, of which £1680 was paid out to the mortgagees William Warne, Henry Wade and William Chapman. The property in Crowhurst was also sold, and the mansion house, Skeynes and the small remaining property were settled to provide an income for Margaret Reddich.[31] Unfortunately, her difficulties were not at an end. Further unpaid loans of £500 from Ann Saxby and £100 from Robert Streatfeild had to be secured against this trust the following year, and three years later, Henry Streatfeild bought a further part of the estate in order that these loans could be repaid.[32] By 1700, a further unpaid loan of £350 was secured against the settled estate, and in 1702 £150.[33] By 1703, even Skeynes had to be sold, and John Reddich had been arrested and was in the Fleet Prison.[34]

John Reddich was not the only gentry mortgagor to lose his estate. Dorothy Powell, a daughter and heiress of the Streatfeild family, widowed early, was another serial borrower, much of whose estate was sold.[35] The Willoughbys were another; they had been at Bore Place, Chiddingstone, since Thomas Willoughby married the heiress Bridget Rede in about 1510. Their grandson, Thomas, mortgaged various parts of the estate in the 1580s and 1590s, but it was his son, Percival, who had to sell the entire Kentish property (Stevenson 1911, p. 584). By 1608, he was at least £12,000 in debt, and the purchaser, Bernard Hyde, complained that encumbrances and other issues had been disguised.[36] Sir Percival had married his cousin, Bridget Willoughby, who was an heiress from the main branch of the family, and attributed part of his problems to the execution of the will of his father-in-law, with whom he had a stormy relationship, involving liabilities which he had personally to meet. Unlike the Reddiches, the family survived and prospered, removing to the estate of the main branch of the family (Stevenson 1911, pp. 570–583). The Seyliards of Delaware, who had been established in Edenbridge and Hever for at least five hundred years and perhaps longer, also came to grief, much of their estate being broken up to pay debts and daughters' portions in 1699.[37] Examples like these engender some sympathy for the notion of a 'crisis of the aristocracy', although not as an occurrence at a particular date and time. There was, perhaps, a structural danger implicit in the way of life of the upper gentry. They lived with risk liable to be made (like the Sidneys of Penshurst Place) or broken (like the Bullens of Hever Castle) by public service, and they were liable to become indebted as a consequence of the political exigencies of the period and the rising social and financial expectations of caste.

These more spectacular gentry debts are not typical of the yeomen, but yeomen could also get into difficulties; John Hollamby of Coles, who as an heir in gavelkind received only a third share of the eighty-acre holding which had been in the family for two centuries, mortgaged the property, and over forty years later the property had to be sold by his sons. The fact that he *could* keep a mortgage running for forty years and find new mortgagees is surely significant.[38] The Wakelin brothers, too, lost their inherited property in Chiddingstone.

Many mortgages were repaid on time and achieved their objectives. In 1685, William Webb, who came from a milling family, purchased a three quarters share of Edenbridge Mill, immediately mortgaging it to his brother Thomas of Chiddingstone Mill; two years later, he was able to purchase the remaining quarter share.[39] In this county of inheritance by all sons, reassembling shares was a frequent pastime; in 1697, Thomas Ashdowne mortgaged his half-share of Whistlers in Hever in order to buy the other half.[40] It is not always possible to do more than speculate on the purposes for which capital was raised. Since the chattels of a testator passed to his executor, the inheritor of the land might need to raise capital to restock his farm. Daniel Defoe's case shows that risky investments might be involved, and in the uncertain times of the seventeenth century, taxes, dues and composition with sequestrators were perpetual risks. Nor can we absolve some of the debtors in this saga of conspicuous consumption. What they demonstrate is that capital could be raised with ease for these sundry purposes.

4.5.2 *Redemption*

The Right of Redemption

The right to redeem the property subsisted under common law up to the point where default had taken place in repayment according to the terms of the agreement. This was a recognised property right; the 1657 remortgage by Sir Charles Waldegrave of the manors of Hever Brocas and Hever Cobham records that he had been mortgagor with his father, 'And whereas shortly after the making of the sayd recited Indenture the revertion and Inheritance of the sayd Mannors and premisses became lawfully vested in the sayd Charles Waldegrave and his heires and thereby the right of Redemption of in and to the premisses did accrew and belong to him the sayd Charles…'.[41]

The problem lay with the nature of the common law which required the terms to be met precisely, hence the intervention of the equity courts where the mortgagor had failed to pay. By the mid-seventeenth century, the right to redeem after default seems to have been in existence in practice, although not named. In 1630, Edmund Medhurst mortgaged Bodes Land and Perryfield near Medhurst Row to his kinsman Thomas Medhurst. In 1655, he finally quitclaimed to the heirs of the assignee Thomas Round, saying that Round had promised to reconvey if he redeemed, but he was unable to do so.[42] It seems as though a *moral* right to redeem might in practice have been accepted much earlier than this; in the 1590 redemption of land at Truggers forfeited by Peter Woodgate in 1578, the mortgagee, Henry Streatfeild (c.1535–1598), says 'Nowe knowe ye that I, Henry Streatfeild, not minding the hinnderance of him the said Peeter in taking benefyt of said proviso, and for the sum of Thirty and fyve poundes of good and lawfull money of England to mee by Johane Bassett of Chedingstone aforesaid, mother in law of the said Peeter in hand paied… Have of myne owne free will and accorde, beeing moved thereunto w[i]th a neighbourlike pitie, delyvered, demised, feoffed and confirmed..'.[43] Law follows society: 'neighbourlike pity' had a moral place before the formal intervention of equity.

The Equity of Redemption

The right to redeem after default developed into a fully fledged interest in land, the 'equity of redemption'. Simpson's dating of this interest as property which could be bought and sold to case law in the early eighteenth century is supported by one example in Somerden: in 1736, a mortgagee, Sarah St John, was chagrined to find that not only had her creditor defaulted and wasted the estate by felling trees and allowing buildings to fall into disrepair, but he had sold the equity of redemption to a third party.[44] The mention of the term 'equity of redemption' as an estate which had to be purchased occurs before the end of the seventeenth century, however; when John Ashdowne purchased the butcher's shop and lands from William Wakelin in 1695 the conveyance specifically mentioned it.[45]

4.5.3 Remedies and Dispute Resolution

Although the majority of mortgages seem to have ended amicably, either with the repayment of the loan or with the sale of the property, they were still a fruitful source of disputes. Most disputes concern multiple debts and conflicting mortgages, reinforcing the view that recording of encumbrances was an issue. Cockburn tells us that actions relating to property, real and personal, were the 'staple diet' of the county assizes' civil cases in the seventeenth century (Cockburn 1972, p. 140). By the seventeenth century, the action for ejectment dominated; this began as an action for recovering property by a tenant under a lease, but was extended to freeholders' claims in the late sixteenth century by means of a fictional lease (Simpson 1986, pp. 146, 242). In a typical debt case, in 1689 one of John Reddich's creditors obtained judgement against him and took out a writ of elegit (attachment) against his lands; an extent was made, and an action for ejectment brought, but by this time most of the property had been sold to repay other debts.[46] A long dispute occurred with the heirs of William Warne, he having apparently accepted alternative security but not cancelled the mortgage; this began as an action for ejectment in the Kent Assizes in 1693 against the purchaser, Henry Streatfeild, who appears to have won the case, but five years later was in Chancery.[47]

Most of the cases coming to Chancery were brought by gentry, but yeomen were not shy of litigation. When Lord Burgh mortgaged his property in 1596 to Richard Streatfeild, yeoman and ironmaster, it was nearly thirty years before Richard's heirs were able to take possession. Until her death in 1622 the widow, Lady Katherine Burgh, was still claiming the land.[48] A dispute also arose in 1614 with another creditor, the East India Company merchant, William Beareblock, claiming on a statute staple of Lord Burgh's from 1596, where the defeasances were exhibited to defeat the claim (for William Beareblock see Rabb 1967, p. 244).[49] The case was not finally settled until 1656 with the dismissal of the claim of the purchaser of the Burgh estate.[50] Meanwhile, the disputed title led to aggravation for all involved; Richard Streatfeild's trustees removed livestock from Buskhopes to prevent damage, and the tenant of the adjacent property sued. The following year the adjacent tenant was himself sued by the tenant of the property following another dispute.[51]

A century later, Henry Streatfeild (1639–1710) was obliged to pay out the Peachey annuity, John Reddich having continued to pay it for a while after selling the property and then defaulting even on that.[52] Actions for debt were taken in the Court of Common Pleas by John Reddich's mother-in-law, Timothea Jemmett for £700; by Anne Saxby of Lingfield for £1000; and by the executor of Roger Meredith for £200, and there were other suits for bond debts (not directly secured on the land).[53]

Cases with their claims and counterclaims could be extremely lengthy. The dispute with Lord Burgh's heirs and purchasers rolled on for sixty years and that with William Warne's for forty-three years. Lord Burgh's debt to John Mabbs of 1582 on a recognisance (a registered debt) was not repaid; it descended to the son of the lender, another John, then to his widow and then to her heir Abigail Payne. In 1634, this heir and her husband, having obtained a writ of elegit, obtained an extent from the High Sheriff of Kent. The following year, this was assigned and conveyed to a third party who took possession of the land, a timescale of 53 years.[54] If a mortgage did lead to a dispute, it was likely to be over alternative encumbrances and was likely to be slow of resolution.

4.6 Conclusions

The picture which emerges from this examination of mortgages in an agricultural community is one of an active but very local market. Lenders and borrowers were largely family and neighbours, outsiders being drawn upon only for the very largest loans and by gentry with metropolitan contacts. There is no evidence of professional intermediaries, although scriveners and lawyers may have played a role, especially after 1670. The evidence supports the impression that mortgages increased in number over the period and particularly after 1630, but there is, for example, only a modest difference between the 1560s and 1630s. The level drops again in the seven decades after 1560, and further lows occur in the 1640s and 1660s (periods of political uncertainty), but in the three decades after 1670 remains high; overall 75% of the total occur after 1625 and 40% after 1675. There is no evidence of an increase after the liberalisation of usury laws. The apparently limited impact of the Usury Act of 1571 is borne out when we look at the relation between the interest rate charged and the statutory maximum. Although the rate seldom exceeds the maximum, it clusters around the level of 5–6%, which suggests a relationship with the return on capital expected from land.

Yeomen were lending and borrowing in the 1630s, 1650s and 1690s, and lent more often than they borrowed. Gentry were also net lenders. The aristocracy are small in number and dominated by two or three large net borrowers, but the main net borrowers were tradesmen. Loans were typically in the low hundreds, though even in the late sixteenth century they could be in the thousands as in the mortgages of Lord Burgh and Percival Willoughby. The smallest loan made by a yeoman was £7.

The medieval form of mortgage with separate defeasance disappeared early in the period. The basic form of conveyance, the mortgage in fee, dominated between 1550 and 1650, but with increasingly sophisticated and complex covenants. After 1650, the mortgage by demise became popular. The inadequacy of enrolment is revealed by the occurrence of hidden encumbrances, leading on several occasions to litigation. Remedies were becoming simpler with the emergence of the action for ejectment, but disputes could roll on for many years.

The story of the Jemmetts and Reddiches was unlikely to have a happy ending and it did not. Devastating as was the financial loss, it was initiated and compounded by the demographic catastrophe. Timothea Jemmett survived all her eight children with the exception of Margaret. From her marriage in 1648 to her death forty years later, she had seen the loss of her husband, her brother-in-law, her father-in-law, seven of her own children and several of her grandchildren. Margaret was in turn survived by only one daughter out of her numerous children, and when she died in 1724 was buried simply. The following year her daughter, Anne, lost her young husband; it is not known what became of her, but her only son was the rector of a Romney Marsh church until his death, unmarried and apparently unlamented, in 1772.

This family failure is clearly not typical. The Webb family were still millers well into the eighteenth century, occupying several of the mills in the south-west corner of Kent at various periods. William Streatfeild, the good neighbour who had purchased Timothea Jemmett's distrained goods for her, and his cousin Henry who had attempted to restructure the family possessions to protect Timothea and Margaret, prospered; the family continues in the area to this day. The Ashdownes remained prominent yeomen for another century. It appears that the mortgage had become a commonplace method of raising capital, and the protections afforded by the courts to the parties were largely effective, difficulty and dispute generally arising from hidden encumbrances, which could occur as a result of the inadequate system of registration or enrolment which was not to be rectified for another two hundred years.

Notes

1. Kent Record Office at the Kent History and Library Centre, Maidstone [hereafter KRO], U908 T22.
2. KRO, U908 L42, T38, L43.
3. TNA, PROB 11/538.
4. The sample was drawn from all the relevant title deed records in the Kent Record Office, with further items from Nottingham University Library Manuscripts Collection; in all over two thousand documents were examined of which just over seven hundred individual documents were found to be within the hundred and in period (references below for materials used). Twenty-four further examples of potential mortgages were found to be duplicates, or with missing or illegible parts, or outside the boundaries of the hundred, and twelve could not be securely identified or contextualised. Mortgages: KRO, U55 T326; KRO, U908 T2, T3, T8, T13, T16, T18, T20, T22, T25, T29, T35, T36, T38, T45, T54, T60, T61, T64, T68, T78, T79, T82, T94, T95, T96, T103, T106, T109, T120, T124, T134, T136, T155, T160, T162, T167, T169, T171, T178, T251; KRO U1823-1 T12; KRO, U1986 T35; Nottingham University Library Manuscripts and Special Collections [hereafter NUL], Mi5 160/22, 27; 161-03/20, 27; 161-2/5, 11, 22, 37, 38; 162/22, 26, 27, 29, 56, 61, 63, 6. Other related title deeds: KRO, U55 T216; KRO, U184 T2; KRO, U908 T33, T104, T130, T267; NUL, Mi5 162-83. Legal cases: KRO, U908 L32, L33, L34, L35, L36, L37, L39, L40, L41, L42, L43, L45, L70. Wills: TNA, PROB 11/48, PROB 11/152, PROB 11/155, PROB 11/538; Lambeth Palace Library [hereafter LPL], VH96/5716.

5. KRO, U908 T29, T22, T36, T38, T20.
6. KRO, U908 T162, T120.
7. See my doctoral thesis, currently in preparation.
8. KRO, U908 T136, T96.
9. KRO, U908 T22, T25, T29, T36, T38, T106, T167.
10. KRO, U908 T60; even by the 1830s an agricultural labourer in the high-wage parish of Chiddingstone was earning only 12*s.* a week: *Answers to Rural Queries* (House of Commons Papers 44, 1834, XXX).
11. KRO, U908 L43.
12. KRO, U908 T25, TNA, PROB 11/155.
13. TNA, E 115/224/70; DD/P/6/1/1/60.
14. KRO, U908 T25.
15. TNA PROB 11/48.
16. LPL, VH96 5716.
17. KRO, U908 T38.
18. KRO, U908 T169-6.
19. KRO, U908 T169-8, 9.
20. KRO, U908 T2, T120.
21. KRO, U908 T78.
22. KRO, U908 T64.
23. KRO, U908 T54.
24. KRO, U908 T33.
25. KRO, U908 T64, U908 T54.
26. KRO, U908 L37.
27. TNA, PROB 11/152.
28. KRO, U908 T38.
29. KRO, U908 T8-3, U908 61-1, U908 T20-1.
30. KRO, U908 T13-9, U908 T162-11.
31. KRO, U908 T20/6.
32. KRO, U908 T21/4 & 5.
33. KRO, U908 T21/21 & 23.
34. KRO, U908 T21/3.
35. KRO, U908 T267.
36. NUL, Mi5 162-83.
37. KRO, U184 T2.
38. KRO, U908 T130.
39. KRO, U908 T171.
40. KRO, U908 T104.
41. KRO, U55 T216.
42. KRO, U908 T64.
43. KRO, U908 T251.
44. KRO, U908 L70.

45. KRO, U908 T94.
46. KRO, U908 L41.
47. KRO, U908 L43, L44; TNA,C 9/432/90.
48. KRO, U908 L33.
49. KRO, U908 L32.
50. KRO, U908 L36.
51. KRO, U897 L34, L35.
52. KRO, U908 L45.
53. KRO, U908 L39, L40, L41.
54. KRO, U908 T3-4.

Acknowledgements I am grateful to Lord Middleton for allowing me special access to his collection, held at the University of Nottingham Manuscripts and Special Collections, to the staff at the University of Nottingham and to the Streatfeild family. I also acknowledge a debt to the research and codification of records for Edenbridge, Hever and Cowden by Lionel Cole, which in many cases has enabled me to locate properties and to reconstruct the boundaries of Somerden Hundred, and to Neil Jones and Craig Muldrew for their comments on the first draft of this paper.

Personal and place names are those used at the end of the seventeenth century, but have been modernised as to spelling. Dates have been modernised with the year deemed to start on 1 January.

References

Primary Sources

Cockburn, J.S., 1980. *Calendar of Assize Records. Kent Indictments: James I* (London: HMSO).

Lambarde, W., 1576. *A Perambulation of Kent* (London).

Tawney, R.H. (ed.), 1925. *A Discourse upon Usury by Thomas Wilson DCL, 1572* (New York: Harcourt Brace and Co.).

Secondary Works

Anon., 1655. *The Complete Clerk's and Scrivener's Guide, Containing Exact Drafts and Presidents* (London).

Baker, J.H., 2002. *An Introduction to English Legal History*, 4th edn (London: Butterworths).

Bridgman, O., 1689. *Conveyances: Being Select Precedents of Deeds and Instruments Concerning the Most Considerable Estates in England*, 2nd edn (London).

Cockburn, J.S., 1972. *A History of English Assizes 1558–1714* (Cambridge: Cambridge University Press.

Coleman, D.C., 1951. 'London scriveners and the estate market in the later seventeenth century', *EcHR*, vol. 4, pp. 221–230.

Cruise, W., 1835. *A Digest of the Laws of England respecting Real Property*, 4th edn, ed. Henry Hopley White (London: Saunders and Benning).

Grose, F., 1787. *A Provincial Glossary: With a Collection of Local Proverbs and Popular Superstitions* (London: S. Hooper).

Habakkuk, H.J., 1952. 'The long-term rate of interest and the price of land in the seventeenth century', *EcHR*, vol. 5, pp. 26–45.

Holderness, B.A., 1975. 'Credit in a rural community, 1660–1800: Some neglected aspects of probate inventories', *Midland History*, vol. 3, pp. 94–116.

Holderness, B.A., 1976. 'Credit in English rural society before the nineteenth century with special reference to the period 1650–1720', *Agricultural History Review*, vol. 24, pp. 97–109.

Jones, N., 1989. *God and the Moneylenders: Usury and Law in Early Modern England* (Oxford: Basil Blackwell).

Kaye, J.M., 1988. 'A note on the Statute of Enrolments, 1536', *Law Quarterly Review*, vol. 104, pp. 617–636.

Kew, J.E., 1967. 'Mortgages in mid Tudor Devonshire', *Report and Transactions of the Devonshire Association*, vol. 99, pp. 165–179.

Matthew, S., 2009. 'Money supply and credit in rural Cheshire c.1600–c.1680', *C&C*, vol. 24, pp. 245–274.

Melton, F.T., 1986. *Sir Robert Clayton and the Origins of English Deposit Banking 1658–1685* (Cambridge: Cambridge University Press).

Muldrew, C., 2001. 'Hard food for midas: Cash and its social value in early modern England', *P&P*, vol. 170, pp. 78–120.

Phelps-Brown, E.H. and S.V. Hopkins, 1955. 'Seven centuries of building wages', *Economica*, vol. 22, pp. 195–206.

Quilter, M., 2004. 'Daniel Defoe: Bankrupt and bankruptcy reformer', *Journal of Legal History*, vol. 25, pp. 53–73.

Rabb, T.K. 1967. *Enterprise and Empire: Merchant and Gentry Investment in the Expansion of England, 1575–1630* (Harvard: Harvard University Press).

Richards, R.D., 1929. *The Early History of Banking in England* (London: P.S. King and Son).

Robinson, T., 1741. *The Common Law of Kent or, the Customs of Gavelkind* (London).

Seymour, C., 1915. *Electoral Reform in England and Wales 1915: The Development and Operation of the Parliamentary Franchise* (Newton Abbott: David and Charles).

Simpson, A.W.B., 1986. *A History of the Land Law*, 2nd edn (Oxford: Oxford University Press).
Stevenson, W.H., 1911. *Report on the Manuscripts of Lord Middleton Preserved at Wollaton Hall, Nottinghamshire* (London: HMSO).
Stone, L., 1965. *The Crisis of the Aristocracy 1558–1641* (Oxford: Oxford University Press).
Trevor-Roper, H., 1951. 'The Elizabethan aristocracy: An anatomy anatomized', *EcHR*, vol. 3, pp. 279–298.
Turner, R.W., 1931. *The Equity of Redemption* (Cambridge: Cambridge University Press).
Waddilove, D.P., 2014. '*Emmanuel College v Evans* (1626) and the history of mortgages', *Cambridge Law Journal*, vol. 73, pp. 142–168.
Wrightson, K., 1982. *English Society 1580–1680* (London: Hutchinson).
Zell, M., 1994. *Industry in the Countryside: Wealden Society in the Sixteenth Century* (Cambridge: Cambridge University Press).

CHAPTER 5

Why the Equity of Redemption?

D. P. Waddilove

5.1 Introduction

The 'equity of redemption' is a legal doctrine that undergirds the law of mortgages in the common law world. It originated in the English Court of Chancery in the early modern period. Exactly when is a matter of some uncertainty, but it seems to have arisen, and slowly crystallised, from the late-sixteenth century to the early or mid-seventeenth century, and was unquestionably in place by the chancellorship of Lord Nottingham (LK 1673–1675, LC 1675–1683). Long before and after the equity of redemption arose, the legal structure of a mortgage took the form of a conditionally defeasible grant of title to land by a debtor (a mortgagor) to a creditor (a mortgagee) at the beginning of a mortgage, which grant was undone by repayment of a debt at a pre-specified time. The common law interpreted mortgages, as with any deed, literally and strictly according to their stated terms. As such, if a mortgagor failed to repay according to the strict letter of the contract, even by repaying a few hours late, the property was forever forfeit. The equity of redemption was a different approach that reshaped the theoretical framework of mortgages. According to the equity of redemption, a mortgagor

D. P. Waddilove (✉)
St. Catharine's College, Cambridge, UK
e-mail: dpw24@cam.ac.uk

C. Briggs and J. Zuijderduijn (eds.), *Land and Credit*,
Palgrave Studies in the History of Finance,
https://doi.org/10.1007/978-3-319-66209-1_5

remained the true owner of mortgaged property throughout a mortgage despite lacking legal title; a mortgagee's interest was mere security for a debt; and a mortgagor was thus entitled to redeem the property at any time—irrespective of the terms of the mortgage—until his or her equity of redemption was declared foreclosed by a court. Perhaps as a result of this doctrine, but at least coincidentally with its rise in the second half of the seventeenth century, mortgages became far more widespread. The equity of redemption has remained the foundational doctrine for mortgages ever since.

Yet along with many aspects of English mortgages, the history of the equity of redemption remains poorly understood. The main accounts of its history were written by lawyers primarily interested in the evolution of legal doctrine who did little to explain its social reality or consider why it arose in the first place (Turner 1931; Yale 1954, 1961, 1965). Several stories therefore exist of its origin. One story is that other equitable doctrines—such as relief given from harshness of the common law, relief given to sureties and expectant heirs, relief given in relation to penalties and orders of specific performance—were so frequently engaged by the structure of the common law mortgage that they crystallised into the equity of redemption (Turner 1931, pp. 21–33; Simpson 1986, pp. 243–245; Holdsworth 1927, pp. 256–257; Plucknett 1956, p. 608; cf. Kiralfy 1958, p. 621; Spence 1846–1849, i, pp. 620–623). While probably partly correct, this story remains solely within the internal logic of legal doctrine and so is perhaps incomplete. It is now widely accepted that even those courts that purport to remain purely within the internal logic of legal rules at least sometimes fail so to do, and the Chancery did not purport to remain within such exclusive scope in the relevant period. Another story is that the doctrine was simply a means for the Chancery to capture territory in a jurisdictional war with the common-law courts and so increase its own business and fees (Turner 1931, pp. 30–33; Megarry and Wade 2012, p. 1118, n. 32; Watt 2007, p. 81 (citing Lord Bramwell in *Salt v Marquess of Northampton* [1892] A.C. at 19 referring to 'piety or love of fees of those who administered equity')). But such a view presumes an enormous degree of self-interested cynicism amongst Chancellors that is in tension with the legal culture of the day, and it is a view that has little support in the evidence beyond the supposedly self-evident logic of a desire for increased business and fees. Yet another story is that the doctrine arose out of concern for the weak bargaining power of mortgagors (McFarlane et al. 2015, p. 1067; Watt

2007, p. 81). While, as discussed below, this might have been relevant, such an idea lacks much contemporary support and seems too narrow to account entirely for the doctrine. In perhaps the most influential origin story, others have suggested that the Chancery created a doctrine to aid powerful landowners (Sugarman and Warrington 1995, 1997; see also McFarlane et al. 2015, p. 1067). By making the forfeiture of land more difficult, so the story goes, the equity of redemption allowed those whose position in society was based upon owning large landed estates, particularly the hereditary aristocracy, to unlock the capital value of their prime asset, while making it less likely that they would lose it. But this theory primarily considers a basic fact of the equity of redemption and infers its cause from its effect.

No one has ever attempted to ground the equity of redemption in primary sources from the period in which it emerged to elaborate the picture of its origins. This chapter aims to do that. It therefore considers a sample of the record of the Court of Chancery from roughly 1580 to 1620 along with existing works of social and economic history.[1] It thereby observes mortgages and mortgage forfeiture in the legal and social context of the nascent equity of redemption, noting relevant aspects of the nature of mortgages as it presents a view of why the equity of redemption might have developed. Grounding the nascent equity of redemption in its social context ought to provide a view of the doctrine not unlike contemporaries' own. Given the lack of any explicit contemporary theoretical reflection upon the doctrine and its origins, creating such a view might be as close as it is possible to come to understanding why the doctrine arose.

Before proceeding further, some caveats are in order. Firstly, to the extent that it is an exploration of why a legal rule arose, created as it was by multiple, semi-coordinated agents, over an uncertain but probably long period of time, in the absence of explicit explanations by those agents, this chapter can achieve only so much. Even undertaking such an exercise raises myriad theoretical issues. This chapter therefore neither purports to provide a definite answer to the question 'Why the Equity of Redemption?', nor does it assert that an answer can necessarily be given. But lest the value in understanding important aspects of history, culture and law expressed in judge-made legal rules be entirely lost through despair at the attempt, this chapter proceeds towards an answer. Secondly, this chapter considers in large part the influence of factors in the development of the equity of redemption other than internalist doctrinal logic, and it leaves aside the question of the relative significance of internal and external factors in such development. This is partly because of the immense theoretical difficulties involved in such questions and partly because assessing internalist development would benefit from greater understanding of the nature and state of doctrine and precedent in early modern England in general and the Court of Chancery in particular. Much of what this chapter therefore does is to ask 'why might the equity of redemption make sense in its social context?'; it uses the answer to infer why, at least in so far as it was not due purely to the internal logic of equity, the doctrine arose. Thirdly, where this chapter makes original observations of social history, they are offered anecdotally; the nature of the primary-source evidence does not necessarily permit valid extrapolation more broadly. This is not because the Chancery record has any clear bias in matters such as geographic region, social class, urban versus rural disputes or other such distinctions, but because the relatively limited numbers of Chancery litigants make them an inapt basis for strong claims about society as a whole. That having been said, anecdotal observations still have the value that they have, and in relatively unexplored territory, it may be more than negligible. In general, it is hoped that what follows makes a contribution to understanding an important aspect of law in history, the consequences of which remain very much alive today.

5.2 The Purpose of Mortgages

The basic purpose of any mortgage was and is, of course, to secure a creditor by providing recourse against particular property in case of failure to repay a debt. But beyond this unremarkable fact, mortgages in the context of the nascent equity of redemption seem to have had particular purposes slightly different from those of modern mortgages.

5.2.1 Acquisition of Property

The stereotypical modern mortgage enables the purchase of a home by immediate mortgage of such home to secure a loan of purchase money. So widespread is the practice that in popular parlance one speaks (catachrestically) of 'getting' and 'paying off' a mortgage to buy a house; 'mortgage' has thus become synonymous with 'home purchase loan'. But this both misunderstands the modern transaction and has little relation to early modern mortgages. A borrower does not, and never did, 'get' a mortgage, but rather gave it: a mortgage was itself the pledge of property that secured a debt; a debtor was a mortgagor—the active doer of a mortgage—and a creditor was a mortgagee—the passive recipient of a mortgage. This is true today as it was in the early modern period. But in contrast to today, in our period mortgages of newly acquired property to secure purchase money, whether of homes or any other property, do not appear to have been common. No acquisition mortgages appeared in the Chancery record surveyed, nor do any appear in William West's influential book of precedents of legal documents called the *Symboleography* (West 1615; Jones 2004; Poole 1984).

This is not to say that no acquisition mortgages took place in our period, but they were the exception rather than the rule. *Cary's Reports* very briefly recount a case in Chancery involving an acquisition mortgage.[2] And literary scholars have long known of another example. On 10 March 1613, William Shakespeare purchased a notorious Roman Catholic meeting place and safe house, the Blackfriars gatehouse, from one Henry Walker, for a recited consideration of £140 (Halliwell-Phillipps 1907, ii, pp. 31–34). The following day, Shakespeare mortgaged the property back to Walker by grant of 100-year lease redeemable by payment of £60 the following Michaelmas (29 September) (Halliwell-Phillipps 1907, ii, pp. 34–36; Schoenbaum 1975, p. 225). The only reasonable deduction is that Shakespeare initially paid only £80 of the purchase money and had a further six months to pay the remaining purchase price, which debt was secured by mortgage of the property. But unlike a stereotypical acquisition mortgage, the vendor in this case was also the creditor. While thus technically taking the form of an acquisition mortgage, this transaction actually bore more substantive similarity to a slightly different type of transaction—a conditional sale.

It was the conditional sale that seems, instead of the acquisition mortgage, to have been the typical transaction to facilitate the purchase of property upon credit in our period. According to a conditional sale, a buyer paid a portion of the purchase price in exchange for an immediate grant of title conditioned upon payment of the remaining purchase price; if the buyer failed to pay the outstanding sum, the condition in the deed of sale invalidated the grant and title returned to the vendor (see, e.g., West 1615, Sect. 415).[3] To the extent that a buyer forfeited the property if he or she failed to pay the sum allowed upon credit, the transaction was similar to a mortgage. But to the extent that it involved only two parties—no third-party creditor took the risk of non-payment that allowed a vendor to drop out of the picture—it was crucially unlike a mortgage. Conditional sales and mortgages also differed in legal technicalities. Most obviously, according to a mortgage, a creditor held title while the debt was outstanding, while according to a conditional sale, the debtor held title. This might have significance for the status of the property in a range of circumstances, especially if third parties made claims upon it. The normality of conditional sales in our period also appears in the fact that while neither the Chancery record nor West's *Symboleography* contains acquisition mortgages, both contain conditional sales. Vendors thus seem to have functioned as creditors when property was purchased upon credit, and conditional sales were more common in our period than acquisition mortgages; more research would be necessary to say anything more definite.

Irrespective of their actual frequency, the Chancery did not appear to consider acquisition mortgages to be the standard or representative type of mortgage for purposes of the equity of redemption. The seemingly total absence of such mortgages in the Chancery record means that either no acquisition mortgages came to Chancery, or the fact of being an acquisition mortgage was irrelevant for Chancery adjudication. The Chancery therefore evidently treated mortgages for purposes of the equity of redemption as mortgages of previously owned property. In the eyes of equity, therefore, mortgage forfeiture was loss of an old asset rather than failure to acquire a new one. Such a distinction might have significance as loss of an old asset might more clearly constitute harm to a mortgagor than failure to acquire a new asset, which might appear more like maintenance of a neutral *status quo ante*. The former more obviously invited Chancery relief than the latter. Furthermore, as discussed below, long ownership of land might trigger an equitable concept called 'ancient inheritance' that functioned like an interest in land. Mortgage of pre-owned property was more likely to induce Chancery relief through this concept as well. In short, in the context of the nascent equity of redemption the Chancery viewed mortgages as the hazard of old property, rather than a failure to acquire new property; this might have encouraged Chancery relief from mortgage forfeiture.

5.2.2 *Obtaining Otherwise Unavailable Credit*

Rather than financing home purchases, mortgages in our period seem to have been used in numbers of cases to induce the extension of credit to borrowers who would otherwise be unable to obtain it. This appears in the relatively numerous instances in the Chancery record of mortgagees extending credit to mortgagors in some extreme circumstance imperilling the mortgagor's finances. For instance, in *Ashebey* v. *Paramore* (1592),

> the said [mortgagor] did show a note in writing of the names of a number of persons to whom [he] was greatly indebted bewailing the Imminent extreme hard case and grievous dangers wherein he then stood in respect of the same his creditors and earnestly entreating [the mortgagee's] friendship to qualify the rigorous courses then set abroad against him by the same his creditors… [Thus] for very pity of the distressed estate of the said [mortgagor] the said [mortgagee] yielded [and granted a loan upon mortgage and allowed the mortgagor to use a house of the mortgagee as a base for his business dealings].[4]

In *Grynkyn v. Bull* (1605), the mortgagor (actually a pawnor, a mortgagor of a chattel), one Cuckson, was in physical, and one presumes concomitant financial, extremity. His creditor alleged that he '(in the last great sickness in London) lent unto one Cuckson… xx^{li} in money in his great necessity [and took] in pawn certain plate to the value of xxij^{li}'.[5] Cuckson failed to repay and soon died 'of the said sickness'.[6] And in *Hanmer* v. *Lochard* (1612), the mortgagor was already in such financial extremity that he was already in debtors' prison upon a statute of £1000 at the time of the mortgage.[7]

Other cases show the link between mortgages and financial extremity because a creditor, after initially making a loan upon non-mortgage security, later required a mortgage because of deterioration of a debtor's financial condition. In *Stanley* v. *Heale* (1605), Mr Serjeant John Heale made a series of loans to Mr James Anton (see Powell 2004; for an incident regarding starch and Mr Anton see Harrison 1931, p. 50): Sjt Heale first lent £1100 upon a bond of £1600; then £300 more upon a bond of £600; then £400 more upon security not named in the Chancery record; then Sjt Heale 'paid 1130^{li} for the said Anton to Sir John Swynnerton for the redemption of his patent of starch', for a total in loans of £2930.[8] Upon the last loan, Sjt Heale required and obtained of Mr Anton a mortgage of 'Barmondsey house worth 2800^{li}' upon condition that Anton repays all sums 'that should fall out upon an account to be due to him the said Mr Sjt Hele'.[9] In short, after a series of increasingly strong securities, Sjt Heale, an individual of obvious legal sophistication, finally required a mortgage. Similarly, in *Knowles* v. *Westwray* (1592):

> the said plaintiff having heretofore borrowed of the defendant at several times the sum of 470 odd pounds and gave the defendant several statutes of great value for payment thereof[;] The same 470 odd pounds in time in respect of the interest which grew for the same came unto 550 pounds[;] whereupon it was agreed between the said parties That the said plaintiff should have nine months after for payment of the said 550^{li} so as he would mortgage the inheritance of certain of his freehold lands to the value of 1000^{li}.[10]

And in *Topcliffe* v. *Lacie* (1604) upon an original loan of £183 secured by (an admittedly proportionally enormous) bond of £600,[11] the borrower 'failed to pay the same[;] whereupon new agreement he got two years further day or thereabouts of the defendant upon mortgage of certain lands therefor'.[12] In *Topcliffe* the creditor thus did not require a mortgage until the debtor had already defaulted on the original loan. In each of these cases, a creditor required a mortgage only after a deterioration in a debtor's financial condition. Overall, common employment of mortgages when mortgagors were in extreme circumstances suggests that mortgages were necessary to induce the extension of the credit in question.

Such use of mortgages could help explain the fact that the effective legal maximum interest rate in our period was also the standard rate for mortgage loans. Ten per cent *per annum* was the effective legal maximum interest rate under the Statute of Usury (1571).[13] Ten per cent also appears to have been the standard rate for mortgage loans in our period,[14] and the Chancery awarded damages for late redemption at the same rate.[15] Indeed, as the plaintiff in *Garnett* v. *Nevill* (1621) put it, his mortgage was redeemable by payment of principal and 'interest after the usual rate of ten pounds in the hundred for forbearance thereof'.[16] The mortgage was nevertheless arguably the strongest security in early modern England (Waddilove, in preparation). According to classical economic theory, such strength of security should have reduced the price of mortgage credit. Instead, mortgage credit cost the same as credit upon normal security: Professor Sir H. John Habakkuk has written that '[t]he legal maximum rate in the early seventeenth century appears to have represented the full market rate for *normal* security' (Habakkuk 1952, p. 33 (emphasis added); Homer and Sylla 1996, p. 113). The 'risk-free' rate of interest in the period was about six per cent (Ibbetson 2012, p. 10, n. 58; Clark 1988, pp. 272–273). The correspondence in price between mortgage credit and credit upon normal security suggests that mortgages' price-reducing function applied particularly to risky borrowers to whom lenders would otherwise not extend credit, or would extend it only above the maximum rate. In other words, mortgages made credit accessible more than particularly cheap.[17]

One might object to such reasoning on the grounds that the Chancery record, as a record of litigation, is necessarily biased towards mortgages that were forfeit, hence those given to riskier debtors in the first place. While the record is undeniably biased towards forfeited mortgages, it may not be so biased towards risky debtors. Almost all mortgages appeared in Chancery in our period because mortgagors exhibited bills for late redemption. Late redemption required repayment of the principal debt plus interest for the late period. Bills for late redemption thus made no sense unless a mortgagor actually had enough money to redeem, a circumstance perhaps less likely for particularly risky borrowers than for others. The Chancery record may therefore not over-represent especially risky mortgagors as one bias balances the other. Furthermore, some research not based on the records of litigation, such as Professors H. R. French and R. W. Hoyle's study of a particular Yorkshire manor, has found evidence of extremity encouraging mortgages at least at certain times of economic distress (French and Hoyle 1999, pp. 374–376). Yet, this is not to say that all mortgages in our period induced extension of otherwise unavailable credit or took place in circumstances of extremity. Many cases show no hallmarks of such a situation, and some comfortable debtors presumably secured their creditors by mortgage. Further research could help clarify the matter, but the relevant point for present purposes is that *one* important function of mortgages was to induce the extension of otherwise unavailable credit.

As it relates to the equity of redemption, the actual prevalence of mortgages used to obtain otherwise unavailable credit may not matter as much as the general impression that mortgages were used for such purpose. Circumstances of extremity arguably represent a vulnerability potentially exploitable by lenders. If the Chancery considered mortgagors categorically vulnerable this way, it might have encouraged strengthening mortgagors' rights via the equity of redemption. It nevertheless remains difficult to say whether this was the Chancery's view of mortgagors in the relevant period. Later, courts certainly referred to mortgagors as 'necessitous men',[18] but no such statements appear in our period. The balance of Chancery sentiment therefore remains an open question. But at least at the margins, the fact that one important function of mortgages was to induce extension of otherwise unavailable credit likely brought at least some vulnerable debtors into Chancery and contributed to the equity of redemption through sympathy with their plight.

5.3 Relation of Property and Debt Values

Logic predicts that the value of mortgaged property would ordinarily exceed the value of a debt secured. A mortgagee ought to demand at least some excess value to compensate both for the risk of ordinary fluctuation in the market value of the mortgaged property and, perhaps more importantly, for inevitable costs in liquidating the asset. Such realities led later equitable doctrine to limit trustees investing trust funds to lending no more than about two-thirds of the value of any property mortgaged to them (Maitland 1909, pp. 97, 268–269).[19] And contemporary law codes in continental Europe in our period required security of 150% of the value of the debt (Zuijderduijn 2009, p. 219). Mental negotiating pressures of the parties also tend to favour mortgage of property of excess value. A mortgagee cannot control whether redemption will occur; that is up to a mortgagor. A mortgagee thus ought to require some premium for the risk associated with uncertainty as to whether a mortgagor will redeem. A mortgagor, on the other hand, both can control whether redemption will occur, absent a change in supervening circumstances, and ordinarily intends it to occur. Redemption naturally renders irrelevant any disparity of value between the property and the debt. A mortgagor thus both controls and ordinarily intends a circumstance that will eliminate the significance of a disparity of value. Such logic does not, of course, pertain to mortgagors in particularly desperate straits: they may be very aware of a significant risk that they will be unable to redeem, which would reduce or eliminate any insouciance on their part as to a disparity of value. But in aggregate, one would expect a negotiated equilibrium that would favour mortgages of property more valuable than the debt.

The Chancery record bears out the logic that mortgaged properties were often more valuable than the debts that they secured. In *Lady Russell* v. *Earl of Lincoln* (1589), the court listed amongst its reasons for relieving the mortgagor: 'that the lands and tenements so mortgaged are of far greater value than the money lent thereupon'.[20] In *Bellamy* v. *Ratclyef* (1597), the court again mentioned reason for granting relief: 'the said manor and lands [mortgaged] were of far greater value' than the debt.[21] In *Byrd* v. *Benyon* (1596), successive mortgages of the same property secured first £500 and then £1000, suggesting a significant disparity of value during at least the first mortgage.[22] And in *Pascall* v. *Clovell* (1589), the mortgagee 'affirmed to the [mortgagor] that he would have nothing but the said Lands for his CCC^{li}[,] The same being worth mmm^{li} at the least[,] which unmentionable kind of Dealing the said Lord Chancellor much misliketh'.[23]

The Chancery record nevertheless must be a basis for only limited inference because only those cases in which the value of the property exceeded the debt would come to Chancery in the first place. As previously mentioned, almost all mortgage cases came to Chancery in our period upon mortgagors' bills for late redemption, i.e. they were requests to repay debts plus interest to redeem properties. In every case, at least the subjective value of a property to the mortgagor, if not to the market in general, must therefore have exceeded the debt, or the mortgagor would not have exhibited the bill in the first place.

That having been said, no reason exists to believe that anything in our period overrode the pre-existing logic that favoured mortgage of property exceeding the value of debts. Mortgages probably therefore did manifest a disparity in value towards mortgage of properties more valuable than the debts that they secured. And somewhat like whether mortgages were for debtors in difficulty, the relevant point for the equity of redemption is more the Chancery's impression of the matter rather than what was objectively true. If the Chancery saw mortgages as pledges of excess value, such a view may have promoted the equity of redemption. Forfeiture of excess value was tantamount to a contract penalty, something that equity disfavoured anyway (Jones 1967, pp. 436–448). And regardless, the basic injustice of extracting a disproportionately large sum from one party to allocate merely as a windfall to another is self-explanatory. The appearance that mortgaged properties were more valuable than their debts would therefore have encouraged the development of the equity of redemption as means of preventing unconscionable loss.

5.4 Ancient Inheritance

A significant background concept in Chancery related to mortgages was the idea that blood ties to land mattered. Indeed, the Chancery seems to have regarded blood ties to land—that is, birthright—sufficiently highly that one might speak of an 'equity of ancient inheritance' that practically amounted to an interest in land. The name comes from the Chancery record's tendency to refer, in so many words, to 'ancient inheritance'. Only the broad contours of the idea can be set out at present; more research must be done. It nevertheless seems that the Chancery recognised a certain sort of interest, based on long familial ownership of land, which inhered in individuals roughly according to ordinary principles of primogeniture. A scion of a family thus had the primary equity of ancient inheritance, with lesser forms resting in other family members by degrees. But many questions of the specifics of the concept remain outstanding.

Two cases show an 'equity of ancient inheritance' that a mortgagor had in forfeited property. In *Ellyot* v. *Nance* (1600), a mortgagor, one Martin Trewinyard, 'was altogether decayed by usurious bargains [made with individuals other than the mortgagee[24]] and died in prison before or about the time that the said lands should have been redeemed'.[25] Mr Trewinyard's children sued to redeem the family's eponymous manor in Cornwall, offering to repay outstanding mortgage principal and reimburse the mortgagee any sums expended on the property, in exchange for both an account of profits received by the mortgagee after forfeiture and reconveyance of the property. The court found the offer reasonable and ordered Sir Francis Godolphin and Mr George Carewe to 'treat between the said parties and to end the cause between them in such so as that the plaintiffs may have the said manor and lands being the ancient inheritance of their ancestors…'.[26] And the court later decreed Trewinyard manor to the Trewinyard children according to the report of Sir Francis and Mr Carewe.[27]

In *Barley* v. *Eyre* (1601), Peter Barley mortgaged the manor of Barley (and various other properties) and provided before his death for trustees to redeem on behalf of his heirs.[28] The trustees, in breach of trust, failed to redeem because such breach benefitted them financially. James Barley, the mortgagor's brother and heir, sued the trustees in Chancery. The enrolled decree describes Egerton LK's view of the trustees' actions as:

> frauds and practices [that] his lordship utterly disliked and condemned[,] tending indeed to the utter ruin & overthrow of the plaintiff[,] being by [the trustees'] means deprived of his ancient inheritance that for the space of four hundred years and better had continued in the ancestors of the plaintiff.

James Barley had not sued for late redemption because he had conveyed away his interest to the earl of Shrewsbury under duress of the situation. Because he felt that he could not recover the manor from 'so great a person',[29] he instead sued the trustees for damages for breach of trust, which he recovered accordingly.

The Chancery recognised an equity of ancient inheritance in mortgage and non-mortgage cases alike, sometimes with significant consequences. In *Power* v. *Power* (1617), a son sued his father because the father, 'being of 80 years of age[,] hath of late taken a young gentlewoman to wife' and had resettled his estate, at the expense of the son, in favour of a daughter begotten of the new wife.[30] Within a matter of days of his appointment, Bacon LK, 'much misliking that such an Ancient Inheritance settled as aforesaid [in favour of the son] should by the means of a Stepmother be thus diverted into another course', ordered *nisi causa* that the lands should descend as originally settled. (Note that the capitalisation of 'Ancient Inheritance' appears in the original.) Similarly, in *Joyner* v. *Joyner* (1616), Ellesmere LC found that a testator, 'the father[,] was drawn to disinherit the Complainant being his son and heir out[*sic*] by the fraudulent practices and Circumventions of the said Defendant [the plaintiff's younger brother]'.[31] Ellesmere therefore remade the entire testamentary settlement, declaring that the land in question, the manor of Cuddesdon, Oxfordshire, 'ought to go to the Complainant being his birthright & inheritance' as elder son.

The equity of ancient inheritance was not limited to a single individual, but applied by degrees to various members of a family. Thus, in *Joyner*, described immediately above, in decreeing lands to the elder son against the younger, Ellesmere nevertheless recognised an interest of the younger son; he therefore restricted the elder son's ability to alienate:

> and his Lordship did now declare his meaning to be that the [elder son] shall not have any power to sell away any of the said lands but that the same shall remain after his death to his brother and next heir if he shall die without issue of his own body.

Similarly, in *Hill* v. *Hill* (1600), Ellesmere restricted a mortgagor's ability to alienate in order to favour the mortgagee who was a 'near kinsman' of the mortgagor[32]; as part of his decree permitting late redemption, Ellesmere ordered that the manor in question:

> or any part thereof shall not be sold granted or leased by [the mortgagor] or his heirs for any term above one and twenty years… to any person except it be to [the mortgagee] and his heirs if he or they will have the same, and give therefor reasonably as two indifferent gentlemen to be Chosen by both the said parties or their heirs after them shall think meet and appoint to the end the same shall still remain in the name and blood of the said plaintiff.[33]

Ellesmere thus established what amounted to an equitable entail in *Joyner* and a permanent right of first-refusal to purchase in *Hill*, in both cases out of concern to preserve ancient inheritance for members of a family other than the holder of the primary interest.

Many questions nevertheless remain about the scope of the equity of ancient inheritance. One such question is the degree of connexion to land necessary to trigger it. In both *Ellyot* and *Barley*, the property in question was an eponymous manor of a family, suggesting a significant connexion. And in both *Power* and *Barley*, references appear to the property having been in the family for over four hundred years, another obviously strong connexion. (One also wonders if the fact that the record refers in both cases to four hundred years, as opposed to any other time frame, has significance.) But in *Hill* and *Joyner*, the degree of connexion of the family to the land is not clear. Logically, someone who had recently purchased a plot might by degrees have more ancient inheritance in it than the rest of the world (with the possible exception of the recent vendor), but whether minimum thresholds, such as specific length of ownership or actual residence upon a property, must have been crossed to establish an initial equity is unclear. And other questions of scope, such as whether the concept could apply to chattels, remain outstanding.

Also unclear are the bounds of the effect of the equity of ancient inheritance once triggered. In *Hill* and *Joyner*, ancient inheritance was used permanently to restrict a freeholder's ability to alienate. Indeed, in *Joyner*, depending on the exact interpretation of Ellesmere's order, it amounted to conversion of a fee simple into an equitable fee tail. Such restriction on alienability was not unknown in law both in the legal fee tail and in the concept of *retrait linager*, which applied or had applied by degrees to certain sorts of lands, like some burgages, at various times and places in England (Hemmeon 1914, pp. 110–126); although it is surprising to see such restriction arising by operation of such equity. In *Power*, the court directly invalidated a voluntary settlement of a living settlor—a settlement in favour of a natural-born daughter no less—on the grounds of ancient inheritance. In these cases, the Chancery seems to have gone very far indeed to protect the equity of ancient inheritance. But limits surely existed. One readily identifiable limit was a mortgagee's right to financial recompense. When a mortgagor voluntarily imperilled his or her ancient inheritance by mortgaging it, Chancery would go only so far to help: unless the mortgagor could repay principal plus interest damages (and possibly costs), Chancery would allow the mortgagor to lose the property.[34] It thus seems that the equity of ancient inheritance was a strong interest but was subject to other interests such as a mortgagee's right to compensation. Beyond this, it is difficult to say exactly what force the equity of ancient inheritance had.

The way that the equity of ancient inheritance related to the equity of redemption is plain. To the extent that equity favoured birthright to land based on blood ties, it would favour allowing mortgagors who, as shown above were mortgaging pre-owned property, to retain their land. The equity of ancient inheritance was thus a background principle tending to promote the equity of redemption.

5.5 Relationships Between Mortgagors and Mortgagees

A particularly important question for the development of the equity of redemption was the nature of typical relationships between parties to mortgages in our period. These relationships were substantially different than modern ones. And they cast the equity of redemption in a particular and important light.

A picture of quotidian credit markets in our period appears in the work of Professors R. H. Tawney and Craig Muldrew (Tawney 1925; Muldrew 1998). Professor Muldrew has described the ubiquity of credit mediated by trust in early modern England, driven in part by a lack of specie that affected everyone (Muldrew 1998, pp. 95–103). As the use of cash for every transaction was practically impossible, virtually everyone required credit for ordinary purchases of basic goods and foodstuffs. Others required credit for their livelihoods: farmers required loans to carry them through the seasons between crops; weavers, fullers, miners and artisans required credit to build up stocks of their products and to float them between markets. Merchants in particular required large amounts of credit because of the turnover inherent in their businesses: Francis Bacon (LK 1617, LC 1617–1621) wrote: 'it is certain that the greatest part of the trade is driven by young merchants upon borrowing at interest; so as if the usurer either call in, or keep back his money, there will ensue presently a great stand of trade' (St. Albans 1857, p. 47). Yet, in our period, '[i]f it is hardly an exaggeration to say that the use of credit was almost ubiquitous, the provision of it, nevertheless, was still decentralised, fluid and unsystematic' (Tawney 1925, p. 88). Banks did not yet exist, and few individuals devoted themselves to full-time money-lending (Muldrew 1998, pp. 111–112, 259). Indeed, most finance remained 'a stage of what may be called semi-capitalism, intermediate between the specialised financial mechanisms of the later seventeenth century, and the casual pawnbroking which, though accompanied, of course, by larger operations, had been most characteristic of the Middle Ages' (Tawney 1925, p. 87). In our period, '[t]he money-lending which concerns nine-tenths of the population is spasmodic, irregular, unorganised, a series of individual, and sometimes surreptitious, transactions between neighbours' (Tawney 1925, p. 22). Indeed, lending 'was normally a venture taken up as a bye-employment by the prosperous tradesman or farmer in the intervals of his ordinary occupation' (Tawney 1925, p. 87, cf. p. 21). 'The needy gentleman found in the tailor, draper, or Merchant Adventurer, a willing, if not an accommodating, mortgagee' (Tawney 1925, p. 96). Borrowers and lenders were therefore often of equal status within the same community, the lenders just 'a little more prosperous than their neighbours' (Tawney 1925, p. 22).

The interpersonal credit markets of our period were simply logical given the circumstances. Without banks and with the-few-existing corporate entities being not mainly commercial in nature but religious, capital both resided with and was used by individuals. And individuals had good reasons to do business with their prior acquaintances. When information travelled no faster than a horse or ship, simply connecting willing lenders and borrowers was relatively difficult; previously acquainted individuals were more likely to find one another. Furthermore, and perhaps most importantly, an individual lender could not have the volume of experience, actuarial data, reserve assets, or diversified portfolio of a modern, institutional lender. Neither did any lender have access to information provided today by credit-rating agencies; the only substitute was the comparatively imprecise information supplied by networks of reputation (Muldrew 1998, ch. 6). Early modern lenders thus had difficulties in both assessing the creditworthiness of potential borrowers and withstanding mistakes in so doing. Personal knowledge addressed this deficiency: as Professor Muldrew has written, 'the most reliable means of judging someone's credit was direct interpersonal contact with the person' (Muldrew 1998, p. 151). In short, lending to known individuals diminished both transaction costs and risk.

The Chancery record corroborates that mortgages took place between prior-acquainted individuals. For instance, in *Hill* v. *Hill* (1600) the mortgagee was a 'near kinsman' (of uncertain degree) who shared a surname with the mortgagor.[35] In *Wilmote* v. *Beckenshawe* (1601), Edward Wilmote mortgaged 'diverse lands in Garforde in the county of Berkshire' to 'Mr Richard Beckenshawe being his brother-in-law in Regard of many favours received of the said Beckenshawe [and £400]'.[36] In other cases, an exception seems to prove the rule of prior acquaintance. In *Tresham* v. *Forthe* (1597), the court made special note that the mortgagor 'was promised from one Sute a Citizen of London whom the plaintiff never knew before that he should have 100^{li} for six months upon interest'[37]; the record seems to mention the unfamiliarity of the parties because it was unusual. Clearer is *Ashebey* v. *Paramore* (1592) where the mortgagee described the beginning of his financial relationship with the mortgagor, Thomas Ashebey, thus:

> Thomas Ashebey repaired unto the said [mortgagee]... and became an earnest suitor... to borrow of him great sums of money[,] which was a

> strange suit unto the said defendant considering that the said Complainant Thomas Ashebie was a stranger unto the said defendant and before that time not known unto him.[38]

Francis Bacon also wrote: 'no man will lend his moneys far off, nor put them into unknown hands' (St. Albans 1857, p. 48). Mortgages in our period were therefore a familiar business in contrast to the systematic, formal and impersonal reality of the present. As considered below, this tended to militate in favour of the equity of redemption.

5.6 Mortgagees' Desire for the Property

In the light of the familiar situation of many mortgage parties, it is not surprising that numbers of mortgagees, instead of viewing mortgaged property merely as a financial security, hoped to acquire it permanently. For example, in *Wood* v. *Effield* (1600), the mortgagor alleged that the mortgagee,

> understanding that the said [mortgagor] had such house and lands as aforesaid[,] and he having a great desire to have the same[,] did utterly refuse to lend to the said [mortgagor] one hundred pounds unless the said [mortgagor] would[,] for security of the same money to be lent[,] mortgage [the premises] to him.[39]

The mortgagee characterised the situation rather differently, but the mortgagor's allegation was plausible enough, and tending to support his view is the fact that the mortgagee took possession upon forfeiture. In *Ellyot* v. *Nance* (1600), the mortgagee's desire for the property was undeniably evident from the fact that he personally took up residence there immediately upon forfeiture.[40] In other cases, a mortgagee showed desire for the property by purchasing or attempting to purchase it at some stage. In *Mollineux* v. *Leake* (1617), the mortgagor exhibited a bill 'that the [mortgagee] might be ordered to make assurance of the said lands' to a purchaser, which the mortgagee 'refused to do[,] alleging no other Cause but that it was agreed that he should have the said premises paying 3000^{li} more'.[41] In *Eaton* v. *Basenett* (1605), after forfeiture the mortgagor 'of his own seeking for a further sum of money' sold the premises to the mortgagee.[42] In *Perton* v. *Dawson* (1596), a mortgagor, evidently believing that the mortgagee desired the property, specifically included in his will that his executors should try to sell the property to the mortgagee.[43] And more cases suggesting, one way or another, that a mortgagee desired the property appear in the record.[44] In each of these cases, it seems that the mortgagee had some desire to acquire mortgaged property for reasons other than simply security for a debt.

But this is not to say that every mortgagee desired mortgaged property. Some mortgagees certainly had finance as an exclusive interest; for them, acquisition of property was more inconvenience than anything else. As discussed below, certain mortgagees even allowed redemption after forfeiture even absent any compulsion to do so presumably as a convenient means of liquidating the asset. And whether it was expression of an exclusive interest in money, or simply to pre-empt an expected Chancery order, numbers of mortgagees in Chancery offered *sua sponte* to reconvey forfeited property upon payment of various sums.[45] Some mortgagees thus wanted property, while others wanted money. As will be seen, this cut both ways for the equity of redemption.

5.7 Variance of Mortgage Terms

Also unsurprising in the light of the familiar circumstances of many mortgages is the fact that parties appear commonly to have treated terms of a mortgage contract with a degree of informality, frequently departing from the strict terms of their initial agreement. Indeed, one gets the impression that willingness to operate flexibly was considered socially the only right and proper attitude. Legal rights were not to be insisted upon; they were merely a guideline for the parties' dealings. Although space does not permit treating the matter more fully, it is worth noting that what follows speaks directly—and in interesting ways—to debates about negotiations between private parties 'in the shadow of the law' and in realms where the law is unknown or ignored (see literature related to Mnookin and Kornhauser 1979; Ellickson 1991; McAdams 1997). For our purposes, it is sufficient to note prevailing practice in the context of the nascent equity of redemption.

5.7.1 *Continuation upon Interest*

An important way that parties treated their mortgages informally was in extension of a debt upon payment of interest. This was common in part because mortgages in our period appear to have been typically of short duration. As far as the Chancery record demonstrates, if there was such a thing as a standard mortgage term, it was a single year, at the end of which the entire debt was due in one, full payment.[46] And Dr Juliet Gayton found in her study of copyhold mortgages in five Hampshire manors described in her chapter of this book that 'the overwhelmingly short-term nature of these copyholder mortgages is a defining feature of them' (Gayton 2018, p. 56). Further investigation of mortgage muniments would provide greater certainty about which structures were most typical, but it nevertheless appears that whatever the specifics, mortgages were commonly of a rather short duration. The need for longer-term financing seems to have been met by a regular practice of rolling over, or 'continuing', in contemporary language, mortgages upon payment of interest. Upon continuation a mortgagor would pay interest, the principal would remain outstanding, and the deal would carry over for another period of time. Such continuation required consent from both sides as either side could insist upon enforcement of the original agreement. But such consent was often sensible. Circumstances making a mortgage desirable one year might very well remain unchanged in the next. And given the transaction costs of mortgage formation discussed above, mortgage continuation was a logical response. If circumstances changed for either side, non-renewal was always possible, but otherwise continuation was a way for both sides to avoid incurring expenses.

The Chancery record and the work of other scholars confirm the view that mortgage continuation was common. Numbers of mortgage forfeitures relieved in Chancery were those in which problems arose upon continuation, such as when parties failed properly to update their legal documents and a dispute later arose.[47] Other cases show continuation as apparently routine. In *Knowles* v. *Westwray* (1592), the mortgagor alleged that he was told 'by the broker that dealt between the said parties That any time upon 14 days warning he would cause the said [mortgagees] to continue the said mortgage'.[48] In *Mason* v. *Wilmott* (1600), the mortgagor described the very nature of the mortgage 'as only meant for security… and to be renewed from time to time'.[49] Although it was a case of a debt secured upon a bond rather than mortgage, *Cornewallis* v. *Swanton* (1601) shows that such expectation of continuation might be clearly pre-agreed. Mr Serjeant Christopher Yelverton (Ibbetson 2004) mediated between the parties so that £100 secured by a bond,

> should Remain still in the hands of the plaintiff and be continued from year to year upon Interest During the lives of him the said Defendant and

> his wife... [and] agreement [was] published on both parts at the time of the then sealing & Delivery of the said bond that the money should be continued & the bond yearly Renewed.[50]

Given that the ultimate beneficiary of this continuation, the defendant's wife, was also Sjt Yelverton's sister, his negotiation of a continuation agreement shows that it was consonant with legal sophistication.[51] Professor Lawrence Stone has also described the continuation of mortgages in our period as routine (Stone 1965, p. 526). And Professors French and Hoyle showed in their study of a Yorkshire manor shortly after our period that a 'mortgage could, potentially, last for decades, albeit with occasional rescheduling of the debt' (French and Hoyle 1999, p. 374). Professor Ian Ward mentioned that the deeds of the earl of Bridgwater suggest that many of his mortgages were continued in the 1660s (Ward 1991, p. 30). And the anonymous author of a treatise called *The Law of Securities* wrote in 1722 that 'Upon a Mortgagor's paying the Interest of the Money borrowed to the Mortgagee, Mortgages oftentimes continue a long Time without disturbing the Possession or Parties' (Anon. 1722, pp. 103–104).

In the light of both the logic for continuation and the evidence that it was in fact a common practice, it may not be going too far to suggest that in our period social norms included a presumption that one ought to agree to continuation in the ordinary course. Both parties needed or wanted the arrangement when it was agreed, and absent a change of circumstances, why should one put the other to the substantial inconvenience and expense of finding an alternative? Refusal to continue by a creditor might especially cause considerable hardship to a debtor who might be expected to struggle to raise the whole principal for repayment unexpectedly. Indeed, Charles Dickens used Grandfather Smallweed's unexpected refusal to continue Mr George's debt (upon bond rather than mortgage) as an example of mean and treacherous dealing in his nineteenth-century novel *Bleak House*, which centred on a Chancery suit. Conversely, a debtor who insisted upon repaying in full at the earliest opportunity might at least surprise and disappoint a creditor hoping to maintain a remunerative arrangement (cf. Maitland 1909, p. 269). The strength of the norm of presumptive continuation and what circumstances were generally thought to justify non-continuation are unclear. Yet, the point remains that continuation seems to have been regular enough to attract some degree of expectation of it.

5.7.2 *Late Redemption Beyond Chancery*

Parties also appear sometimes to have varied from the original terms of their mortgages in allowing late redemption in the absence of Chancery compulsion. Late redemption and continuation were two sides of the same coin. Both involved charging interest for forbearing principal for a period after an original redemption date. Indeed, Professor Stone has noted both a similarity and commonality to the practices (Stone 1965, p. 526). The difference between the two was that continuation was agreed before the original redemption date had passed, while late redemption was not. Both nevertheless appear regular in our period.

The Chancery record contains numbers of examples of privately agreed late redemptions. In *Burgoyne* v. *Beecher* (1592), the mortgagor continued to occupy the premises for four years after forfeiture until reaching a 'second agreement' with the mortgagee by which the mortgagor could redeem upon repayment of the mortgage principal plus interest; Chancery litigation ensued when the mortgagor failed to redeem according to the second agreement.[52] In *Kynder* v. *Clarke* (1616), the parties agreed after forfeiture to an absolute conveyance to a trustee 'but with this Condition[,] agreement[,] and trust between all the said parties that the [mortgagor] might redeem the said lands' at another date[53]; Chancery litigation focussed on a later refusal, in breach of trust, to honour the new condition of redemption. Other cases refer to private arbitrations awarding late redemption. In *Clapham* v. *Walthye* (1592), 'an award was made after the forfeiture of the said mortgage whereby the plaintiffs were to pay the said [unpaid principal] and costs to have their land again'.[54] And in *Crowther* v. *Adams* (1604), an 'arbitrament of certain Citizens in London awarded that if the said [mortgagor] paid the 469[li] pounds to the said [mortgagee] That then the said [mortgagee] should reconvey the said houses' despite forfeiture.[55] Beyond the Chancery record, West's *Symboleography* even includes an example of a deed for late redemption: 'A Bargain and sale of lands forfeited upon a Mortgage', which named both the forfeiting mortgagor and the buyer as 'R.B.', thus indicating that the deed was a form of late redemption (West 1615, Sect. 395).

It may seem at first sight surprising that mortgagees would consent to late redemption: their strict legal rights put them in an excellent position upon forfeiture, with a clear and simple right to take property absolutely. Irrespective of whether a mortgagee was primarily interested in finance or acquiring a property permanently, insisting on such right would seem logical for the gain that would result. But three interrelated considerations help explain late redemption, all three of which apply to mortgagees primarily interested in finance, and the latter two of which apply to mortgagees interested in acquiring a property.

Firstly, late redemption was the cheapest way to liquidate a mortgaged asset. Substantial transaction costs attended any attempt to raise cash from a relatively illiquid asset like realty because either selling the land or managing it to take profits involved significant labour and/or time. But transaction costs could be virtually eliminated by allowing late redemption: the buyer was already in place and the terms of the deal essentially prearranged, assuming one applied the original interest rate for the period during which the mortgagor was late. The simplest and hence cheapest manner for a mortgagee to recover his or her debt was therefore to allow a mortgagor to redeem late, with payment of interest for the forbearing at the rate previously agreed, irrespective of legal rights.

Secondly, in purely moral terms, separating debtors from their property seems to have had negative significance in our period. Such morality went beyond the concept of 'ancient inheritance' discussed above, although it was obviously intimately related to it. The fact that the value of mortgaged property usually exceeded, sometimes significantly, the value of the debt secured meant that in many cases taking mortgage forfeiture was problematic disgorgement of wealth from someone who was almost by definition financially vulnerable. And the moral significance of mortgage matters was viscerally heightened by the typical familiar relations between mortgage parties discussed above; a mortgagee could therefore hardly claim that denying late redemption was 'nothing personal'—it was a decision immediately impacting a neighbour with all the immanent import thereof. Moreover, in our period, finance and business were still intimately bound up in a theological matrix giving all such issues vastly greater moral valence than the later view that treats such matters as dry questions of morally neutral business (Tawney 1925). The moral significance of late redemption in our period is confirmed in the perhaps surprising fact that the Chancery record contains numbers of instances of deceased mortgagees providing for late redemption in their wills[56]: a last will was of course the last point to remedy the 'hard and unchristianly dealing' (Dasent 1899, p. 185) of taking mortgage forfeiture.

Finally, the greater interrelation of moral and economic realms in our period mutually intensified the significance and effect of the other. The physically and socially intimate business world described above was, as Professor Muldrew has set out, bound together with trust in economic relations. As perceptions of trustworthiness were affected by perceptions of moral conduct, the moral significance of late redemption would redound again upon purely economic matters. Similarly, the economic importance of a mortgage increased the moral significance of late redemption because of the major impact that forfeiture might have on the life of a mortgagor who was likely a neighbour. In short, a mutually reinforcing cycle of economics and morality heightened the significance of both and tended to militate in favour of late redemption.

In such an atmosphere, one imagines that a cultural norm of allowing late redemption might also have existed. As with continuation upon interest, mortgagors might have reasonably expected mortgagees to allow late redemption absent special circumstances. Indeed, given the close relation between the two norms, one might imagine that if one existed it would tend to reinforce the other. But irrespective of their potential normativity, it seems that continuation upon interest and allowing late redemption absent court compulsion were at least fairly common in our period, at least on a view from the Chancery. They thus formed part of the background of the equity of redemption in our period irrespective of their objective situation in wider society.

5.8 Conclusion

Returning to the question 'Why the Equity of Redemption?', it is worth reviewing what this article has observed of the nature of mortgages in the social context of the nascent equity of redemption. We have seen that the purpose of mortgages was often allowing risky borrowers to obtain otherwise unavailable credit by hazard of pre-owned property rather than enabling acquisition of new property by financing purchase money. The values of mortgaged properties often exceeded the values of the debts that they secured. Mortgages took place in a context in which the Court of Chancery, if not society at large, viewed blood ties to land as creating an interest of 'ancient inheritance' that rendered it per se equitable to maintain connexions of families to land according to ordinary principles of primogeniture. Parties to mortgages in our period were generally individuals who already knew one another, and were often neighbours or family members. In light of such relationships some mortgagees unsurprisingly desired to acquire mortgaged property to keep permanently rather than for mere financial security; however, such a desire was not universal. And parties treated their mortgages with a degree of informality, varying their terms, particularly through routine continuation upon payment of interest and allowance of late redemption absent court compulsion. Indeed, the context and seeming frequency of such practices suggest that consent to continuation and late redemption in the ordinary course might have been cultural norms.

While this picture confirms aspects of the traditional answer to why the equity of redemption arose (to the extent that such an answer has existed), it provides a different and, it is submitted, more important answer. Consonant with traditional views is the fact mortgages that were ordinarily of pre-owned property, the value of which exceeded the debt, which the Court of Chancery would wish to maintain in the ownership of long-established proprietors. Consonant also is the idea that mortgages were not infrequently a tool for those in some financial difficulty. But such realities do not perhaps explain totally—or even primarily—the emergence of the doctrine. Of greater significance is the prevailing context of social credit of the day. With mortgages taking place between neighbours of prior acquaintance, and social norms presumptively favouring continuation upon interest and late redemption, the equity of redemption appears to be something like enforcement of prevailing social views of proper mortgage dealings irrespective of legal technicality. One might say that the equity of redemption was judicial enforcement of reasonable 'real-world' expectations surrounding mortgages. The equity of redemption thus appears to be the Chancery attenuating strict legal rights in favour of a more social approach. Particularly given that a core Chancery jurisdiction was the enforcement of substance over legal form (see, e.g., Baker 2002, pp. 102–103; Bryson 2001, p. 310 at 119.230), this is arguably a better view of the equity of redemption than prior views. Such a view renders the equity of redemption an explicable, if not natural, response to cases of mortgage forfeiture in Chancery. Why it arose is then because it was the most obviously 'fair' or intuitively 'reasonable' way to address cases of mortgage forfeiture at the time. It was the layman's response to mortgage forfeiture rather than the lawyer's.

One point might militate in the other direction: the social situation of mortgage parties meant that a mortgagee might have bargained for a mortgage in specific and *prima-facie* legitimate hope of acquiring a mortgaged property not for financial security, but to keep. Such a negotiation might have been open, honest, forthright and thus worthy of enforcement. Equity nevertheless found that on balance the right thing was to allow late redemption—with appropriate compensation for the delay in repayment—and thus required mortgagees so to do. But it is worth noting that equity's eventual, rather inflexible, position of 'once a mortgage, always a mortgage' with concomitant prohibition of 'clogs and fetters upon the equity of redemption', which together manifested a strong unwillingness to allow mortgagees to acquire mortgaged property, was a later development. In our period, the Chancery would happily uphold purchase of mortgaged property by a mortgagee and even in some cases granted mortgagees, apparently *sua sponte*, rights of first refusal to purchase mortgaged property.[57] Perhaps it was the march of doctrinal logic that took the court further towards a thoroughgoing hostility to mortgagees acquiring mortgaged property. In our period, the Chancery remained at ease with the ordinary social practice of its litigants, which included both rights similar to the equity of redemption and the possibility of a mortgagee acquiring mortgaged property.

For lawyers, it is also worth noting that the view of the equity of redemption presented here tends to render equity more predictable and less threatening than some other views. Lawyers often, and naturally, take the common law as a baseline against which to contrast equity. Such a manoeuvre casts equity as a departure from a given, which may make it look like a dangerous aberration. But the view of the equity of redemption in this chapter is of something less capricious. Instead of riding roughshod over agreements freely formed according to established rules—and thereby radically reshaping settled expectations in potentially arbitrary ways—equity appears merely as enforcement of 'real-world' or 'common sense' values instead of legal technicality. A layperson's reasonable expectations simply became the law instead of technical doctrine. And one might argue that laymen's widely held common expectations might be no less stable or clear than the law itself; but that is an argument for another day. The point is merely that considering the equity of redemption in social terms, as this chapter has done, renders equity both less threatening and more explicable than starting with a view from the common law.

Notes

1. The sample considered includes TNA, C 33/60 (Michaelmas 1579–Trinity 1580); C 33/75 (Michaelmas 1587–Trinity 1588); C 33/83 (Michaelmas 1591–Trinity 1592); C 33/91 (Easter 1596–Easter 1597); C 33/99 (Michaelmas 1600–Trinity 1601); C 33/108 (Michaelmas 1604–Trinity 1605); C 33/131 (Michaelmas 1616); C 33/132 (Hilary 1616/7).
2. Anon., Cary 8–9; 21 E.R. 5.
3. Further examples of conditional sales appear in *Grynkyn* v. *Bull*, C 33/107 f. 314, 21 January 1605; *Denton* v. *Easington*, C 33/132 f. 46, 19 October 1616. Other forms of conditional sale existed in various times and places; see, e.g., Helmholz (1987, p. 331).
4. C 78/74/13, membrane 49, lines 49–54, 59–60, 26 January 1592.
5. C 33/107 f. 314, 21 January 1605.
6. Ibid. The vendors alleged 'that the information whereupon the said order was grounded is in many parts untrue', C 33/108 f. 370v, 25 January 1605. The matter settled without ever making clear which, if any, facts in the information were untrue, C 33/108 f. 707v, 22 April 1605.
7. C 33/122 f. 1177, 22 June 1612; cf. Tothill 132; 21 E.R. 145. For an explanation of statutes, see Waddilove (in preparation).
8. C 33/108 f. 369, 26 January 1605.
9. Ibid.
10. C 33/83 f. 425v, 14 April 1592.
11. C 33/105 f. 417, 8 February 1604.
12. Ibid.
13. 13 Eliz. I, c. 8; see also 37 Hen. VIII, c. 9. In fact, the Statute of Usury 1571 allowed disgorgement of interest at 10% or below and penalized charging of interest above 10%. In this sense, it did not allow charging of interest at any rate. But in practice interest at 10% and below was tolerated.
14. See, e.g., *Williams* v. *Bates*, C 33/75 f. 59v, 20 October 1587; *Ashebey* v. *Parramore*, C 78/74/14 membrane 48, 26 January 1592; *Sculthorpe* v. *Desborrowe*, C 33/91 f. 402v, 5 November 1596; *Byrd* v. *Benyon*, C 33/92 f. 562, 10 December 1596 (referring to two separate mortgages at 10%); *Davye* v. *Chamberlen*, C 33/91 f. 762, 20 April 1597; *Mason* v. *Wilmott*, C 78/111/11; C 33/99 f. 239v, 15 November 1600; *Courtman* v. *Convers*, C 33/99 f. 628, 17 June 1601; *Rye* v. *North*, C 33/108 f. 906v, 10 June 1605; *Sherley* v. *Wintershall*, C 33/131 f. 88, 15 October 1616; *Flendon* v. *Grunwyn*, C 33/131 f. 35, 19 October 1616; *Parkins* v. *Digges*, C 33/132 f. 424v, 25 January 1617; *Garnett* v. *Nevill*, C 78/218/18, 13 October 1621; *Westbrooke* v. *Cranley*, C 78/434/10,

18 October 1621; *Winter* v. *Smith*, C 78/237/1, mortgage of February 1621; see also *Bowyer* v. *Bancroft*, C 33/132 f. 679, 5 April 1617 (9.35%; £30 interest due on £350 after eleven months); *Bellamy* v. *Ratcylef*, C 33/92 f. 748v, 14 April 1597 (9.875%); cf. *Parsey* v. *Bartholomewe*, C 33/95 f. 270, 27 October 1598 (in which a mortgagee provided for late redemption in his will at any time if the mortgagor paid 10% damages). A pair of loans at the end of our period reflect an interest rate of only 9%: *Harris* v. *Rolfe*, C 33/131 f. 260, 22 November 1616; *Mollineux* v. *Leake*, C 33/132 f. 661, 19 March 1617. And one loan, between brothers-in-law, was for a mere 5%: *Wilmote* v. *Beckenshawe*, C 33/99 f. 556, 20 May 1601.

15. See, e.g., *Burgoyne* v. *Beecher*, C 33/83 f. 615, 6 June 1592; *Knowles* v. *Westwray*, C 33/83 f. 653, 1 June 1592; *Bellamy* v. *Ratclyef*, C 33/92 f. 748v, 14 April 1597 (note that the underlying interest rate on the mortgage loan was only 9.875%). In *Bird* v. *Benyon*, the Chancery ordered 'Interest or Damages for the forbearing' of mortgage money without specifying the rate, which tends to suggest an understanding of a 10% standard; C 33/92 f. 563, 10 December 1596.
16. C 78/218/18, 13 October 1621.
17. Modern empirical scholarship suggests that the same may be true in the twenty-first century, see Armour (2008), text at nn. 22, 29.
18. *Vernon* v. *Bethell*, (1762) 2 Eden 110, 113; 28 E.R. 838, 839 (Ch.).
19. *Palmer* v. *Emerson*, [1911] Ch. D. 758. Such limits were eventually enshrined in several statutes, e.g. the Trustee Act 1925s. 9, but were repealed by the Trustee Act 2000, see Pearce et al. (2010, pp. 745–746).
20. C 33/78 f. 806, 13 June 1589.
21. C 33/91 f. 748v, 14 April 1597.
22. C 33/92 f. 562, 10 December 1596.
23. C 33/99 f. 814, 11 July 1589.
24. C 78/132/6 membrane 16 (specifically noting that the mortgagee-defendant was not himself a usurer).
25. C 33/99 f. 58v, 23 October 1600.
26. Ibid.
27. C 78/132/6 membrane 16, 13 November 1600.
28. C 78/118/4 membrane 42, 7 July 1601.
29. Ibid. at membrane 43.
30. C 33/132 f. 660, 19 March 1617.
31. C 33/131 f. 261v, 9 November 1616.
32. C 78/113/23, membrane 2, 17 December 1600.
33. Ibid. at membrane 4.
34. See, e.g., *Gigger* v. *Cowper*, C 33/75 f. 764v, 20 June 1588; *Knowles* v. *Westwray*, C 33/83 f. 653, 1 June 1592; *Colt* v. *Wood*, C 33/108 f. 462,

28 January 1605; cf. *Lynfield* v. *Adams*, C 33/131 f. 104v, 8 November 1616. Foreclosure decrees never could have developed without such fundamental limitation on a mortgagor's interest.

35. C 78/113/23 membrane 2, 17 December 1600, the mortgagor had first borrowed from a non-relative whom the 'near kinsman' replaced as mortgagee; cf. Muldrew (1998, p. 113), regarding credit amongst kin.
36. C 33/99 f. 556, 20 May 1601.
37. C 33/91 f. 735, 13 April 1597 (emphasis added).
38. C 78/74/14 membrane 49, 26 January 1592.
39. C 78/101/3 membrane 9, 15 November 1600.
40. C 78/132/6, 13 November 1600.
41. C 33/132 f. 661, 19 March 1617.
42. C 33/108 f. 818, 2 May 1605.
43. C 33/91 f. 191, 18 June 1596.
44. *Gwillyams* v. *Hopkyns*, C 78/104/12, 8 February 1598; *Cockeyne* v. *Asheley*, C 33/99 f. 226, 7 December 1600; *Bowyer* v. *Bancroft*, C 33/132 f. 679, 5 April 1617.
45. See, e.g., *Hide* v. *Sidley*, C 33/108 f. 787, 11 May 1605; *Parsey* v. *Bartholomewe*, C 33/108 f. 453v, 7 February 1598; *Maytam* v. *Whitfield*, C 33/99 f. 72, 24 October 1600; *Mawchell* v. *Deane*, C 33/99 f. 113, 10 November 1600; *Bushopp* v. *Dover*, C 33/131 f. 99v, 4 November 1616; *Mathewe* v. *Jenkins*, C 33/132 f. 403v, 24 January 1617.
46. See, e.g., *Day* v. *Murrell*, C 78/116/3, 13 November 1600 (one year); *Barker* v. *Barker*, C 33/99 f. 295v, 30 January 1601 (one year); *Sherley* v. *Wintershall*, C 33/131 f. 88, 15 October 1616 (one year); *Bowyer* v. *Bancroft*, C 33/132 f. 679, 5 April 1617 (eleven months); *Hanmer* v. *Lochard*, Tothill 132; 21 E.R. 145; C 33/122 f. 1177, 22 June 1612 (approximately thirteen months); *Mason* v. *Wilmott*, C 33/99 238v, 15 November 1600 (approximately thirteen months); *Killingford* v. *Hallett*, C 33/38 f. 76, 175, 307, 432 (1591–92) (approximately fourteen months). See also Stone (1965, pp. 528–529).
47. See, e.g., *Fathers* v. *Horwoode*, C 33/60 f. 239v, 6 February 1580; *Donne* v. *Pendree*, C 33/83 f. 80, 26 October 1591; *Brawnche* v. *Brudenell*, C 33/85 f. 421, 21 May 1593; *Adams* v. *Adams*, C 33/132 f. 614v, 15 February 1617; cf. *Bellamy* v. *Ratclyef*, C 33/91 f. 409v, 6 November.
48. C 33/83 f. 425v, 14 April 1592.
49. C 78/111/11, 15 November 1600.
50. C 33/99 f. 300v, 27 January 1601.
51. C 33/99 f. 320, 6 February 1601. The Chancery eventually ordered a new arrangement, C 33/99 f. 468v, 8 May 1601.
52. C 33/83 f. 615, 6 June 1592.
53. C 33/131 f. 223v, 28 November 1616.

54. C 33/83 f. 596, 1 June 1592.
55. C 33/108 f. 88, 22 October 1604.
56. See, e.g., *Parsey* v. *Bartholomewe*, C 33/95 f. 270, 27 October 1598; *Wood* v. *Effield*, C 78/101/3 membrane 11, 15 November 1600; *De la Pynde* v. *Lady Glover*, C 33/108 f. 268, 28 November 1604; *Parry* v. *Lewis-David*, C 33/131 f. 143v, 19 November 1616.
57. See, e.g., *Hill* v. *Hill*, C 78/113/23, 17 December 1600; *Ashebey* v. *Parramore*, C 78/74/14 membrane 49, 26 January 1592; *Byrd* v. *Benyon*, C 33/92 f. 562, 10 December 1596; *Bruncker* v. *Taylor*, C 33/91 f. 555, 18 December 1596.

References

Primary Sources

Bryson, W.H. (ed.), 2001. *Cases Concerning Equity and the Courts of Equity 1550–1660, Vol. I* (London: Selden Society, vol. 117).

Dasent, J.R. (ed.), 1899. *Acts of the Privy Council of England, New Series, Vol. XVIII 1589–1590* (London: HMSO).

Harrison, G.B. (ed.), 1931. *A Second Elizabethan Journal; Being a Record of Those Things Most Talked of During the Years 1595–1598* (London: Constable and Co.).

Tawney, R.H. (ed.), 1925. *A Discourse upon Usury by Thomas Wilson DCL, 1572* (New York: Harcourt Brace and Co.).

West, W., 1615. *The First Part of Simboleography* (London: Stationers' Company).

Yale, D.E.C. (ed.), 1954. *Lord Nottingham's Chancery Cases, Vol. I* (London: Selden Society, vol. 73).

Yale, D.E.C. (ed.), 1961. *Lord Nottingham's Chancery Cases, Vol. II* (London: Selden Society, vol. 79).

Yale, D.E.C. (ed.), 1965. *Lord Nottingham's Manual of Chancery Practice and Prolegomena of Chancery and Equity* (Cambridge: Cambridge University Press).

Secondary Works

Anon., 1722. *The Law of Securities* (London).

Armour, J., 2008. 'The law and economics debate about secured lending: Lessons for European lawmaking?', *European Company and Financial Law Review*, Special Volume 2: The Future of Secured Credit in Europe.

Baker, J.H., 2002. *An Introduction to English Legal History*, 4th edn (London: Butterworths).

Clark, G., 1988. 'The cost of capital and medieval agricultural technique', *Explorations in Economic History*, vol. 25, pp. 265–294.

Ellickson, R.C., 1991. *Order Without Law: How Neighbors Settle Disputes* (Cambridge, MA: Harvard University Press).

French, H.R. and R.W. Hoyle, 1999. 'The land market of a Pennine manor: Slaidburn, 1650–1780', *C&C*, vol. 14, pp. 349–383.

Gayton, J.D., 2018. 'Mortgages Raised by Rural English Copyhold Tenants 1605–1735'. In *Land and Credit* (New York: Palgrave Macmillan) (this volume, Chapter 3), p. 31.

Habakkuk, H.J., 1952. 'The long-term rate of interest and the price of land in the seventeenth century', *EcHR*, vol. 5, pp. 26–45.

Halliwell-Phillipps, J.O., 1907. *Outlines of the Life of Shakespeare.* 2 vols, 11th impression (London: Longmans, Green, and Co.).

Helmholz, R.H., 1987. *Canon Law and the Law of England* (London: Hambledon Press).

Hemmeon, M. de Wolf, 1914. *Burgage Tenure in Medieaval England* (Cambridge, MA: Harvard University Press).

Holdsworth, W.S., 1927. *An Historical Introduction to the Land Law* (Oxford: Clarendon Press).

Homer, S. and R.E. Sylla, 1996. *A History of Interest Rates*, 3rd edn (New Brunswick, NJ: Rutgers University Press).

Ibbetson, D.J., 2004. 'Yelverton, Sir Christopher (1536/7–1612)', in *Oxford Dictionary of National Biography* (Oxford: Oxford University Press).

Ibbetson, D.J., 2012. 'The Earl of Oxford's Case (1615)', in C. Mitchell and P. Mitchell (eds.) *Landmark Cases in Equity* (Oxford: Hart), pp. 1–32.

Jones, N.G., 2004. 'West, William (c.1548–1598)', in *Oxford Dictionary of National Biography* (Oxford: Oxford University Press).

Jones, W.J., 1967. *The Elizabethan Court of Chancery* (Oxford: Clarendon Press).

Kiralfy, A.K.R., 1958. *Potter's Historical Introduction to English Law*, 4th edn (London: Sweet and Maxwell).

Maitland, F.W., 1909. *Equity*, ed. A.H. Chaytor and W.J. Whittaker (Cambridge: Cambridge University Press).

McAdams, R.H., 1997. 'The origin, development, and regulation of norms', *Michigan Law Review*, vol. 96, pp. 338–433.

McFarlane, B., N. Hopkins, and S. Nield, 2015. *Land Law: Texts, Cases, and Materials*, 3rd edn (Oxford: Oxford University Press).

Megarry, R. and W. Wade, 2012. *The Law of Real Property*, 8th edn, ed. C. Harpum, S. Bridge and M. Dixon (London: Sweet and Maxwell).

Mnookin, R.H. and L. Kornhauser, 1979. 'Bargaining in the shadow of the law: The case of divorce', *Yale Law Journal*, vol. 88, pp. 950–997.

Muldrew, C., 1998. *The Economy of Obligation: The Culture of Credit and Social Relations in Early Modern England* (Basingstoke: Palgrave).

Pearce, R., J. Stevens, and W. Barr, 2010. *The Law of Trusts and Equitable Obligations*, 5th edn (Oxford: Oxford University Press).

Plucknett, T.F.T., 1956. *A Concise History of the Common Law*, 5th edn (Boston: Little, Brown and Company).

Poole, E., 1984. 'West's *Symboleography*: An Elizabethan formulary', in J.A. Guy and H.G. Beale (eds.), *Law and Social Change in British History* (London: Royal Historical Society), pp. 96–106.

Powell, D.X., 2004. 'Hele, Sir John (1541/2–1608)', in *Oxford Dictionary of National Biography* (Oxford: Oxford University Press).

Schoenbaum, S., 1975. *William Shakespeare: A Documentary Life* (Oxford: Oxford University Press).

Simpson, A.W.B., 1986. *A History of the Land Law*, 2nd edn (Oxford: Oxford University Press).

Spence, G., 1846–1849. *The Equitable Jurisdiction of the Court of Chancery*, 2 vols (London: V. and R. Stevens and G.S. Norton).

St. Albans, Francis Bacon, first viscount, 1857. 'Of Usury', in B. Montagu (ed.), *The Works of Francis Bacon,* 3 vols (Philadelphia: Parry and McMillan), i, p. 47.

Stone, L., 1965. *The Crisis of the Aristocracy 1558–1641* (Oxford: Oxford University Press).

Sugarman, D. and R.A. Warrington, 1995. 'Land law, citizenship, and the invention of "Englishness". The strange world of the equity of redemption', in J. Brewer and S. Staves (eds.), *Early Modern Conceptions of Property* (Abingdon: Routledge), pp. 111–143.

Sugarman, D. and R.A. Warrington, 1997. 'Telling stories: Rights and wrongs of the equity of redemption', in J.W. Harris (ed.), *Property Problems: From Genes to Pension Funds* (London: Kluwer Law International), pp. 207–224.

Turner, R.W., 1931. *The Equity of Redemption* (Cambridge: Cambridge University Press).

Waddilove, D.P., in preparation. 'The "mendacious" common-law mortgage'.

Ward, I., 1991. 'Settlements, mortgages and aristocratic estates 1649–1660', *Journal of Legal History*, vol. 12, pp. 20–35.

Watt, G., 2007. 'The lie of the land: Mortgage law as legal fiction', in E. Cooke (ed.), *Modern Studies in Property Law, Vol. 4* (Oxford: Hart), pp. 73–96.

Zuijderduijn, C.J., 2009. *Medieval Capital Markets: Markets for Renten, State Formation and Private Investment in Holland (1300–1550)* (Leiden and Boston: Brill).

CHAPTER 6

Credit and Land: The Jews of Zaragoza 1383–1400

Michael Schraer

6.1 Introduction

Jews provided a significant component of the supply of credit to urban and rural clienteles in the lands of the crown of Aragon during the thirteenth and fourteenth centuries. Their lending and other economic activities have been the subject of numerous studies, focusing on both communities resident in small market towns, whose prime clients were rural, and those in major cities such as Barcelona, Girona and Valencia, who served the local, urban market as well as the rural hinterland (see Emery 1959; Guilleré 1984; Hinojosa Montalvo 1985a, b; Ollich i Castanyer 1985; Casas i Nadal 1985; Assis 1988; Rich i Abad 1999; Fernández-Cuadrench 2007). These studies draw on notarial and other archival sources, mostly from the late thirteenth and early fourteenth centuries. Although lending against the pledge of land is not unknown in these cases, it appears to have been the exception rather than the rule.

This study takes as its subject selected members of the Jewish community of Zaragoza, capital of Aragon, during a later time period (1383–1400).

M. Schraer (✉)
Independent Scholar, London, England
e-mail: michaelschraer@gmail.com

C. Briggs and J. Zuijderduijn (eds.), *Land and Credit*,
Palgrave Studies in the History of Finance,
https://doi.org/10.1007/978-3-319-66209-1_6

It offers a contrast to previous studies in a number of respects. The general political and economic climate, the credit market in general and the status and prosperity of the Jewish communities had undergone fundamental transformations. Crucially, the majority of loans studied here were secured in whole or part by land pledges.

The methodology deployed is to compare the lending business of these individuals with the results of the earlier studies, including the mix of clienteles by geography, typical loan size and security employed, in order to assess and explain the impact of economic and market changes, specifically, the rationale for the apparent growth in mortgages. The individuals and families selected for analysis were not only amongst the most prolific lenders in the sources under review but were also active in the property market, facilitating explanation of any direct or indirect linkages between lending and property investment.

6.2 Loan Guarantees and Pledges—Theory and Practice

Loans made by both Jews and Christians in the crown of Aragon were variously secured by oaths; personal guarantees (submitting oneself as hostage); third-party guarantors; general pledges of goods; specific pledges of moveables and by the pledging of specific land. From the viewpoint of the creditor, the primary economic considerations in the choice of security would be cost and efficiency of enforcement; guarantee of the adequacy and reliability of value of assets pledged or guaranteed; and the attached property rights. These, in turn, revolve in part around the social status of creditor and debtor, with greater separation likely to result in more formal and tangible means of guarantee (compensating for lower levels of trust and informal information) and on legal factors (not only the effectiveness of the courts in enforcement but also the specific rights of creditors to enforce and to hold and trade pledged property).

Evidence presented below indicates that use of guarantors was common in supporting much Jewish lending up to the mid-fourteenth century, implying both trust and availability of information on assets and wealth. The growth in pledging of property may be attributable to a number of factors: a decline in trust and creditworthiness individually and inter-communally; borrowers having strong and documented legal rights in their land, under law codes dating from the late twelfth and thirteenth centuries; and an active market in land and property, which also comprised the most valuable part of their asset base.

The ability of the creditor to exercise land rights was a particular consideration for the Jews, with their peculiar legal status. In England, for example, Jews acquired large quantities of land pledges but enjoyed limited property rights, in effect taking a rent charge on the land (Richardson 1960, pp. 102–106). From 1271, English Jews were forbidden to own freeholds, but the main result was that, in settlement of loans with land pledges, landed interests tended to pass directly from heavily indebted knights to wealthy religious institutions or noblemen, with considerable political and social implications. In the crown of Aragon, by contrast, Jews had the legal right to own allodial land and are frequently found in the record so doing, thus taking away a potential bar to the use of land as security (Mieres 1533, First Collation, Chap. 6, p. 3 and Second Collation, Chap. 52, pp. 62–63).

From the debtor's viewpoint, pledging of land is more attractive where landholdings are fragmented, so that the loss of pledged lands would not necessarily leave the borrower with no source of subsistence (Briggs, this volume). Royal grants of land in small subsistence packages in Aragon, accompanied by an active market in land may, therefore, have facilitated the mortgage market.

From a legal perspective, the key issues with the form of land pledge are, firstly, which of the parties holds the land, and receives its income, during the term of the loan and, secondly, the rights afforded to the creditor by the loan deed in the event of default. Meir Kohn argues that the land pledge or *pignus*, in which the creditor holds the land, was the norm in medieval Europe, as opposed to the classic Roman law mortgage (*hypothec*) where the debtor remains in possession until default, because the courts would seldom allow the lender to seize the land for repayment when there was a superior seigniorial interest that might potentially be lost. In sixteenth-century England, however, the mortgage contract was a conditional deed of bargain and sale dated on the date of repayment, rendered null and void if the loan was repaid; the borrower retained possession and kept the income for the duration of the loan (Kohn 1999, pp. 1–3). The *pignus*, on the other hand, did have significant economic advantages, reducing the costs of enforcement and allowing the creditor to evade usury laws by taking the fruits as 'hidden' interest. This is most widely found in pawn-broking; especially for small loans, the expedient of passing the asset to the creditor not only avoided enforcement costs out of proportion to the loan value but usually avoided costly documentation altogether.

Mortgage lending was, on occasions, employed (notably by religious houses) as a means of acquiring land and land rights. Van Werveke and Hoffman Berman describe examples in Flanders, Lotharingia and Southern France, in some cases arising from knights having to borrow to finance crusades. These examples highlight the importance of creditor appetite for real estate investment in the decision to lend against land pledges. Church rents and tithes were also commonly pledged (Van Werveke 1968; Hoffman Berman 1986).

On the other hand, the limited evidence to hand on Christian lending in the crown territories in the early fourteenth century suggests that land pledges were not common, most loans being backed by personal or third-party guarantees, with relatively infrequent cases of any sort of pledge, including animals, jewellery or a share of crop (García Marsilla 2002, p. 53; Guilleré 1984). Bensch argues that the thirteenth century saw a move away from mortgaging of agricultural land to Barcelona's urban patriciate, towards pledging of urban rents against loans and other forms of security which rested on the wider sharing of both risks and returns (Bensch 1995, pp. 199–201).

6.3 Jewish Lending and Developments in the Credit Market

6.3.1 Background—c.1250–1350

The late thirteenth century represents the zenith of economic fortunes for the Jews of the crown of Aragon. Healthy demographic, economic and trade growth was enhanced by territorial expansion, with conquests of Mallorca and Valencia accompanied by substantial land grants, including a significant number to Jews, notably courtiers. This environment supported strong growth in the demand for credit. Until 1283, Jews were permitted to serve in treasury roles, and during the reign of Pere *el Gran* (from 1276), members of elite Jewish families occupied almost all of the important treasury positions for the crown and within Catalonia, Aragon and Valencia, as well as enjoying substantial incomes from tax farming (Romano 1983). The crown relied heavily on Jews, not only as financial administrators, but also as a source of revenue, both through taxes dependent on their income and wealth and through loans. In either case, they needed Jewish lending to continue, albeit strictly regulated. Jaume I (1213–1276) passed various pieces of legislation setting limits on the return from Jewish lending (notably in 1228, covering Catalonia, and the *Corts* of Girona of 1241, covering the entire crown territory). In almost all cases, a 20% interest rate was established, although the 1241 edict, whilst setting monthly interest at 1.66%, also limited interest to 16.66% in any one year (Riera i Sans 2010). Other restrictions applicable from time to time included a bar on compound interest and the requirement for interest not to exceed capital. In 1254, Jaume (as an act of piety) went so far as to confiscate all Jewish debts (Baer 1992, i, pp. 149–150 and pp. 407–408, n. 28).

This period of prosperity and political power coincided with copious recorded lending by Jews. Although aided by the tightening of usury laws in relation to Christian lending, it was in all likelihood a positive response to a growing market opportunity, as opposed to a forced move resulting from a bar on other income sources, such as land ownership or trade (Emery 1959, p. 101, cites the contrary views of Isidore Loeb). A number of sources suggest that Jews enjoyed a high and rising share of the credit market. Bensch's analysis for Barcelona suggests that the share of Jewish lending rose from around 10–20% in the early part of the century to a peak of around 86% in the 1250s, then remaining above two-thirds between 1271 and 1290 (Bensch 1995, p. 284, Table 7.1). Milton's study of Santa Coloma de Queralt estimates that, between 1276 and 1313, of 1584 recorded loans, Jews made 70% and Christians 29% (Milton 2012, p. 87, Table 4.4).

However, assessing credit market shares from notarial records is problematic. On the one hand, records undoubtedly understate the volume of Christian lending, since usury laws meant Christian loans were commonly disguised or simply not notarised. Christians primarily used *comanda* and *mutua* which, in pure legal form, carried no interest, as well as credit sales and real estate transactions, in which rent in cash or kind could stand in for interest. In Milton's analysis of Santa Coloma, noted above, 98.8% of credit sales were made by Christians, underlining that loans by themselves are not a reliable guide to the total credit market. A similar finding emerges from Guilleré's analysis of notarial data for Girona between 1321 and 1330, with Jews making around two-thirds of loans but these being far out-numbered by credit sales made by Christians, who also dominate loans made under the *comanda* and *amical* legal forms. Adding sales on credit by Christians, mainly of cloth, to these loans, the overall Jewish share of the credit market by volume was around 34% (by comparison, Jews constituted around 7–10% of the total population) (Guilleré 1984, p. 369, Table I and p. 370). García Marsilla's somewhat later analysis of lending in Valencia indicates Jewish lending in 1341 at 41% of the total number of loans notarised (García Marsilla 2002, p. 89).

Christian lending may also be under-estimated because the high cost of parchment and the services of notaries further discouraged notarisation which, for Jews, was an essential form of legal cover (Bensch 1995, p. 286). This is most marked in the case of villages or small towns where networks of informal lending, especially by wealthier peasants, are likely to have been common. As a result, Jewish lending dominates the notarial record in these locations. On the other side, it is certain that much of the smaller-scale Jewish pawn-broking was itself not notarised (not only was notarisation uneconomic for small loans but unnecessary protection for a lender who held the pawn for the term of the loan). Some evidence of it is found in the *fueros* and royal edicts, which contain various privileges for Jews in relation to stolen gages and reclamation of gages (e.g. Régné 1978, docs. 43, 180, 343).

6.3.2 *Previous Studies of Jewish Lending*

Table 6.1 summarises the key results of selected, localised studies of Jewish lending, mostly relating to the period 1261–1334, but with one study in the post-Black Death years, encompassing both the major cities and smaller market towns. Excluded from Table 6.1 are the studies of Jewish lending in Valencia in the 1380s by Hinojosa Montalvo, as these cover a rather smaller and less representative sample, including less comprehensive analysis. They do, however, indicate a substantial majority of loans to agriculturalists.

Table 6.1 includes over 5900 separate loans. Some are drawn from notarial sources, which represent a reasonable sample for the time and place concerned, others for which no notarial records survive (notably in Barcelona before the 1290s) are based on the less complete surviving deeds and other related documentation held in royal, church and other archives. Nevertheless, some important common themes emerge.

Table 6.1 Some studies of Jewish lending in the crown of Aragon: key data

Location	*Years covered*	*No. of loans analysed*	*No. of documented Jewish lenders*	*Estimated Jewish population*	*Percentage of all loans by Jewish creditors made to rural borrowers*	*Average loan (sous)*
Perpignan	1261–1286	1643 (1321 new loans)	203	Around 200 adult males, 100 families	65% by volume (43% by value) to villagers	65*s.* (median)
Santa Coloma de Queralt	1293–1299	1002	64	30–50 families, 110 adults in notarial record	78% of loans to towns and villages outside Santa Coloma, 155 locations in total	59*s.* (mean)
Vic	1266–1278	490	33	Only 7 regular lenders resident in Vic from 4 families	82% by volume (53% by value) to peasants; 27 locations in 1266, 51 in 1278	66*s.*
Cardona	1330–1334	324	11 (4 main lending families, 5 minor lending families)	13 families, 58 individuals	Around 45–52% outside Cardona, villages within a 10–15 km radius	90*s.*

(continued)

Table 6.1 (continued)

Location	*Years covered*	*No. of loans analysed*	*No. of documented Jewish lenders*	*Estimated Jewish population*	*Percentage of all loans by Jewish creditors made to rural borrowers*	*Average loan (**sous**)*
Barcelona—1	1196–1300	371	167 (but note, tiny sample spread over a very long period)	c. 250–500 families	Around 20% to peasants, average loan 166s. 68% of loans to Barcelona residents, 29% with the surrounding territories	341*s.*
Barcelona—2	1349–1390	c. 760	33 individuals account for 456 loans	c. 250–500 families	n/a but, in addition to Barcelona itself, 5 surrounding towns had over 20 debtors, 3 had 10–20 debtors and around 35 locations with up to 10 debtors, up to 25–35 km from the city	193*s.*
Girona	1321–1330	1304	n/a	c. 200 families	92% by volume, 91% by value to villagers	92*s.*

Sources Perpignan: Emery (1959); Santa Coloma de Queralt: Assis (1988); Vic: Ollich i Castanyer (1985); Cardona: Casas i Nadal (1985); Barcelona 1: Fernández-Cuadrench (2007); Barcelona 2: Rich i Abad (1999); Girona: Guilleré (1984)

Firstly, in virtually all cases, rural borrowers (including villages around the city) account for either the dominant or, at least, a highly significant proportion of the loans recorded. This is true even for Jews resident in the major cities. Secondly, it is noticeable that the lending business often covered quite broad geographical areas, typically up to 10–20 km from the centre of Jewish settlement, but occasionally up to 30–40 km. Thirdly, lending was, if not ubiquitous amongst the Jewish population, certainly recorded by a significant proportion, although analysis indicates that, in most cases, a few families dominated the lending business. In the thirteenth-century samples, the typical loans in the market towns were around 60–70 *sous* (*s.*), whilst Barcelona has a much higher average, reflecting the predominance of urban loans to merchants and nobles. The fourteenth-century samples ranged from 90*s.* in Cardona and Girona to 190*s.* in Barcelona where, as in the earlier period, urban merchants and artisans predominated, albeit with a significant minority of loans to rural residents, covering the '*hort i vinyet*' area of cultivation around the city, up to a 25–30 km radius (Rich i Abad 1999, p. 250–257). By way of comparison, a workman in the late thirteenth century might have earned around 4*d.* per day and an artisan around 1*s.*, placing the median loan in the studies outside Barcelona at anywhere from two to nine months' pay (Burns 1996, p. 9; Emery 1959, p. 49, Table 6 and p. 129). By the late fourteenth century, wage inflation meant that the typical day wage of an unskilled worker in Aragon was 22–25*d.* and of a master mason up to 42*d.* per day (Hamilton 1975, Appendix XI, p. 281; Zulaica Palacios 1994, Table 10, p. 361).

6.3.3 *Security*

Although there is evidence of lending against pledges of land, it is relatively rare. Where gages were deployed, they were often animals or other moveable property. Indeed, for Perpignan, Emery notes that many villagers borrowed without specific surety, implying that their creditworthiness was underpinned either by their own good standing or by general assets (Emery 1959, p. 62). He cites just three cases of mortgages and argues that the tiny proportion of property transactions by Jews in the registers (thirty-one notarial acts, versus 1643 debts) reflects the normal practice of defaulting debtors with land selling in the market to raise the settlement funds, rather than pledging or selling direct to the creditor. The registers also contain only three cases of moveable property gages turned over to creditors, although, as noted previously, pawn-broking was probably largely unnotarised (Emery 1959, especially p. 32).

In Vic, Ollich observes various forms of security, including personal guarantees, renunciations, goods pledged and guarantors. Just seven loans secured against houses are noted, with total values varying between 50*s.* and 260*s.* A larger number (thirteen) were secured against animals and often for relatively high-value loans (such as a mule securing 90–120*s.*, a horse 200*s.*), in addition to further loans secured against, and settled in, crop (commonly wheat or spelt) (Ollich i Castanyer 1985, especially p. 15).

Similarly, in the loans documented in Cardona, guarantees and pledges of goods were common, whilst mortgages seem to have been rare, though not unknown. Of 327 documents transcribed by Casas i Nadal, only eight explicitly note land pledges, although where the surviving document is a receipt or acknowledgement, full details of security may not be known. The eight documented examples include a house under construction held in pledge, with the creditor making a contribution to the construction costs and the borrower also providing general security of all his goods. Other examples of *mutua* loans include pledges of houses, houses with garden and other properties (including one loan between Jews, with the creditor paid a rent of 9*s.* on a loan of 100*s.*, no doubt to avoid the religious bar on usury between Jews) (Casas i Nadal 1985, docs. 24 (pp. 170–171), 102 (pp. 203–204), 104 (p. 205), 118 (pp. 211–212), 123 (p. 214), 166 (p. 232), 222 (pp. 262–263) and 274 (p. 289)). Where details of the mortgage are specified, the creditor is granted full alienation rights without having to go to court in advance, if the loan is not paid in the due term (ibid., doc. 102, p. 204, states '… *nisi in dicto termino solverimus vobis dictum debitum, vos et vestri possitis vestra propria auctoritate sine aliqua requisicione Curie vendere et alienare et impignorare* …'). In one example, a house is pledged but the lender holds the property for rent income and takes the fruits, with similar alienation rights (ibid., doc. 72, p. 191).

Assis' study of Santa Coloma de Queralt also documents security variously provided in the form of witnesses, guarantors, pawns, bonds and rents pledged, mortgages, promissory notes and power of attorney. Whilst Assis notes a few cases of mortgages, no statistical analysis is presented (Assis 1988, pp. 91–93).

Lenders in the larger cities seem to have relied more heavily on third-party guarantors, with a few cases of personal guarantee of the borrower, as noted by both Cuadrench and Rich Abad for Barcelona (in the latter study, guarantors are present in almost all loans, pledging the entirety of their goods, immoveable and moveable, although less than 4% are actually settled by them). A small number of pledges are documented, typically clothes or items of silver (Rich i Abad 1999, p. 264, Table 32, and pp. 266–267). Similarly, in Girona, Jewish loans were secured in most cases by general or specific obligations or guarantors, with records of only around twelve gages of any description (Guilleré 1984, pp. 364–366).

To conclude, previous studies of Jewish lending (drawing on examples from both the thirteenth and fourteenth centuries) find a significant rural clientele and a broad range of types of security, dominated by personal guarantees, sometimes backed by general pledges of moveable and immovable property. Mortgages seem to have formed a very small element of the credit market, for both Jewish and (more understandably given their direct contravention of usury laws) Christian lenders.

6.3.4 Developments in the Credit Markets During the Fourteenth Century

The key development of the fourteenth century, particularly the latter half, was growth in the annuity (*censal*) as a form of financing, in both the private and public debt markets. The original form of the *censal* derives from the common emphyteutic tenure in the crown of Aragon, in which the tenant holds long-term usage rights to land, in return for payment of rent, but the seigneur retains both a pre-emption right and the right to receive a transfer fee when the tenancy changes hands (known respectively as *fadiga* and *lluisme* or *foriscap*). The legal form underpinning the *censal* is the conveyance of the emphyteutic rights attached to the property, excluding these seigniorial rights. Thus, the buyer of the *censal* effectively acquires the right to receive rent payments, whilst the seigneur retains ultimate control of the land. A separate document usually sets out the terms of redemption of the *censal*, on repayment of the capital sum (García Marsilla 2002).

The system of public finance up to the early fourteenth century relied primarily on the revenues of the royal patrimony—rents and dues—supplemented by irregular levies, with financial crises met by the wholesale mortgaging of royal domains and by subsidies raised from municipalities and Jewish communities (through their local councils, or *aljamas*).

This system was put under intolerable pressure by the spiraling costs of wars, including the invasion of Sardinia in 1321, wars with Genoa, civil wars with the Aragonese nobility and, most importantly, the ruinous war with Castile between 1356 and 1375 (Sánchez Martínez et al. 2008). These put particular financial stress on the Jewish communities, who had long accounted for around 20–25% of total crown revenues (Baer 1992, i, p. 179). For example, the Jews of Girona paid tribute of 430,000*s.* between 1309 and 1327; from 1327 to 1348, the *aljama* paid 225,000*s.* in tribute and almost 1 million *s.* in extraordinary subsidies, significantly higher burdens than those imposed on the Christian municipalities (Guilleré 1997, pp. 375–376). These non-systematic revenue sources ultimately proved inadequate and thus, progressively, particularly from the 1350s, a more structured system developed. Key municipal taxes effectively became permanent, covering all crown territories, not just the royal domain. These included indirect imposts, plus taxes on income and assets, all of which developed into municipal taxes, de facto regular and of a fairly fixed amount, to meet specific royal demands. Taxes were supplemented by borrowing, initially through the use of short-term usurious loans. These were gradually replaced by two forms of annuity: the *censal mort*, which had no fixed term, and the *violari*, which survived either for the life of the holder or a defined heir, both forms occasionally being redeemable by the issuer.

The censal mort and *violari* offered three advantages to the borrower: lower rates, generally accepted moral lawfulness and long-term security of revenues (see, e.g. Furió 1993; García Sanz 1961). A canonically acceptable rate of 7.14% was established on *censals* (14.28% on the non-perpetual *violaris*), whilst existing *censals* commonly traded at yields of up to 10% (Schraer 2016, Table 10, pp. 166–167), interest rates much lower than the maximum permitted 20% charged on Jewish loans. Both the lower rate of interest and the formal status of the *censal* as the sale of a right to receive an annuity, rather than as a loan, resulted in its acceptance under usury laws (Noonan 1957, especially Chap. 7).

Although the original *censals* were backed by real property, those issued by municipal and other public bodies were commonly secured by the assignment of patrimonial and tax revenues and thus required the imposts, particularly indirect taxes, to be formally transformed into ordinary, regular and stable income. In effect, the assignment of taxes meant that all assets of the municipality were pledged against these loans. It also established a large rentier class holding these instruments and the growth of a major new market in tradeable debt, held predominantly by Christian creditors, presenting serious competition to Jewish lending. Crucially, the *censal* became the predominant form of public finance (taxes fell from 84% of *censal* sales in 1359 to 27% in 1400 and 5% in 1427, resulting in the application of the vast majority of tax revenues to annuity payments) (Salvat Editores 1978–1979, iii, p. 187).

One measure of the rise of the *censal* is found in the records of the *Justicia Civil de Valencia*. Between 1361 and 1372, they document 119 repayment claims, comprising 104 usurious loans, eleven *violaris* and four *censals* but, in the following decades, these proportions were inverted, especially after 1391 with the destruction of the Jewish community of the city of Valencia, along with many others across the crown of Aragon (García Marsilla 2002, p. 314, Table 40 and pp. 358–359).

This development of an 'alternative' credit market would have affected Jewish lenders both through rate competition and increased supply of funds, backed by readily marketable securities. It exacerbated the impact of the tributes and subsidies in impoverishing the Jewish communities and eroding their capital base for lending. For instance, up to 1348, the notarial record of Girona shows members of the Jewish *aljama* involved in 35–40% of notarial acts, a proportion which declined to less than 10% by the end of the century, whilst sale of *censals* rose to 15% of all such acts (Guilleré 1997, p. 380). From 1348, the tax contribution of the *aljamas* fell and they resorted increasingly to issuing their own *censals* to meet their tributes and expenses. By the outbreak of the Castile war, the contribution of the *aljamas* was far outweighed by the new sources of finance.

Thus, the backdrop to Jewish lending in the late fourteenth century was negative in many respects: loss of political power, Jews having been barred from public office as far back as 1283; the economic pressure of over-taxation; and an apparent loss of share in the credit market (although note that this loss of political power was not absolute as, despite the legal restrictions, some continued to hold positions of influence, notably Alazar Golluff in late fourteenth-century Zaragoza, included in the analysis that follows (see Blasco Martínez 2009)). Furthermore, the period of study straddles the anti-Jewish riots of 1391, which not only produced large-scale forced conversion and the destruction of several major *aljamas* but undoubtedly led directly to substantial economic loss to those Jews who did survive.

6.4 The Jews of Zaragoza, 1383–1400

Consonant with its status as capital of Aragon, Zaragoza had one of the largest Jewish populations. Baer estimates 200 families, whilst Martínez finds 313 registered houses in the *judería* in 1369, rising to 347 'hearths' in 1404, all consistent with a total population of between 1000 and 1700, not dissimilar in scale to the Jewish populations of Barcelona, Huesca and Valencia (Baer 1992, i, p. 193; Blasco Martínez 1988, pp. 11 and 27). The rise in the number of Jewish households reflects the fact that not only was Zaragoza spared the attacks of 1391 (the king being in residence), but gained migrants fleeing other communities.

This study draws on the notarial records held in the *Archivo Histórico de Protocolos de Zaragoza* (AHPZ). Records are drawn from five notaries widely used by the Jews, namely Domingo Martín de Aguilón, Juan de Capilla, Blasco Aznárez de Anso, Juan Blasco de Azuara and Juan López de Barbastro, during the period 1383–1400. The analysis covers 28 individuals from eight families, amongst the most economically active Jewish individuals and families, particularly as lenders and also documented as real estate investors.

6.4.1 The Lenders

The Alazars and Bienvenist/de la Cavallerias were two of the leading Jewish families of Aragon, with high levels of wealth, special tax privileges and strong political ties (Blasco Martínez 1992). The thirteen documented members of the Alazar family over this short period (with some 200 acts in total) include two physicians; members of the family are recorded as owners of seven properties in the *judería*, as well as renting out vineyards to Christians for substantial rents (in one case, 65*s*. per annum recorded as being received for two years). Five members of the intermarried Bienvenist and de la Cavalleria families feature in eighty-five acts; amongst them, a widow (Orovida) was one of the most active. As with the Alazars, they are recorded receiving rents over prolonged periods (in one case, as least four years), trading in grapes and as both principals and agents in significant real estate transactions.

A third important family is the Abnarrabis, comprising Salamon, a leading financier, merchant, administrator and prominent member of the *aljama*, and his two sons. This family has the most documented real estate activities, with numerous sources of rent income (including the grants of four long leases), in one case held for at least eleven years, plus sales and purchases, one with a leaseback clause to the previous owner, which must have been a form of financing (Schraer 2015).

Another family of high status were the Golluffs: father (Açach), a wealthy cloth trader who served several times on the *aljama* and Jewish religious court and lent, inter alia, to the king; son (Alazar) who served the *infant*, the Queen and the archbishopric of Zaragoza as a financial administrator, also making significant royal loans (Blasco Martínez 2009, see, in particular, pp. 488, 490–491, fn. 90 and fn. 93, pp. 493–498 and 505–508; also, see Blasco Martínez 2005, pp. 605–606).

Two other significant lenders are from the artisan or merchant class. Açach Amato, for whom forty loans and a number of property transactions are recorded, is noted as a tailor by occupation. Açach Almachuqui, also a tailor and a member of the *aljama*, is one of the best documented lenders (well over 100 surviving acts of credit, plus two real estate transactions), whose business was primarily with Muslim residents of the Zaragoza hinterland, almost half of the loans with a crop element.

6.4.2 Scope of Economic Activities

The sources under consideration include a total of 723 relevant transactions for these individuals, encompassing a variety of economic activities. The largest element comprises loans (576 acts, 80% of the total). The majority of these (487) are cash-only loans, mostly using a standard loan deed (*carta de deudo*), with a further 26 loans repayable in a combination of cash and crop and 18 in crop only. An additional 27 loans use the *comanda* form. As noted above, this legal form was used more by Christians, to circumvent usury laws, than by Jews. When employed by the Jews of Zaragoza, it was often in mercantile business ventures. A further 21 deeds encompass pledging agreements and redemptions, cessions of loans and the transactions related to existing loans.

The second largest category is real estate related, with a total of 53 transactions (7% of the total). These predominantly reflect Jews acting as landlords to Christian tenants, including 21 rent receipts, seven lease grants and one sale of rents. The next largest category is property purchases (11) and sales (three). The balance includes one house construction, one intra-family gift and four land cessions. Higher average value of property purchases and sales than loans, and their longer-term nature as an investment mean that the economic significance of real estate transactions is disproportionate to their numerical quantity.

Remaining transactions include 23 purchases of grapes; 21 borrowings (including 10 *comanda*); 20 official dealings, mostly collections of taxes and tributes; 14 trade transactions; five relating to cession of holdings of *censals*; three pledge deeds; and eight others.

6.4.3 Loan Deeds

Earlier studies of Jewish lending commonly identified the main legal form to be the *mutuum*, in which interest is not explicitly stated. The *carta de deudo* used most frequently in Zaragoza generally specifies 'profit' (*ganancia*) to be '*al coto et mandamiento del senyor rey*', that is, 'in accordance with the edict and order of the lord king'. As noted above, this was almost always stated as 20% in the *fueros* and *Corts* edicts; the actual percentage is seldom mentioned in the deed. The deed specifies a repayment term, always as a single bullet repayment, almost always less than one year. In practice, however, many loans are seen outstanding long after these terms. The deed usually contains standard wording, obliging the borrower to support the lender in legal suits, at his own cost. It also generally contains some form of security, discussed below.

6.4.4 Analysis of Loans

Of the 576 recorded loans, we have sufficient data for analysis (including the amount of the loan, either full or summary terms, usually the date of the loan and the identity of both lender and borrower) in 550 cases of new loans, in either *carta de deudo* or *comanda* forms, made between 1383 and 1400. In 319 of these cases, the surviving documentation is the borrower's acknowledgement of the debt, usually with an abbreviated summary of the main terms (abbreviated to varying degrees). In just two cases, it is the lender's confirmation. A full copy of the loan deed, or comprehensive summary of the main terms, is available for 95 loans. In 107 cases, surviving documentation is a receipt, for repayment of interest and/or capital. In 27 cases, we have other loan-related documentation which includes the key data on the original loan.

Table 6.2 Value of loans in Zaragoza

(a) Loans by value					
Total value of loans (s.)			*Mean loan (s.)*	*Median loan (s.)*	
454,752			858	190	
(b) Loans by value ranges					
	20–50s.	*51–100s.*	*101–500s.*	*501–1000s.*	*>1000s.*
Number of loans	46	105	238	65	76
% of loans by volume	8.7	19.8	44.9	12.3	14.3
% of loans by value	0.4	1.8	11.7	10.5	75.6

Note The two largest loans are both equal to 3000 florins (approximately 27,000*s.*)
Source AHPZ, notaries Domingo Martín de Aguilón, Juan de Capilla, Blasco Aznárez de Anso, Juan Blasco de Azuara and Juan López de Barbastro, 1383–1400

Cash loan amounts are known for 530 loans, summarised in Table 6.2. This excludes crop-only loans and does not attempt to value the crop element of mixed loans. Based on the range of wheat prices over the period, the crop element of mixed loans would add between 15 and 30% to the overall loan value of the mixed loans, but, given their relatively small number and value, it is not a material adjustment to the overall analysis.

It is immediately clear that the average loan was very much higher than the credit in small market towns discussed above, where typical loans were 60–90*s.*; indeed, the average loan is even substantially higher than that observed in thirteenth-century Barcelona. However, much of this increase in loan size would appear to be explicable by wage inflation; compared with the higher levels of wages in the late fourteenth century noted above, the median loan represents around three months' pay of an unskilled labourer and about two months' pay of an artisan, at the lower end of the scale for the market towns.

The unusually large gap between mean and median reflects the significant business in very large loans, some municipal, some to groups of leading members of the patriciate and some clearly representing investments in mercantile ventures. Despite competition from Christian loans at much lower interest rates, all of the surviving evidence is that Jewish lenders continued to charge 20% on their loans, in accordance with the legally permitted maximum interest rate, implying either that they served debtors unable to access other sources of funds or that demand exceeded the supply from non-Jewish sources.

6.4.5 *Borrowers*

Very few of the loan deeds indicate the occupation of the borrower, but in most cases (495 in total), the location of residence of the borrower is known, mapped in Fig. 6.1. Of these, 220 (44%) were made to urban borrowers, almost all to residents or citizens of Zaragoza and a handful to residents of Daroca. Thirty-one loans were made to residents of '*villas*', towns such as Zuera and Alcañiz. A further nine have multiple borrowers, one in Zaragoza and one in either a town or rural area. In total, therefore, almost

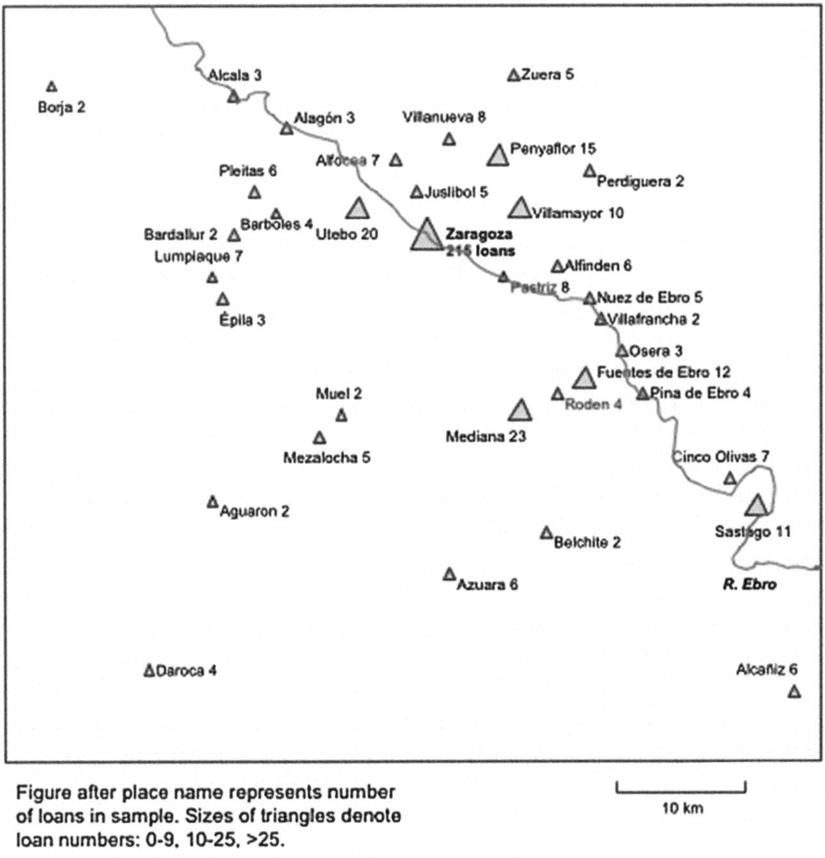

Fig. 6.1 Main places of residence of borrowers from Jews of Zaragoza 1383–1400 (495 loans)
Source see Table 6.2

exactly 50% of the loans where the residence of the borrower is known were made to urban residents, leaving 50% to rural residents. The clientele is notably less urban than the small Barcelona samples, a fact that might be expected to lead to smaller average loans, but, in fact, the reverse is true. Although rural borrowers unsurprisingly comprise a smaller percentage of the total number of debtors than in some of the smaller market towns, the gap is less marked than might be expected.

Of the non-urban borrowers, 57 resided in '*aldeas*' of Zaragoza, villages in its hinterland (although the documentation uses the terms '*aldea*' and '*lugar*' somewhat interchangeably). A further 178 loans were made to residents of various '*lugares*' or '*poblas*', small rural locations in the Zaragoza province. Ninety-four of these were loans to Muslims, who were largely displaced from the city following the re-conquest and formed a sizeable part of the rural population (commonly found in the fertile lands of the Ebro Valley, including such places as Cinqolivas (modern Cinco Olivas), Mediana, Pleitas, Sastago, Roden, Nuez and Osera). Twelve loans are also recorded to Muslims residing in the *morería* of the city of Zaragoza itself. The most commonly occurring locations are Huytevo (Utebo), with 15 cases; 12 in Penyaflor, a village some 12 km from the city; seven in Villamayor, 10 km from the city; and others from Azuara, Fuentes, Pastriz, Villanueva de Burjazud (part of Villanueva de Gallego) and Mezalocha. These are in a ring, with a concentration in the Ebro valley, 10–60 km from the city centre, as shown in Fig. 6.1.

The highest median loan is found in the towns (*villas*), at 600*s*., the distribution being skewed by 13 loans over 1000*s*., four of which were to town councils or *aljamas*. By comparison, the median loan to Zaragoza residents was 210*s*. As one would expect, the median loan in rural locations was lower, 125*s*. in the *aldeas* of Zaragoza and 100*s*. in the other villages (*lugares* and *poblas*). Muslims represent a significant element of the rural market, accounting for 108 loans with a median cash value of 102*s*. (the 66 cash-only loans have a median value of 130*s*., more representative of all rural loans). As Table 6.1 illustrates, even these median rural loans are 1.5–2 times higher than those recorded in the previous studies of market towns with mainly rural clientele.

This higher typical loan value, although consistent with wage growth, runs against the tide in two other respects. Over time, as we have seen, the municipal debt market moved away from usurious loans to the issue of *censals* and *violaris*, a development expected to reduce the share of Jewish lenders in a market with relatively high average loans. In fact, the Zaragoza data do include a reasonable element of municipal lending, albeit more to Muslim *aljamas* than Christian councils. Also, the progressive impoverishment of Jewish communities and erosion of their capital base might be expected to push them downmarket, into smaller loans, but the converse is observed.

6.4.6 Security Underpinning Loans

In addition to the high average loan size, the most striking aspect of the loans under consideration is the predominance of land pledges as the sole or prime means of security, as indicated in Table 6.3, which covers the 267 loans for which the form of security is known. Land was the sole element in 73% of cases and at least one element in 84% of cases. This is a completely different picture from most of the other case studies of Jewish lending. It seems that the mortgage emerged as the main type of loan during this period and in this location, begging the question as to how far it reflects social conflict and thus the lowering of inter-communal trust, the relatively high average loan value in Zaragoza, requiring stronger asset backing than the traditional guarantee, or the growth in a broader economic role of property. Table 6.3 also illustrates that the lowest value transactions were secured by guarantor alone and the highest value by pledge of land and/or other property, although the differential between average value of the sample and that of mortgages is not dramatic. Indeed, the proportion of very large loans backed by land is very similar to the average. Of the loans valued over 500*s.*, security is known for thirty-four cases (out of sixty-five), five backed by pledge of goods only, twenty-six by land only (76%) and three by both land and goods.

Table 6.3 Loan security

	Number	*Total value (s.)*	*Mean loan (s.)*	*Median loan (s.)*
Security (excl. crop-only)				
Land only	193	60,626	314	140
Land and goods	14	4102	293	153
Land and guarantor	16	2623	164	138
Goods only	19	5713	301	145
Guarantor only	24	2625	109	85
Guarantor and goods pledged	1	62	62	62
Total	267	75,751	284	135

Source see Table 6.2

For the relatively large municipal loans, security is not stated in most extant documents although, in at least one example, it is backed by goods of each of the leading citizens (*honrats*).[1]

Of the loans to Muslim borrowers, four were backed by goods pledged, 14 by guarantors, 12 by land pledges only and two by both land pledges and guarantors. Muslim borrowing was less dependent than average on pledges of land, no doubt partially reflecting the low value of their rural property holdings and, perhaps, limited property rights as tenant farmers; nevertheless, mortgages were not uncommon. The 14 documented cases of land pledges are disproportionately urban (seven in Zaragoza and seven in rural areas), presumably reflective of higher urban property values. An unusually high proportion of these loans to Muslims (76 loans) have no documented security, even (in a few cases) where we have a full loan deed. As well as the nature of surviving documentation, this may well reflect the relatively low median value of these loans (100*s.*) and the presence of crop-only loans in this group, with the produce of the land effectively acting as security, rather than the land itself.

Table 6.4 shows the type of land used as security for loans. As one might expect, mixed plots of urban land and property (presumably larger in size than houses alone) supported the largest average loans and loans supported by houses display higher values than fields, olive groves or vineyards. There is a wide spread of property types used for such mortgages. Of the loans backed by houses, the majority (sixty) are located within Zaragoza, eight in the surrounding *aldeas* and ten in *lugares* or *poblas* (most of the balance in *villas*). The Zaragoza houses support a median loan of 223*s.*, slightly above average but not dramatically so.

Table 6.4 Type of land used as security

	Number of loans	*Median loan (s.)*
Houses	85	195
Mixed houses with cellars, gardens, field, yards and/or vineyards	10	490
Vineyards	52	153
Young vineyards ('*malluellos*')	20	137
Fields/fields and vineyards	34	113
Olive groves	12	128
Gardens/gardens and vineyards	4	252
Other/not known	6	170
Total	223	140

Source see Table 6.2

The loan-to-value ratio provides a key measure of the strength of security provided by the land pledged. Although we do not know the market value of the actual land pledged against each loan, we can compare these loans with the average values of properties separately traded in Zaragoza by the creditors, based on the AHPZ records. Of 48 relevant land transactions, the mean price was 1552*s.* and the median 825*s.* The 21 sales and purchases of vineyards had a considerably lower average value (mean 608*s.* and median 325*s.*). Houses, unsurprisingly, attracted far higher average prices (overall mean 2295*s.*). Sales of houses (median price 1290*s.*) were typically of much higher value than purchases of houses (median price 750*s.*) (Schraer 2016, pp. 60–65). This may simply reflect a profitable trade or, if directly related to mortgaged property, possible hidden returns above the permitted 20% interest ceiling, with properties acquired at below market price and quickly on-sold (e.g. see Blasco Martínez 1988, pp. 205–206; further detail and discussion in Schraer 2016, pp. 267–269 and discussion below). In most cases, however, it is not possible to verify this from the records by tracing the original acquisition of the properties sold.

If these values were also typical of the mortgaged properties, it would imply average loan-to-value ratios of 17% for all properties, 15–25% for houses but rather higher for vineyards at almost 50% (based on the median loan and sale price). If, on the other hand, the high values of land transacted reflect a desire to hold only the best land as an investment, reflective of quality, location and plot size, the mortgage loan-to-value ratio might be under-stated by this calculation. By way of comparison, Van Werveke's sample of mortgage loans by religious houses indicates an average loan:value ratio of just under 60%, compared to an average of around two-thirds in Génestal's sample for Normandy (Van Werveke 1968, p. 180). Archival sources for Barcelona also document seven cases of land sold in Barcelona in 1242 to settle outstanding debts owed to Jews. Assessment is complicated by the loans and sale prices being in different currencies; at the then exchange rate of *morabatins* to *sous doblenc*, the outstanding loans were (in six cases) between 60 and 77% of the value of the property sold. To the extent that the data reliably indicate over-collateralisation, it can readily be explained by the need to provide additional security against short-term land price volatility. It may also have been a way of achieving returns above the legal limit, but this is, understandably, not indicated explicitly by the wording of the loan deeds (see below).

Table 6.5 Loan security by type of location

Number of loans by type of location	*Aldeas*	*Lugares*	*Cities*	*Villas*	*Mixed*	*Not known*	*Total*
Pledge type							
Land only	28	37	117	3	4	4	193
Land and goods	4		7		1	2	14
Land and guarantor	5	2	6	1		2	16
Goods only		6	10		2	1	19
Guarantor only		18	4	2			24
Goods and guarantor			1				1
Total	37	63	145	6	7	9	267

Source see Table 6.2

For 258 loans, the sources reveal both the type of security and residency of borrower (see Table 6.5). Of 215 of these cases supported by a land pledge (as part or whole of security provided), 139 are urban (city, town or mixed) and 76 rural (*aldea* or *lugar*). Thus, whilst the mortgage here was predominantly an urban phenomenon, around one-third occur in purely rural locations. We should also note throughout that the urban/rural distinction is different from the modern idea, given the ubiquitous presence within or just outside the city walls of vineyards, *huertas* and fields serving the urban population and the unity of the city with its rural hinterland (Ray 2006, p. 37).

6.4.7 *The Terms of Land Pledges*

Most of the surviving documents are in highly abbreviated form, stating that property is placed in special tenancy (*metemos en special tenencia*), or even merely *en special* before description of the property pledged (similar terminology to the Latin *specialiter* indicating a pledge of specific assets, as opposed to a general pledge of the goods of a borrower or guarantor). However, in some cases, we have the full wording, from which the broad mortgage pledge can be inferred:

> … for your greater strength and security, we oblige to you in special tenancy, to be returned [on repayment], in place of guarantors, for the above-mentioned debt, interest and costs, [the mortgaged property], in such a manner that, if we or any of us do not pay to you or whoever you wish the said debt, interest or costs, you are empowered, by

> your own authority, following the passing of the said term, and without licence, order of any judge, without penalty or fines [*calonia*] and without announcement of the 30 days [required in the laws of pledges and property rights, to permit any pre-emption or other rights to be exercised], to sell the said property which we place in special tenancy, to be returned, in place of guarantors, to whomever you wish and for the amount of the price which is obtainable; and of the price which is obtained, that which remains of the said debt, interest and costs and any matter, to be delivered by hand to you, without deferral, that which is recovered, all which we promise to you. And we are obliged to you completely to perfect the sale which you make of the said properties, we will be established at that moment as guarantors and principal sellers of those which are required to be sold.[2]

This language establishes that the effective, temporary legal control of the property is placed in the hands of the creditor, pending repayment. It is not clear from the wording whether the creditor took physical control of the property; however, his explicit right is only to sell the property in order to recover his debt, not to exploit the land, to take its fruits in lieu of interest, nor indeed to retain ownership after default. This may suggest the right was more akin to a *hypothec* than a *pignus* but is not definitive. There is also a specific term that the debtors undertake to bear all the legal obligations both as guarantors and as principals of the sale, further underlining that they remain beneficial owners and that the creditor's interest is a lien over the property, not actual ownership. The total absence from the notarial record of any deeds of enforcement of pledges would seem to imply that this legal wording was effective in permitting the sale of the property without further legal recourse, as it was clearly intended to do. It is true that these creditors are also observed purchasing properties on a scale not documented amongst other Jewish communities of the crown and some might infer that these purchases were, therefore, directly related to the credit business, but this remains a matter of conjecture. It is, of course, possible that the creditors chose to purchase the properties themselves in settlement of the loan, either because the market at the time offered further potential for gains or because their relative market power meant that they could sell at a profit, but it is equally possible that some properties were acquired independently, to exploit an attractive market opportunity.

6.4.8 Relationship to the Wider Property Business

A number of real estate transactions can be explicitly or implicitly connected to lending, with sources indicating different economic functions in individual cases. As noted above, Blasco Martínez discusses one example, in which Açach Amato purchased a piece of land for 1000*s.* on the same day as lending, in the *comanda* form, 500 florins (approximately 4500*s.*) to the vendor. Seven months later, Açach sold the same land for 1290*s.*, a substantial capital gain. In this case, the land was in all probability purchased at an artificially low price in order to enhance the return achieved on the loan. On the other hand, the precise link between the two transactions (of such different sizes) is not entirely clear—the capital gain is much lower than the potential interest accrual under a *carta de deudo* over that period—and the lapse of seven months before sale suggests that at least some risk was being taken. Indeed, from these sources, it is a rarity to be able to link the land purchases specifically to a loan, either by correspondence of date or by loan size. This may, in part, be a function of the incompleteness of the surviving record and, in part, a deliberate desire to divorce the two halves of linked transactions which might, in effect, have transgressed usury laws. On the other hand, the lack of positive evidence must leave open the possibility, noted above, that real estate was being held as an attractive asset class in its own right, at least in part independent of credit. Whilst the presence of numerous cases of land, especially vineyards, rented by Jews to Christians for cash rents, may also be seen as linked to credit (as rents often were a means of subverting usury laws), there is no direct evidence to that effect in these records.

In a number of cases, land sales were made to settle outstanding debts. For example, Salamon Abnarrabi purchased land from a Christian family with whom he had more than one outstanding debt. Although not explicitly in settlement, this seems a probable motive.[3] One of his sons, Samuel, transferred several lands to Bonafos de la Cavalleria in explicit settlement of outstanding loans.[4]

An example of an indirect link between lending and land is seen in a series of purchases of properties in Alagón for a total price of 15,000*s.*, undertaken by Bonafos de la Cavalleria, apparently as agent for a Christian. The wording of the deed indicates that these lands had been acquired under redeemable pledges and that the consequent land transactions offered substantial gains for several parties. On the same date,

Salamon Abnarrabi sold houses and vineyards to Bonafos for 7000*s*. in the same location, apparently pledged to him by a Christian, no doubt part of the same speculative trade.[5]

A final explicit link is seen in at least one 'sale and leaseback' transaction under which Salamon Abnarrabi purchased vineyards for 1800*s*. and leased them back to the vendors, on a 9% yield.[6] Although this return appears far below the normal return on loans, Salamon would have enjoyed both seigniorial rights and potential capital gains to enhance his return, whilst offering a headline rate closer to that of the *censal*.

6.5 Conclusions

The lending of the Jews of Zaragoza in the last two decades of the fourteenth century offers a particularly interesting case study. The political and economic environment was markedly less attractive than that enjoyed by earlier Jewish lenders, and competition from Christian credit was undoubtedly increased by the rise of *censal*, in addition to other credit instruments. Widespread and highly destructive anti-Jewish riots occurred in 1391, the very middle of the period of study. Whilst Zaragoza escaped destruction, and indeed attracted immigrants from other communities, the resultant fear and uncertainty must have been considerable. Yet, we find a healthy credit business, built in large part on pledges of land and with a close apparent link to a lively real estate business. These mortgage loans were of large average size and engaged with both urban and rural clientele, mostly in and around the city of Zaragoza, but with a substantial business in a ring 10–25 km around the city, some to borrowers up to 50–60 km away.

The reasons for the increased prominence of large mortgages to both rural and urban clients are a matter of speculation. However, given the growing uncertainty, both in the status of the Jewish community and in the wider economy, it may reflect reduced inter-communal trust and the need for stronger, more valuable and reliable security. The apparent over-collateralisation of the loans supports this contention. If this trend was primarily defensive, it does also seem to have had positive results in facilitating an active real estate business. Following the depopulation resulting from the Black Death of 1348 and subsequent plague outbreaks, the rise in the land:labour ratio seems to have resulted in rents falling relative to wages, which may have made the pledging of land more attractive to debtors (Álvarez-Nogal and Prados de la Escosura 2013, pp. 8–9).

However, information on the trend in land values during this period is limited. If land values were more robust than rents, given an apparently active land market, the trend to mortgage lending may well also have been supported by a recognition on the part of creditors that overall returns could be enhanced as a result of combining lending and land investment.

Conversely, economic theories relating to minority group behaviour would imply a general preference for portable over fixed assets, in view of the risks of unreliable property rights, confiscations and persecution, particularly favouring investment in human rather than physical capital, with its advantages of portability and low confiscation risk (Brenner and Kiefer 1981; Botticini and Eckstein 2005, 2007). This theory helps to explain the generally high investment by Jews and other minorities in education. However, in this case, when choosing between investment in lending or real estate, several factors run counter. Firstly, the apparent liquidity of the property market may have meant that the portability issue was less serious than with lending, which could not readily be realised before maturity, other than by assignment, and suffered from both high costs of enforcement and material risk of delayed repayment. Secondly, although property rights were often partial and transitory, the legal framework, both civil and religious, offered a reasonable platform to support land as a tradeable asset, source of reliable income and store of wealth. In some cases, Jews were granted the right to act as absentee landlords in re-conquered territories (Ray 2006, pp. 18–19), and there is plentiful evidence of their acting as landlords to Christian tenants, including in the Zaragoza records, analysed above. Even though the incidence of Jews acting in official court positions had fallen sharply by the late fourteenth century, their regular appearance as tax and rent farmers and collectors would have required them or their agents to travel widely and to possess the power and authority to collect dues and enforce property rights, vital attributes for landlords.

We have also seen that lending carried a risk of confiscation, whilst officially sanctioned moratoria and delayed repayment were regular features of the market. Thirdly, the longevity of settlement of the Jews in Iberia may have meant that the risk of forced resettlement was discounted, at least prior to 1391 (for examples of the 'normality' of commercial relations between Christians and Jews in the unstable period leading up to 1391, see Guerson de Oliveira 2012). Thereafter, that risk could not be discounted, but still investment in real estate continued unabated.

Overall, it does seem that the land pledges offered the lender greater security than a guarantee, oath or general pledge, in value, liquidity and dependability. It may have assisted Jewish lenders in competing with the growing Christian credit by tapping into a different market, whilst contributing to overall return on investment. It allowed the creditors to take advantage of a major asset class owned by both urban and rural borrowers, to the benefit of both parties to the debt.

Perhaps most surprisingly, faced with stiff competition, Jews were able to maintain a high-volume, high-value business, with a full 20% return, not forced downmarket to smaller loans. The use of land pledge (far less noticeable in earlier case studies of Jewish lending) opened up a market of both urban and rural borrowers who may not have had ready access to the *censal*, but could tap into their most valuable asset to raise credit. Credit was the largest and, in all probability, most lucrative business for the Jews, but the real estate business that emerged from it and alongside it offered healthy, reliable, long-term returns, coupled with valuable portfolio diversification.

Notes

1. Archivo Histórico de Protocolos de Zaragoza (hereafter AHPZ), notary: Juan de Capilla, 1390 f. 67r–68r. Loan of Mose Alazar.
2. Author's translation; AHPZ, Juan de Capilla, 1384 f. 6v–8v. Loan of Açach Golluff: '*…amayor firmeza et seguridat vuestra, obligamos avos en special tenencia et retorno [en lugar de fiança] porel sobredito deudo, ganancia et misiones … [details of property mortgaged] tal manera que si nos o qualquier de nos non pagaremos avos o a qui vos queredes el dito deudo, ganancia o misiones que vos por vuestra proprio actoridat pasado el dito termino et sines licencia et mandamiento de algun juge et sines penayr calunya alguna et sines crida d' xxx dias podades vender las ditas [property] que nos en special tenencia et retorno [et en lugar de fiança] metemos aqui queredes et pro quantia precio que trobardes et del precio que de havedes que vos enquedes del sobredito deudo ganancia et misiones et alguna cosa vos entregado en so br[azo] que lo restituyades si nos et sin de tri[n]guata todo aquello vos prometemos et nos obligamos complidament emendar dela vendicion que vos faredes delas ditas [properties] agora porla hora nos stableremos seyer fianças et principals vendedors de aquellas aqui quiere que las vendredes*'.
3. AHPZ, Domingo Martín de Aguilón, 1391 f. 152v–153v.
4. AHPZ, Domingo Martín de Aguilón, 1391 f. 159rv.
5. AHPZ, Domingo Martín de Aguilón, 1391 f. 157v–158v and f. 168v.
6. AHPZ, Domingo Martín de Aguilón, 1394 f. 151rv.

References

Primary Sources

Mieres, T., 1533. *Apparatus Super Constitutionibus Curiarum generalium Cathaloniae* (Barcelona: Carolum Amorosum).

Régné, J., 1978. *History of the Jews in Aragon: Regesta and Documents 1213–1327*, ed. and annotated Y.T. Assis (Jerusalem: Magnes Press).

Secondary Works

Álvarez-Nogal, C. and L. Prados de la Escosura, 2013. 'The rise and fall of Spain (1270–1850)', *EcHR*, vol. 66, pp. 1–37.

Assis, Y.T., 1988. *The Jews of Santa Coloma de Queralt: An Economic and Demographic Case Study of a Community at the end of the Thirteenth Century* (Jerusalem: Magnes Press).

Baer, Y., 1992. *A History of the Jews in Christian Spain*, 2 vols, trans. Louis Schoffman (Philadelphia: Jewish Publication Society).

Bensch, S.P., 1995. *Barcelona and Its Rulers, 1096–1291* (Cambridge: Cambridge University Press).

Blasco Martínez, A., 1988. *La judería de Zaragoza en el siglo XIV* (Zaragoza: Institución Fernando el Católico).

Blasco Martínez, A., 1992. 'Las Expulsiones Señoriales: Los Caballería y los Alazar de Zaragoza, vasallos del Orden del Hospital', *Proceedings of the Conference: Expulsion of Jews from Spain, 1474–1516, Jerusalem, 1992.* At: http://www.unizar.es/cema/recursos/expulsiones.pdf, accessed 3 May 2016.

Blasco Martínez, A., 2005. 'Judíos Zaragozanos comerciantes de Tejido en Siglo XIV: anotaciones biográficas', *Acta historica et archaeologica mediaevalia*, vol. 26, pp. 587–612.

Blasco Martínez, A., 2009. 'Alazar Golluf, regente de la tesorería de la reina de Aragón, y su entorno familiar (siglos XIII–XI)', in F. Sabaté and C. Denjean (eds.), *Cristianos y judíos en contacto en la Edad Media: Polémica, conversión, dinero y convivencia* (Lleida: Milenio), pp. 481–580.

Botticini, M. and Z. Eckstein, 2005. 'Jewish occupational selection: Education, restrictions or minorities?', *JEH*, vol. 65, pp. 922–948.

Botticini, M. and Z. Eckstein, 2007. 'From farmers to merchants, conversions and diaspora: Human capital and Jewish history', *Journal of the European Economic Association*, vol. 5, pp. 885–926.

Brenner, R. and N.M. Kiefer, 1981. 'The economics of the diaspora: Discrimination and occupational structure', *Economic Development and Cultural Change*, vol. 29, pp. 517–534.

Burns, R.I., 1996. *Jews in the Notarial Culture: Latinate Wills in Mediterranean Spain, 1250–1350* (Berkeley, LA and London: University of California Press).

Casas i Nadal, M., 1985. 'El "Liber Iudeorum" de Cardona (1330–1334). Edició i estudi', *Miscel·lània de Textos Medievals*, vol. 3, pp. 121–350.

Emery, R.W., 1959. *The Jews of Perpignan in the Thirteenth Century: An Economic Study Based on Notarial Records* (New York: Columbia University Press).

Fernández-Cuadrench, J., 2007. 'El crèdit jueu a la Barcelona del segle XIII', *Barcelona Quaderns d'Història*, vol. 13, pp. 157–196.

Furió, A., 1993. 'Crédito y endeudamiento: el censal en la sociedad rural valenciana (siglos XIV-XV)', in E. Serrano Martín and Sarasa Sánchez, E. (eds.), *Señorío y feudalismo en la Península Ibérica siglos XII-XIX*, 4 vols (Zaragoza: Institución Fernando el Católico), i, pp. 501–534.

García Marsilla, J.V., 2002. *Vivir a crédito en la Valencia medieval* (Valencia: Universitat de València).

García Sanz, A., 1961. 'El censal', *Boletín de la Sociedad Castellonense de Cultura*, vol. 37, pp. 281–310.

Guerson de Oliveira, A., 2012. 'Coping with Crises: Christian-Jewish Relations in Catalonia and Aragon 1380–1391', unpublished PhD thesis, University of Toronto.

Guilleré, C., 1984. 'Le crédit à Gérone au début du XIVe siècle (1321–1330)', in E. Eiras Roel (ed.), *La documentación notarial y la historia: actas del II Coloquio de Metodologia Histórica Aplicada*, 2 vols (Madrid: Junta de Decanos de los Colegios Notariales de España), ii, pp. 363–371.

Guilleré, C., 1997. 'Fiscalité et société à Gérone du XIVe siècle', in M. Sánchez Martínez and A. Furió (eds.), *Actes: Col·loqui Municipis i Fiscalitat a la Baixa Edat Mitjana* (Lleida: Institut d'estudis Ilerdencs), pp. 367–382.

Hamilton, E., 1975. *Money, Prices and Wages in Valencia, Aragon and Navarre, 1351–1500* (Philadelphia: Porcupine Press).

Hinojosa Montalvo, J.R., 1985a. 'Actividades judías en la Valencia del siglo XIV', *En la España Medieval*, vol. 7, pp. 1547–1567.

Hinojosa Montalvo, J.R., 1985b. 'El préstamo judío en la ciudad de Valencia en la segunda mitad del siglo XIV', *Sefarad*, vol. 45, pp. 315–340.

Hoffman Berman, C., 1986. 'Medieval agriculture, the southern French countryside, and the early Cistercians: A study of forty-three monasteries', *Transactions of the American Philosophical Society*, vol. 76, pp. 1–179.

Kohn, M., 1999. 'The capital market before 1600', Working Paper 99–06, Department of Economics, Dartmouth College. At: http://www.dartmouth.edu/~mkohn/Papers/99-06.pdf, accessed 12 April 2016.

Milton, G.B., 2012. *Market Power: Lordship, Society and Economy in Medieval Catalonia (1276–1313)* (New York: Palgrave Macmillan).

Noonan, J.T., 1957. *The Scholastic Analysis of Usury* (Cambridge, MA: Harvard University Press).

Ollich i Castanyer, I., 1985. 'Aspectes econòmics de l'activitat dels jueus de Vic segons els "Libri Iudeorum" (1266–1278)', *Miscel·lània de Textos Medievals*, vol. 3, pp. 1–118.

Ray, J., 2006. *The Sephardic Frontier: The 'Reconquista' and the Jewish Community in Medieval Iberia* (Ithaca, NY: Cornell University Press).

Richardson, H.G., 1960. *The English Jewry Under Angevin Kings* (London: Methuen).

Rich i Abad, A., 1999. *La comunitat jueva de Barcelona entre 1348 i 1391 a través de la documentació notarial* (Barcelona: Fundació Noguera).

Riera i Sans, J., 2010. 'The Regulations of James I concerning the Jewish moneylenders: A preliminary report', *Imago Temporis, Medium Aevum*, vol. 4, pp. 263–285.

Romano, D., 1983. *Judíos al servicio de Pedro el Grande de Aragón (1276–1285)* (Barcelona: Universitat de Barcelona).

Sánchez Martínez, M., A. Furió and Á. Sesma Muñoz, 2008. 'Old and new forms of taxation in the Crown of Aragon (13th–14th centuries)', in S. Cavaciocchi (ed.), *La fiscalità nell'economia europea. secc. xiii-xviii. - fiscal systems in the European economy from the 13th to the 18th centuries* (Florence: Florence University Press), pp. 99–130.

Salvat Editores (ed.), 1978–1979. *Història de Catalunya*, 6 vols (Barcelona: Salvat Editores).

Schraer, M.A., 2015. 'Salamon Abnarrabi—A Jewish rentier in late fourteenth-century Zaragoza', *Journal of Medieval Iberian Studies*, vol. 8, pp. 94–109.

Schraer, M.A., 2016. 'Real Estate and the Jews of the Crown of Aragon, 1150–1400', unpublished PhD thesis, University of Cambridge.

Werveke, H. Van, 1968. 'Le mort-gage et son rôle économique en Flandre et en Lotharingie', in H. Van Werveke, *Miscellanea Mediaevalia: verspreide opstellen over economische en sociale geschiedenis van de middeleeuwen* (Ghent: E. Story-Scientia), pp. 159–190.

Zulaica Palacios, F., 1994. *Fluctuaciones Económicas en un Período de Crisis: Aragón en la Baja Edad Media (1300–1430)* (Zaragoza: Institución "Fernando el Católico").

CHAPTER 7

Not Only Land: Mortgage Credit in Central-Northern Italy in the Sixteenth and Seventeenth Centuries

Giuseppe De Luca and Marcella Lorenzini

7.1 Introduction: The Land Rush in Sixteenth-Century Northern Italy

During the early modern age, substantial innovations emerged in the mortgage system that played a pivotal role in the development of the credit market. The first decisive stimulus came from rural areas around the middle of the sixteenth century when steady demographic growth, combined with the increased availability of silver coming from the New World, caused the price revolution that affected most European countries. The steep rise in crop prices and the ballooning of land values led on the one hand to a concentration of capital investment in the agricultural sector and to a general land rush carried out by the urban

G. De Luca (✉) · M. Lorenzini
University of Milan, Milan, Italy
e-mail: giuseppe.deluca@unimi.it

M. Lorenzini
e-mail: marcella.lorenzini@unimi.it

C. Briggs and J. Zuijderduijn (eds.), *Land and Credit*,
Palgrave Studies in the History of Finance,
https://doi.org/10.1007/978-3-319-66209-1_7

aristocracy and well-to-do farmers, and on the other to an increase in the pressure on small rural landowners.

These effects yielded different outcomes. Nobles, patricians, well-off merchants and members of the elite in general started to divert their capital from commercial and industrial activities, then the most profitable, to agriculture. Land became very attractive for those who had financial resources and ambition to improve their economic and social condition. Indeed, land, apart from continuing to represent a status symbol and a means pursued by *homines novi* to climb the social ladder and become part of the urban oligarchy, was the emblem that exemplified the dynamism and entrepreneurship of powerful and active individuals (Roveda 2012, p. 16; Lanaro 1992, p. 61). The increasing demand for land, as a consequence of population growth, led to the reclamation of new stretches of terrain that had once been barren, uncultivated or swampy.[1] In the second half of the sixteenth century, especially in northern Italy, large and important drainage projects were undertaken, which were accompanied by the introduction of irrigation systems, the building of artificial canals and in general by the improvement of the soil quality in order to gain new stretches of land and to increase productivity (Ventura 1970; Ciriacono 1994). In the Republic of Venice, the land rush was paired with a parallel 'water rush' that manifested itself as a rise in the number of request for water concessions.[2] The price of land rose consistently. In the dominions of *La Serenissima* in the mid-sixteenth century, a marshy plot of land cost between three and six ducats; sixty years later, after being reclaimed, it could sell for 120 ducats (Bolognesi 1984, p. 83).[3]

This return to land that characterized the sixteenth-century economy has long been regarded in much of the literature as a sort of fall-back choice. The actions of the most industrious bourgeoisie who redirected their investments from business, trade and manufacturing activities to agriculture have usually been interpreted as an attempt by the emerging upper classes to imitate a *more nobilium* lifestyle, passively settling for rents. Likewise, aristocrats who invested in land (labelled a safe haven asset by historians) have often been seen as acting passively, or as driven by non-economic motivations. More recent research, however, has shed new light on the Renaissance land market, highlighting the entrepreneurial spirit that underpinned these new capitalist investments in the primary sector. This activity (aimed at improving real estate by enlarging properties) brought about the concentration of property titles in the hands of a few families of the urban elite, who were the protagonists of a process of redistribution and centralization of land ownership in the countryside.

The vast estates of the prestigious families who were part of the patriciate were taking shape during the long sixteenth century. The D'Addas of Milan, a noble family that became enriched thanks to trade and merchant activity, boasted—in the second half of the sixteenth century—real estate holdings of 25,000 pertiche, the value of which amounted to one million lire.[4] The Areses, who belonged to the Milanese aristocracy, had properties that totalled 11,000 pertiche. The Serbellonis, with roots in the notarial and trade world, tried to climb the social ladder by holding public offices and obtaining control over notarial duties. Their social and political success was achieved through strategic marriages and by undertaking military and diplomatic missions. The family reinforced their prestige by expanding their estate. After buying a lordly palace in Milan, for 81 million imperial lire, they started to increase their land holdings in the countryside. From the second half of the sixteenth century onwards, they adopted a policy of broadening their patrimony through purchases, auctions, inheritance and dowries (Cerini 1994, pp. 9–13). The Trivulzios, one of the richest and biggest landowner families of the city, had by the sixteenth and seventeenth centuries accumulated a patrimony of several thousands of pertiche that they had started to assemble in the fifteenth century both by force and legal methods. The land they possessed was not only extremely extensive but also the most fertile. This new high-quality soil was obtained through works of improvement, like the reclamation of marshy lands, the removal of wooded areas and the building of drainage canals and ditches. The methods they employed to gather such a vast patrimony were varied, namely purchases and seizures from common property and from small landowners (Roveda 2012, pp. 114–126).

There are many other examples of high-ranking families, like the Stampas of Soncino (Dionisio 1997, p. 213), or the Melzis, Malingegnos, Caravaggis and Littas, who invested hundreds of thousands of lire to expand their holdings in rural areas (Bolognesi 1984, pp. 78–79). The enlargement took place via different strategies, from the purchase of new plots of land to inheritance (as is widely known, aristocratic families were very careful to prevent the fragmentation of their estates and made every effort to bequeath them intact for the heirs), and from exchanges (or *permute*, literally two parties exchanging plots of land) to the acquisition of the estates of insolvent debtors.

Dispossessing insolvent mortgagors was a phenomenon with very ancient roots and was generally done through fictitious sales contracts, namely sales agreements that included a clause stipulating that the seller could recover the real estate ('cum pacto de recupera') if he returned the money to the buyer. If the seller was unable to repay the loan, the purchaser would automatically become the owner of the real estate without having to go through auctions or draw up formal documents (Vendrame 2009, p. 122). After studying the economic structure of the Paduan countryside in the fourteenth and fifteenth centuries, Silvana Collodo concluded that 'liens, mortgages and transfers to pay off debts created a continuous flow of property exchange powered by credit and by unscrupulous operations that modified the distribution of estates, creating and destroying wealth'.[5] Studies of early modern economies likewise maintain that the concentration of landed properties occurring from the mid-sixteenth century was the outcome of a similar process (Corazzol 1979, p. 50; Cattini 1983, p. 126; Vendrame 2009, p. 122). However, at present, there is no robust evidence that the massive process leading to the creation of large estates during the sixteenth- and seventeenth-century land rush was due to confiscations of insolvent borrowers. Much literature has emphasized that the expropriations linked to mortgages featured mainly as an element of the ideological debate on the relationship between the city (where the rich lenders lived) and the countryside (populated by poor and exploited borrowers), but there is not enough quantitative data to enable us to make broader inferences. Gian Maria Varanini, for instance, who examined the financial condition of peasants and farmers in the Veronese countryside, stated that the transfer of land to lenders, through the expropriation of insolvent mortgagors, was neither an automatic process nor an inevitable event. In some cases, the eviction could take a long time, taking place only after the rent had gone unpaid for many years. Moreover, sometimes landowner-creditors who wanted to keep debtors (often their tenants) under close control chose not to push the borrowers to return the money. They profited from the borrower's weakened position, making them do work for free such as digging, planting or transporting agricultural goods (Varanini 1987, p. 111; Lanaro 1987, p. 210).

As a matter of fact, the general conditions of peasants were deteriorating by the mid-sixteenth century in the Italian countryside; small landowners in particular entered a troubled period (Malanima 2002, pp. 111–113; De Maddalena 1992, pp. 43–165). Demographic growth during the middle ages had demolished the holdings of traditional farmers, dividing them among a growing number of heirs and undermining the economic independence of small landowners. Such people were used to growing agricultural products that barely met the basic needs of their households. In these areas, the circulation of money was scarce, and the only wealth families were able to produce was chiefly in kind, which they usually consumed immediately. Cash was necessary, however, to pay taxes, to pay for goods in the city markets, to cover unexpected expenses and also to buy seed, farming tools and draught animals such as oxen or mules. The demand for credit started to increase particularly in the second decade of the sixteenth century. The interest rates on secured loans were calculated in currency, but usually paid in kind. However, the cost of one unit of wheat could rise or fall by one hundred percent from one harvest to the next. In March 1529 in Arezzo, in central Italy, one bushel of wheat cost 128 soldi; five months later, after an abundant harvest, the price fell to 30 soldi. In the Pavese countryside, people who borrowed five sacks of wheat, at a price of 420 imperial soldi each, had to pay back 10 sacks just one year later as a result of the drop in price (to 197.5 soldi).[6] The interest rates paid in kind could reach 20–40% (Cattini 1983, p. 124). In 1546, the Marcuzzi brothers of Portogruaro (a village near Venice) pledged a plot of land for a 10 ducat loan, on which they had to pay an interest rate of two bushels of wheat. The price of wheat underwent such sharp fluctuations that the brothers ended up paying rent that, had it been monetized, amounted to 19.3% in 1546, 33.8% in 1550, 20% in 1553 and 38.7% in 1557 (Vendrame 2009, p. 121). As noted, rents and interest rates on loans were commonly paid in kind, mainly wheat, wine or oil. The combination of frosts and droughts that affected the hill country of Verona, Vicenza and Padua in the 1540s severely damaged olive crops.[7] Those who had to pay their obligations in oil rebelled and asked the Venetian Senate for measures to protect themselves. These actions may have played an important role in the events that occurred in rural areas in the years that followed. The bad harvests of 1548 and 1550 also caused a rapid rise in wheat prices. The unexpected disasters that affected the countryside of the north at the dawn of the sixteenth century (due to the so-called Little Ice Age) brought about great fluctuations in the market value of crops.

Small- and medium-sized farmers in the Venetian Republic rose up and asked for interest rates from loans to be paid in money, instead of in kind, while the elites lobbied to keep remittances in commodities, which were inflation-neutral. Eventually, in 1551, the Senate of the *Serenissima* responded to complaints and requests from rural areas by issuing new reforms that imposed the payment in cash of leases and interest rates on mortgages entered into from 1520 onwards. The latter could not exceed a maximum cap, the amount of which would be set by the authorities in each city. The law was adopted in different years across the Venetian dominions. In Venice, the interest rate on mortgages could not exceed 5.5%.[8] On 19 May 1553, the Great Council of Verona set the ceiling for interest rates at 6%, the same rate used in Vicenza (1551), Bassano (1551) and Padua (1553). In Friuli, the rate was 7% (Pedrinelli 1768, p. 48). The higher interest rates were probably due to the greater shortage of capital in those areas (Corazzol 1979, p. 71).

Rental reform, aimed at protecting small landowners and farmers, was not a phenomenon limited to the Italian countryside, but a Europe-wide trend. Similar measures were undertaken in Denmark, England, France and Spain (Nelson 1967, pp. 94–119; Schnapper 1957, p. 119). These new norms did not put a stop to the charging of interest in kind; however, they contributed to a significant curb in rates and paved the way for far-reaching credit innovations.

7.2 The New Success of an Old Credit Instrument

Between the tenth and sixteenth centuries, a wide range of different forms of instrument linking land and credit emerged under the stimulus of an expanding market and of the simultaneous development of financial techniques. These developments helped place the Italian Peninsula at the forefront of Europe in this sphere (Felloni 2008, p. 101). The different categories of instrument, which were described by terms that over time assumed overlapping meanings, essentially comprised two types of money loan: the *census* and the *mutuum*.

The *census* was originally linked to a contract for lease of a plot of land or a building (such as a house, palace or shop). The first kind of *census* was the *c. reservativus*, where the landowner gave his real estate (or more often a portion of it) to the lender, and the interest (in the form of rent) was paid from the revenue generated by that property. In most cases, the obligation to pay rent to the original lender or to his heirs could last for generations and remain embodied in the property itself, until the principal sum was repaid by the initial owner or his successor. Loans at interest began to be banned in a strict fashion by the Church in the thirteenth and fourteenth centuries, when usury became a byword for heresy. The charging of any amount, however small, which exceeded the sum lent was considered usury; this idea gave rise to intense debates that lasted for centuries.[9] Nonetheless, the form of loan described above was deemed legitimate (Felloni 2008, p. 102).

Beside the *c. reservativus*, another form emerged and became soon prevalent. This was the *c. consignativus*, which was designed on the basis of an 'emptio cum locatione', literally a sale followed by a lease. It was in effect a type of mortgage credit whereby the borrower (seller) sold a plot of land to the lender (buyer) and then became the lessee of the land, paying rent that was actually the interest on the loan. The agreement stipulated the seller's right to reacquire the estate, and indeed after a fixed term, the borrower could buy back his property by returning the capital to the lender. The buyer promised to sell the land back to the seller, once he had returned the money, and the presence of this promise proves that this kind of agreement was not a simple sale, but a concealed loan. For instance, on 20 January 1591, Gio. Maria q. Iacobo from Lugo di Valle Pantena (in the Veronese countryside) sold a piece of land, containing willow trees, for 50 ducats to Paolo q. Sebastiano in Corrubio Stallavena.[10] The contract ended with a clause that allowed the seller to regain ownership of the land, after having returned the capital.[11] This commercial (or more aptly financial) transaction could prove very risky for debtors, especially small farmers. This is because, as previously mentioned, if the debtor was unable to gather the capital and repay it by the deadline, he might definitively lose the property. While during preceding periods the lender was usually inclined to renew the deed, the higher land values of the sixteenth century tended to make him more interested in gaining possession of the collateral, which was usually land.

In addition to the *census* (in its two different forms), the second type of money loan, probably more ancient, was in use: the *mutuum*. The essential content of this contract was very simple: the creditor gave a sum of money to the debtor, who promised to return it in the same place and in the same type of coin, with added interest, that could be in kind or in labour. However, the agreement could not openly display the nature of the operation, because of the canonical ban on interest. For this reason, the writing underpinning the deal could assume various forms. Very often there was no mention of the interest rate; sometimes, only the sum to be repaid was indicated; and at other times, the agreement took the form of a sale of real estate which included the right of the debtor to regain the property once he had paid back the money ('cum pacto de recupera'). In the tenth and eleventh centuries, this contract always involved the pledge of a piece of real estate, which resembled the form of the *pignus* (Felloni 2008, pp. 104–105). Yet the instrument was substantially distinct from the *c. consignativus* because the pledged land did not remain to the use of the debtor, and consequently, there was no payment of rent by the latter.[12]

The remarkable spread of *c. consignativus*, which allowed one to bypass the interest prohibition via a 'sale and lease' transaction, focused attention from the early thirteenth century on the question of its legitimacy. As a consequence of this discussion, the *c. consignativus* was definitively regulated and reinforced in 1569 when the pope, Pius V, issued the bull *Cum Onus* (Placanica 1982, pp. 210–214). This contract granted the creditor the *dominium directum* ('right to direct'), while the *dominium utile* ('right to use') was ceded to the debtor, who continued to cultivate the estate as tenant (Alonzi 2011, p. 30). Thanks to the *c. consignativus*, which—as required by the papal bull—had to be drawn up by a notary, the borrower could ask for a loan by using as collateral a piece of real estate which could yield an annual rent that in effect constituted the yearly interest payment. The bull stated that in the case of the *c. consignativus*, 'the annuity can be constituted only if backed by real estate, which must have a revenue-generating nature and whose borders must be clearly defined in the contract. It must be created exclusively in exchange for cash, in the presence of witnesses before a notary and be put down in the public record, with honest obligation and at a fair price'. Moreover, the borrower was allowed to extinguish the annuity whenever he chose, by returning the capital to the lender, with two months' notice.[13] This redesigned version of the *c. consignativus* openly mentioned a rate of interest, which had to be charged and could not exceed a maximum cap, which was set by the government.[14]

The most innovative and significant element of the *c. consignativus* following its remodelling in the 1569 bull was its redeemability and the right of the borrower to extinguish the obligation *quandocumque* (whenever) he wanted and was able to. Contracts usually stipulated a perpetual pact allowing the tenant and his heirs to extinguish the debt and be set free whenever they wished from the aforementioned annuity. In relation to this point, the debtor could decide when to close the contract. In essence, the restyled form of *c. consignativus* meant the rebalancing of the tension between lender and borrower in favour of the latter.

In Verona, in the second half of the seventeenth century, mortgage contracts of this type made up 90% of all loans transacted by notaries (Lorenzini 2016). The agreement was divided into three parts: in the first (*emptio*), the debtor, technically the seller, sold his real estate (or part of it) to the creditor, officially the buyer. In the second part of the contract (*locatio*), the borrower received the real estate back and in turn contracted to pay an annual rent to the lender which was tantamount to the interest rate on the principal sum that he had just received. The final part of the act laid out its redeemability, i.e. the possibility for the debtor to regain that part of estate if he paid off the debt.

Subsequently, the setting of a deadline for return of the capital became very common in some territorial states of the Peninsula; the term, agreed by the parties, generally ranged from three to nine years. So, if the borrower was unable to return the full amount, several scenarios could occur. First, the lender could come into possession of the collateralized estate, thereby executing the expropriation. Second, a debtor could be forced to return money and unpaid interest by giving a plot of land instead of grain or cash, according to a procedure known as *datio in solutum*.[15] Eventually, if the debtor could not repay the money he owed, he could seek out a new creditor willing to finance him. In such cases, the notary played a critical role, helping the borrower find a new lender (most likely selected from the ranks of his customers) willing to offer finance (Lorenzini 2016, p. 305). The notary very often played an active part in the arrangement of agreements, operating like an informal financial intermediary in credit markets (Hoffman et al. 2000). Overall, the new type of mortgage instrument legitimized the levying of interest on cash loans and, although some contracts included a fixed repayment deadline, it generally safeguarded borrowers by allowing them to extinguish the debt whenever they wished, and therefore removed them from the clutches of greedy lenders who aimed to seize the collateral, which typically was a cultivated plot of land (Bolognesi 1988, p. 286).

The framework of the *census consignativus* echoes that of the government bonds created in the Italian Republics during the middle ages. The emerging city states of Genoa, first, and subsequently Venice, Florence and Milan, were sucked dry by growing expenses. Frequent wars required large quantities of capital. In addition to taxation, in order to raise funds, the cities had recourse to forced loans, and thus became indebted. Lenders (usually the wealthiest citizens) received high interest rates in exchange for their loans. The interest rates were paid with the yields from fiscal revenues. Governments considered indebtedness a temporary solution, but when wars started to become ever more frequent and require greater amounts of capital, forced loans proved insufficient, and new stratagems were devised. New forms of borrowing were made possible through the alienation of revenue-generating real estate that represented both the source of finance and the collateral. In the same manner as government bonds, the *census consignativus* became a redeemable, heritable and tradable loan, as well as a method of payment that helped the credit market become more liquid and to expand (De Luca and Moioli 2008).

The Church's interest in regulating lending activity can be partly explained by the fact that ecclesiastical bodies were some of the main actors in local credit markets and were among the most concerned with the legitimization of interest rate loans. Many of their assets, especially those of the regular orders and the female monasteries, were made up of capital that came from generous bequests, dowries and donations from the faithful. Religious institutions, far from wanting to keep money idle (*inopia pecuniae*), wanted to make it profitable, and one of the safest and most remunerative ways was by investing in the mortgage market.[16] Mortgages were as safe as land, easier to manage and more profitable. While land had a return of 3–5% at most, lending could yield between 6 and 7%, even 10% in Rome (Faccini 1988, p. 113; Vaquero Piñeiro 2007, p. 72). It was also more lucrative than investing in the mint, or in the *monti di pietà* (civic pawnshops), which provided returns of 3–4% (Pezzolo 2006, pp. 89–90; Lorenzini 2016, pp. 49–50; Cattini 1983, p. 128; Borelli 1974, p. 361).

In addition, the *censi* soon became tradable and were able to support a kind of secondary market, as was seen in Florence at the end of the sixteenth century. The Medici Bank crisis in 1573, which lasted for almost twenty years, made it difficult to obtain credit and worsened the unstable condition of the industrial sector, especially wool manufacturing. This financial impasse, along with social and economic instability, led people to use the *censi* on a massive scale to overcome the hardships of that period. Similarly, creditors who were in trouble and had signed *censi* began to alienate to other financiers their right to receive interest rates.

All this contributed to the rapid spread of the use of *censi* across the entire fabric of society, not just among small farmers in tough financial straits, but also among those who had liquid funds to invest and decided to use it in lending activities, diversifying their holdings to include not just assets. *Censi* contracts became so widespread that they overshadowed all other forms of investment in Italian cities and were responsible for the remarkable increase in the recourse to credit across all strata of society.

7.3 The Versatile Nature of *Censi Consignativi*: From a Defensive Instrument to a Driving Force

Currently, quantitative data are not available to allow one to estimate precisely and assess the diffusion of the *c. consignativus* compared to the other instruments of mortgage credit. Yet the phenomenon was clearly widespread, and the fiscal sources in particular prove that the use of *c. consignativi* was becoming pervasive, especially from the end of the sixteenth century and during the two following centuries. It is also thanks to their use that credit became an increasingly characteristic feature of society in the Italian States. The *c. consignativus* underwent transformation from money loan into a negotiable instrument. In addition to creating a secondary market, this provided the credit system with resilience. This process was in effect possible because the instrument came to be used in ways not solely connected to land.

In the notarial records where *censi* credit contracts were normally registered, the specific motivation that drove the borrower to ask for a loan is very rarely mentioned. Drawing upon a survey of a thousand contracts concerning debts on landed collateral drawn up in Verona during the seventeenth century, the most frequent reasons given by debtors were the payment of arrears, the creation of a dowry for a daughter who was going to be married or enter the convent, the payment of taxes and legal expenses (Lorenzini 2016). Therefore, mortgages were chiefly used for coping with necessities linked to everyday life, mainly basic or financial needs. The late seventeenth-century economic system of Verona was recovering from years of hardship caused by the plague of the 1630s, wars and famine, and thereafter the motivations that underpinned a mortgage began increasingly to be tied to production activities. The medium- to long-term duration of *c. consignativi* (also called *livelli* affrancabili in some Italian States, such as the Republic of Venice, which was not aligned with the Pope)[17] was one of their principal characteristics. Therefore, those who wanted to carry out large and capital-intensive projects could benefit from the use of this credit instrument.

Censi and *livelli* soon began to be used to open shops in the city, aimed at meeting the growing demand that resulted from population growth and the trend towards urbanization. In keeping with a phenomenon that was seen all over Europe, in northern Italy, the Baroque age was also a period characterized by an increasing number of bakers, butchers, shoemakers and artisans who 'conquered and devoured' the cities and villages in which they settled, as Fernand Braudel put it (Braudel 1981, p. 43). Likewise, in Verona, at the end of the seventeenth century, the number of craftsmen, apothecaries and retail shops was slowly rising. The capital necessary to open a commercial retail activity was not especially high, amounting to about 200 ducats for a bakery and 450 ducats for an apothecary (Lorenzini 2016, pp. 255–257). The *livello affrancabile* was very widely used in the Venetian mainland by merchants to finance their activities. For instance, Giuliano Piovene of Vicenza—the owner of a large estate, a renowned international businessman and merchant—used many financial tools to raise capital to fund his commercial activities, including *livelli affrancabili* (Demo 2014, p. 117; Caracausi 2007, pp. 294–295). Another major Venetian merchant and entrepreneur, Giorgio Sola, raised a total of 4000 ducats through *livelli* to finance his businesses (Vianello 2004, p. 181).

Moreover, city councils resorted to debt (derived from *censi* or *livelli*) in order to fund extremely expensive infrastructure projects. At the end of the seventeenth century, after the Adige River violently broke its banks, the city of Verona needed to quickly collect a huge sum of money in order to repair the riverbanks destroyed by the flood. The capital was originally granted 16,000 ducats at 4% interest by Francesco Manzoni, a nobleman from Padua.[18] Some years later, the city wanted to extinguish its debt. To do so, it withdrew half of the sum from the city *monte di pietà* to pay Manzoni and borrowed the other half from another nobleman of Verona, Earl Piero Zazzaroni, who in those years was also a member of the municipal administration. Zazzaroni lent 9000 ducats for ten years at 4%, in return for which the city pledged its butchers' shops and ghetto houses.

There was a significant use of *censi* by the municipalities in the countryside in order to cover growing expenses, much of which came from central governments that had to meet the rising cost of state building. The total debt, in *censi consignativi*, of the State of Milan's municipalities in 1636 was 27 million imperial lire (Faccini 1988, p. 110). The recourse to *censi*, especially notable from the second half of the sixteenth to the mid-seventeenth century, was due to needs and urgent expenditures arising from an increase in the taxes levied by the state. The costs imposed by frequent wars and by the growing bureaucratic apparatus that would shape the modern state were reflected in the intensification of levies. In particular, the cities, which had more independence when it came to setting their fiscal and lending policies and enjoyed greater bargaining power than the rural municipalities, were able to shift their tax burden onto small communities in the countryside.

Up until the early decades of the seventeenth century, the growing indebtedness of municipalities was not particularly worrying. They had large real estate holdings that could be used as collateral. Interest rates ranged from 6 to 8%, which were the same as market rates, achieving one percentage point higher or lower depending on the bargaining power of creditors and debtors. Financiers were normally members of the urban elite, or rather the most active members of it, such as patricians and affluent merchants. The financial state of local institutions worsened in the third and fourth decades of the seventeenth century; the most feared risk was that they would become insolvent, in turn reducing the revenues flowing into city coffers. This represented another element that could cause crisis and economic instability. The potential collapse of municipalities was addressed by central governments through the issuing of certain measures that set a ceiling for interest rates on *censi* taken out by local governing bodies. In the Venetian Republic, the Doge issued specific laws in order to protect the growing obligations of rural villages and lowered the interest rate cap on loans drawn up by municipalities. In June 1673, the city of Verona issued a *Parte* (measure) stipulating that the interest rates of debts contracted by local administrations had to be lowered from 6 to 4.5%. The document reads: 'the generous concession made by the *Serenissimo Principe* with the law of 10 June 1673, [enabled us to] take money through *census* at 4.5%, which must be free from tax and which will serve to extinguish previous debts (*censi*) at 6%, therefore giving the benefit of a reduction in levies'.[19]

One of the rules imposed by the papal bull of 1569 in its definition of the *census consignativus* was that the loan had to be backed by 'an immovable thing, fruitful in its nature', in other words, all or part of an estate that generated revenue. Indeed, this was in effect the most common practice. Almost all mortgage contracts drawn up in the early modern period concerned a plot of cultivated land, with fruit trees, a house, a shop, a mill or anything that could guarantee a revenue stream. This would serve to pay the annual rent to the mortgagee. Real estate ownership, and therefore the land itself, became indeed an engine of credit. In 1676, Domenico Rambaldi of Verona received a loan of 50 ducats from the lawyer Lorenzo Porta to whom he gave five *campi* of land (about 15,200 square metres).[20] This estate had been bought by Domenico and his brother shortly before signing the loan contract.[21]

The preferred form of collateral was in fact land, which was very meticulously described. The contract indicated the property's borders, the total area, the type of cultivation and the presence of any vines, mulberry trees or other fruit trees that would increase the value of the collateral. When comparing the description of the collateral, more specifically the surface area of the land, to the sum borrowed, a lack of correlation between the two variables emerges. The total amount of farmland mortgaged for a loan of 50 ducats could range from 3 to 24 *campi*.[22] The types of terrain could undoubtedly differ depending on to the land's geographical position and the crops grown on it, which affected its productivity. The price of one *campo* could range from a few dozen to hundreds of ducats. Pastoral lands had a higher value, which could increase further if they included water, houses, wells, and so on. However, an analysis which compares similar parcels of land (similar in terms of position, crop, surface area and contractual terms, and therefore homogeneous with regard to key variables) with the amount of money loaned shows a clear lack of consistency in the relationship between area of land pledged and value of loan.

Brigida Montresori, widow of Antonio, pledged four *campi* for a loan of 100 ducats.[23] For the same sum, Francesco Tegnali pledged more than twice the amount of land, namely 10 *campi*.[24] In both cases, the land was located in the same area, the interest rate was 6%, and the duration of the contract was five years. The difference between the collateral pledged for another 100 ducat credit was even more evident; in one case, Giovanni Salvador pawned three *campi*,[25] in another, Donato Zucchi offered as collateral 24 *campi*.[26] In these two situations, the type of land was the same, and for both, the interest rate was 6% and the duration three years. The evident difference between one loan and the other, where the terms and collateral are the same, serves to convince us that there were other elements, apart from the collateral that contributed to mitigating risk, namely trust, reliability and the reputation of the debtor.[27] On the other hand, the protagonists of early modern societies did not always act according to economic criteria alone. Equity, 'rational' behaviour, distributive and commutative justice coexisted and interconnected in complex ways. Often connections based on money were entwined with personal and blood relations and were also strengthened by physical and spiritual proximity.

Urban residents borrowed against real estate they owned in the city like houses, buildings or shops. In order to obtain a loan of 1500 ducats from Earl Francesco Montanari, Gio. Battista Turco, a member of a noble family from Verona, collateralized his entire palace called San Fermo, in the centre of the city.[28] In a contrasting example, the widow of an apothecary (*speziale*) asked for a loan of 304 ducats, for which she had to pawn 'the entire shop, with its implements and everything pertaining to the use of the apothecary shop'.[29] Not just private citizens but also guilds, institutions and organisations resorted to debt. The Jewish community of Verona had to pledge 'all the houses and capital that it possessed in the ghetto' to have a loan of 5000 ducats from earls and brothers Verità and Pietro Zenobi.[30]

Real estate had always been favourably viewed in the credit market. Nevertheless, the idea of collateral was slowly moving away from its traditional formula and encompassing different types of goods. Collateral became more liquid, even going so far as to include revenues like tolls or tithes. In 1681, Earl Lorenzo Pullé of Verona took out a loan for 250 ducats, for which he collateralized a 'portion of the tithe and the right to levy tithes on grains'.[31] Francesco Marogna, who lent 100 ducats to Giacomo Castorio, received as collateral 'all the mulberry trees' that were present on the borrower's estates.[32]

In other larger, more entrepreneurial areas like the State of Milan, it is clear that the collateral used was shaped by an economy that was developing and growing, where agricultural and industrial activities, along with an expanding international trade network, were hungry for capital. The property that was pledged was therefore further and further detached from real estate and increasingly linked to intangible assets like public bonds, tolls or fiscal revenues. This was the case for the merchant and iron entrepreneur Niccolò Cipriani. In 1575, in order to obtain a loan of 7000 scudi[33] from the banker Marco Antonio Rezzonico, in addition to a beech tree, he pledged a furnace ('forno colandum ferrum'), the revenue from duties on a mill ('dazio macina') and the licence to use and graze horses in order to 'cercare vene di metalli' (search for veins of ore). The loan stipulated a 7% interest rate, which Cipriani paid until 1584.[34]

Thus, an increasing number of *censi* began to be backed by government bonds, a feature that was due also to the increasing reliance of the State of Milan on public debt around the end of the fifteenth and the beginning of the sixteenth century. Figure 7.1 shows 241 *censi* contracts for a total amount of 2,116,000 lire drawn up between 1575 and 1611. All these used state bonds as collateral, albeit with different levels of coverage. The interest rates ranged from 7% for 20-year *censi* to 9%

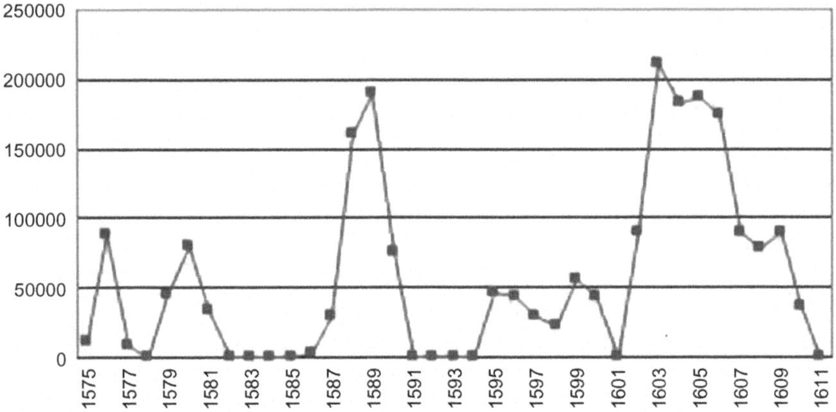

Fig. 7.1 *Censi consignativi* contracts backed by state bonds in Milan, 1575–1611 (current lire)

Sources Asmi, N., f. 13102 (1576–1588) notary: Rolando Mazza; 13710–13711 (1575–1577) Giovanni Battista Bombelli; 13880–13895 (1575–1597) Dionigi Oldoni; 14766–14784 (1575–1594) Ambrogio Ferni; 14922–14929 (1591–1598) Ventura Solari; 14937–14944 (1575–1584) Ottaviano Castelletti; 15432–15441 (1575–1591) Giacomo Filippo Cattaneo Vaiani; 15505–15515 (1575–1601) Cesare Borsani; 15505–15515 (1575–1607) Cesare Borsani; 16296–16300 (1575–1607) Bernardo Quarantini; 16471–16483 (1575–1598) Giovanni Giacomo Fedeli; 16612–16623 (1575–1606) Cesare Guidi; 16939–16958 (1575–1607) Francesco Massarola; 17030–17031 (1573–1608) Polidoro Mantelli; 17569–17581 (1575–1592) Giovanni Paolo Pellizzari; 17676–17683 (1575–1607) Girolamo Martini; 17782–17787 (1575–1607) Benedetto Barbavara; 18928–18938 (1575–1607) Paolo Girolamo Fontana; 19594–19603 (1578–1607) Giovanni Battista Baruffi; 20651–20667 (1583–1611) Giuseppe Martignone; 23715–23719 (1597–1611) Dionigi Capra; 23821–23824 (1597–1604) Pietro Luigi Merlato; 23950–23956 (1598–1611) Francesco Rugginelli; 23982–23991 (1598–1611) Giovanni Ambrogio Caccia; 24779–24780 (1603–1611) Francesco Brofferio, ad vocem censo for 10-year loans (these were the most common after 1595). To meet the considerable demand for arms in the period from 1575 to 1577, Milanese entrepreneurs were encouraged to integrate vertically by opening new mines or reopening old ones: in this way, they could produce weapons using their own and local iron mineral, joining together the different stages of production in order to reduce costs and improve efficiency. Since in this industry the quantity of fixed assets was negligible and liquidity was necessary in order to buy raw materials and individual parts, having working capital in the form of short-term loans was essential. However, when the promised financial assistance from the state failed to materialize, the capital required for processing the ore could be obtained only through the *censi* credit system. Starting in the 1570s, the total and average sums of *censi* gradually rose because they were the only viable way to finance the mining of local iron in Valsassina for the war effort; in effect, the first peak of the curve in 1589 mirrors the boost in demand for weapons connected to the geopolitical strategy of the Spanish monarchy, while in the second upsurge of the curve during the first decades of the seventeenth century, the borrowers were mainly large merchants who used the capital to open silk production facilities.[35] In the case of Milan, public bonds (which had become especially attractive thanks to the guaranteed payment of interest, their alienation rate, easy tradability and tax-exempt status) played a major role in credit representing almost the entirety of the mobile assets that *censi consignativi* borrowers sold to lenders as security for loans. So, state securities not only constituted additional income but were also used as collateral for credit by the world of industry.

7.4 Concluding Remarks

Under the stimulus of a booming interest in agriculture, which was triggered by the rise in crop prices during the mid-sixteenth century in particular, the complex system of lending activities backed by real estate in Italy was struck by a wave of radical changes. After centuries in which similar forms of mortgage credit coexisted and overlapped—giving rise also to a confused terminology—there slowly began to emerge a refinement of the *census consignativus*, an instrument that had been in use for a long time.

This was due in large part to the papal bull of 1569, which laid down the framework and introduced some new features: redeemability of the loan within a defined period of time, which favoured the borrower; a modest interest rate; and full moral legitimacy. An instrument thus emerged that gave a large part of the population access to credit in a more resilient way. All that needed was to own a revenue-generating plot of land or real estate that could be pledged.

Until now, the economic history literature has maintained that the main reason for the creation and diffusion of this instrument was the need to defend indebted small landowners from an assault on their land carried out by the urban elite. Yet, this perspective is more the result of an ideological view based on the power imbalance between the city and the countryside, rather than a thesis backed by robust empirical evidence. The growth of real estate holdings and the dispossession of small farmers occurred by other means. Meanwhile, the *c. consignativus* and its many incarnations (during the period of economic expansion beginning in the 1520s in central-northern Italy) acquired a structure that was less defensive and less tied to the management of financial emergencies and served more as a driving force that enabled the parties to pay for improvements in soil productivity, the setting up of irrigation and drainage systems and infrastructure, and to finance industrial and commercial activities.

The full moral legitimacy, solid legal basis and low interest rate made this kind of lending activity the preferred tool of religious institutions, chiefly monasteries and female convents, which during this time were among the most important sources of credit. The use of *censi consignativi* became increasingly widespread and pervasive; they began to be used to meet the financial needs of rural municipalities. The primary goal of lenders, who were an heterogeneous group, was no longer that of gaining ownership of the mortgaged assets, but rather the establishment of a source of revenue. These creditors perfectly attest to the progressive development of a diversified way of making money profitable, which the spread of income generated from public debt also shows. In addition, the versatility inherent in the structure of the *c. consignativus* led to a broadening of the definition of collateral to include other types of revenue-generating assets such as public bonds, thus revenue went from being property-based to asset-based. Thanks to its simple scaffolding, this credit instrument went on to become the focus of the various reciprocal interests that determined its success. In effect, it perfectly permitted the potential complementarity of public finance, private credit and economic production (Neal 2015, p. 43), and the Milanese case fully embodies this, showing how the *c. consignativus*, an instrument born and designed to help and protect the peasant classes, quickly turned into a tool that supported economic expansion in manufacturing, trade and infrastructure.

Notes

1. For an analysis of the Italian agrarian world in the early modern period, see Malanima (2002, pp. 93–149).
2. The increasing number of requests to obtain a licence for water use in defined zones was a consequence of the growth in farming that characterized many areas of northern Italy, especially the Po Valley region. For the Venetian dominions, see Lanaro (1992, p. 247) and Ciriacono (1998).
3. One ducat equalled six lire and four soldi.
4. One pertica equalled 654.52 square metres.
5. Collodo (1983, p. 20). For the Lombardy area, see Roveda (2012, pp. 140–150).
6. Similar situations can be found in rural areas across central and northern Italy, such as Udine, Bassano, Modena and Parma (Cattini 1983, p. 124).
7. Olive oil was one of the most prized goods exported (passing through Venetian harbours) to northern European countries.
8. Literally 'metter denaro a livello più di 5.5% se si fondi sopra beni di questa Città e Dogado' (Pedrinelli 1768, p. 48).
9. The bull that finally legitimized interest rate loans was the *Vix Pervenit* issued in 1745 by Pope Benedetto XIV: Vismara (2004, p. 253).
10. Literally: 'asserens se habere ius in re infrascritta ex suis iustis titulis, ex maxime vigour [...] de ea facta ab Angelo q. Ioannis de Zambellis de Ecclesia Nova ex infrascritto redemptionis manu mea [...] Per se heredes suos [...] ex nomine venditis iure proprio [...] dedit, vendit et tradit Paulo fq. Sebastiani a Corubio Stallavena': Archivio di Stato di Verona (hereafter Asvr), Notarial Archive (hereafter N.), notary Agapito Borghetti, f. 1007, 20 January 1591.
11. In the same example, the relevant text is as follows: 'Cum pacto perpetuo quandocumque ex sine aliquos temporis estintione concesso detto Gio. Maria de redimendo anted. rem vendit ducatos quinquaginta'.
12. In the seventeenth century, the term *census* replaced the older term *mutuum*. The latter type of contract had become widespread during the thirteenth century and contributed significantly to medieval economic growth. This tool allowed for the growth of the credit market, enabling maritime cities like Genoa to finance commercial and manufacturing activities. As noted, the contract clearly stated the amount of money lent, the lien and the deadline. In some *mutuum* contracts, the interest rate

was added to the final sum that the borrower had to return to the lender, so for example if the amount borrowed was 10 *dinari*, at the end of the contract the debtor had to return 11.5 *dinari*. In other cases, the interest rate was clearly stated using the *per centum* formula (Palermo 2008, pp. 119–120). The word *mutuum*, which was strictly forbidden from any kind of deed throughout the early modern period, came into use again in the eighteenth century, signalling a change in mentality and a different attitude towards money and credit. The idea of money as the devil's excrement ('sterco del demonio'), as it was called by the Catholic Church, had been overtaken by a new mindset that saw money as a key factor for economic growth (Palermo 2008, p. 120).

13. The key text is as follows: 'Annuum redditum creari constituive nullo modo posse, nisi in re immobili aut quae pro immobili habeatur, de sua natura fructifera, et quae nominatim certis finibus designata sit. Rursum, nisi vere in pecunia numerata, praesentibus testibus ac notario, et in actu celebrationis instrumenti, non autem prius, recepto integro iustoque pretio' (Alonzi 2005, p. 88).
14. The borrower continued to pay taxes on the portion of the real estate that had been used as collateral. The contract usually contained a clause that clearly stated the debtor's obligation to pay the *gravezze* (taxes) on the land.
15. See for instance the contract drawn up in 1686 by the noble Verità Poeta brothers. They gave ('per titolo di dà in pagamento') to Bartolomeo Peverelli a plot of land in return for 100 ducats that they used for their sister's dowry. Since they did not have the cash to pay him back ('e non havendo gli stessi il commodo di liberarsi dal detto debito'), they ceded ('per titolo di dà in pagamento in virtù del loro diretto dominio') a plot of land; Asvr, N., notary Francesco Bernardi, f. 1458, 12 January 1686.
16. This was in effect a practice common to almost all the regular orders; see Landi (1996, 2005). For the use of *censi* by the regular orders in Friuli, see Monte (2000, pp. 253–284). See also the credit activity undertaken by the Dominicans in Verona: Lorenzini (2017).
17. For the original and juridical structure of the *livello* instrument in the Italian peninsula, see Pertile (1892).
18. Asvr, N., notaries: Gio.Francesco Vidali and Domenico Moretti, f. 11.295, 10 February 1681.
19. The '... gratiosa concessione fattali dal Serenissimo Principe nella Parte del dì 10 Giugno 1673 [prevedeva] ch'è di poter pigliar denari a censo di 4,5% libero da gravezze per estinguer il capitale per li quali è tenuto pagar il 6% et così goder il beneficio delle minorazioni degli aggravi'; quoted in Asvr, N., notary Vincenzo Ferro, f. 5248, 5 June 1676.
20. One *campo* equalled 3047 square metres.

21. Asvr, N., notary Francesco Bernardi, b. 1428, 17 September 1676.
22. That means, from 9000 to more than 73,000 square metres.
23. Asvr, N., notary Francesco Bernardi, b. 1426, 30 April 1676.
24. Asvr, N., notary Francesco Bernardi, f. 1428, 26 September 1676.
25. Asvr, N., notary Nascimbene Bajetta, f. 1532, 16 May 1676.
26. Asvr, N., notary Vincenzo Ferro, f. 5246, 7 May 1676.
27. These constituted in effect the key factors that underpinned early modern credit markets; see Muldrew (1998).
28. Asvr, N., notary Filippo Filippini, f. 5143, 7 May 1681.
29. Literally 'il negozio intero con utensili e altro al medesimo pertinenti ad uso di speciaria', Asvr, N., notary Francesco Bernardi, f. 1458, 20 March 1686.
30. Asvr, N., notary Giovanni Bernardi, f. 1681, 24 December 1686.
31. He mortgaged a 'porzione di decima et ragione di decimare grani minuti et ogni altra cosa solita decimarsi nella villa di San Pier in Carian': Asvr, N., notaries Gio.Francesco Vidali and Domenico Moretti, f. 11297, 9 October 1681.
32. Asvr, N., notary Gianfilippo Gianfilippi, f. 6034, 18 December 1681.
33. One scudo equalled six lire imperiali.
34. Archivio di Stato di Milano, Fondo Commercio, carta 221, f. 16, 12 September 1580.
35. The silk industry, which included the production of raw silk and silk cloth, was expanding rapidly during the sixteenth century. Much of it was produced for export. The decline of the wool industry in the previous century was soon counterbalanced by the expansion of silk manufacturing, which reached its apogee in the mid-sixteenth century in several regions of northern Italy.

References

Secondary Works

Alonzi, L., 2005. 'I censi consegnativi nel XVI e nel XVII secolo tra "finzione" e "realtà"', *L'Acropoli*, vol. 6, pp. 86–102.

Alonzi, L., 2011. *Economia e finanza nell'Italia moderna. Rendite e forme di censo (secoli XV–XX)* (Rome: Carocci).

Bolognesi, D., 1984. 'Le campagne dell'Italia padana nel Seicento', *Cheiron*, vol. 3, pp. 77–99.

Bolognesi, D., 1988. 'Attività di prestito e congiuntura. I censi in Romagna nei secoli XVII e XVIII', in *Credito e sviluppo economico in Italia dal medioevo all'età contemporanea* (Verona: Società Italiana degli Storici dell'economia), pp. 283–306.

Borelli, G., 1974. *Un patriziato della terraferma veneta tra XVII e XVIII secolo. Ricerche sulla nobilita' veronese* (Milan: Giuffré).

Braudel, F., 1981. *Civiltà materiale, economia e capitalismo (secoli XV–XVIII)* (Turin: Einaudi).

Caracausi, A., 2007. 'Capitali e mercanti imprenditori in Italia settentrionale nei secoli XVII e XVIII', *Annali di storia dell'impresa*, vol. 18, pp. 283–299.

Cattini, M., 1983. 'Problemi di liquidità e prestito ad interesse nelle campagne emiliane (secc. XVI–XVIII)', *Studi Storici Luigi Simeoni*, vol. 33, pp. 121–130.

Cerini, F., 1994. 'I Serbelloni nel XVIII–XIX secolo: un grande patrimonio e la sua dissoluzione', *Storia in Lombardia*, vol. 12, pp. 5–42.

Ciriacono, S., 1994. *Acque e agricoltura. Venezia, l'Olanda e la bonifica europea in età moderna* (Milan: FrancoAngeli).

Ciriacono, S. (ed.), 1998. *Land Drainage and Irrigation* (London and New York: Routledge).

Collodo, S., 1983. 'Credito, movimento della proprietà fondiaria e selezione sociale a Padova nel Trecento', *Archivio storico italiano*, vol. 141, pp. 3–72.

Corazzol, G., 1979. *Fitti e livelli a grano. Un aspetto del credito rurale nel Veneto del '500* (Milan: FrancoAngeli).

De Luca, G. and A. Moioli, 2008. 'Il potere del credito: reti e istituzioni in Italia centro-settentrionale fra età moderna e decenni preunitari', *La Banca. Annali di Storia d'Italia*, vol. 23, pp. 212–255 (Turin: Einaudi).

De Maddalena, A., 1992. 'Il mondo rurale italiano nel Cinque e nel Seicento', in A. De Maddalena, *La ricchezza dell'Europa. Indagini sull'antico regime e sulla modernità* (Milan: Egea).

Demo, E., 2014. '"Prexe dinari a cambio et anco da altre private persone." Il problema del finanziamento all'impresa nella Terraferma veneta del '500', in M. Carboni and M.G. Muzzarelli (eds.), *Reti di credito. Circuiti informali, impropri, nascosti (secoli XIII– XIX)* (Bologna: Il Mulino), pp. 109–124.

Dionisio, A., 1997. 'Gli Stampa di Soncino. Politiche territoriali di una famiglia aristocratica nella Lombardia dell'Ottocento', *Archivio Storico Lombardo*, vol. 12, pp. 193–232.

Faccini, L., 1988. *La Lombardia fra '600 e '700. Riconversione economica e mutamenti sociali* (Milan: FrancoAngeli).

Felloni, G., 2008, 'Dall'Italia all'Europa: il primato della finanza italiana dal Medioevo alla prima età moderna', *La Banca. Annali di Storia d'Italia*, vol. 23, pp. 93–149 (Turin: Einaudi).

Hoffman, P., G. Postel-Vinay and J.-L. Rosenthal, 2000. *Priceless Markets. The Political Economy of Credit in Paris (1660–1870)* (Chicago: University of Chicago Press).

Lanaro, P., 1987. 'Reddito agrario e controllo fiscale nel Cinquecento: la Valpolicella e Verona', in G.M. Varanini (ed.), *La Valpolicella nella prima età moderna (1500 c.–1630)* (Verona: La Grafica), pp. 205–242.

Lanaro, P., 1992. *Un'oligarchia urbana nel Cinquecento veneto. Istituzioni, economia, società* (Turin: Giappicchelli).

Landi, F., 1996. *Il Paradiso dei monaci. Accumulazione e dissoluzione dei patrimoni del clero regolare in età moderna* (Rome: La Nuova Italia Scientifica).

Landi, F., 2005. *Storia economica del clero in Europa. Secoli XV–XIX* (Rome: Carocci).

Lorenzini, M., 2016. *Credito e notai. Capitali per l'economia veronese del secondo Seicento* (Bologna: Il Mulino).

Lorenzini, M., 2017. *Patrimonio e finanza di un convento in età moderna. I Domenicani di Santa Anastasia di Verona* (Milan: FrancoAngeli).

Malanima, P., 2002. *L'economia italiana. Dalla crescita medievale alla crescita contemporanea* (Bologna: Il Mulino).

Monte, M., 2000. 'Costo del denaro e tassi d'interesse nell'attività di credito dei Regolari nel Friuli', *Ce Fastu?*, vol. 2, pp. 253–284.

Muldrew, C., 1998. *The Economy of Obligation: The Culture of Credit and Social Relations in Early Modern England* (Basingstoke: Palgrave).

Neal, L., 2015. *A Concise History of International Finance. From Babylon to Bernanke* (Cambridge: Cambridge University Press).

Nelson, B., 1967. *Usura e cristianesimo. Per una storia della genesi dell'etica moderna* (Florence: Sansoni).

Palermo, L., 2008. *La banca e il credito nel Medioevo* (Milano: Bruno Mondadori).

Pedrinelli, G., 1768. *Il Notaio Istruito nel suo Ministero secondo le leggi, e la Pratica della Serenissima Repubblica di Venezia. Opera Umiliata al Magistrato Gravissimo degl'Ill.mi et Ecc.mi Signori Conservatori ed Esecutori delle Leggi da Giovanni Pedrinelli Avvocato Fiscale del medesimo Magistrato* (Venice: Carlo Todero).

Pertile, A., 1892. *Storia del diritto italiano. Dalla caduta dell'Impero romano alla codificazione* (Turin: Unione Tipografico-Editrice).

Pezzolo, L., 2006. *Una finanza d'ancien régime. La Repubblica veneta tra XV e XVIII secolo* (Naples: Edizioni Scientifiche Italiane).

Placanica, A., 1982, *Moneta, prestiti usure nel Mezzogiorno modern* (Naples: Società Editrice Napoletana).

Roveda, E., 2012. *Uomini, terre e acque. Studi sull'agricoltura della 'Bassa lombarda' tra XV e XVII secolo* (Milano: FrancoAngeli).

Schnapper, B., 1957. *Les rentes au XVIe siècle. Histoire d'un instrument de crédit* (Paris: S.E.V.P.E.N).

Vaquero Piñeiro, M., 2007. 'I censi consegnativi. La vendita delle rendite in Italia nella prima età moderna', *Rivista di storia dell'agricoltura*, vol. 40, pp. 57–94.

Varanini, G.M., 1987. 'Problemi di storia economica e sociale della Valpolicella nel Cinquecento e primo Seicento', in G.M. Varanini (ed.), *La Valpolicella nella prima età moderna (1500 c.–1630)* (Verona: Centro di documentazione per la storia della Valpolicella), pp. 47–155.

Vendrame, L., 2009. 'Aspetti del credito rurale a Fossalta nel '500', in V. Gobbo and E. Martin (eds.), *Fossalata nei secoli* (Fossalta di Portogruaro: Comune), pp. 117–130.

Ventura, A., 1970. 'Considerazioni sull'agricoltura veneta e sulla accumulazione originaria del capitale nei secoli XVI e XVII', in *Agricoltura e sviluppo del capitalismo. Atti del convegno organizzato dal'Istituto Gramsci (Roma 20–22 aprile 1968)* (Rome: Editori Riuniti), pp. 519–560.

Vianello, F., 2004. 'Mercanti, imprese e commerci nel Cinque e Seicento', in G.L. Fontana (ed.), *L'industria vicentina dal Medioevo a oggi* (Padua: Cluep), pp. 187–229.

Vismara, P., 2004. *Oltre l'usura. La Chiesa moderna e il prestito a interesse* (Soveria Mannelli: Rubbettino).

CHAPTER 8

Rural Credit Markets in Eighteenth-Century France: Contracts, Guarantees and Land

Elise M. Dermineur

8.1 Introduction

Historians of early modern France have long taken an interest in rural credit and debt; many of the great monographs of the *Annales* era covered this topic extensively (Saint Jacob 1998; Boehler 1995). These have not only shown the weight of indebtedness in rural communities throughout the period, but also emphasized the intrinsic link between debt and land (Béaur 1984, 2009). Building upon their work, traditional historiography has underlined that indebted peasants, unable to meet their engagements, had to cede their land to their rapacious creditors, who in turn were always ready to deprive peasants of their plots. Land was also a means to access capital in the credit market as it was traditionally used to back loans. Recently, however, scholars have begun to readdress this relationship between credit and land, and have advanced the idea that borrowing did not necessarily embody distress on the

E. M. Dermineur (✉)
Umeå University, Umeå, Sweden
e-mail: elise.dermineur@umu.se

C. Briggs and J. Zuijderduijn (eds.), *Land and Credit*,
Palgrave Studies in the History of Finance,
https://doi.org/10.1007/978-3-319-66209-1_8

part of the borrowers but could be a way to sustain investment—notably in land—and that lending did not imply a will to expropriate as its end. Credit, in fact, became a means to achieve a social and economic profit (Béaur 1994; Brennan 2006; Fontaine 2001; Hoffman et al. 1992, 2000; Hoffman 1996). This perspective applies particularly to the eighteenth century. As a result, the significance of land in financial transactions seems to have changed.

In order to show the significance of land in relation to credit, the chapter provides first an overview of the early modern French rural credit market and its characteristics, including the various types of contracts available to agents in which land served as collateral. Then, it examines in more detail the credit market of one specific rural area as a case study. Finally, the chapter takes a closer look at the meaning and evolution of guarantees, especially land, throughout the eighteenth century in this particular area. It is argued that the significance of land as collateral decreased throughout the eighteenth century. Through a close examination of notarial contracts covering loans and credit practices, the study seeks to examine the significance of land in credit exchanges.

8.2 Rural Credit Markets in Early Modern France

In rural communities, where credit was dynamic and widespread, peasants resorted to loans for various reasons. Scholars have demonstrated that there was a positive correlation between land and credit (Béaur 1994). Purchasing land often required substantial financial means, and only a few could afford to pay outright. Most land acquisitions had to be financed through credit. Rural dwellers also resorted to loans to make ends meet, either to pay their taxes or to defer payments on goods purchased. Occasional events such as a marriage, a succession, or the payment of a dowry, could also be financed through loans. In other words, credit sustained investment and provided means in difficult times. On most occasions, these loans were backed thanks to land.

8.2.1 Circuits of Credit

In early modern rural France, which is the focus of the research presented here, several channels of credit coexisted, comprising the institutionalized credit market on the one hand, and informal channels on the other. Where informal credit exchanges are concerned, many small credit transactions between individuals still elude us, either because the records of them were not archived or because they were often verbal agreements between parties (Pfister 1994, p. 1342). Creditor and borrower often knew each other and were bound either by family ties or by geographical proximity; thus, they often exempted themselves from the burden of registering their transaction (Dermineur 2015). We can track part of these transactions with the help of the probate inventories. Such transactions were often called '*contrat sous seing privés*'. The inventory of Pierre Malraget, who died in 1711, gives us an idea of such a transaction. Malraget owed money to Jean Jacques Cathey for seeds, to the nailer of Saint André for several small *obligations*, to the surgeon for 'medications' and to Pierre Desronces, who inscribed in his '*livre de raison*' a debt amounting 3 *livres* 10 *sols* 9 *deniers*, among others.[1] Many of these transactions never appeared in official documents. The amounts exchanged were also often small and did not necessarily require the official seal of the notary, for which a charge had to be paid, for the promise to be respected. These exchanges likely involved more flexibility in terms of negotiations regarding the terms of the contract, especially when it came to interest rates that were outside any official regulations.[2] One may suppose that the parties could have agreed to pay the interest—if any—in kind. Many of these loans were in fact deferred payments for commodities and various types of goods, highlighting the resort to credit in times of cash shortage. In these agreements, guarantees could be part of the deal but this does not appear to have been necessary. The amount exchanged was usually small, and it does not appear that these informal exchanges were used as a means to invest in land. It was not their main purpose.

The notary, on the other hand, was the official channel and institution for credit transactions (Hoffman et al. 1994, 2000). Throughout the early modern period, the French crown had attributed greater prerogatives to notaries.[3] Since 1566 and the reform of justice, loans superior to 100 *livres* had to be registered before the notary for a fee or had to be written down between private parties (Hardwick 1998, p. 5). This legal disposition underlines the effort of the state to rule out verbal agreements and control exchanges. But it does not seem that peasants took up the habit of registering their loans with the notary on a regular basis before the beginning of the eighteenth century. At that point, they steadily started to register most of their financial transactions, even loans inferior to 100 *livres*.

Religious institutions constituted another institutionalized circuit of credit (Ammannati 2012). Locally, parish vestries in each village also allocated resources and extended money. Very few studies have examined these transactions, mostly because they have been outshone by the richness of those in the notarial records but also because many parish vestry records have been destroyed and/or lost. Yet, the parish vestries' credit activities are extremely interesting, as we shall see.

Other channels of credit, such as pawnbroking, for instance, gravitated to the margins of the institutionalized credit market. Finally, one must note that the notary and these alternative circuits of credit did not compete with each other as they responded to different needs.

8.2.2 The Main Credit Instruments

In early modern France, at least four major different types of notarized and official financial tools coexisted: *obligations*, *rente perpétuelle*, *rente constituée* and *rente viagère*. The *rente viagère* (life annuity) was certainly the least common of the three types of annuity contract in the eighteenth century. The lender paid the borrower a certain capital, usually a significant sum. The lender made an interest payment annually until the creditor's death. Following the death of the creditor(s), the payment stopped; the heirs had no claim on the borrower. But if the debtor died before his creditor, his heirs had to continue the annual payments. This financial tool often served as a retirement pension, and its modern form and variant can still be found. The *rente perpétuelle* (perpetual annuity) worked differently. A payment was made annually, including interest, until the principal was totally repaid. Usually, the amount paid every year was fixed, giving the lender the assurance of a fixed annual income. The lender could not ask for the repayment of the capital but the borrower had the possibility to repay the principal of his *rente* at once (Béguin 2005, p. 1231). The annuity was backed by specific pieces of land. The *rente* was transmissible to heirs in case of the lender's death and if the capital had not been repaid by then. Taylor has labelled this instrument as 'archaic', underlining its very modest return compared to other instruments available (Taylor 1967, p. 481). The *rente constituée* (annuity) resembled the *rente perpétuelle*. It was attached to a specific piece of land. With a *rente constituée*, a lender extended money to a borrower until the latter decided to repay the capital in full. In the meantime, fixed interest payments—supposedly the revenues of the land—were made every year. Ferrière argues that this type of contract resembled a 'sale with the option to re-purchase' the land (Ferrière 1771, p. 548). The *rente constituée* functioned therefore somewhat like a medieval English mortgage and was often confused with the *rente perpétuelle* (Servais 1994). The land could be transferred to the buyer until full repayment of the *rente* (de Ferrière 1728, pp. 451–465). But the buyer often let the tenant continue working the land. Each of these three annuity contracts required collateral, usually in the form of land.

The last credit instrument was probably the most common and popular. *Obligations* were notarized promissory notes, widely used by artisans and peasants because they were used for small amounts repayable in the short term. Hoffman, Postel-Vinay and Rosenthal highlight the fact that 'over the course of the eighteenth century, they [*obligations*] grew larger and more common, and by the nineteenth century, they came to dominate the credit market' (Hoffman et al. 2000, p. 15). These authors, among others, argue that *obligations* could not legally bear an interest rate (Hoffman et al. 2000, p. 15). In practice, however, the interest could be hidden in the capital or arranged on the side (Rosenthal 1993, p. 132).[4] *Obligations*, which had to include a specific deadline for repayment—usually short term—could not also bear an interest rate, as the combination of both a deadline and interest constituted the crime of usury (Homer and Sylla 1996). Only an annuity contract allowed the lender to ask for interest because the annuity had no fixed limit in time regarding the repayment of the capital. The annuity contract (*rente constituée* or *rente perpétuelle*) gave the lender the right to collect a sum of money every year, known as *rente*. In order to circumvent the rules of the Church, an annuity contract had to include a specific piece of property (*bien immeuble*) on which the contract would be based, it had to have an interest rate with a maximum ceiling of 5%, and had to be 're-purchasable' by the debtor whenever he wished—or rather whenever he could. This aspect made the annuity a priori unlimited in time, that is 'perpetual'. These conditions therefore assimilated the annuity contract with a partial sale of the mortgaged land, which was allowed by the Church. Incidentally, it was the land mortgaged which bore the annuity, not the debtor. For instance, the land could be sold or inherited but would continue to be mortgaged, and the new owner would have to pay the annual *rente* to the lender. It is safe to argue that in the eighteenth century, all types of contract could potentially bear interest, concealed or not (Hoffman et al. 1992, p. 296). We shall return to this point shortly.

This rigid typology of contracts was undermined in practice (Dermineur and Svetiev 2015). In early modern France, similar credit instruments had different names and various characteristics. The *obligation* had a polymorphous and complex definition, and Jean-Laurent Rosenthal recognizes that 'even within the notarial system, the links between obligations and *rentes* remain unclear' (Rosenthal 1994, p. 291). For instance, in the seigneurie of Delle, discussed further below, the term *obligation* was widely used and did not strictly fit the definition given above. Peasants used the term *obligation* for all sorts of loans, both short term and long term, and with both fixed duration and undetermined duration. They used it for cash loans and for deferred payments, and they even used it for informal transactions, though normally, the *obligation* featured security of some kind. *Rentes* and *obligations*, therefore, displayed great porosity in their respective definitions and their uses. This appears clearly in our sample of transactions.

8.3 A Rural Credit Market in the Eighteenth-Century France

8.3.1 A Local Credit Market

As a case study, the seigneurie of Delle, located in Alsace, has been selected (Fig. 8.1). From the end of the seventeenth century, this seigneurie, a grouping of 19 villages, was the property of the Mazarin family (Colney 1989; Dermineur 2011). In 1720, approximately 2200 inhabitants populated the area, while in 1766 the rural dwellers were about 3400.[5] Most of the inhabitants of this rural seigneurie were farmers. Delle was the main town (roughly populated by 300–400 inhabitants in the middle of the eighteenth century), in which several artisans and merchants lived and worked, as well as a few millers and tanners. Delle was also the administrative centre of the lordship, where a local court, one notary and most of the seigneurial agents could be found.[6] Their numbers tended to increase in the eighteenth century. Agriculture and craft activities, with marginal textile production, were the main occupations.[7]

In this particular seigneurie, partible inheritance applied, and strict equality among heirs, regardless of sex, was respected (Dermineur 2011, 2016). The seigneurie also followed local customs for all sorts of legal arrangements.

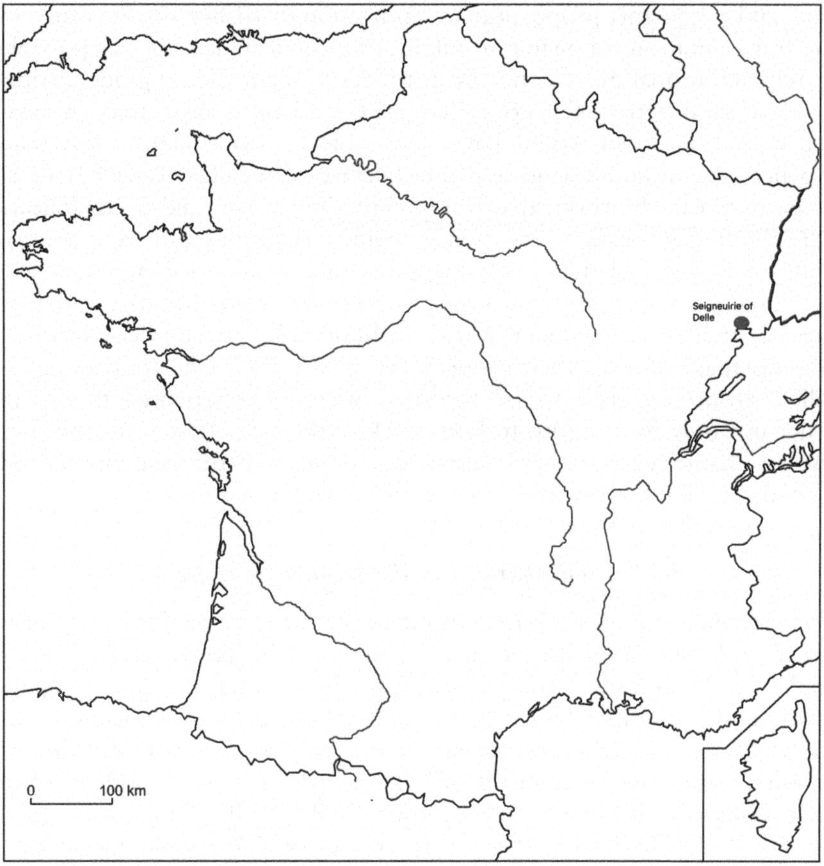

Fig. 8.1 The seigneurie of Delle

In the absence of proper tax registers for this region (such as *compoix* for instance), it is difficult to assess exactly the nature of land tenure. Jean-Michel Boehler estimates that about 60% of the land in Alsace was owned by peasants (Boehler 1999, p. 45). Among the other groups of proprietors, we can find lords, nobles, religious institutions and, to a lesser extent, urban elites. The relative distance of the seigneurie of Delle from the closest urban centre of Belfort might have dissuaded the urban bourgeois from investing in land there. Most of the peasants owned their land and when this proportion was not enough to live on—because of the fragmentation following an inheritance for instance—it was possible to rent additional plots either from the lord, from the religious institutions or from better-off fellow villagers. Calculations show that on average each household would have been able to work slightly less than five hectares of arable land and one hectare of meadow each.[8] It must be pointed out, however, that if fragmentation of land did occur following inheritance, peasants resorted to coping strategies and were able to trade with their relatives—offering plots in exchange for money, or in exchange for other plots—in order to redress the conditions created by the inheritance (Dermineur 2011). Additionally, peasants could alienate, mortgage and sell their property. However, their land transactions—called *mutations*—had to be recorded with the seigneurial notary in order not only for the lord to keep track of the taxes levied on land, but also to charge a fee for the transaction. If most of the peasants indeed owned their land, most of them were also charged with taxes.

8.3.2 Obligations in the Seigneurie of Delle

The vast majority of *obligation* contracts state the names, places of residence and sometimes the occupation of both the borrower(s) and the lender(s), the amount of money lent, the interest rate, the date of repayment, and the guarantees offered (guarantors and assets pledged). In the seigneurie of Delle, *obligations* were largely preferred to any kind of annuity (*rente*) at the notary's office. Record has been found of 1463 *obligations* for the eighteenth century (1733–1790), amounting to a total of 442,473 *livres* for the entire period, or 7763 *livres* per annum. As a comparison, 138 million *livres* were exchanged annually in Paris (Hoffman et al. 1999, p. 76). There was only one notary operating at a time in the seigneurie of Delle throughout the eighteenth century. Therefore, one can assume that most of the official loans in this seigneurie were recorded in this office. Our sample is thus quite complete. While it was theoretically possible to lend and borrow money in another seigneurie, evidence suggests that peasants tended to apply to the notary in their own seigneurie. Access to other seigneuries' credit markets proved to be more difficult.

Throughout the eighteenth century, not only did the number of loan contracts increase but the volume exchanged also rose (see Table 8.1). After the 1760s, a rapid increase both in terms of volume and number of

Table 8.1 Overview of the *obligations* in the seigneurie of Delle in the eighteenth century

	1730–1739	*1740–1749*	*1750–1759*	*1760–1769*	*1770–1779*	*1780–1789*
Volume (*livres*)	23,667	44,812	46,909	48,972	100,287	177,926
Number of contracts	131	179	194	207	280	472
Mean size	180.6	250.3	241.8	236.6	358.2	376.9
Median size	126	150	126.5	144	200	241

Sources ADTB, 2E4/155–159, 2E4/194, 2E4/222–223, 2E4/245–246, 2E4/257–258 and 2E4/279–280

Table 8.2 Distribution by size of *obligations* in the seigneurie of Delle, 1730–1789

	Number of contracts	*%*	*Median*
Size (*livres*)			
Below 50	52	(3.5)	40
50–99	156	(10.6)	72
100–199	505	(34.5)	120
200–229	307	(21.0)	212
300–399	166	(11.3)	300
400–1000	205	(14.0)	500
Over 1000	72	(5.0)	1420

Sources see Table 8.1

credit exchanges occurred. Hoffman and his co-authors have observed the same phenomenon in the credit market in Paris (Hoffman et al. 2000). A combination of several factors such as inflation, greater monetization and an emerging category of investors explains this sharp rise. Simultaneously, the median size of each contract rose rapidly after the 1760s. Taking a closer look at the distribution of *obligations* according to their size, it appears that 50% of the contracts involved sums between 100 and 300 *livres* (see Table 8.2).[9] In Delle, the notary seemed to offer only obligations to his clients. The number of *rentes* found is very negligible. We shall return to this point shortly.

Notaries only rarely specified the purpose of a loan.[10] Therefore, it is difficult to assess whether an obligation was in fact a deferred payment for goods, or an actual loan in cash.[11] We note nonetheless, based on the few contracts which specified purpose, that the volume of exchange for deferred payments began to decrease in the middle of the eighteenth century, while loans in cash rose impressively, which could indicate a greater penetration of money into rural areas.

Creditors and borrowers agreed on short-term loans. Most of the contracts stipulated a deadline for repayment of either one year (45%) or three years (28%). But in practice, it took longer for borrowers to repay, and some loans were renewed either informally or formally.[12] The case of 'on-demand' repayment ('*à première requisition*') is interesting. An on-demand repayment meant that the creditor could ask for the repayment of his capital whenever he pleased, with agreed amount of advance notice. Only a very few loans were repayable on demand.

Obligations usually mentioned collateral in the form of land, livestock, real estate property such as houses, or simply in the form of all the borrower's goods ('*tous ses biens meubles et immeubles*'). A co-signer could also be added to the deed. The debtor remained in possession of the land pledged. In the last part of this chapter, this subject of guarantees is explored in detail.

The credit market in the seigneurie of Delle worked almost in complete isolation, that is most of its agents were inhabitants of the seigneurie. Capital from beyond the seigneurie's borders was therefore marginal. We must also note that 30% of the loans were made between people living in the same village, tied by strong norms of cooperation, emotional norms and kinship (Dermineur 2017).

The vast majority of the *obligations* specified an interest rate of 5% (or 4% between 1766 and 1770), which corresponded to the legal ceiling. Only a few loans were interest free, or at least in appearance. In January 1735, Richard Baré bought several meadows. He asked a bourgeois of Delle to lend him 600 *livres* for this transaction, which he promised to reimburse within two years. The agreement between the two was interest free, but the meadows were mortgaged, and it was specified that the lender would make use of them until the repayment was complete. In June 1740, the same type of agreement occurred when Alexis Gladieu sold two steers to Jacques Monnier and his wife Jeanne Feriez for 87 *livres*. The couple agreed to pay Gladieu within a year without interest, and they pledged two specific plots of land. Gladieu would make use of the plots until full payment for the steers was made. In the cases where contracts specified a 5% interest, we can also assume that additional and hidden interest could be included in the agreement, either in kind or in the capital.

Various scholars underline the predominance of annuity contracts in the notarial archives (Hoffman et al. 2000; Schnapper 1957; Servais 1994). Hoffman and his co-authors argue that this specific credit instrument dominated the credit market both in terms of volume and in number until the last third of the eighteenth century (Hoffman et al. 2000, pp. 58–68). The *obligations* in our sample stipulated both an interest rate *and* a specific repayment date. As the province of Alsace was attached to the French kingdom after the Thirty Years' War by the treaty of Westphalia, it was decided to render the integration as smooth as possible. The '*us et coutumes*' of Alsace, therefore, remained, for the most part, unchanged. Alsatians had previously applied interest rates to what they called *obligations*, and this seemed to have continued after 1648. Despite the fact that an interest rate was applicable to an *obligation* contract in this region, annuities and *obligations* remained two different credit instruments. In the light of this, how do we explain the fact that annuities do not appear in the notarial registers?

8.3.3 Annuities Versus Obligations?

In order to explain the specificities of *obligations* in the seigneurie of Delle, we must first underline the absence of annuities in the notarial registers. Indeed, the number of *rentes*—annuities—was extremely low; fewer than 30 contracts or so for the period can be found here and there in different notarial records. How can we explain such a contrast with the *obligation* contracts? Why did peasants prefer to resort to *obligations* instead of annuities? Was it something specific to this particular region? Why did the notary offer *obligations* instead of annuities? Was it a trend peculiar to the eighteenth century? What does it mean when it comes to the involvement of land? And finally, were *obligations* really different from annuities?

First, we cannot completely discard the idea that annuity registers might have been lost. But surely traces of such contracts could be found in the judicial records in cases of conflict, for instance. While a good deal of debt litigation has been identified in research for this chapter, the vast majority of it concerned *obligation* contracts.

Second, we might question the extent to which our sample is representative of credit practices throughout early modern France. Despite the interest of the *Annales* historians in reconstructing peasants' lives and experiences, and despite the fact that all those scholars note the importance of credit in traditional communities, only partial information is currently available regarding contract practices and choices over agreements.[13] For Burgundy, Jean-Laurent Rosenthal has examined about

8100 loan contracts for the period 1757–1776. In Nuits-Saint-Georges, he found that 56% of the notarized credit contracts were *obligations*, accounting for 39% of the volume exchanged, while only seven per cent of the contracts were annuities, but these accounted for 21% of the volume exchanged. However, Rosenthal also found that 80% of the peasants resorted to *obligations* rather than annuities as borrowers (Rosenthal 1994, p. 291). One can only regret that Rosenthal remains vague about the exact definitions of *obligations* and annuities in his sample. Future studies will no doubt tell us more about rural credit contract practices.

Third, as the notary in Delle almost always offered the *obligation* to his clients as an instrument of credit, and very seldom annuities, it seems logical to assume that the weight of habit may have played a significant role, not only on the part of the peasants but also that of the notary, in reproducing contract practices. In the northern part of France, Postel-Vinay has noted that some notaries preferred to use *obligations* while others mainly resorted to annuities, depending on the 'characteristics of their clients' (Postel-Vinay 1998, p. 39). In Paris, in the second half of the eighteenth century, it seemed that notaries encouraged their clients to switch from *rentes* to *obligations* (Hoffman et al. 2000). In Delle, the notary might have had good reason to offer *obligations* rather than annuities. We may assume that the nature of land tenure (involving small parcels of property) encouraged the resort to *obligations* rather than annuities. This may have made sense because creditors may have preferred small loans to various debtors, so as to diversify their portfolios and therefore spread risks. It also seems logical to assume that peasants *did* in fact prefer to resort to *obligations* rather than annuities for strategic reasons. Some borrowers might not have wanted to engage their property in a long-term annuity, as this might have complicated the division of estates at death. On the other hand, lenders might not have wanted to place their capital with just one borrower, and/or for a lifetime. Lenders might have had a better chance of getting paid annual interest if they spread their capital over various borrowers, despite the fact that this involved risks and despite the fact that transaction costs might have been higher.

All these explanations might be complementary. The aim now is to advance another explanation: Peasants did not resort to annuities with the notary, because they could negotiate annuities elsewhere.

8.3.4 *Parish Vestries and Annuities*

Annuities were tools intended for better-off individuals, households and families that were able to immobilize their capital in the long run. Therefore, we may assume that only a few peasants could contract annuities. The problem, however, was not so much the demand for annuities, but rather their supply; the former may have exceeded the latter.

We can find annuity contracts in the registers of the parish vestries, which were called *fabriques* (Boccard 2015; Restif 2015; Constant 1938; Hoëttick-Gadbois 2006; Merlin 2001). These organizations existed from the thirteenth century at least and could be found in each parish throughout France (Bos 1998). In the late middle ages, the Church decided to transfer a quarter of its revenue to the parishes in order to repair and maintain religious buildings there. Scholars have shown that at least since the thirteenth century, laypersons—called *fabriciens* or *marguilliers*—administrated these revenues (Goujard 1982). Parishioners donated small amounts of money for the repose of their souls (*fondation de messe*), but they could also bequeath land, estates and money to the Church. Obviously, the revenue of each parish vestry depended on the size of the parish, the number of its inhabitants and their wealth. The *Fabrique* Saint Etienne in Courtelvant, in our sample, for instance, counted less than 500 inhabitants in the eighteenth century; its revenue in 1715, for example, amounted to 1944 *livres* in cash. There were two types of revenue. First, there was the revenue from collections during services, funerals, pew-renting and sale of produce from the cemetery, for instance. Second, the vestry also collected revenue from renting out land bequeathed by the faithful, and from the annual payment of annuity contracts extended to hundreds of individuals. Part of this money went to the repair and maintenance of the parish church but also to the purchase of candles, religious ornaments, payment of the priest for the service of the mass and payment to the administrators of the parish vestries. As the revenue could exceed expenses, the administrators were able to lend cash to individuals. In order to respect the Church's rules on usury, only annuities were accepted. Peasants pledged a piece of land to the *fabrique* in exchange for capital received, and then every year, they paid the parish vestry a *rente*. For the seigneurie of Delle, the annuity registers of the parish vestries have disappeared. Some account books are left for a few years but they only give partial information on the contracts. It has proved possible to find a copy of such a contract in a record of judicial proceedings. Adam Meyet from the village of Courtelvant borrowed 12 *livres bâloises* from the *fabrique* at 4% interest in 1670. He had not repaid the capital, and his heir and grandchild, Pierre Bettevy, had to renew the annuity contract with the parish vestry in 1715. For this, six *journeaux de champs* were mortgaged.[14] Such a loan could be interpreted in fact as a rent paid every year to the *fabrique* (Taylor 1967, p. 474).

A rapid and non-exhaustive survey of probate records in Delle throughout the eighteenth century reveals that 63% of the decedents were indebted to a parish vestry. Some owed only small amounts, but others owed significant sums.[15] An example is Joseph Rapiney, who died in 1703. Among other things, he owed to the parish vestry 269 *livres* 15 *sols bâloises*, a very significant amount of money.[16] Dizier Bandelier died in 1764. He was indebted to several individuals and to the parish vestry, to which he owed 54 *livres.*[17] The majority of the probate inventories examined for the last quarter of the seventeenth century mention a debt to a vestry, while fewer such debts can be found after the second half of the eighteenth century.

Further research needs to be undertaken on the parish vestries, especially regarding the strategies behind the distribution of credit to certain individuals within the community, and the allocation of different interest rates. In the few account books which do survive, indeed, money was granted to various borrowers with different interest rates, suggesting cronyism, perhaps nepotism and/or risk assessments which took account of the reputations of debtors. Jacques Henningue, for instance, had borrowed 250 *livres.* In 1761, he owed 12 *livres* 10 *sols* as interest. In this case, Henningue paid 5% interest to the *fabrique.* Jacques Herbelin paid 10 *livres* as interest on 150 *livres* borrowed, that is to say, 4%. The widow Elisabeth Franquin paid 6 *livres* and 14 *sols* as interest on a capital sum of 101 *livres*, that is to say, more than 6.5% in interest.[18] It is unclear why certain individuals were granted preferential rates. In some cases, the parish vestry seemed to be able to offer interest rates that were more attractive than the maximum rate that the notary was legally obliged to apply.

As the parish vestries' surplus cash was limited in volume, the lay administrators might have privileged certain individuals, such as their own clients and solvent borrowers, so that the *marguilliers*' account would not suffer from conflict over repayments; the *marguilliers* were accountable for the management of funds during their tenure. For instance, to judge by the account books of the *fabrique* of Delle, it appears that women did not enjoy access to the capital of the parish vestry. Widows appeared in the records, but this was usually because they were required to reimburse the debts of their deceased husbands. They had inherited land to which the *rente* was attached.

Those who were able to secure their loans with land could have access to the parish vestry funds. As the annuity contracts had no fixed limit in time, we can presume that loans were substantial, as the sample of post-mortem inventories suggests. It is unclear whether or not the value of the land pledged had an effect on the size of the transaction. Katia Béguin has shown that the value of land often exceeded the principal sum loaned in the *rente* (Béguin 2005, p. 1234). It could be argued that those who could not access parish vestry funds might have turned as an alternative to the notary.

Borrowers necessarily had to look to the long term when they contracted annuities, and ask themselves whether they really wanted to burden their land with *rentes*. Annuities did exist alongside *obligations*, but they were clearly reserved to a happy few. They served therefore a rather different purpose to *obligations*. While annuities had been used since the middle ages, they do not seem to have changed much in the eighteenth century. A rapid and admittedly incomplete survey of probate inventories shows that annuities extended by parish vestries were less numerous in the second half of the eighteenth century. On the other hand, *obligations* did develop after 1760 and perhaps really began to differentiate themselves from *rentes* in that period.

8.4 Changes and Challenges in the Second Half of the Eighteenth Century

8.4.1 The Ultimate Need for a Guarantee

In considering the sample of *obligations* for the seigneurie of Delle, a closer look at the guarantees used to secure loans reveals changes over the course of the eighteenth century, especially regarding the role of land.

In traditional societies, in order to lend money, creditors needed to be assured that, in addition to the payment of regular and certain interest, they would recover their capital in due time. Trust, nonetheless, was mostly based on information about the debtor's assets, competences, intentions and reputation (Dermineur 2015). Existing information asymmetry between a lender and a borrower, however, produced situations of high uncertainty where it was difficult to generate trust, mostly on the creditor's side (Yamagishi 1991). However, in small communities, where the borrower and the creditor likely knew each other beforehand, and where we can assume that pre-existing trust and access to reliable information was present, uncertainty revolved mostly around the conditions of repayment, since external and uncontrollable factors might provoke temporary or definitive defaults (these factors include death, disease and the consequent inability to produce an income, bad harvests, climatic shocks and an increase in tax rates). Moral hazard could still have an impact, but its risk was somehow reduced thanks to social ties and the availability of information. Members of the same community, or of the same network, could reduce asymmetry and uncertainties through social exchange. In Bourdieu's perspective, for instance, social capital helped to abbreviate moral hazard (Bourdieu 1980).

Social proximity, strong endogamy, kinship ties, strong norms of cooperation and easy access to information were the characteristics of rural communities that enabled creditors and debtors to reach mutual trust without resorting to unnecessary guarantees. Moreover, a good reputation as an honest person—having credit—enabled the debtor not only to find credit more easily but also to ensure that fewer guarantees were required on the deed, as a good reputation and personal credit determined trustworthiness (Crowston 2011). In a small community, reputation constituted a critical factor, and this key information was easy to come by, thanks to high degree of social proximity. Reputation showed the creditor the willingness of the debtor to repay his debts, and this secured the transaction (Smail 2004). Information, reputation, competences and guarantees were therefore the four pillars of trust in the traditional rural credit market (Muldrew 1998).

As a result, in traditional communities, guarantees offered accompanying a loan did exist but remained reduced, flexible and negotiable (Dermineur and Svetiev 2015). Peasants who lived within the same community, and worked together, shared many social norms. Their social and geographical proximity, family ties, high rate of endogamy, and their relative knowledge of each other created strong bonds within the community, including trust. Many authors have highlighted that a society which shared norms created expectations of trustworthiness, and this therefore reduced the transaction costs related to infringement of norms (Coleman 1988; Ogilvie 2004; Yamagishi 2011).[19] Indeed, the infringement of norms by a group member would provoke in return social stigma and punishment by the community, through ostracism, for instance (Coleman 1988, p. 99;

Table 8.3 The proportions of *obligations* involving different types of guarantees, 1730–1790

	Co-signer(s)		*Specific piece(s) of land pledged*		*Specific piece(s) of land pledged and co-signer(s)*		*All movable and immovable goods pledged*	
	N	%	N	%	N	%	N	%
1730–1739	20	15.3	48	36.6	13	9.9	50	38.2
1740–1749	42	23.5	55	30.7	25	13.9	57	31.8
1750–1759	54	27.8	35	18.0	20	10.3	85	43.8
1760–1769	86	41.5	8	3.9	2	0.9	111	53.6
1770–1779	112	40.0	7	2.5	5	1.8	156	55.7
1780–1789	247	52.3	10	2.1	4	0.8	211	44.7

Sources see Table 8.1

Bicchieri 2006; Elster 1989, 1999). A peasant who borrowed money from another and did not repay the loan while he had the means to do so, would lose his credit and good reputation and consequently fail to establish further loans with community members in the future, and perhaps would also fail in other business transactions. Knowledge of default was assured through discussion in the community, but also through resort to a judicial institution (Smail 2004). Yet despite the strong norms of cooperation existing among peasants, we should however not be surprised to find collateral backing loans, as defaults did occur.

Collateral in the form of land dominated the guarantees offered until around the middle of the eighteenth century (see Table 8.3). It is safe to assume that the choice of the plots specified in the deed as collateral had been negotiated between the parties beforehand, and perhaps even without the intermediation of the notary. Pledging a particular plot in the deed might also have been a form of commitment which engaged the borrower on an emotional level. Historians have argued that in partible inheritance regions, peasants were not attached to specific plots but rather to the notion of possession. While this argument sounds reasonable, engaging a particular plot of land, perhaps inherited, perhaps bought, in a risky and uncertain credit transaction could have had an emotional dimension. More work in this area needs to be done since it might inform us further on the meaning of land and property. Finally, it is worth noting that borrowers remained in possession of their pledged land.

Before the middle of the eighteenth century, we note a great diversity in the guarantees offered, reflecting not only the needs and strategies of both creditors and debtors but also the great flexibility in terms of arrangements in the contract (Dermineur and Svetiev 2015). For example, in June 1733, the widow Marie Barbe Tourtelier borrowed from the physician Lacour the sum of 300 *livres* in 'real' money.[20] The widow promised to reimburse her creditor in a year and engaged some of her meadows and arable lands as guarantees. The parties also agreed that the lender would receive hay and new growth from the mortgaged meadows and 20 carp in addition as interest. In this case, the mortgaged lands served to pay interest in kind to the creditor. In October 1733, Jean Henri Feriez bought two steers from Alexis Gladieux for 120 *livres*. Feriez promised to pay the whole sum to him in a year and backed his purchase with several specific meadows mortgaged in addition to all his goods. No interest was specified. We can hypothesize that the meadows mortgaged might have served to pay the interest—especially if the borrower took longer to repay than the period initially planned—since on the face of it the contract itself was merely a deferred payment and a debt recognition.[21] In March 1734, Jean Pierre Chaumé recognized that he owed Marc Vareschat 81 *livres*. Chaumé had bought two young mares from Vareschat. He promised to pay him within two years with an interest at 5%.[22] He backed this deferred payment by pledging all his goods as well as a plot of meadow '*à titre précaire*', which means that the lender could use this land until full repayment. Here, it is interesting to note that in addition to the legal interest, a piece of land apparently also indirectly served to pay interest. Either the revenue of the land was considered to be the 5% interest specified or, and this seems plausible, the piece of land was given in addition to the 5% interest. In this way, the legal ceiling could be circumvented (cf. Flandreau et al. 2009).

In the event that the debtor could not meet the payment deadline and fell behind in his repayments, the creditor could bring him to the local court. This solution for recovering the capital likely occurred after negotiations between parties, and appeared as the last available resort. The judge examined the contract and usually ruled in favour of the creditor after the first hearing in almost all the cases. After a long process, auction of the mortgaged land took place. However, most litigation stopped after the first hearing; peasant evictions were uncommon (Holderness 1975; Postel-Vinay 1998, p. 33). Often, peasants preferred to solve their contention privately. In 1765, Elisabeth Gainon extended a loan of 50 *livres* to a couple living in her village for their '*affaires et besoins*'. Jacques Bonjean and Suzanne Vuilaumier, however, could not repay her after the three-year deadline. They preferred to execute a land sale and cede one of their pieces of land to Gainon.[23] One may also assume that this pattern of flexibility could also have applied to larger loans such as *rentes.* If a debtor missed an annual payment, negotiations could ensue, and consensus could be reached. The creditor might agree to receive the annual payment in kind for instance.

It should be pointed out that the land mortgaged in the loans did not necessarily match the value of the capital borrowed. It was either far superior to it, which could indicate a demanding attitude on the part of the lender, or inferior to the capital borrowed, which could indicate perhaps that the land was used to pay the interest in kind.

These diverse arrangements were common before the 1760s; there are many variations and specificities pertaining to each contract. Borrowers and lenders seemed to have enjoyed latitude of action, decisions and choices regarding their loan deals which was far superior to the situation they would experience in the second half of the eighteenth century (Dermineur and Svetiev 2015).

8.4.2 Changes in the Second Half of the Eighteenth Century

As we have seen, borrowers had to add guarantees to the deed in order to secure their transactions and reassure their creditors. If, in the first half of the eighteenth century, borrowers usually pledged specific plots of land to secure their transaction, and in the second half of the eighteenth century, they began to pledge their entire present and future goods exclusively, without the mention of any specific piece of land (see Table 8.3). The pledge of a specific piece of land before 1760 appears in almost 40% of the contracts (specific piece of land pledged 27.4%, *and* specific land pledged and co-signers, 11.5%). After 1760, however, pledges of specific pieces of land dropped markedly (see Table 8.3). We shall come back to this point shortly.[24]

Meanwhile, third-party co-signers were also added in large numbers to the deeds after 1760. In the 1730s, only 15% of contracts mentioned the presence of an external guarantor, while in the last decade of the century, this proportion reached 52.3% of the contracts signed.

But perhaps more strikingly, we can observe another feature. From the 1730s to the 1760s, the data show that peasants represented 65% of the total creditors, while in the last decade of the Old Regime, they represented only 35% of the creditors. This major change can be explained by the involvement of a new type of creditors, from the liberal professions (related to administration and services) and seigniorial agents (judges, clerks and so on). It seems that only a handful of these people, such as the seigneurial judges, for instance, had good information on potential borrowers. In the 1730s, these judges lent 10.7% of the volume exchanged (the equivalent figure for peasants was 48.16%), while in the last decade of the Old Regime, they lent 30% of the total volume, in comparison with 31% for the peasants (Dermineur 2015).

This new group of investors, coming from a different socio-professional category, had different goals, financial strategies and expectations, which did not match the traditional pattern of cooperation and norms of reciprocity of the peasants. Above all, they had different priorities regarding the guarantees required to secure their transactions. We have seen that the amount of land mortgaged dropped suddenly, which can be explained partly because most of it had already been mortgaged before, but also, one can argue, because the new creditors, who were not farmers, did not want to have to deal with land (Postel-Vinay 1998, p. 123). This might be because land would have been hard to sell or to rent in a difficult economic context, but also, and above all, because creditors did not want the peasants to use pledged land to pay interest in kind. Payment in kind might have entailed complications, transaction costs, difficulties of storage, and so forth. This aspect also explains why the data show more guarantors, after 1760, who could provide extra security if the initial borrower defaulted. However, it can also be suggested that the guarantor could have provided not only the repayment of the sum borrowed in case of default, but might also have provided an incentive for repayment, as part of a social mechanism whereby cooperation and coercion among peers would have yielded better and more efficient results than external coercion—from a judge, for example.

In addition, we must note that the number of married couples who borrowed money increased throughout the period from 22% of the total amount borrowed in 1730–1739 to almost 50% in 1780–1789, meaning that men progressively attached their wives' names to deeds and fewer and fewer men borrowed alone in the credit market (Dermineur 2014). Married women's properties in the form of dowry, cash or inherited property became an interesting additional guarantee in the eyes of many creditors (Dermineur 2009), perhaps because the land contained in women's dowries might not yet have been over-collateralized. Moreover, repayment could be sought by turning to the widow for her share of the debt, in the case of her husband's death, as she was legally involved in this process and therefore liable for half of the loan.

As a new group of investors emerged, the amount of debt litigation at the local court increased, which tends to indicate not only the growing indebtedness on the part of peasants but also the impatience of creditors. Bringing proceedings for the repayment of a debt did not necessarily include seizing the debtor's goods, which was a long process, but could instead be a strategy to reach the co-signer. It should be stressed that in case of default, the legal procedure could be long, with uncertainty on the part of the creditor that he would recover his capital in its entirety. In case of default, indeed, the creditor could also face competition with other potential lenders. In a drawn-out legal process, the judge would have to decide on the matter, assess the priority of claims of various creditors, and land would have to be auctioned. Expropriation per se remained exceptional (Postel-Vinay 1998, p. 33). The time lost and the uncertainty in recovering the totality of their capital—if they recovered any—in this scenario may have discouraged creditors from accepting land as mortgages.

Therefore, the nature of guarantees changed and evolved after the 1760s. Land, while still an important security, did not appear as attractive a guarantee as previously, and no longer sufficed. Borrowers continued to offer all their goods as collateral, but it seems that creditors did not wish to deal with specific plots in case of default. Land was often already mortgaged and charged with annuities, and characterized by uncertainty concerning yields and harvests, high transaction costs and fears concerning payment of interest in kind, all of which pushed creditors not only to ask for greater guarantees but also for guarantees that would give them easier access to cash.

As the new category of investors turned their backs on traditional collateral in the form of land, we might then question the value of land. Surely, it remained a critical asset for peasants for production and survival, but as the new category of creditors disregarded it in favour of cash, one may suggest that bartering and flexible arrangements concerning the payment of interest were relegated to the background. Moral economy and strong norms of cooperation, traditional characteristics of early modern rural communities, were thus challenged.

8.5 Conclusion

This chapter has shown that the peasants of the seigneurie of Delle largely resorted to notarial *obligations* contracts. Annuities, on the other hand, could be found only in the parish vestry registers and seemed to have been the privilege of a few. We may argue that annuities were in fact rare instruments while *obligations* were easier to provide. Two different channels of credit coexisted therefore and gave peasants a choice over their credit strategies. Annuities required the land pledged to be burdened with a *rente*, while on the other hand, land pledged in *obligations* could be used to pay interest in kind or to be left in the hand of creditors until repayment as a usufruct only.

In the second half of the eighteenth century, however, a group of new investors, from the emerging bourgeoisie, socially and often geographically remote from the local community, began to extend credit and to demand stronger guarantees to secure their investments, as well as rigid deadlines for repayment. As a result, not only did the saving capacity of these creditors flood the local credit market, leading to an increase in the number of loans, but their exigency towards repayment and guarantees also changed the moral and emotional norms traditionally experienced by ordinary debtors and creditors, witnessing a sharp increase in guarantees that did not involve solely land. This group of new investors changed the norms of cooperation and introduced more rigidity in agreements, especially regarding guarantees, leading, for example, to the increasing requirement of a co-signer. They might also have changed the meaning and significance of land. However, much more work needs to be done regarding credit contract practices in early modern France. The results of this study cannot be extrapolated to other regions without great caution; we would be wrong to assume that credit tools were used the same way in the various parts of the kingdom or equally throughout time.

Notes

1. Archives Départementales du Territoire de Belfort (hereafter ADTB), 2E4/85, 26 March 1711, Inventory of Pierre Malraget.
2. It should be noted, however, that an interest rate superior to 5% was legally considered usurious. The legal cap for notarized loans was 5%, with the exception of the years 1766–1770 when it was 4%. See Isambert (1829, p. 406).

3. Royal notaries coexisted with seigneurial notaries, often called *tabellions*, whose legal capacities were similar.
4. However, in Delle (the locality studied in this chapter), it was found that these contracts, just like *rente*, specified an interest rate; in the eighteenth century, this was usually equal to the 5% legal rate and almost never under that level. This can be explained by the fact that Alsace retained most of its legal norms and customs after the French conquest in 1648.
5. ADTB, 21J1, Dénombrement 1720 and 1766.
6. During the eighteenth century, the seigneurie of Delle had its own local courts; these courts met frequently in its towns. Peasants could seek justice very easily as all the villages were located near the towns. As the seigneurie was part of Alsace, there was no royal justice in this particular region (one specificity of this area). Instead, seigneurial courts of justice offered their services to the peasants, who found themselves satisfied with both its quality and service; see Dermineur (2011).
7. The putting-out system is rather difficult to establish for this particular region. We have evidence of small-scale familial production, thanks notably to probates. It likely generated complementary revenue for those families that could afford a weaving loom. The merchants of Mulhouse, located less than 50 km away, might have provided outsourcing contracts for the peasants of the seigneurie. Mulhouse was nicknamed the French Manchester because of its important textile production.
8. Based on ADTB, 21J.
9. Only 14% of the loans were below 100 *livres*. This can be explained by the fact that the law obliged agents to resort to a notary for loans superior to 100*l*.
10. Notaries were not obliged to specify the purpose of the loan (Ferrière 1771, p. 250).
11. Under the category loans (cash), can be found loans that were made in cash but also loans where it cannot be certain that the loan was in cash. Those mentioned only a 'just and legal loan of money' ('juste et légal prêt d'argent'). In the absence of other information, it is assumed that the money was delivered in cash.
12. The rise of debt litigation in the eighteenth century indicates the difficulty borrowers had in repaying their debts on time.
13. To date, Hoffman et al. (2000), remains the key reference for the examination of credit practices in early modern France. Their sample, however, focuses on Paris, and their conclusions cannot be applied in other regions without great caution.
14. ADTB, 12B182.

15. ADTB, 2E4/56 (1675–1707), 85 (1713–1728), 211 (1761–1763) and 287 (1779–1788). The sample comprises 57 post-mortem inventories.
16. ADTB, 2E4/56.
17. ADTB, 2E4/211.
18. ADTB, 12B182.
19. Here, transaction costs refer to the costs associated with the making of an economic exchange, such as search and information costs, bargaining costs, but more specifically enforcement costs.
20. ADTB, 2E4/155.
21. ADTB, 2E4/155.
22. ADTB, 2E4/155.
23. ADTB, 2E4/257.
24. It is interesting to note that Postel-Vinay has observed the contrary in Maubeuge, where specific guarantees were required. He does not specify whether this specific guarantee involved land (Postel-Vinay 1998, pp. 123–124).

Acknowledgements The author would like to acknowledge the financial support of Riksbankens Jubileumsfond and the Swedish Collegium for Advanced Study for this research. She would also like to thank the editors for their helpful suggestions and their constructive comments.

References

Secondary Works

Ammannati, F., 2012. *Religion and Religious Institutions in the European Economy, 1000–1800* (Florence: Florence University Press).

Béaur, G., 1984. *Le marché foncier à la veille de la Révolution: les mouvements de propriété beaucerons dans les régions de Maintenon et de Janville de 1761 à 1790* (Paris: Editions de l'Ecole des Hautes Etudes en Sciences Sociales).

Béaur, G., 1994. 'Foncier et crédit dans les sociétés préindustrielles: des liens solides ou des chaînes fragiles?', *Annales. Histoire, Sciences Sociales*, vol. 49, pp. 1411–1428.

Béaur, G., 2009. 'Credit and land in eighteenth-century France', in P.R. Schofield and T. Lambrecht (eds.), *Credit and the Rural Economy in North Western Europe, c.1200–c.1850* (Turnhout: Brepols), pp. 153–167.

Béguin, K., 2005. 'La circulation des rentes constituées dans la France du XVIIe siècle', *Annales. Histoire, Sciences Sociales*, vol. 60, pp. 1229–1244.

Bicchieri, C., 2006. *The Grammar of Society: The Nature and Dynamics of Social Norms* (Cambridge: Cambridge University Press).

Boccard, M., 2015. 'Commande et financement des œuvres d'art: à travers les comptes des fabriques de Saint-Melaine et Saint-Mathieu de Morlaix', in J.-C. Cassard, Y. Coativy, A. Gallicé and D. Le Page (eds.), *Le Prince, L'argent, Les Hommes Au Moyen Âge: Mélanges Offerts À Jean Kerhervé* (Rennes: Presses Universitaires de Rennes), pp. 313–322.

Boehler, J.-M., 1995. *Une Société Rurale en Milieu Rhénan: la Paysannerie de la Plaine d'Alsace (1648–1789)* (Strasbourg: Presses Universitaires de Strasbourg).

Boehler, J.-M., 1999. 'De la reconstruction agraire à la mise en vente des biens nationaux: possession de la terre, conjoncture agraire et rapports sociaux dans la plaine d'Alsace (XVII e–XVIII e Siècles)', *Histoire, Économie et Société*, vol. 18, pp. 43–62.

Bos, A., 1998. Les archives des fabriques parisiennes à la fin du Moyen Âge et à l'époque moderne. *Bibliothèque de l'Ecole des chartres*, vol. 156, pp. 369–405.

Bourdieu, P., 1980. 'Le capital social', *Actes de la recherche en sciences sociales*, vol. 31, pp. 2–3.

Brennan, T., 2006. 'Peasants and debt in eighteenth-century Champagne', *Journal of Interdisciplinary History*, vol. 37, pp. 175–200.

Coleman, J., 1988. 'Social capital in the creation of human capital', *American Journal of Sociology*, vol. 94, pp. 95–120.

Colney, M., 1989. *Delle au XVIIIe Siècle* (Strasbourg: Coprur).

Constant, G., 1938. 'Les registres de marguilliers', *Revue D'histoire de l'Église de France*, vol. 24, pp. 170–183.

Crowston, C., 2011. 'Credit and the metanarrative of modernity', *French Historical Studies*, vol. 34, pp. 7–19.

de Ferrière, C.-J., 1728. La science parfaite des notaires, ou Le moyen de faire un parfait notaire (Paris: Osmont). http://gallica.bnf.fr/ark:/12148/bpt6k9679357t.

Dermineur, E., 2009. 'Female peasants, patriarchy, and the credit market in eighteenth-century France', *Proceedings of the Western Society for French History*, vol. 37, pp. 61–84.

Dermineur, E., 2011. 'The civil judicial system in early modern France', *Frühneuzeit-Info*, vol. 22, pp. 44–53.

Dermineur, E., 2014. 'Les femmes et le crédit dans les communautés rurales au 18e siècle', *Traverse Revue d'Histoire - Zeitschrift für Geschichte*, vol. 2, pp. 53–64.

Dermineur, E., 2015. 'Trust, norms of cooperation, and the rural credit market in eighteenth-century France', *Journal of Interdisciplinary History*, vol. 45, pp. 485–506.

Dermineur, E., 2016. 'Widows' political strategies in traditional communities: Negotiating marital status and authority in eighteenth century France', in J. Daybell and S. Norrhem (eds.), *Gender and Political Culture in Early Modern Europe, 1400–1800* (Abingdon: Routledge), pp. 123–141.

Dermineur, E., 2017. 'Indebtedness', in S. Bromhall (ed.), *Early Modern Emotions: An Introduction* (Abingdon: Routledge), pp. 195–198.
Dermineur, E., and Y. Svetiev, 2015. 'The fairness of contractual exchange in a private law society: A case study of early modern credit markets', *European Review of Contract Law*, vol. 11, pp. 229–251.
Elster, J., 1989. 'Social norms and economic theory', *Journal of Economic Perspectives*, vol. 3, pp. 99–117.
Elster, J., 1999. *Alchemies of the Mind: Rationality and the Emotions* (Cambridge: Cambridge University Press).
Ferrière, Claude-Joseph de Ferrière, 1728. *La science parfaite des notaires, ou Le moyen de faire un parfait notaire* (Paris: Osmont). http://gallica.bnf.fr/ark:/12148/bpt6k9679357t.
Ferrière, C., 1771. *Dictionnaire de droit et de pratique*, vol. 2 (Paris: Bauche).
Flandreau, M., C. Galimard, C. Jobst and P. Nogués-Marco, 2009. 'The bell jar: Commercial interest rates between two revolutions, 1688–1789', in J. Atack and L. Neal (eds.), *The Origins and Development of Commercial Markets and Institutions: From the Seventeenth Century to the Present* (Cambridge: Cambridge University Press), pp. 161–208.
Fontaine, L., 2001. 'Antonio and Shylock: Credit and trust in France, c.1680–c.1780' *EcHR*, vol. 54, pp. 39–57.
Goujard, P., 1982. 'Les fonds de fabriques paroissiales: une source d'histoire religieuse méconnue', *Revue D'histoire de l'Église de France*, vol. 68, pp. 99–111.
Hardwick, J., 1998. *The Practice of Patriarchy: Gender and the Politics of Household Authority in Early Modern France* (University Park: Pennsylvania State University Press).
Hoëttick-Gadbois, G., 2006. 'Les marguilliers, "chevilles ouvrières" de la vie paroissiale d'après les visites archidiaconales de Josas, 1458–1470', *Revue d'Histoire de l'Eglise de France*, vol. 92, pp. 25–46.
Hoffman, P., 1996. *Growth in a Traditional Society: The French Countryside, 1450–1815* (Princeton: Princeton University Press).
Hoffman, P., G. Postel-Vinay and J.-L. Rosenthal, 1992. 'Private credit markets in Paris, 1690–1840', *JEH*, vol. 52, pp. 293–306.
Hoffman, P., G. Postel-Vinay and J.-L. Rosenthal, 1994. 'What do notaries do? Overcoming asymmetric information in financial markets: The case of Paris, 1751', UCLA Economics Working Paper. UCLA Department of Economics.
Hoffman, P., G. Postel-Vinay and J.-L. Rosenthal, 1999. 'Information and economic history: How the credit market in old regime Paris forces us to rethink the transition to capitalism', *AHR*, vol. 104, pp. 69–94.
Hoffman, P., G. Postel-Vinay and J.-L. Rosenthal, 2000. *Priceless Markets. The Political Economy of Credit in Paris (1660–1870)* (Chicago: University of Chicago Press).

Holderness, B.A., 1975. 'Credit in a rural community, 1660–1800: Some neglected aspects of probate inventories', *Midland History*, vol. 3, pp. 94–116.

Homer, S., and R.E. Sylla, 1996. *A History of Interest Rates*, 3rd edn. (New Brunswick, NJ: Rutgers University Press).

Isambert, F., 1829. *Recueil général des anciennes lois françaises: depuis l'an 420 jusqu'à la révolution de 1789* (Paris: Belin-Le-Prieur).

Merlin, J., 2001. 'Les plus anciens comptes de fabrique de l'eglise paroissiale de Lambersart (1483–1513)', *Revue du Nord*, vol. 340, pp. 295–317.

Muldrew, C., 1998. *The Economy of Obligation: The Culture of Credit and Social Relations in Early Modern England* (Basingstoke: Palgrave).

Ogilvie, S., 2004. 'How does social capital affect women? Guilds and communities in early modern Germany', *AHR*, vol. 109, pp. 325–359.

Pfister, U., 1994. 'Le petit crédit rural en Suisse aux XVIe–XVIIIe Siècles', *Annales. Histoire, Sciences Sociales*, vol. 49, pp. 1339–1357.

Postel-Vinay, G., 1998. *La terre et l'argent, l'agriculture et le crédit en France du XVIIIe au début du XXe siècle* (Paris: Albin Michel).

Restif, B., 2015. *La révolution des paroisses: culture paroissiale et réforme catholique en Haute-Bretagne aux xvie et xviie siècles* (Rennes: Presses Universitaires de Rennes).

Rosenthal, J.-L., 1993. 'Credit markets and economic change in southeastern France 1630–1788', *Explorations in Economic History*, vol. 30, pp. 129–157.

Rosenthal, J.-L., 1994. 'Rural credit markets and aggregate shocks: The experience of Nuits St. Georges, 1756–1776', *JEH*, vol. 54, pp. 288–306.

Saint Jacob, P., 1998. *Les paysans de la Bourgogne du Nord au dernier siècle de l'Ancien Régime* (Rennes: Presses Universitaires de Rennes).

Schnapper, B., 1957. *Les rentes au XVIe siècle. Histoire d'un instrument de crédit* (Paris: S.E.V.P.E.N).

Servais, P., 1994, 'De la rente au crédit hypothécaire en période de transition industrielle. Stratégies familiales en région Liégeoise au XVIIIe siècle', *Annales. Histoire, Sciences Sociale*, vol. 49, pp. 1393–1409.

Smail, Daniel L., 2004. *The Consumption of Justice: Emotions, Publicity, and Legal Culture in Marseille* (Ithaca: Cornell University Press), pp. 1264–1423.

Taylor, G.V., 1967. 'Noncapitalist wealth and the origins of the French Revolution', *AHR*, vol. 72, pp. 469–496.

Yamagishi, Toshio, 1991. *Trust the Evolutionary Game of Mind and Society* (Tokyo: Springer).

Yamagishi, T., 2011. *Trust: The Evolutionary Game of Mind and Society* (Tokyo and London: Springer).

CHAPTER 9

The Use of Perpetual Annuities in Rural Brabant in the Fifteenth and Sixteenth Centuries

Michael Limberger and Nicolas De Vijlder

9.1 Introduction: The Role of Credit in the Rural Economy of Brabant

Research on rural credit markets in the Southern Low Countries in the middle ages and the early modern period is still scarce and comes down to a handful of articles. The study of rural credit is generally integrated into studies of the land market, a field of research which has received increasing attention during the past several decades. Notably, in 2003, the 35th 'Settimana di Studi' of the Istituto Datini at Prato was dedicated to the study of land markets. Within the framework of this conference, E. Thoen and T. Soens provided a treatment of the situation in medieval Flanders. While mentioning the existence of different forms of formal and informal credit arrangements, they mainly focused on constituted rents or annuities (in Dutch *renten*) as being the most frequent form of registered credit transactions in the late middle ages in Flanders (Thoen and Soens 2004).

M. Limberger (✉) · N. De Vijlder
Ghent University, Ghent, Belgium
e-mail: Michael.Limberger@ugent.be

C. Briggs and J. Zuijderduijn (eds.), *Land and Credit*,
Palgrave Studies in the History of Finance,
https://doi.org/10.1007/978-3-319-66209-1_9

Constituted rents were also very popular in urban environments, and they became more and more used not only on a personal level, with real estate as security, but also for the issuing of public debt by village and town authorities and, by the sixteenth century, even of the Estates of large territorial states (Tracy 1985; Boone et al. 2003).

The legal basis of the sale of annuities in Brabant was analysed as early as 1960 by P. Godding in his PhD thesis on the real estate law in fifteenth-century Brussels (Godding 1960). Also, in 1957, Schnapper wrote a study about the phenomenon in France, where annuities were known as *rentes* (Schnapper 1957). The principle of selling rents was known in Flanders and Brabant from the middle of the thirteenth century and consisted originally of a cession of a plot of land as the mortgage of a loan, and an immediate retrocession to the seller against the payment of a yearly rent or annuity. This form of cession to the lender continued to be used in the coastal area of Flanders, while in the interior it disappeared during the fourteenth century. Hence, we have to deal in theory with a combination of two real estate transactions, which in practice, however, came down to one; that is, the sale of an annuity on a plot of land, the price being the capital sum of a loan, and the plot of land serving as mortgage (Thoen and Soens 2004; Godding 1960, 1987). Renten could be sold for the duration of the life of the buyer (lijfrente) or for an indefinite term, in which case, the obligation to pay the annuity passed on to the heir of the plot (perpetual annuity or *erfelijke rente*). In return for the longer duration, perpetual annuities paid a lower interest rate. Life annuities were frequently used especially in the fourteenth century, while the sale of perpetual annuities became increasingly popular in the fifteenth and sixteenth centuries. From the fourteenth century onwards, perpetual annuities could be cancelled by paying back the capital sum. From 1529 onwards, this option was guaranteed by law (Van Bavel 2010, p. 187). Annuities were a means to obtain relatively large quantities of credit, but it was limited to those who had some real estate to mortgage. They therefore were only one of the several means of obtaining credit, although the most formal and therefore the best documented. Furthermore, the registration of the transaction as well as the transaction fee that had to be paid were obstacles that limited the use of this credit instrument to more substantial loans. Hence, by focussing on the sale of annuities or renten only a particular segment of the rural credit market can be highlighted. Other, more informal arrangements will not be considered here.

Historians do not quite agree to what extent land markets and related credit markets can actually be considered as markets like others, because of the strategic role of land in the household patrimony. Instead, some scholars prefer to see sales and mortgages of land rather as part of the patrimonial household strategies inherent to the rural society of the Old Regime. Land and credit were exchanged frequently among members of rural society as well as between them and townsmen or urban institutions. The effects of participation in these land and credit markets could vary: it could lead to a more flexible relationship towards landed property, but it could also lead to indebtedness and to the long-run expropriation of the rural population. Within the medieval Low Countries, the two dynamics can be distinguished. In highly commercialized zones with large capital investments, such as the coastal area of Flanders, land transfers took place between local landowners and wealthy institutions or individuals, such as townsmen. These transactions led to a process of accumulation of landed property in these areas (Thoen and Soens 2004). A similar development took place in the closer surroundings of big cities, where urban capital was abundant and found its way into investments in land, such as in the case of Antwerp. H. Soly, in his work on the Antwerp real estate market in the sixteenth century, showed that Antwerp citizens were very interested in accumulating real estate, and among others they frequently invested their money in annuities secured on rural goods. However, as far as purchases of land were concerned, a preference for investments in larger farms and capital-intensive forms of exploitation such as polders along the river Scheldt can be observed (Soly 1977; Limberger 2001, 2008). In areas where smaller peasant holdings were predominant, such as in the interior of Flanders or in Brabant, land and credit markets were rather a function of the needs of the local community and were designed to provide for the changing requirements of households. Thoen and Soens describe the two models of development for different parts of Flanders. In the coastal area, ecological pressure related to the maritime environment required high levels of investment, which was only possible by means of credit. In the fourteenth century, the adverse economic circumstances led many landowners to default and eventual expropriation and the introduction of leasehold. In the interior of Flanders, on the contrary, the local peasantry used the land market in order to provide for the needs of their households. Especially, young households, which had not yet inherited, acquired a holding on their own through sale of annuities and by other means of credit. The creditors could be townsmen, but also members of the local community, often older inhabitants who invested their surplus in order to obtain annuities as a kind of retirement plan (Thoen and Soens 2004).

To what extent do these models of development apply to the Duchy of Brabant, which generally corresponds with the circumstances of inner Flanders rather than with the coastal area, but which also shows considerable internal differences? The Duchy of Brabant was of considerable size (more than 110 km from north to south, and approximately 100 km from west to east at its greatest extension) and consisted moreover of geographically distinctive areas. Much of the northern part of the Duchy, actually the largest part of the territory, was characterized by sandy plains, which were not suited for intensive agriculture. In fact, these were only thinly populated, with about 15–25 inhabitants per square kilometre (Klep 1981). Further south, more or less south of Antwerp, the soil was more fertile, and as a consequence population density was considerably higher. Here, a dense network of sizeable towns was to be found, among which were the cities of Brussels, Louvain, Mechlin (Mechelen) and Antwerp. North of Antwerp, the diked banks of the river Scheldt formed yet another distinctive area. In the different parts of Brabant, quite distinctive factors intervened in the dynamics of the local land and credit markets. The different environmental features of these three geographical sub-areas of Brabant affected the agrarian structures and resulted together with specific social property relations in what Thoen described as 'social agro-systems'. However, it would go too far to claim that social property relations were the immediate result of the environmental particularities of an area; they also were the result of historical developments, such as the presence of particular landowning elites, the proximity of cities and others (Thoen 2004).

The available literature allows us to shed some light on three different parts of Brabant and their land and credit markets: on the one hand, recent research on the Campine area by Van Onacker and De Keyzer allows us to distinguish some general characteristics of that area. The Campine area was characterized by its sandy soil, which resulted in a low population density and only limited agrarian activity. Large parts of the land remained uncultivated and were used as commons for grazing (Van Onacker 2014; De Keyzer 2014). The area was furthermore characterized by a predominance of peasant smallholders who had a strong control over their property rights. Rural elites consisted of farmers with relatively large farms, without, however, being comparable to the dominant figures of areas like the Île de France, described by authors such as Moriceau (1994). The wider surroundings of Antwerp, situated in the north–west of Brabant, were the subject of Limberger's research on the social and economic transformations in the hinterland of the rising metropolis between the fifteenth and sixteenth centuries. In one study, he analysed the market for annuities in the village of Aartselaar, some 10 km south of Antwerp (Limberger 2009). Finally, within the framework of a study of the dynamics of the land and credit markets in the Southern Low Countries, De Vijlder provides data concerning the villages of the manor of Kruikenburg or Overzenne, only a few kilometres west of Brussels, which we will present in this chapter (De Vijlder 2012, 2013). The design of the above studies is not identical in each case, which means that we cannot make precise comparisons. However, we still can discern common and divergent features of the different areas by taking account of the distinctive local circumstances.

9.2 The Problem of Sources

A requirement for analysing the effects of the development of factor markets for land and capital is the availability of comparable and quantifiable source material. By means of a relatively little-known source, namely the accounts of transaction fees due to the seigneur, or in many cases the prince, we undertook a research project in which different local case studies within Flanders and Brabant are compared for the period between 1400 and 1600.[1]

In the above-mentioned study of the annuity market in the village of Aartselaar, south of Antwerp, published extracts from the registers of the Antwerp aldermen (schepenregisters) were used. These extracts helped to overcome the almost unsurmountable problem of the huge quantity of documents contained in this exceptionally rich source (Soly 1974). They were extremely useful for collecting information on qualitative aspects of the transactions, that is, the names of the parties involved, their mutual relations and the description of the mortgage. Hence, a qualitative analysis could be undertaken in addition to a purely quantitative approach. Therefore, strategies of individual actors or specific groups become visible, and credit transactions can be seen in the light of other related transactions of the same person or group. These sources are, however, not so precise on economic and juridical details concerning the transactions. This is because the transactions are summarized only in a very short form. The greatest inconvenience of the Antwerp letters of aldermen is their limited representativeness. The registration of real estate transactions in the rural areas surrounding the town in the urban registers was not obligatory. It was rather before the aldermen of the corresponding seigniorial administration that registration had to take place (Cerutti 1969, pp. 78–79). In particular, it was Antwerp citizens or individuals related in one way or another to the city who chose registration by the Antwerp aldermen. The letters of aldermen therefore tend to overestimate the degree of urban involvement in the rural real estate market. Another inconvenience is the lack of the mention of the amount of the loan. Only the value of the annuity is mentioned. For a calculation of interest rates, we therefore have to turn towards alternative sources.

Within the framework of the aforementioned project on the real estate market in the Southern Low Countries, we also made use of another type of source to study annuities, that is, the conveyance taxes levied by local lords and the prince, within the princely demesne, which allows a complete survey of the transactions within a particular domanial jurisdiction. The income from this fee was registered in the domanial accounts of lay landlords as well as in the accounts of the ducal demesne. Within the limits of Brabant, we focus on the holdings of the demesne of Overzenne, near Brussels. Data concerning 3000 transactions for the period between 1405 and 1553 are available, among which there are 700 sales of mortgage rents (De Vijlder 2012, 2013). This combination of real estate transactions and annuity sales allows us to get a better contextualization of the mortgage sales as well as a better view of the socio-economic profile of the actors involved. However, this requires a careful prosopographical analysis, which is very time-consuming. Here, we will therefore only be able to give a first impression of the relationships among the different parties involved in this market. Further in-depth research will be for a future occasion.

9.3 The Surroundings of Antwerp

In Aartselaar, situated 10 km south of Antwerp, at the beginning of the fifteenth century, we find distinguished members of the local nobility, the gentry as well as urban patricians not only among the buyers but also among the major sellers of annuities (Limberger 2009). The transactions mainly took place within the same social group. Throughout the fifteenth century, we could observe the emergence of a local middle class, which had an increasing hold on the annuity market. It was only from c.1520 that the number of townsmen among the creditors increased. This can be seen in the context of the increasing investments in rural property by inhabitants of Antwerp during the economic rise of the city throughout the sixteenth century. Throughout the research period, the local market for annuities concentrated around a few dominant families.

The spread of annuity sales in the surroundings of bigger cities was closely linked with the investments of townsmen in rural real estate. In that way, it affected the dynamics of the land market and could contribute to a transfer of land from local landowners to urban proprietors. On the other hand, the spread of annuities was part of broader process of economic integration. By changing attitudes towards credit, as well as its availability, it changed the dynamics of the land market. This in turn led to a spread of credit transactions among the rural population at the same time as increasing investments by townsmen. Annuities were not only created but also transferred to third parties. Hence, annuities circulated and became a popular financial instrument especially among the urban population. The values of the annuities varied, but there was still an evident tendency for high proportion of them to be expressed in kind. It is not certain, however, whether the payment was actually in kind or in money. This high percentage of payments in kind was typical for Brabant and was in sharp contrast with the county of Flanders (Thoen and Soens 2004). The same discrepancy can be observed for land leases, which were also to a much higher degree payable in kind in Brabant than in Flanders during the fifteenth and sixteenth centuries. The ratio between the size of the mortgage and the annuity was not fixed. It is remarkable, however, that a considerable number were set at one *sister* (i.e. approximately 292 litres) of rye per *bunder* (1.33 hectares)—which corresponds more or less with 20–25% of the gross yield.[2]

9.4 The Campine Area

More recently, Van Onacker looked at the situation in the Campine area, a sandy plateau with an extensive agrarian structure east of Antwerp. Within the framework of her study of the role of rural elites, she looked, among other things, at the dynamics of factor markets. Her study of two villages in the Campine was based on court records, in combination with rent registers and lists of taxation. Her results differed in some points from those of Aartselaar due to the different agrarian and socio-economic structures in these two cases. Van Onacker found fewer urban buyers of annuities involved than in the village near Antwerp. The local elites—that is, the wealthiest 50%—had a predominant position in the land and credit markets, without, however, fully dominating them. They had a relatively high share in the number of loans, both as creditors and as debtors, which shows that they mainly undertook credit transactions with other members of the higher property groups rather than lending money to the poorer peasants. Interestingly, she detected at the same time a tendency of increasingly equal property structures for the period between the fifteenth and sixteenth centuries. The frequency of annuity sales was rising during the sixteenth century, so that in the fifteenth century in the village of Rijkevorsel there were 0.31 transactions per hundred inhabitants and by the sixteenth century the frequency had risen to 1.14. Interest rates rose from 5.9 to 6.25%, which was the official rate in the second half of the sixteenth century (Van Onacker 2014, and this volume).

9.5 West of Brussels: The Villages of the Manor of Kruikenburg

The archives of the ducal domain of Brabant provide us with another sample of registered sales of both land and annuities. The seigneurie of Kruikenburg contained the villages of Ternat, St-Katherina-Lombeek and Wambeek, situated approximately 15 km west of Brussels. Together, these villages had some 1250 inhabitants (250 households). From the fourteenth century onwards, the seigneurie was held by the 't Serclaes, a prestigious patrician family from Brussels, and from 1562 by Charles de Fourneau, the son of the chamberlain of Charles V (Wauters 1855). At the same time, the villages were part of the ducal domain of Overzenne, which included a larger area than the three villages of Kruikenburg.[3] Many of the seignorial fees were split between the lord of Kruikenburg and the receiver of the ducal domain. The accounts of the ducal domain are available for the period 1404–1796. During the period 1404–1553, real estate transactions are registered as a consequence of a conveyance tax (*pondgeld*), which represented five per cent of the value, but the receiver of Overzenne yielded only half of the amount, because the income was shared with the lord of Kruikenburg.[4] The pondgeld was only levied on real estate purchases on censal land, that is, land that was subject to a fixed annual rent. It included also annuity sales mortgaged on such land; this means that freehold land was not included. The accounts contain the names of the two contracting parties, the description of the property and the price for which it was sold. In the case of an annuity sale or mortgage rent, the annual amount of the annuity is mentioned, and the total amount of the capital loan can be calculated via the amount of the fee. By using the tariff mentioned in the account (2.5%), the total amount of the transaction and the relation between the annuity and the total amount, i.e. the interest rate, can be calculated. In practice, the calculation is sometimes complicated, as annuities were often payable or expressed in amounts of grain or in a variety of different currencies.

9.5.1 Land and Credit Markets

In terms of geographical features, the Kruikenburg area was characterized by a slightly hilly landscape with altitudes reaching from 20 to 50 metres above sea level, with a very fertile sandy clay soil and numerous small creeks and streams. The population of the area increased in the later middle ages, which led to a relatively high population density by the fifteenth century of around 50 inhabitants per square kilometre. From the thirteenth century onwards, therefore, large parts of the remaining forests and heaths were transformed into farmland and meadows. Around 1570, the village of St-Katherina-Lombeek, one of the three villages of the Kruikenburg manor, consisted of 64% arable land, 21% water meadows, which were periodically flooded, and seven per cent meadows. An interesting feature is the existence of hop-gardens, which made up eight per cent of the surface. The spread of the cultivation of hops was a relatively recent development of the sixteenth century, which can be related to the demographic growth of Brussels and the resulting urban demand for beer. The size of holdings was small. Fifty-two per cent of the holdings contained less than one hectare, and 31% between one and three hectares. Only 17% were larger than three hectares, and therefore capable of producing an agrarian surplus. Furthermore, only one-third of the land was held in direct ownership, the rest being leased out. Between 1404 and 1553, 3131 land sales were registered in the domanial accounts. After that, the registration of transfer fees stops. The early fifteenth century and the beginning of the sixteenth century were especially characterized by increases in activity, while between 1470 and 1499, the activity declined. The land market of the villages of Kruikenburg during the fifteenth and sixteenth centuries was characterized by an increasing degree of participation. While in the fifteenth century, the average household was involved in a real estate transaction once every ten years, the frequency doubled in the sixteenth century. Around the middle of the sixteenth century, roughly 11.7 hectares of land were traded each year, that is, 0.43% of the total surface area. At the same time, the variety of types of land in the registered transactions also increased during the sixteenth century, so that besides farms, farmland and meadows, which were the basic types of land in the fifteenth century, we increasingly find gardens, orchards and hop-gardens. In the sixteenth century, ecclesiastical institutions and local noblemen enhanced their landed property in the area strongly, while the number of other townsmen was quite small (see Table 9.1) (De Vijlder 2013).

The number of annuity transactions also rose steadily throughout the fifteenth century, from an average of 2–3 sales per year in the beginning of the fifteenth century to an average of 5–10 at the end of the century. After a period of stagnation and even decline in the beginning of the sixteenth century, the activity increased further to reach an average of 20 transactions per year in the 1550s, the end of our research period (Fig. 9.1). Considering the population size of the Kruikenburg area of roughly 250 households that means that each household would have been involved on average in one annuity transaction, either as seller or as buyer, per 50 years in the early fifteenth century, and in one transaction in only six years in the middle of the sixteenth century. This shows that annuity sales became a quite common transaction during the sixteenth century, reaching almost the same frequency as land sales. However, the transactions were not equally spread among the inhabitants. While in general the same person did not sell more than one or two annuities within his/her lifetime, some did buy several and some individuals even a quite considerable number, such as Roelant de Weert, who bought no fewer than 29 annuities between 1527 and 1553 with a total value of 270 lb. (pounds) Brabant groats.

Table 9.1 Property relations in St-Katherina-Lombeek, 1570

Social group	*Share of total surface area (%)*
Religious institutions	31
Townsmen	3
Nobility	23
Local population	43

Source De Vijlder 2013

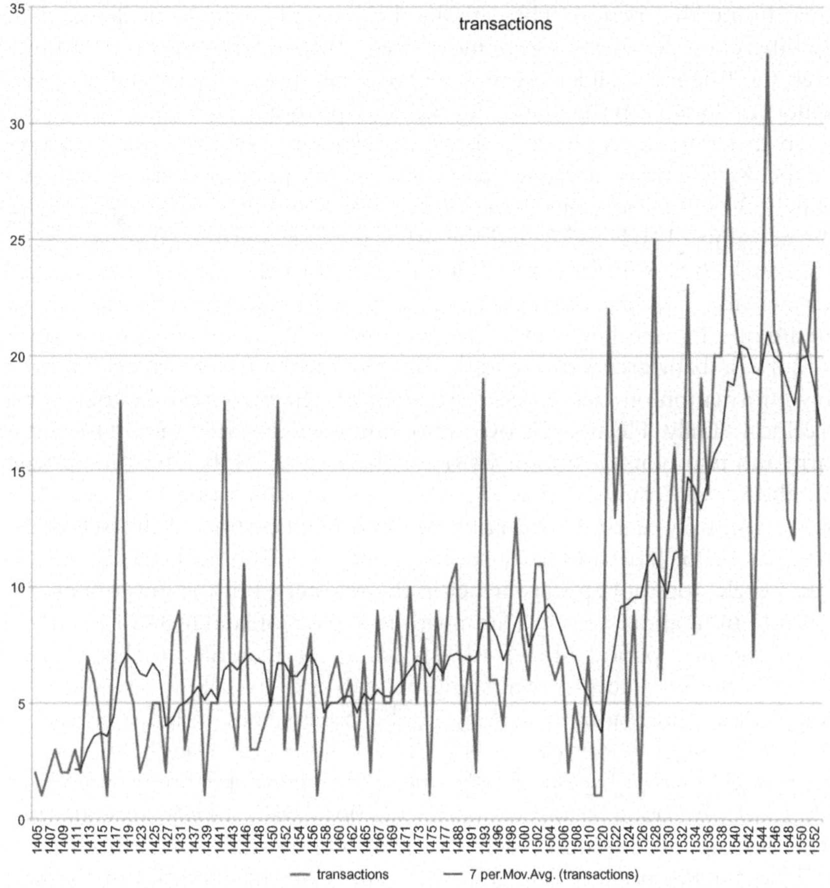

Fig. 9.1 Number of annuity sales in the manor of Kruikenburg per year, 1405–1553
Source State Archives of Belgium, Chamber of Accounts, Registers, 4739–4742

Annuities were payable either in kind, that is, mostly in quantities of grain, or in money. In the fifteenth century, payments in kind were more frequent than money payments. Besides grain, the annuities could be expressed in capons, geese or in two cases even in labour services, more specifically two days of haymaking and 12 days of service with horses. Payments in money were expressed in the different currencies that were in use in the area during that period. Throughout the fifteenth century, no fewer than 33 different types of coins were mentioned. At the end of the century, however, the Rhenish Guilder became the most common currency and was used almost exclusively in the sixteenth century (Appendix, Table 9.2).

In order to get a closer look on the dynamics of the annuity market in the Kruikenburg area, we compared two sample periods of approximately 30 years each, one covering the first years that were registered in the accounts (1404–1432) and the other the last available 30 years, 1523–1553, which was at the same time the period of the greatest rise in market activity. The first transaction, recorded in 1405, concerns the sale of an annuity by one Janne Den Hoecke, who sold an annuity for the price of 2 lb. Brabant groats to Hendrik Van den Berghe. While we do not have any information on Den Hoecke, Van den Berghe was a member of a notable local family. He bought two more annuities in 1407 and 1414 and a farm and two plots of land in 1431 for the sum of 24 lb. The same is true for the second transaction of the same year, in which one Velde Cassaert sold an annuity of 10 lb. to Master Thomas Henkenshoet, a Brussels patrician. In 1406, Jan Van Ossele sold an annuity of 3 lb. to Gielis De Cock. Van Ossele does not appear further in the registers, but the buyer does. De Cock bought annuities and a farm with four plots of land in 1411.

In the first period (1404–1432), the great majority of the 91 sellers of annuities sold only one annuity, with just six selling two and only one selling three annuities. Among the buyers, not much more accumulation can be observed: among the 78 buyers, six bought two annuities, one bought three and only one four. The major buyer was Gielis De Cock: he bought four annuities (1406, 1418, 1419), though they were for modest amounts. In 1411, he also bought a farm and four plots of land for the price of 21.75 lb. The purchases of annuities in the first period, between 1404 and 1423, generally were of a modest nature. The average value of the annuities was 12.7 lb. Brabant groats, which is the equivalent to the price of a small farm. This average value, however, is influenced by one outlier, that is, the sale of an annuity by a certain Jan Van Leeuw for no less than 201 lb. to Everaard 't Serclaes, lord of Kruikenburg, in 1429. The median value was only 6.5 lb. Based on an interest rate of 5%, which was the most common in the fifteenth century, the average annuity payments were 6.5 shillings (78 pennies) per year.

We can distinguish a number of members of the Brussels nobility among the buyers of annuities, like Everaerd 't Serclaes who bought another annuity of 5 lb. in 1420. Among them, we also find Willem Van Heetvelde, who bought an annuity for 5 lb. in 1417, and the widow of Wouter Van der Noot, from another prestigious noble family, who bought an annuity for 59 lb. from the heirs of her deceased husband. Finally, there is Lord Aard Van Pede, a debtor who sold an annuity for 30 lb. to the priory (*godshuis*) of Oudergem. Other townsmen can only be distinguished in some cases when their origin is mentioned explicitly in the sources, such as in the case of Aerd Vanden Loeren 'in Brussels', or Gielis Hooghe, described as 'master', a title generally associated with lawyers. We also find ecclesiastical and charitable institutions among the creditors, among which several were situated in Brussels, such as the abbey of Coudenbergh or the Beguinage and the hospital of St. Claire. Other ecclesiastical institutions were the abbey of Affligem, situated seven km from Kruikenburg, and the priory of Oudergem, situated south of Brussels. At the same time, we find very few transactions among kin: in 1415, Jan Van Eengaarde sold an annuity for 2 lb. to Jan Faes, his brother-in-law. In 1424, Gielis De Bloyere sold one for 160 d. to his father Peter De Bloyere. In 1431, Jan De Horne the elder sold an annuity to his son of the same name. In 1426, Hendrik De Zadele sold an annuity for 360 pennies to Janne Vande Eede, his brother-in-law. Finally, in 1425, the widow of Wouter Van der Noot, of one of the leading noble families from Brussels, bought a sizeable annuity for 59 lb. from the heirs Van der Noot.

In the second sample period, covering the period 1523–1553, the market activity had increased considerably. Five hundred annuity sales were registered. There were 305 sellers, of whom one, Gillis Van der Gucht, sold 15, another 15 persons between 5 and 10. Six persons sold four annuities each, but the great majority sold one (212, i.e. 70%), two (47, i.e. 15%) or three (24, i.e. 8%) annuities. The most likely motive to contract a loan in the form of an annuity sale was the purchase of a plot of land. Indeed, 103 of the sellers of annuities bought real estate within the Kruikenburg manor, but only 53 did so in the same year as their annuity sale. In four transactions, the price of the purchase coincided exactly with that of the loan. In the other cases, the proportion between the loan and the price of the real estate purchase varied between 16 and 1400%, the median being 90% (quartile 1 = 51.7%, quartile 3 = 145%). At the same time, there were 240 buyers of land without any related annuity sale, and 193 sellers of annuities without any related land purchases. That means that there was no automatic link between mortgage loans and real estate transactions as is the case today. Annuities could be used for a variety of purposes, in particular as a means to settle balances among heirs (Hoppenbrouwers 1992, pp. 226–231, 2004). In order to find evidence of such settlements, we looked at sellers of annuities whom we could identify as kin or as collective heirs of a property. In fact, 62 sellers of annuities were identified as heirs and usufructuaries of a decedent, and 45 more as widows or children of the decedent. In one case, an annuity was sold to pay a mass. In 1529, Godevaert De Pape sold an annuity for the considerable amount of 24.5 lb. to the church of Wambeek to pay for a mass in the church of Wambeek for his uncle Jan de Pape, and another, of 10 lb. to the Wambeek poor table. The situation may have been similar in other cases when the heirs of the deceased sold annuities to ecclesiastic or charitable institutions, like Katelijne Bocxoers, the widow of Gielis Van Blijdenberghe, who sold an annuity for the price of 5.5 lb. to the church of Ternat in 1532. Furthermore, there were of course many other ways to use annuities to obtain a loan, but these are not mentioned in our sources.

As far as the buyers of annuities are concerned, there were 274 in this period, buying 1.78 annuities on average. Among the creditors, some individuals stand out to an even greater extent than in the fifteenth century. We have already mentioned Roelant de Weert, who bought 29 annuities between 1527 and 1553 and 12 plots of land between 1536 and 1550. De Weert seems to have local origins or at least family ties in the area. Already in 1416, one Roelant De Weert, most probably his ancestor, bought eight plots of land. It is also interesting to see that the sellers of the annuities which De Weert bought were among the most active players on the annuity market, Jan and Kerstian Van de Gucht and Claes De Vlaemink. Lenaart Danoot was another interesting figure. He bought 13 annuities, making up a total capital sum of 265 lb. between 1528 and 1536. He also bought a farm for 26 lb. from the children of Claes Buyskens, in 1532. Besides these two big players, there were eight more who bought between five and 10 annuities. Everaard Nagels (d. 1552) bought eight annuities between 1526 and 1551. He also figures as the buyer of several plots of land between 1538 and 1547. Another notable buyer of annuities was the priest Goes De Cuyper, who bought eight annuities between 1528 and 1533, which together comprised a total value of 28 lb. Hence, there were only 30 individuals who bought annuities on more than one occasion.

In most cases, these buyers of multiple annuities were of local origin or at least strongly integrated into the local society. Most of them were frequently involved in real estate and credit transactions, had kin or family (based on surname evidence) in the area or were linked by marriage (Müller 2009, 2014). Some of these families assumed a key position in the local land and credit markets, such as the Van den Cleygates and the Van der Guchts. We find 11 different members of the Van Gucht family in 50 different credit transactions. Four of them were married to members of local families. Twelve members of the Van den Cleygate family bought 49 plots of land and were involved in 59 annuity sales either as seller or as buyer. Other families belonging to this local elite were the Bockxoers, Nagels, Metermans and De Vlemincks. They constituted the group of wealthy inhabitants of the village, which P. Schofield identified in his work on the rural credit market in England as being the most active creditors (Schofield 2004, p. 793). This coincides to some extent with the findings concerning the other Brabantine regions mentioned before. Van Onacker identified a similar local elite in the Campine, the 'leaders of the pack' or 'coqs de village' as she described them (2014, p. 191). In Aartselaar, these local elites were also recognizable, although they were less prominent due to the strong impact of Antwerp citizens on the land and credit markets. In the Kruikenburg area, despite the close proximity to Brussels, the urban presence was less prominent. As in the fifteenth century, we find some urban patricians and noblemen among the buyers of annuities but their activities were rather isolated, although sometimes their transactions could be quite sizeable, such as the annuity of 201 lb. bought by Everaard 't Serclaes, lord of Kruikenburg, or the annuity of 100 lb. sold by Lady Johanna Baelde and her son Joris de Glymes, member of the high Brabantine nobility, to Gillis Van Busleyden, in 1523. This could partly be due to problems of identification, but the predominance of the leading local families remains quite clear.

9.6 Conclusion

The Kruikenburg area, near Brussels, therefore fits quite well into the picture of the Brabantine areas presented in existing studies. The land and credit markets were already well established by the time our documentation begins, around 1400. During the fifteenth century, but in particular during the first half of the sixteenth century, the activity increased quite strongly. In the surroundings of Antwerp, the exceptional growth of the city had a strong impact on the local market for land and credit via the massive participation of townsmen. In the surroundings of Brussels, this urban presence can also be perceived but to a much lesser degree. Here, the urban elites that were active on the rural land market had a rather noble or patrician profile, while in the surroundings of Antwerp they had rather a commercial background. In all areas, we can identify a strong local upper class, consisting of a small number of interrelated families. They were active as buyers and sellers of land and of annuities on a large scale. The effects on local property relations seem, however, to have differed between the different areas. While in the Antwerp and Brussels areas, the sixteenth century was characterized by an increasing concentration of landed property, the more remote Campine area rather maintained its egalitarian character.

Notes

1. The project 'A comparative study of the rural land market in the Southern Low Countries (15th–16th century)' was funded by the Special Research Funds of Ghent University between 2012 and 2015, within the framework of a Start Credit.
2. This assumes a gross yield of between 1200 and 1500 litres/hectare.
3. In addition to the three villages of Kruikenburg, the domain of Overzenne also included the villages of Asse, Kapelle-op-den-Bos, Hombeek, Zemst, Merchtem, Liezele, Lippelo, Malderen, Steenhuffel, parts of Wolvertem and Rossem, all situated in an array 10–20 km north and west of Brussels.
4. State Archives of Belgium, Chamber of Accounts, Registers, 4739–4742, Accounts of the Ducal Domain of Overzenne, 1404–1553.

Appendix

See Table 9.2.

Table 9.2 Currencies in which annuities were expressed, 1405–1499

Currency	*Frequency*	*Years*
Rhenish guilder	42	1442–1499
Peter	35	1405–1498
Crown	25	1418–1499
Cijnsgulden	15	1409–1497
Guilder	13	1407–1488
Shilling	13	1431–1461
Oude groot	10	1423–1476
Rijder	9	1438–1470
Stuivers	8	1474–1499
Golden crown	6	1451–1469
Payment	5	1417–1440
Plak	4	1417–1460
Mottoen	3	1414–1438
Holland guilder	2	1418/1466
Leeuw	2	1468–1478
Leuven peter	3	1451–1474
Old guilder	2	1418
Saluyt	2	1442
Golden frank	1	1499
Golden peter	1	1451
Golden rijder	1	1459
Golden saluyt	1	1467
Light crown	1	1450
Light schilling	1	1448
Light shield	1	1452
Old shield	1	1425
Old guilder	1	1460
Old crown	1	1472
Old shilling	1	1456
Parisis	1	1441
Flemish crown	1	1462
Borsgeld	3	1460–1468

References

Secondary Works

Boone, M., K. Davids and P. Janssens (eds.), 2003. *Urban Public Debts: Urban Government and the Market for Annuities in Western Europe (14th–18th Centuries)* (Turnhout: Brepols).

Cerutti, F.F.X., 1969. 'De schepenbank in de Brabantse stad en de overdracht en bezwaring van onroerende goederen', *Varia Historica Brabantica*, vol. 3, pp. 47–87.

De Keyzer, M., 2014. 'The common denominator: Regulation of the community of users of common waste lands within the Campine area during the 16th century', in F. Aparisi (ed.), *Beyond Lords and Peasants. Rural Elites and Economic Differentiation in Pre-Modern Europe* (Valencia: Universitat de València), pp. 217–245.

De Vijlder, N., 2012. 'The Rural Land Market in the Southern Low Countries. Fifteenth to Sixteenth Centuries', unpublished MSc thesis, Ghent University.

De Vijlder, N., 2013. 'De rurale grondmarkt in Zuid-Brabant (15de–16de eeuw): een braakliggend stuk prijzengeschiedenis', *Eigen Schoon en de Brabander*, pp. 477–500.

Godding, P., 1960. *Le droit foncier à Bruxelles au Moyen Âge* (Brussels: Institut de sociologie Solvay).

Godding, P., 1987. *Le droit privé dans les Pays-Bas méridionaux du 12e au 18e siècle* (Brussels: Palais des académies).

Hoppenbrouwers, P.C.M., 1992. *Een middeleeuwse samenleving. Het Land van Heusden (ca. 1360–ca. 1515)* (Groningen: Stichting Nederlands Agronomisch-Historisch Instituut).

Hoppenbrouwers, P.C.M., 2004. 'Family affairs. Passing property under an egalitarian system. The case of the land van Heusden (the Netherlands) in the late medieval and early modern period', in S. Cavaciocchi (ed.), *Il mercato della terra secc. XIII–XVIII. Atti delle 'Trentacinquesima Settimana di Studi' 5–9 Maggio 2003*, (Florence: Le Monnier), pp. 951–978.

Klep, P.M.M., 1981. *Bevolking en arbeid in transformatie. Een onderzoek in Brabant 1700–1900* (Nijmegen: SUN).

Limberger, M., 2001. 'Merchant Capitalism and the countryside: Antwerp and the west of the Duchy of Brabant - (XVth–XVIth centuries)', in P. Hoppenbrouwers and J.L. Van Zanden (eds.), *Peasants into Farmers? The Transformation of Rural Economy and Society in the Low Countries (Middle Ages-19th Century) in Light of the Brenner Debate* (Turnhout: Brepols), pp. 158–178.

Limberger, M., 2008. *Sixteenth-Century Antwerp and Its Rural Surroundings. Social and Economic Changes in the Hinterland of a Commercial Metropolis (ca. 1450–ca. 1570)* (Turnhout: Brepols).

Limberger, M., 2009. 'Credit, the land market and the connection between the rural and urban economy. The use of perpetual annuities in Aartselaar (Brabant) from the fourteenth to sixteenth century', in P.R. Schofield and T. Lambrecht (eds.), *Credit and the Rural Economy in North Western Europe, c.1200–c.1850* (Turnhout: Brepols), pp. 63–73.

Moriceau, J.-M., 1994. *Les fermiers de l'Île-de-France. L'ascension d'un patronat agricole (XVe–XVIIIe siècles)* (Paris: Fayard).

Müller, M., 2009. 'Peasants, lords and developments in leasing in later medieval England', in B.J.P. Van Bavel and P.R. Schofield (eds.), *The Development of Leasehold in North-Western Europe, c.1200–1600* (Turnhout: Brepols), pp. 155–178.

Müller, M., 2014. 'Communal structures, lordship and peasant agency in later medieval England: Some comparative observations', in F. Aparisi (ed.), *Beyond Lords and Peasants. Rural Elites and Economic Differentiation in Pre-Modern Europe* (Valencia: Universitat de València), pp. 69–86.

Schnapper, B., 1957. *Les rentes au XVIe siècle. Histoire d'un instrument de crédit* (Paris: S.E.V.P.E.N).

Schofield, P., 2004. 'Credit and the peasant land market in the medieval English countryside', in S. Cavaciocchi (ed.), *Il mercato della terra secc. XIII–XVIII. Atti delle 'Trentacinquesima Settimana di Studi' 5–9 Maggio 2003* (Florence: Le Monnier), pp. 785–796.

Soly, H., 1974. 'De schepenregisters als bron voor de conjunctuurgeschiedenis van Zuid- en Noordnederlandse steden in het Ancien Régime. Een concreet voorbeeld: de Antwerpse immobiliënmarkt in de 16de Eeuw', *Tijdschrift voor Geschiedenis*, vol. 87, pp. 521–544.

Soly, H., 1977. *Urbanisme en kapitalisme te Antwerpen in de 16e eeuw. De stedebouwkundige en industriële ondernemingen van Gilbert van Schoonbeke* (Brussels: Gemeentekrediet van België).

Thoen, E., 2004. '"Social agrosystems" as an economic concept to explain regional differences. An essay taking the former county of Flanders as an example (Middle Ages-19th Century)', in B.J.P. Van Bavel and P. Hoppenbrouwers (eds.), *Landholding and Land Transfer in the North Sea Area (Late Middle Ages-19th Century)* (Turnhout: Brepols), pp. 47–66.

Thoen, E. and T. Soens, 2004. 'Appauvrissement et endettement dans le monde rural: Etude comparative du crédit dans les différents systèmes agraires en Flandre au bas moyen âge et au début de l'epoque moderne', in S. Cavaciocchi (ed.), *Il mercato della terra secc. XIII–XVIII. Atti delle 'Trentacinquesima Settimana di Studi' 5–9 Maggio 2003* (Florence: Le Monnier), pp. 703–720.

Tracy, J., 1985. *A Financial Revolution in the Habsburg Netherlands.* Renten *and* Renteniers *in the County of Holland, 1515–1565* (Berkeley: University of California Press).

Van Bavel, B.J.P., 2010. *Manors and Markets, Economy and Society in the Low Countries, 500–1600* (Oxford: Oxford University Press).
Van Onacker, E., 2014. 'Leaders of the pack: A typology of village elites in the fifteenth and sixteenth century Campine area' in F. Aparisi (ed.), *Beyond Lords and Peasants. Rural Elites and Economic Differentiation in Pre-Modern Europe* (Valencia: Universitat de València), pp. 189–216.
Wauters, A., 1855. *Histoire des environs de Bruxelles ou description historique des localités qui formaient autrefois l'ammanie de cette ville* (Brussels: Vanderauwera).

CHAPTER 10

Proactive Peasants? The Role of Annuities in a Late Medieval Communal Society: The Campine Area, Low Countries

Eline Van Onacker

10.1 Introduction

In the pre-industrial Low Countries, annuities ('*renten*') were the most important instrument when it came to procuring long-term debt. Nearly all those owning land, from wealthy townsmen to smallholding peasants, made use of this instrument; this included copyholders, who paid a small yearly rent (*cijns*) to be able to till the land. The widespread usage of these annuities indicates the clear possibility to take on long-term debt as well as the presence of a lively capital market, both of which have often been put forward as vital for economic growth—both past and present. This view is strongly linked to the rise of New Institutional Economics in historical research (Ogilvie and Carus 2014; Van Bavel et al. 2012). Furthermore, the work of Hernando de Soto, which points to the importance of clear property rights allowing ordinary people to use their houses and land as collateral for mortgage loans (de Soto 2000),

E. Van Onacker (✉)
University of Antwerp, Antwerp, Belgium
e-mail: eline.vanonacker@uantwerpen.be

C. Briggs and J. Zuijderduijn (eds.), *Land and Credit*,
Palgrave Studies in the History of Finance,
https://doi.org/10.1007/978-3-319-66209-1_10

as well as the rise of microfinance, with its emphasis on small loans to develop small businesses, has sharpened historians' focus on the development of credit markets and their role in the lives of ordinary people. The emancipating potential of the market, and more specifically of the credit market, has recently been emphasised by Laurence Fontaine, as she compares the pre-industrial use of credit by women to contemporary microfinance initiatives (Fontaine 2014). The Dutch 'solution' to the 'de Soto problem'[1] has been linked to this region's remarkable growth potential, as in Holland titles to land were protected by a property rights system based on ratification by local authorities, thus allowing a large part of the Dutch population to enter the capital market (Van Zanden et al. 2012).

However, the emancipatory potential of easy access to (micro) credit has been severely nuanced and criticised, not only by economists, but also by historical research. The economists Milford Bateman and Ha-Joon Chang refer to the 'illusion of development', arguing that current microfinance initiatives often constitute a poverty trap, locking people into low-paying jobs, and leading to a downward spiral of competition between microfinance initiatives, thus lacking any growth potential (Bateman and Chang 2012). History, furthermore, provides extra proof that microfinance has severe shortcomings, as it lacked the capacity to function as a tool for social mobility (Deneweth et al. 2014). It remains to be seen, furthermore, whether all those with sound property rights engaged in the search for long-term credit, and why they did or did not.[2] The credit market is therefore not necessarily emancipatory.

Indeed, what markets do and how they function can differ greatly between different types of societies. Several recent studies have suggested that the exact functioning of markets was strongly dependent on the social context, as this shaped the role markets played in different types of society. Congost, for example, stresses that the effectiveness of property rights and the land market strongly depends on the social context in which they are embedded (Congost 2003, p. 90); or as formulated in Van Bavel et al: 'it [the organisation of markets] is the result of very specific social conditions. Differences in these conditions result in markedly different organisational arrangements, even between regions situated close to each other' (Van Bavel et al. 2012, p. 370). Not only social structures, but also differences in the balance of power between different social groups played a part in this (Ogilvie 2007). It is furthermore important to note that 'real' market economies, where the market was the prime allocation mechanism not only for commodities, but also for land, labour and capital, were not the norm in pre-industrial times (Van Bavel 2016).

Long-term credit functioned differently in different types of societies, as the social structure and power balance acted as a prism through which this standard set of institutions created an effect. This is meticulously illustrated by Erik Thoen and Tim Soens, who have focussed on the differences between the credit markets of Coastal and Inland Flanders. In the Coastal region, the villages were characterised by a serious upheaval in the fifteenth and sixteenth centuries. During this period, the Coastal polders underwent large-scale commercialisation, causing the expropriation (and later on even proletarianisation) of small-scale peasants and the rise of large, commercial tenant farms in the hands of absentee landowners. Land and credit markets played an essential part in this polarisation process since they enabled the accumulation of wealth by a minority of farmers, while at the same time accelerating the structural impoverishment of a large part of the Coastal inhabitants. In Inland Flanders, a completely different situation can be perceived. Land and credit markets mainly perpetuated the existing structures. This region was characterised by a symbiosis between some large farmers and a large majority of small peasants. Using land and credit markets, these small peasants were able to maintain their business model, based on domestic, non-specialised production, whereas large farmers could use the credit market to strengthen their position vis-à-vis their peasant fellow-villagers (Thoen and Soens 2009).

This chapter will focus on the functioning of long-term credit in a society in which the market was not the predominant allocation mechanism, but in which communal structures played a vital part; a region furthermore that kept the same structural features up until the end of the eighteenth century. It was a region that remained 'peripheral', as it continued to be characterised by a peasant-dominated mixed-farming economy, strongly dependent on the use of commons. As we will see, the Campine peasants had a strong grip on their land and were able to use it as collateral for a long-term loan. The market for annuities furthermore enjoyed a relatively favourable institutional framework. We will, however, sketch how the Campine credit market never played its part in tipping the scales towards accumulation, expropriation or (modern) economic growth. The role the Campine market for long-term credit played was embedded in a very specific social structure and power balance that clearly shaped its functioning. This study will illustrate how the position of economic actors, their interests and strategies, and their relations—among themselves and with the outside world—determined the functioning of institutions. This chapter will zoom in on the market for annuities to assess similarities and differences with equivalent markets in other parts of the Low Countries. The following questions will be central. How was the Campine credit market organised, and was this similar to or different from the Low Countries' core regions? How did the Campine credit market evolve? Who were the creditors and debtors, were they locals or not, and what was their social position? And what was long-term credit used for? Two case-studies have been selected: the villages of Gierle and Rijkevorsel. The source material that will be used has the advantage that it starts relatively early and is almost continuously preserved. For the village of Gierle, credit transactions were recorded by the manor courts (1456–1497)[3] and by the bench of aldermen (1513–1558).[4] In Rijkevorsel, all transactions could be found in the register of the bench of aldermen, which is almost continuously preserved from 1465 to 1585.[5] These registers allowed me to construct an overview of the yearly number of transactions in order to assess the general evolution of the market for annuities. Furthermore, a database was compiled for two sample periods—1465–1485 (for Rijkevorsel) and 1538–1558 (for Gierle)—which lists all information on creditors, debtors and credit conditions to make an in-depth analysis possible.

10.2 The Campine Area: Characteristics of a Communal Peasant Region in the Heart of Urbanity

The Campine area was situated in the Duchy of Brabant, to the north-east of the sixteenth-century metropolis of Antwerp, and was dotted by small towns and innumerable villages (Fig. 10.1). The subsoil consisted mostly of dry and wet sandy soils, alternated by peat marshes. Due to its infertile and challenging nature, medieval colonisation here started rather late. The typical Campine socio-institutional structures were shaped during the thirteenth to fourteenth centuries, especially the period around 1350. What was formed then remained more or less intact up until the beginning of the nineteenth century. Around 1350, the population increased, partly through an influx of migrants from the very populated County of Flanders and from the south of the Duchy of Brabant. Due to the rising population, more and more wasteland was reclaimed.

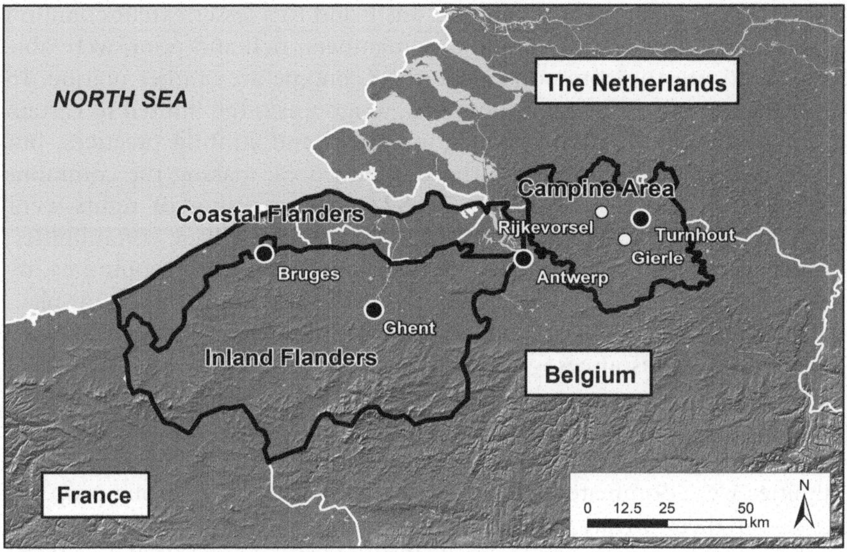

Fig. 10.1 Map of the Campine area, in relation to Inland and Coastal Flanders
Source Map made by Iason Jongepier (Gistorical Antwerp, Hercules Foundation)

This drastically altered the Campine landscape, which before had been characterised by expansive woodlands. The village centres shifted from the fertile higher grounds to the lower brook valleys, and larger blocks of arable land were exploited. The total amount of privately owned arable land and pastures increased 4.5 times between 1210 and 1340, and the woodland slowly transformed into what would become common heath land (Spek and Vangheluwe 2008). A mixed-farming economy emerged, combining arable production, animal breeding and the use of the common waste.

The feudal structure was and remained fragmented, with the Duke of Brabant, ecclesiastical and local lords all trying to get a grip on the region. This stimulated competition, which turned out to be quite advantageous to local communities. The different types of lords (ducal landlord, local lords and ecclesiastical lords)—busy trying to outdo one another and attract new inhabitants for their seigneuries in order to maximise their income—granted all rural community members extensive usage and management rights on the common lands that defined this region. These consisted of common waste and to a lesser extent common pasture. The fact that all community members, rich and poor, were able to and did use the commons made the Campine area rather unique. In most regions with extensive commons, usage was often limited to certain social groups or by the introduction of fees and stinting practices, but this was clearly not the case in the Campine area, making the commons essential (De Keyzer 2014, pp. 78–82). This granting of rights went hand in hand with the formal institutionalisation of village communities, as they were given responsibility for the government of the commons. By the fourteenth century, village communities had become important players in their own right, with elaborate responsibilities in governing themselves and their resources.

During the same period, a specific social structure and power balance came into being within these communities themselves, characterising the region throughout the fifteenth and sixteenth centuries. The village communities were dominated by peasants: smallholders with strong property rights on their private land. Campine villages were economically relatively egalitarian, with Gini indexes fluctuating between 0.50 and 0.56. Still, different types of peasants can be distinguished. Farm sizes serve as an excellent tool to illustrate these evident differences (Table 10.1).[6] First of all, there was a significant minority of nearly landless inhabitants. A large part of them lived in, or on the verges of, poverty and were partially dependent on poor relief and the use of the commons for survival. Furthermore, there was a significant group of cottagers, owning between one and three hectares and struggling to reach subsistence. The group owning over three hectares can be labelled as 'independent peasants'. They were able—more or less—to make a living from the

Table 10.1 Property composition of the village of Gierle (1554)

	Relative number of households per property group (%)	*% of total village surface per property group*
<1 hectare	31.3	6.2
1–3 hectares	28.3	18.8
3–5 hectares	13.9	18.2
5–10 hectares	12.7	27.3
≥10 hectares	6.6	26.8
Unknown	7.2	2.7

Source SAA, OMA Gierle, 344. Pieces concerning the Xth and XXth penny, 1554

combined use of their own lands, animal breeding and the commons. In particular, those owning over five hectares probably were relatively well off. This last group was also able to dominate village office holding, as over 80% of village aldermen (the de facto village government), tax officials, poor masters and so on belonged to this category. In some villages, tenant farmers, tilling somewhat larger farms, were also present, but they were unable to completely direct village life, as the Campine peasants were able to govern their own communities and commons (Van Onacker 2014, pp. 89–96).

The most intriguing aspect of Campine social stratification is therefore its lack of a true 'one per cent', an elite that was able to distinguish itself economically, politically, socially and culturally. No social group was powerful enough to remove the privileges of other social groups; as such, the specific power balance of this region resulted in a 'common denominator', an equilibrium in which all social groups (lords, tenant farmers, peasant elites and small cottagers) were able to get something out of the arrangement, but were unable to completely dominate affairs and fundamentally alter them. This equilibrium did go hand in hand with a lot of quarrelling, small-scale frictions and an elaborate array of formal and informal conflict regulation mechanisms, but the core was never shaken (De Keyzer 2014, pp. 290–302). The Campine structural features, the presence of commons, strong village communities dominated by peasant smallholders and mixed farming remained predominant up until the nineteenth century. This impressive structural stability is one of the most striking features of the Campine area, setting it apart from the Low Countries' core regions—of which Holland is perhaps best known—which all underwent a transition towards a more commercial, even capitalist, economy.

10.3 Annuities: The Institutional Context

The annuity ('*constitution de rente*')—a type of mortgage quite typical for pre-industrial continental Europe—was a loan for which the debtor used real estate as collateral. The creditor surrendered the principal in exchange for a fixed annual interest payment. The main contrast with an ordinary loan was that the lender had no right to demand repayment of the principal. Some annuities were perpetual, while others had to be paid until the stipulated contractor died (Hoffman 1996; Soly 1974, p. 524). For the debtor, this was a relatively straightforward way of acquiring capital, allowing him or her to make the necessary investments without having to use savings or enter into much more expensive short-term debt. Especially in times of rising land and house prices, this makes good economic sense. In Antwerp and Ghent, economically prosperous periods therefore went hand in hand with a rise of the registration of annuities. Furthermore, there was also a lively secondary market, in which these annuities were resold (Dambruyne 1989, p. 189; Soly 1974, p. 532).

On an institutional level, the Campine credit market was very similar to that of other, more commercial regions in the Low Countries; it was certainly not subject to more rigid constraints. As already mentioned, secure property rights, for example, are often identified as one of the prerequisites for smoothly functioning land and credit markets. In the Campine area, land held in customary rent was predominant, and this could be sold and inherited without any need for lordly consent or consent of the community as a whole. As leasehold was still a rather marginal phenomenon even in the sixteenth century (with numbers never exceeding 25% of all land), many peasants had land at their disposal to use as collateral.[7] It is however important to note that the common waste was not part of the private property regime. Neither Campine villagers (who had usage rights) nor their lords (who possessed the bare ownership) were able to sell or mortgage this land. For credit transactions, institutional constraints were virtually non-existent. In some villages, there were, however, some constraints on the functioning of the land market, as land held in customary rent was subject to a tax when sold, the so-called *pontpenningen*.[8] For our fifteenth- and sixteenth-century case-studies, however, it was not possible to find proof that this tax was collected. For the village of Gierle, for example, the ducal domain accounts systematically recorded the word *nyet* ('nothing') in the *pontpenningen* category of the account. In all likelihood, the aforementioned struggles between different types of lords, who were trying to attract peasants to their lands, had an impact on the relatively low degree of lordly interference on the Campine land and credit markets. The only exception was the manor of Westerlo, owned by the influential de Merode family, where the *pontpenningen* tax was indeed collected.[9] This seems to have had a rather limited effect on the liveliness of the land market, since the number of transactions was not remarkably lower. This stands in striking contrast to other more peripheral regions in a European context, such as Württemberg, where borrowing (mostly short-term credit) was limited by very formal constraints, as permission had to be obtained from the community council and local state officials (Ogilvie et al. 2012, p. 163).

Contracting organisations form another relevant aspect of the institutional framework. The organisations competent to register formal credit transactions were not the same throughout late medieval Europe. In southern Europe, notaries were the prime agents of credit registration (Hoffman et al. 1999), whereas in north-western Europe, various 'civil' courts were responsible for this. When it came to these civil courts, differences can also be perceived. The medieval English manor courts (Briggs 2009) were much more lord-dominated than the Holland, Flemish or Brabant benches of aldermen or feudal courts. Zuijderduijn, who focussed on credit in late medieval and early modern Holland, notes that the bench of aldermen had a 'virtual monopoly' on civil and voluntary jurisdiction in this region. Landed property and its division were essential to pre-modern communities, which explains why land and credit transactions were so meticulously recorded (Zuijderduijn 2009). Even though the Campine area was a late developer, its land and credit institutions were relatively similar to those in Holland. The bench of aldermen was the primary recorder when it came to transactions bound to land, including the registration of annuities. However, some further details need to be mentioned. Many benches of aldermen, for example, had a feudal court as their predecessor, which is contrary to the situation in Holland, a 'region without feudalism' (Van Bavel and Van Zanden 2004). These courts were qualified to register transactions linked to landed property, such as the buying and selling of land, but also credit transactions, since these required an immovable as pawn. Even when most villages witnessed the establishment of a bench of aldermen, many of these courts remained in operation (Byl 1965; Van Asseldonk 2002). In Gierle, for example, there was a bench of aldermen responsible for ducal property, but there were also two feudal courts, recording transactions linked to the property of two local lords: the lord of Tielen and the lord of Poederlee. Peasants owning customary land belonging to one of these local lords had to register their transactions in the appropriate court. It seems, however, that this practice died out during the sixteenth century, when benches of aldermen became predominant. Most villages furthermore had one or more notaries, but in the notarial archives, no land or credit transactions could be traced. Notarial deeds offered little legal security, as they lacked power of execution, which explains their absence in facilitating land and credit markets in the Low Countries (Zuijderduijn 2009, p. 188).

A specificity of the strongly urban-dominated County of Flanders and Duchy of Brabant is that annuities were also often registered by urban benches of aldermen. Technically this was illegal, as all land transactions had to be registered in the locality where the land was situated, but due to the cities' greater power and their more elaborate ability to sue transgressors, such registration had a certain appeal, much to the dismay of local lords who were thus deprived of income. During the fifteenth century, a compromise was forged between the Duke of Burgundy, the urban and local courts, and local lords. Transactions could be registered at urban courts, but this had to be accompanied by a registration at the local level as well (Godding 1954, p. 348; Coppens 2000, p. 744). Another interesting phenomenon is the discrepancy between norm and practice when dealing with defaulters, those unable to pay the yearly interest. Technically, the collateral was installed for precisely these circumstances, allowing foreclosure. However, the evidence gathered in research for this study suggests that these benches of aldermen were rather lenient in dealing with default. For the village of Gierle, only fifteen out of 491 entries in the registers of the bench of aldermen (between 1538 and 1558) dealt with arrears in payment. A century earlier, in Rijkevorsel (1460–1485), the number amounted to seven out of 558 transactions. Defaulters were usually granted extra time to make the necessary payments and could even install extra collateral or find guarantors. No single example of foreclosure could therefore be found in the aldermen's registers that are at the core of this research. It is perhaps possible that discussions on defaulting and foreclosure made their way to 'higher' courts, such as the Council of Brabant. However, for individuals the use of this court was quite expensive, and therefore, it was mainly used by groups and communities of peasants, rather than by individuals.[10] The Campine ability to (in)formally regulate conflicts was thus apparently also present when it came to dealing with the issue of foreclosure. Benches of aldermen thus had no 'virtual monopoly' on transactions bound to land, but the institutions responsible for registration were extremely accessible and reliable. They were furthermore strongly embedded within village society as they were—preponderantly—dominated by the elite of independent peasants and relatively shielded from external interferences, especially that of lords.

10.4 General Credit Market Trends

Institutionally, the Campine credit market was very similar to its counterparts in the rest of the Low Countries. The Campine market for long-term credit furthermore followed the broader developments present in the Low Countries as a whole, albeit with a slight delay when compared to cities. In the fourteenth-century cities, annuities became redeemable, as this made the credit instrument easier to apply and more attractive. In 1520, this redeemability was decreed by law in the entire Duchy of Brabant, followed by the County of Flanders in 1529 (Soly 1974, p. 527). Another trend characterising credit markets throughout western Europe—monetisation—could be perceived in the Campine area as well, albeit again somewhat later and slower than in other regions. In fifteenth-century Gierle, most annuities were paid off in kind: only 21.43% were paid off in money. In the sixteenth century, this already amounted to 71.43%. Still, the ongoing presence of annuities in kind makes sense in the context of a mixed-farming peasant society. For the one receiving the yearly interest, income in kind offered much more stability, as it was less vulnerable to depreciation and inflation. Campine poor tables were a clear example of this. Every Campine village had its own poor table, responsible for alleviating poverty within the community and governed by elite laymen. They had a clear preference for income (also largely derived from annuities) in kind, as this was much more reliable during times of crisis (Van Onacker and Masure 2015, p. 79). The annual interest rate—another strong indicator of institutional efficiency—was strikingly similar to that in other regions. In Gierle (1538–1558), this rate came to 5.9% and in Rijkevorsel (1538–1558) 6.25%. This is almost identical to the interest rate in the Inland Flanders village of Haaltert (6.25%) (Thoen and Soens 2004, p. 713) and to the 'sixteenth penny' (6.25%), the legally binding interest rate, established in 1573 by a royal edict (Britz 1847).

Let us now take a look at the evolution of the number of transactions (Figs. 10.2 and 10.3). Throughout the Low Countries, annuities became generally more widely used throughout the late medieval period. In the Campine area, the trend also seems to have been one of increase, but quite liable to fluctuations. The same mounting trend was discerned for Inland Flanders by Erik Thoen and Tim Soens (Thoen and Soens 2009, pp. 28–29). In the Inland Flanders village of Haaltert, between 1465 and 1480, there were on average 0.15 transactions per 100 inhabitants

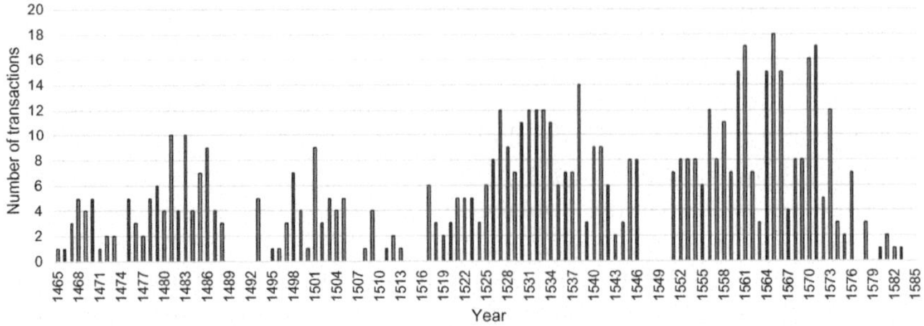

Fig. 10.2 Annuities in Rijkevorsel (1465–1585), N = 626
Note for the periods 1489–1492/1514–1516/1547–1550, no registers were preserved
Source SAA, OMA Rijkevorsel, 145–180. Aldermen's letters, 1465–1609

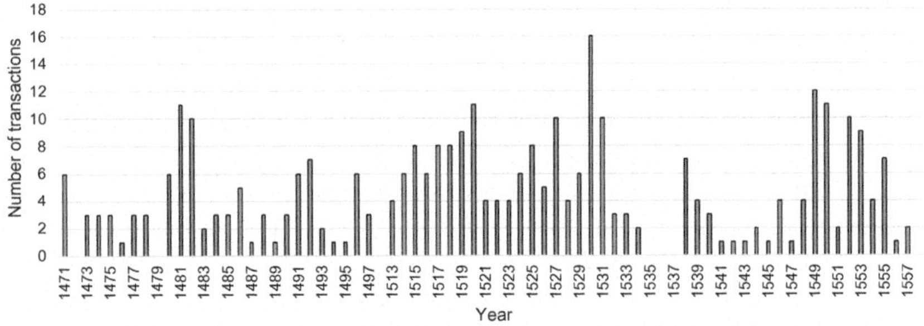

Fig. 10.3 Annuities in Gierle (1471–1558), N = 328
Note for the periods 1498–1512 and 1535–1537 no registers were preserved
Source SAA, OMA Gierle, 627. Manorial records (Court of Lord Daneel Van Ranst), 1454–1497; SAA, OMA Gierle, 630. Manorial records (Court of Lord Peeter Van Brimeu), 1471–1501 and SAA, OMA Gierle, 349 and 350. Aldermen's registers, 1512–1558

per year (De Brouwer 1968, pp. 30–31). In the Campine village of Rijkevorsel, this number was somewhat higher, with 0.31 transactions per 100 inhabitants. In the sixteenth century (1561–1570), the number of transactions was significantly higher. In Haaltert, the average was 0.72 transactions per 100 inhabitants and in Rijkevorsel, 1.14 transactions. In Mijnsherenland in Holland, between 1534 and 1543, the number of transactions amounted to 1.07 per 100 inhabitants (Zuijderduijn, this volume). Other regions with populations that still, but decreasingly so, had land to use as collateral, such as Inland Flanders and Holland, thus had comparable numbers. It is possible that the seventeenth and eighteenth centuries would provide us with another image, as many Flemish and Dutch peasants were more and more engaged in leasehold. Perhaps counter-intuitively, the Campine market for annuities was much more lively than that of contemporary Coastal Flanders, at that time a polarised region characterised by commercial farms, increasingly specialising in cattle-breeding for the market. Soens, however, gives us a convincing explanation for this discrepancy. As landholding in the coastal area was limited to only a handful of very large landowners per village, engaged in leasing out farms and plots of land, hardly any inhabitant of this region was able to use property as collateral, as they simply did not have any (Soens 2015). This was in striking contrast to Inland Flanders, where approximately half of the peasants still owned land, and to the Campine area, where leasehold remained a marginal phenomenon. On the other hand, a striking difference can be noted with Dutch town Edam and its surrounding countryside (*De Zeevang*) where a staggering 120 annuities were established in the year 1564—or 7.21 per 100 inhabitants per year (Van Zanden et al. 2012, p. 17). This clearly indicates a discrepancy between the ever commercialising towns and villages in Holland and the still strongly peasant-dominated agricultural regions of Inland Flanders and the Campine. All three of these regions were characterised by strong property rights, suggesting that de Soto's exclusive focus on its importance cannot account for the variety in the use of long-term credit. Therefore, we turn to social structures.

10.5 The Role of Factor Markets: The Absence of Accumulation

Since we want to find out why and how the Campine credit market was employed within the specific context of a peasant society with commons, the decision was made to look at these institutions from a micro-perspective. Sources do not directly shed light on the motivations and strategies of Campine peasants, so following the lead of scholars such as Thomas Brennan, the study will reconstruct which socio-economic groups were active on the credit market (Brennan 2006). The historiography is highly divided on the 'social function' of credit markets. Often, studies suggest that land and credit markets were dominated by the economically better-off, so as to accumulate land and money and make their fellow-villagers economically dependent on them. According to this view, land and credit markets thus played a vital part in a process of social polarisation (Ogilvie 2007). Eighteenth-century Inland Flanders is a striking example of this. Flemish villages were characterised by an interdependency of large tenant farmers and small peasants. Tenant farmers acted as middlemen for small peasants, bringing their goods to the market and acting as creditors. In exchange for these services, peasants worked on these tenant farms, especially during the harvest (Lambrecht 2003). The influence of social organisation and relations on the way credit functioned was not limited to rural society. In a recent article, Wouter Ryckbosch and Ellen Decraene have convincingly shown how social relations and hierarchy within post-Tridentine confraternities in the city of Aalst clearly had their impact on credit relations, with deans often providing credit for ordinary members (Ryckbosch and Decraene 2014, pp. 23–24).

Others, most notably Craig Muldrew, suggested factor markets created a web of interdependence, binding together different social strata. For urban societies, Muldrew even states that 'the market… introduced a degree of "effective equality" into an otherwise stratified society' (Muldrew 1993, p. 36). For rural societies, similar statements have been made by Trevor Dean (on the fourteenth-century Italian countryside) (Dean 2002) and Chris Briggs (on the fourteenth-century English countryside) (Briggs 2009). They suggest that credit relations were mainly horizontally organised and hardly contributed to a polarisation process. The role credit played within a society is thus not unambiguous, and it diverged greatly, shaped by the social structures and power balance within societies.

To assess whether the Campine credit market played its part in accumulation strategies or was used in a more egalitarian way, the registers of the benches of aldermen of the villages Rijkevorsel and Gierle are used. For the two sample periods (Rijkevorsel, the registers of 1465–1480, for Gierle the registers of 1538–1558), all details from annuities were collected. Creditors and debtors were subsequently linked to sources shedding light on the social stratification of these villages. For Rijkevorsel, the ducal tax registers of about the same period (1465–1474) were used to divide the population into quartiles.[11] For the village of Gierle, the records of a tax on land use (a *penningkohier*) of 1554 were employed to divide the population into property groups.[12] A proportion of the people mentioned in land or credit transactions could be linked to these findings, shedding light on the socio-economic position of creditors and debtors. For Rijkevorsel, 33.9% of those engaging in transactions could be identified, in Gierle 21.6%.

These numbers might seem somewhat limited. Several explanations can be given to frame these findings. First, the sample period used for the registers of the benches of aldermen is somewhat wider than that of the taxation list—most notably this is the case for Gierle, using a list of 1554 and registers of 1538–1558. Quite naturally, we miss out on some people. Furthermore, it is quite a challenge to identify Campine inhabitants. Names are often very inconsistently used, making identification difficult. And furthermore, many of the people engaging in the credit market were women and children (see below). Since taxation lists only enlisted household heads, who were mostly men, women and children are very hard to trace. Finally, some of the people registering transactions probably came from outside the village and could thus not be traced in the village's tax lists. In reality, this group was probably only of limited importance.

If we focus on the socio-economic position of creditors in fifteenth-century Rijkevorsel, it quickly becomes visible how the independent peasants, belonging to quartiles 3 and 4, were the dominant forces (Table 10.2). In sixteenth-century Gierle, the same trend can be discerned (Table 10.3). People owning between five and ten hectares were especially overrepresented, since 29.41% of all creditors came from this group, though it formed only 11.11% of the total population. This is not hugely surprising—to act as a creditor, you must have had some significant assets. Still, quite a significant share of the creditors came from lower social groups. In fifteenth-century Rijkevorsel, debtors also predominantly came from the highest quartiles and thus the group of independent peasants. In sixteenth-century Gierle, we can perceive the same predominance of this group, since 37.04% of all debtors owned between five and ten hectares. But yet again, the 'lower classes' were by no means absent from the credit market, especially as the credit market became more widely used in the sixteenth century. In Gierle, 23.53% of all creditors owned less than a hectare while 17.65% owned between one and three hectares. As lower status creditors and debtors are somewhat harder to identify in taxation lists than their richer counterparts, the real number of 'poorer' peasants engaging in this market might even have been slightly higher. This implies that they were underrepresented

Table 10.2 Economic position (in quartiles) of credit market participants (creditors/debtors vs. total population, based on tax registers), Rijkevorsel, 1464–1485

	Number of creditors, absolute & (relative)	*Number of debtors, absolute & (relative)*	*Total population, absolute & (relative)*
Continuously Q1	4 (18.2%)	3 (16.7%)	128 (25.39%)
Continuously Q2	1 (4.5%)	0 (0.0%)	60 (11.90%)
Continuously Q3	5 (22.7%)	3 (16.7%)	69 (13.69%)
Continuously Q4	6 (27.3%)	5 (27.7%)	71 (14.09%)
Highest Qs	3 (13.6%)	2 (11.1%)	46 (9.13%)
Lowest Qs	1 (4.5%)	1 (5.6%)	57 (11.31%)
Middle Qs	2 (9.2%)	4 (22.2%)	38 (7.54%)

Note For this table, the Rijkevorsel population was divided into four quartiles, based on a series of tax registers. Those continuously belonging to the same quartile are included in 'continuously Q 1/2/3/4'. Those switching between Q3 and Q4 are included in 'highest Qs'. Those switching between Q2 and Q3 in 'middle Qs' and those switching between Q1 and Q2 in 'lowest Qs'

Source SAA, OMA Rijkevorsel, 145–180. Aldermen's letters, 1465–1609 and SAA, OMA Rijkevorsel, 3244–3256. Royal taxation, 1464–1475

Table 10.3 Economic position (based on land use) of credit market participants (creditors/debtors vs. total population, based on *penningkohier*), Gierle, 1538–1558

	Number of creditors, absolute & (relative)	*Number of debtors, absolute & (relative)*	*Total population, absolute & (relative)*
<1 hectare	4 (23.53%)	6 (22.22%)	69 (36.51%)
1–3 hectares	3 (17.65%)	8 (29.63%)	52 (27.51%)
3–5 hectares	4 (23.53%)	1 (3.70%)	24 (12.70%)
5–10 hectares	5 (29.41%)	10 (37.04%)	21 (11.11%)
≥10 hectares	1 (5.88%)	2 (7.41%)	11 (5.82%)

Source SAA, OMA Gierle, 349 and 350. Aldermen's registers, 1512–1558 and SAA, OMA Gierle, 344. Pieces concerning the Xth and XXth penny, 1554

to some extent, but they were by no means an insignificant group. Independent peasants were thus somewhat overrepresented, but they were by no means the only group using annuities as an instrument, either as creditor or as debtor.

However, we still need to ascertain whether a small group of rich villagers used the credit market to create dependency. This would imply a tendency for the same people to reappear constantly as creditors. To get an insight into this matter, an effort was made to ascertain how many people were involved in several transactions. Furthermore, land transactions were included in this analysis, in order to enable us to assess whether dominance of one market coincided with dominance over the other. Only included were those people involved in at least two transactions (one land and one credit transaction). The results are interesting. In Gierle, the proportion of the population engaged in more than two transactions witnessed a minor increase, from 10% in 1471–1497 to 13.4% in 1538–1558. In Rijkevorsel, the increase was even more striking: from 2.8% in 1465–1480 to 15.4% in 1538–1558. This is perhaps unsurprising, as the number of transactions also increased during this period; the use of annuities seems to have become more widespread from the end of the fifteenth century onwards. It therefore does not really suggest an increasing level of dependency creation. When we focus more closely on the group of people involved in several transactions, we can furthermore note the fact that the average number of transactions they engaged in slightly increased in Rijkevorsel (from 2.9 to 3.6) and remained more or less constant in Gierle (around 3.6). It is, however, remarkable that the outliers—peasants involved in a significantly higher number of transactions—were involved in many more transactions in the sixteenth century, although the total number of people in this group remained rather limited. In fifteenth-century Rijkevorsel, the two most active users of the market could each be traced in 6 transactions, whereas in the sixteenth century, this augmented to 10 and 12 times. In the village of Gierle, a similar increase can be noted, from seven and eight transactions to 12 and 13. Yet again, this links up with the general tendency towards increase throughout our research period. So, even though several villagers were more active in these factor markets, long-term credit was not limited to the happy few. An Inland Flemish system, with only a couple of people acting continuously as creditors and large mass of poorer peasants dependent on them, could by no means be discerned for the Campine area. As the Campine area was a region with a relatively low degree of inequality, it is perhaps not surprising that polarisation or complete dominance by a small upper layer was not perceived. The region's specific power balance—the above-mentioned 'common denominator'—furthermore played its part in ensuring no social group was truly able to get the upper hand. In a society where land and power were relatively equally divided and where no one was able to tip this balance, credit was not a tool of subjugation.

10.6 The Absence of Urban Domination

But what about another group often put forward as steering rural credit markets: (wealthy) townsmen? In the strongly urbanised Low Countries, many townsmen were eager to invest in the countryside, be it through the buying of land or by acting as creditors. For the southern Brabantine village of Aartselaar, Limberger has found that during the sixteenth century, of the sellers of annuities recorded in the registers of the Antwerp bench of aldermen, only some 50% came from the village itself; for the buyers, this number was even lower, with 20% (Limberger 2009, p. 68). Many of the latter came from the cities of Mechelen, Leuven and especially Antwerp (De Nave 1978). A close scrutiny of the registers of the bench of aldermen of the Campine town of Turnhout suggests that the Campine area was void of urban investors as hardly any transactions could be found which involved inhabitants of the town of Turnhout.[13] However, given the fact that the Campine area was situated relatively close to one of the most important urban centres of its time, Antwerp, one would immediately be inclined to suspect a certain urban influence. The source shedding light on this topic is the registers of the bench of aldermen of the city of Antwerp. The transactions recorded by this bench (of which a significant part were annuities) were collected in a database and analysed by De Nave (1394–1402) (De Nave 1978) and Bisschops (1491–1494). This will be supplemented with some findings of Michael Limberger for sixteenth-century Antwerp (Limberger 2008). The drawback is of course that these findings were not compiled and analysed in the same way by these different authors, but even so, they shed light on the general patterns.

For the late fourteenth and early fifteenth century, De Nave has reconstructed the ownership of annuities of Antwerp citizens outside of Antwerp. Her research shows that 20% of all transactions were linked to the fertile Polder region to the west of Antwerp, 44.3% took place in the Flemish sandy region[14] and 35.7% in the Campine area. The number is not impressive, but not negligible either. This might be linked to the fact that many Antwerp burghers had a Campine background and perhaps retained links with their native settlements, resulting in credit relations. Michael Limberger, for example, states that, between 1520 and 1530, 60% of all official new Antwerp burghers (the so-called *poorters*) came from the Campine area (Limberger 1993, pp. 95–105), although the number was perhaps rather lower in the fourteenth and fifteenth centuries. Jan De Meester calculated for the entire sixteenth century that approximately 10% of all new burghers came from the Campine area (De Meester 2011, p. 119). Furthermore, several transactions might not have included townsmen, but could have been registered with the Antwerp bench of aldermen as this was more powerful and 'trustworthy' than its rural counterparts.

Unfortunately, de Nave's findings do not allow us to assess the weight of Campine transactions and the number of transactions per year recorded in the Antwerp aldermen's registers. Luckily, the data of Tim Bisschops do allow this exercise for the late fifteenth century. By using his database, we were able to reconstruct the number of annuities registered at the Antwerp bench of aldermen with a plot of land in the Campine area as security.[15] The boxplot in Fig. 10.4 indicates that these numbers were indeed quite low, with a median of 1.1 per village per year. The outliers—with transactions exceeding the third quartile—are mostly larger towns or villages. The most outstanding example is Brecht, an exceptionally large village, with over 2000 inhabitants. In most other villages, the number of transactions per year was extremely limited.

In any case, urban dominance of the Campine market for annuities was not impressive, considering the low number of transactions per year. Antwerp burghers had more lucrative channels through which to invest their money: engaging in the urban market for annuities, buying up property in the fertile polder region or the more immediate environment of the city (Limberger 2008). Furthermore, the Brabantine cities never had the same strong grip on their rural surroundings as their Flemish counterparts, as they were never a worthy match for the expanding powers of the Dukes of Burgundy (Van Uytven 1976). The Campine credit market thus predominantly played a part in the strategies of the Campine villagers themselves. But what were these strategies and how did they link up with the region's specific structures?

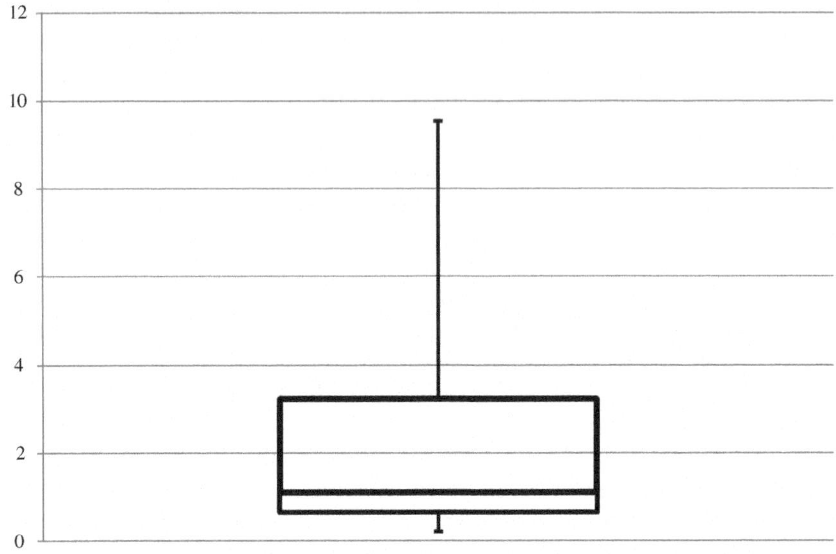

Fig. 10.4 Boxplot showing number of transactions (land and credit) per year, per Campine village, 1491–1495 (average = 2)
Source Database of Dr. Tim Bisschops

10.7 The Role of Factor Markets: Part of a Peasant Strategy

The Campine credit market was not a vehicle in the hands of a tiny village elite or a group of wealthy townsmen. Peasants themselves—as creditors and as debtors—were the main users. The argument offered here is that the Campine market for long-term credit mainly functioned within the context of distinct peasant strategies. In a society with a relatively low degree of inequality and relatively shielded from lordly and urban interference, credit relations were not a tool of polarisation. In a region where many inhabitants had access to land they could use as collateral, a broad layer of society was able to access long-term credit. Long-term credit was therefore used by all social groups, albeit to different extents. So the question remains: What was the function of long-term credit within a communal peasant society? What was credit used for by creditors and by debtors?

Let us first take a look at the motivations of creditors. To reconstruct these, it is enlightening to concentrate on the 'types' of people lending out money in the form of an annuity. In sixteenth-century Gierle, some groups were remarkably active on this front. Institutions such as the poor table ('Holy Spirit table') or fraternities were eager creditors, making up 4.35% of the total. For them, acting as a creditor and receiving the yearly interest was a valid strategy to secure a stable yearly income. Orphaned children under guardianship (14.13%), and women—often widowed (39.13%), and also accompanied by a guardian—were also remarkably active. The impressive number of women participating is consistent with the findings of Hoffman, Postel-Vinay and Rosenthal for eighteenth-century Paris. Often, women used this rent-income to preserve their independence and provide for themselves (Hoffman et al. 1999). In one of the Campine records, this motivation is explicitly stated; in 1472, Aernout Van Bavel and his sister Katelijn and her daughter Digne appeared before the bench of aldermen. As part of the registration of an annuity, Aernout promised to pay his sister a yearly interest of three *viertel* of rye—to provide for her livelihood.[16]

In the village of Rijkevorsel, this specific behaviour of creditors could not be traced. But there is a perfectly logical explanation for this. In Rijkevorsel, the above-mentioned groups (institutions, orphaned children and women) used *erfgevingen* (*bail à rente*) to secure their income. This is in essence a sale of an immovable. Instead of paying in cash, an annuity was established as a form of payment, so the seller received a yearly interest and the buyer did not have to pay the purchase price all at once (Dambruyne 1989, pp. 160–161). In Rijkevorsel, on a yearly basis on average 2.6 *erfgevingen* were recorded before the bench of aldermen. In 1467, for example, Bertelmeeus Van Bavel decided to 'sell' all his immovable goods to his children, in exchange for a yearly interest of seven crowns and a 'bed and place in front of the hearth' with one of his children.[17] Family members were often the buyers in this type of transaction. In 1468, Henric Vanden Aerde appeared before the village aldermen to sell his immovable goods to his nephew, Gheert Vander Meert, in exchange for two *zester* rye per year (707.8 litres).[18] Yet again, women often acted as *erfgevers*, namely in 34.8% of these *bails à rente* in Rijkevorsel. So, to summarise, credit transactions (and by extension *erfgevingen*) were essential building blocks of a peasant's economic strategy. At the important moments of life—when parents died and the inheritance needed to be divided, when one's life's partner died, or when one retired—Campine peasants could opt to act as a creditor and use the yearly income of an annuity to ensure a stable income.

When it comes to the debtor's side of the story, it is extremely difficult to reconstruct the reasons why Campine peasants chose to plunge into debt. Therefore, only some preliminary hypotheses are presented here. First of all, it is safe to say that annuities were not used to buy land. The aldermen's and feudal court's registers were used to examine whether land transactions (which were also recorded in the database) followed credit transactions, but not a single individual who first borrowed money before buying land could be traced. Land and credit markets evolved in completely different ways (Van Onacker 2013, p. 62). This matches the findings of Erik Thoen for Inland Flanders, where peasants also did not borrow money to invest in extra land (Thoen 1988a, pp. 933–934). The exceptions to this are of course the *bails à rente*. This specific type of annuity was specifically designed to purchase land (see above). The size of the annuities was however not negligible, as can be appreciated from Table 10.4. In sixteenth-century Gierle, a peasant on average borrowed the equivalent of the wages of a mower working for 176.5 days or of 353 days of haymaking. In Rijkevorsel, the average loan amounted to the wages from 229.2 days of mowing and 458.4 days of haymaking. These were quite substantial sums, to say the least. Thoen suggests that these loans were predominantly used for 'in-depth investments': investments in the purchase of agricultural implements,

Table 10.4 Size of loan (in brabantine groats and agricultural daily wages), Gierle and Rijkevorsel, 1538–1558 (Rijkevorsel: N = 130; Gierle: N = 87)

	Gierle, brabantine groat	*Gierle, daily wage mower*	*Gierle, daily wage haymaker*	*Rijksevorsel, brabantine groat*	*Rijkevorsel, daily wage mower*	*Rijkevorsel, daily wage haymaker*
Average	2118.1	176.5	353	2751	229.2	458.4
Minimum	180	15	30	240	20	40
Quartile 1	1080	90	180	1500	125	250
Median	1620	135	270	2400	200	400
Quartile 3	2400	200	400	3840	320	640
Maximum	9720	810	1620	6720	560	1120

Source SAA, OMA Gierle, 349 and 350. Aldermen's registers, 1512–1558 and SAA, OMA Rijkevorsel, 145–180. Aldermen's letters, 1465–1609. Rural wages derived from: State Archives Brussels (hereafter: SAB), Chambre de comptes, 5213. Domain accounts of the Land of Turnhout, 1552–1559

livestock, seedcorn or improvement of the farmstead (Thoen 1988a, pp. 933–934). Since a significant number of Campine peasants—mainly the so-called independent peasants—owned some livestock (cows and sheep), often also a plough, and all had arable land that had to be sown, it seems reasonable to hypothesise that Campine credit played its part in purchasing these things. This is supported by the findings of Thomas Brennan for the eighteenth-century Champagne. Since these loans were long-term loans, it seems quite likely that they were used to invest, whereas short-term loans were often used to alleviate urgent needs (Brennan 2006). Due to the fact that Campine peasants were able to use their land as collateral, a relatively broad layer of Campine society was thus able to make the necessary investments to keep their farm up and running smoothly.

10.8 Conclusion

The Campine area was relatively peripheral within the context of the Low Countries. It was and remained furthermore a communally organised region, in which the market was but one of many allocation mechanisms and by no means the dominant one. The institutional framework of its market for long-term credit was however hugely similar to that of the core regions. Institutional constraints were limited, and long-term credit was quite easily obtained, especially since a significant part of the Campine commoners had such strong rights on their land they were able to use it as collateral. The Campine credit market did however lack the potential for polarisation, accumulation and dependency creation, nor did it function as a motor for growth. It was furthermore also quite sheltered from urban control. The number of urban burghers investing in the Campine area was very low. Other regions and strategies generated much more profit, and Brabantine cities were nowhere near strong enough to encroach on the neighbouring countryside the way Flemish cities did. The Campine area's social structure with its relatively low inequality and its power balance—in which no social group was able to dominate the others—is pivotal in explaining the role long-term credit played.

The Campine credit market thus mainly reflected the region's social structure. Independent peasants were somewhat overrepresented in the use of the credit market, but by no means monopolised it, as all social groups were able to use it—something which holds true for all Campine institutions and organisations. Long-term credit mainly played a part in the peasant life cycle, making typical peasant strategies possible. Creditors used it to ensure themselves of a stable income, which explains why women, orphans and peasants on the verge of retirement made ample use of the instrument. Debtors used the extra money they obtained for in-depth investments in their farm or in livestock, perhaps especially at the beginnings of their careers. Markets therefore were quite malleable and were used in different ways in different societies and by different social groups. The Campine credit market was thus no agent of change, but played its part in the continuation of a communally organised society.

Notes

1. The 'de Soto problem' refers to the situation whereby imperfect property rights hamper possible entrepreneurs from using certain assets as collateral.
2. On the complex interaction between property rights and economic growth; see Ogilvie and Carus (2014).
3. State Archives Antwerp (hereafter: SAA), Old Municipal Archives (hereafter: OMA) Gierle, 627. Manorial records (Court of Lord Daneel Van Ranst), 1454–1497, and SAA, OMA Gierle, 630. Manorial records (Court of Lord Peeter Van Brimeu), 1471–1501.
4. SAA, OMA Gierle, 349 and 350. Aldermen's registers, 1512–1558.
5. SAA, OMA Rijkevorsel, 145–180. Aldermen's lettres, 1465–1609.
6. The findings here are for the village of Gierle, but they are representative for the entire region; see Van Onacker (2014).
7. This is in striking contrast to Coastal Flanders, where the market for annuities was not very vibrant during the sixteenth century, as the majority of the population was nearly landless, or only able to lease a tiny plot of land; see Soens (2015).
8. This was rather common in Inland Flanders; see Thoen (1988b).
9. State Archives Brussels, Merode-archief, pontpenningen Westerlo.
10. See De Keyzer (2014).
11. SAA, OMA Rijkevorsel, 3244–3256. Royal taxation, 1464–1475.
12. SAA, OMA Gierle, 344. Pieces concerning the Xth and XXth penny, 1554.
13. City Archive Turnhout, 973–1025. Goedenisboeken, 1444–1600.
14. Which refers, confusingly enough, also to the region to the south of Antwerp, which was part of the Duchy of Brabant.
15. For a sample of 42 villages: Arendonk, Balen, Beerse, Bouwel, Brecht, Broechem, Essen and Kalmthout, Geel, Gierle, Grootloo, Halle, Herentals,

Herenthout, Hoogstraten, Houtven, Hulshout, Kasterlee, Lille, Loenhout, Meere, Meerle, Merksplas, Minderhout, Mol, Olen, Oostmalle, Poederlee, Pulle, Retie, Rijkevorsel, Tielen, Tongerlo, Turnhout, Veerle, Vlimmeren and Wechelderzande, Vorselaar, Vosselaar, Vremde, Westmalle, Wuuswezel and Zandhoven.

16. SAA, OMA Rijkevorsel, 145, f. 176.
17. SAA, OMA Rijkevorsel, 145, Aldermen's lettres, 1465–1487, f. 44.
18. Calculations based on Vandewalle (1984, p. 54).

References

Secondary Works

Bateman, M. and H.J. Chang, 2012. 'Microfinance and the illusion of development: From hubris to nemesis in thirty years', *World Economic Review*, vol. 1, pp. 13–36.

Brennan, T., 2006. 'Peasants and debt in eighteenth-century Champagne', *Journal of Interdisciplinary History*, vol. 37, pp. 175–200.

Briggs, C., 2009. *Credit and Village Society in Fourteenth-Century England* (Oxford: Oxford University Press).

Britz, M.J., 1847. *Code de l'ancien droit Belgique ou histoire de la jurisprudence et de la législation, suivie de l'exposé du droit civil des provinces Belgiques* (Brussels: Van Daele).

Byl, R., 1965. *Les juridictions scabinales dans le Duché de Brabant (des origines à la fin du XVe siècle)* (Brussels: Presses Universitaires de Bruxelles).

Congost, R., 2003. 'Property rights and historical analysis: What rights? What history?', *P&P*, vol. 181, pp. 73–106.

Coppens, H., 2000. 'Schepenbanken en dorpsbesturen' in R. Van Uytven, C. Bruneel, H. Coppens and B. Augustyn (eds.), *De gewestelijke en lokale overheidsinstellingen in Brabant en Mechelen tot 1795* (Brussels: Algemeen Rijksarchief), pp. 712–780.

Dambruyne, J., 1989. 'De Gentse immobiliënmarkt en de economische trend, 1590–1640', *Bijdragen en mededelingen betreffende de geschiedenis der Nederlanden*, vol. 104, pp. 157–183.

De Brouwer, J., 1968. *Demografische evolutie van het Land van Aalst 1570–1800* (Brussels: Pro Civitate).

De Keyzer, M., 2014. 'The Common Denominator. The Survival of the Commons in the Late Medieval Campine Area', unpublished PhD thesis, University of Antwerp.

De Meester, J., 2011. 'Gastvrij Antwerpen? Arbeidsmigratie naar het zestiende-eeuwse Antwerpen', unpublished PhD thesis, University of Antwerp.

De Nave, F., 1978. 'Antwerpen, stad en land (1394–1402). De innerlijke vervlechting van stedelijk en landelijk milieu in de late Middeleeuwen op basis van het privé bezit aan gronden en renten en andere soorten van goed', unpublished PhD thesis, Free University of Brussels.

De Soto, H., 2000. *The Mystery of Capital. Why Capitalism Triumphs in the West and Fails Everywhere Else* (London: Black Swan).

Dean, T., 2002. 'Wealth distribution and litigation in the medieval Italian countryside: Castel San Pietro, Bologna, 1385', *C&C*, vol. 17, pp. 333–350.

Deneweth, H., O. Gelderblom and J. Jonker, 2014. 'Microfinance and the decline of poverty: Evidence from the nineteenth-century Netherlands', *Journal of Economic Development*, vol. 39, pp. 79–110.

Fontaine, L., 2014. *Le marché. Histoire et usages d'une conquête sociale* (Paris: Gallimard).

Godding, P., 1954. 'Les conflits à propos des lettres échevinales des villes brabançonnes (xve–xviiie Siècles)', *Tijdschrift voor Rechtsgeschiedenis*, vol. 22, pp. 308–353.

Hoffman, P., 1996. *Growth in a Traditional Society: The French Countryside, 1450–1815* (Princeton: Princeton University Press).

Hoffman, P., G. Postel-Vinay and J.-L. Rosenthal, 1999. 'Information and economic history: How the credit market in old regime Paris forces us to rethink the transition to capitalism', *AHR*, vol. 104, pp. 69–94.

Lambrecht, T., 2003. 'Reciprocal exchange, credit and cash: Agricultural labour markets and local economies in the Southern Low Countries during the eighteenth century', *C&C*, vol. 18, pp. 237–261.

Limberger, M., 1993. 'Weltwirtschaft, nationaler und regionaler Markt: die Metropolenstellung Antwerpens im 16. Jahrhundert', in *Bericht über den Neunzehnten Österreichischen Historikertag in Graz Veranstaltet vom Verband Österreichischer Geschichtsvereine in der Zeit vom 18. bis 23. Mai 1992* (Vienna), pp. 95–105.

Limberger, M., 2008. *Sixteenth-Century Antwerp and Its Rural Surroundings. Social and Economic Changes in the Hinterland of a Commercial Metropolis (ca. 1450–ca. 1570)* (Turnhout: Brepols).

Limberger, M., 2009. 'Credit, the land market and the connection between the rural and urban economy. The use of perpetual annuities in Aartselaar (Brabant) from the fourteenth to sixteenth century', in P.R. Schofield and T. Lambrecht (eds.), *Credit and the Rural Economy in North Western Europe, c.1200–c.1850* (Turnhout: Brepols), pp. 63–73.

Muldrew, C., 1993. 'Credit and the courts: Debt litigation in a seventeenth-century urban community', *EcHR*, vol. 46, pp. 23–38.

Ogilvie, S., 2007. '"Whatever is, is right"? Economic institutions in pre-industrial Europe', *EcHR*, vol. 60, pp. 649–684.

Ogilvie, S. and A.W. Carus, 2014. 'Institutions and economic growth in historical perspective: Part 1', CESifo Working Paper 4861, Munich University, pp. 1–55.

Ogilvie, S., M. Küpker and J. Maegraith, 2012. 'Household debt in early modern Germany: Evidence from personal inventories', JEH, vol. 72, pp. 134–167.

Ryckbosch, W. and E. Decraene, 2014. 'Household credit, social relations, and devotion in the early-modern economy. A case study of religious confraternities and credit relations in the Southern Netherlands', *Tijdschrift voor Sociale en Economische Geschiedenis*, vol. 11, pp. 1–28.

Soens, T., 2015. 'Between fragmentation and engrossment. Transfers of peasant land in times of flood disaster in the late medieval Low Countries', paper presented at Rural History Conference, Girona, September 2015.

Soly, H., 1974. 'De schepenregisters als bron voor de conjunctuurgeschiedenis van Zuid- en Nordnederlandse steden in het Ancien Régime. Een concreet voorbeeld: de Antwerpse immobiliënmarkt in de 16de Eeuw', *Tijdschrift voor Geschiedenis*, vol. 87, pp. 521–544.

Spek, T. and D. Vangheluwe, 2008. 'De laatmiddeleeuwse transitie van landbouw en landschap in de Noord-Brabantse Kempen', *Historisch-geografisch Tijdschrift*, vol. 26, pp. 1–23.

Thoen, E., 1988a. *Landbouwekonomie en bevolking in Vlaanderen gedurende de late Middeleeuwen en het begin van de moderne tijden. Testregio: de Kasselrijen van Oudenaarde en Aalst* (Ghent: Belgisch Centrum voor landelijke geschiedenis).

Thoen, E., 1988b. 'Rechten en plichten van plattelanders als instrumenten van machtspolitieke strijd tussen adel, stedelijke burgerij en grafelijk gezag in het laat- middeleeuwse Vlaanderen. Buitenpoorterij en mortemain-rechten ten persoonlijken titel in de Kasselrijen van Aalst en Oudenaarde, vooral toegepast op de periode rond 1400', in *Les structures du pouvoir dans les communautés rurales en Belgique et dans Les Pays Limitrophes (12e–19e Siècle): Actes du 13e Colloque International, Spa, 3–5 Sept. 1986* (Brussels: Gemeentekrediet), pp. 469–490.

Thoen, E. and T. Soens, 2004. 'Appauvrissement et endettement dans le monde rural: Etude comparative du crédit dans les différents systèmes agraires en Flandre au bas moyen âge et au début de l'epoque moderne', in S. Cavaciocchi (ed.), *Il mercato della terra secc. XIII–XVIII. Atti delle 'Trentacinquesima Settimana di Studi' 5–9 Maggio 2003* (Florence: Le Monnier), pp. 703–720.

Thoen, E. and T. Soens, 2009. 'Credit in rural Flanders, c.1250–c.1600: Its variety and significance', in P.R. Schofield and T. Lambrecht (eds.), *Credit and the Rural Economy in North Western Europe, c.1200–c.1850* (Turnhout: Brepols), pp. 19–38.

Van Asseldonk, M., 2002. 'De ontwikkeling van bestuur en dorpsgrenzen in de Meierij van 'S-Hertogenbosch (ca. 1200–1832)', *Taxandria*, vol. 74, pp. 221–234.

Van Bavel, B.J.P., 2016. *The Invisible Hand? How Market Economies Have Emerged and Declined Since AD 500* (Oxford: Oxford University Press).

Van Bavel, B.J.P. and J.L. Van Zanden, 2004. 'The jump-start of the Holland economy during the late-medieval crisis, c.1350–c.1500', *EcHR*, vol. 57, pp. 503–532.

Van Bavel, B.J.P., J. Dijkman, E. Kuijpers, and J. Zuijderduijn, 2012. 'The organisation of markets as a key factor in the rise of Holland from the fourteenth to the sixteenth century: A test case for an institutional approach', *C&C*, vol. 27, pp. 347–378.

Van Onacker, E., 2013. 'Bedrijvige boeren? Peasants en de land- en kredietmarkt in de vijftiende- en zestiende-eeuwse Kempen', *Tijdschrift voor Sociale en Economische Geschiedenis*, vol. 10, pp. 40–70.

Van Onacker, E., 2014. 'Leaders of the Pack? Village Elites and Social Structures in the Fifteenth- and Sixteenth-Century Campine Area', unpublished PhD thesis, University of Antwerp.

Van Onacker, E. and H. Masure, 2015. 'Unity in diversity. Rural poor relief in the sixteenth-century Low Countries', *Tijdschrift voor Sociale en Economische Geschiedenis*, vol. 12, pp. 59–88.

Van Uytven, R., 1976. 'Vorst, adel en steden: een driehoeksverhouding in Brabant van de twaalfde tot de zestiende eeuw', *Bijdragen geschiedenis hertogdom Brabant*, vol. 59, pp. 93–122.

Van Zanden, J.L., J. Zuijderduijn and T. De Moor, 2012. 'Small is beautiful: The efficiency of credit markets in late medieval Holland', *European Review of Economic History*, vol. 16, pp. 3–22.

Vandewalle, P., 1984. *Oude maten, gewichten en muntstelsels in Vlaanderen, Brabant en Limburg* (Ghent: Belgisch Centrum voor Landelijke Geschiedenis).

Zuijderduijn, C.J., 2009. *Medieval Capital Markets: Markets for* Renten, *State Formation and Private Investment in Holland (1300–1550)* (Leiden and Boston: Brill).

CHAPTER 11

The *Other* Fundamental Problem of Exchange: Mortgages, Defaults and Debtor Protection in Sixteenth-Century Holland

Jaco Zuijderduijn

11.1 Introduction: The *Other* Fundamental Problem of Exchange

Imagine the following: for whatever reason you have to borrow €5000. There are three potential creditors who all charge the same interest rate: a family member asks 10% per annum, as does a bank, and a loan shark who is known to have strong ties with local mobsters. If you cannot repay them in time, you may either risk disturbing family relations, the bank taking possession of your goods, or a mobster breaking your thumbs. From whom do you borrow?

In 2000, Avner Greif coined the term 'the fundamental problem of exchange': for exchange to occur, a party has to be sure the counterparty will fulfil his obligations. In the words of Greif:

J. Zuijderduijn (✉)
Lund University, Lund, Sweden
e-mail: cornelis_jaco.zuijderduijn@ekh.lu.se

C. Briggs and J. Zuijderduijn (eds.), *Land and Credit*,
Palgrave Studies in the History of Finance,
https://doi.org/10.1007/978-3-319-66209-1_11

> For individuals to enter into mutually beneficial exchange relationships they have to recognise them as such and they have to be able to commit to fulfil their contractual obligations. A lender will not lend without being assured that the borrower will not invest the money in a hopeless venture or take the money and run; an investor will not invest unless assured that the government will not *ex-post* expropriate his assets. (Greif 2000, p. 251)

Whereas Greif's definition focuses on the lender, the question of borrowing from a family member, bank or loan shark suggests that there is also a different side to the story here. This chapter will state the case for taking into account the risks incurred by debtors as well. One could argue that we should expand Greif's definition by adding:

> A debtor will not borrow without being assured that the lender will not impose harsh penalties.

This addition is important because by failing to take into account the perspective of debtors, and considering only that of creditors and investors, economic historians miss out on the incentives and restraints of half of the participants in markets. Yet this is what has happened during the past decades, when it seemed that economic historians equated the 'fundamental problem of exchange' to the risk of the debtor taking the money and running off, or going bust. To secure creditors and investors against this risk, and to convince them to enter into transactions, there should be 'rules of the game': the formal and informal constraints that make up the institutional framework of markets, made famous by Douglass North. These 'rules of the game' (also known as the 'institutional framework') are held to determine the profitability of exchange, and hence also the incidence of market exchange and possibilities for economic growth (North 1990). Following the work done by North and Greif, many scholars set out to reconstruct the 'rules' that solved the 'fundamental problem of exchange', often looking at complicated transactions where payments were postponed and where the party that extended credit ran considerable risks. This research greatly contributed to our understanding of economic institutions and economic change in the long run, uncovering many informal and formal techniques that participants in exchange could use to limit risk. However, by focusing on the credit side and disregarding the debit side, this literature only explains what conditions are needed for creditors and investors to engage in transactions. It says nothing about circumstances under which individuals decide to incur debts.

This chapter addresses the question, under what circumstances were individuals willing to mortgage their real estate? The rise of mortgage credit and mortgage markets is an important topic in economic history and development economics: lending with real estate as collateral has been intricately linked to property owners' possibilities for investment (de Soto 2000). To acquire expensive capital assets such as land, livestock, ships or tools, many individuals had to make use of credit, which often required providing the creditor with security through the mortgaging of real estate. Although economists have long realized this also entailed risk for the debtor (or mortgagor), there has not yet been a proper assessment of how real the danger was of losing collateral due to foreclosure.

The current chapter does two things: it elaborates on the framework for the study of the use of real estate as collateral, by referring to the four types of contract that were also discussed in the introduction to this volume (Briggs and Zuijderduijn, this volume). Fullest attention will be given to the two types of contracts that appear to have been used most throughout history: the *fiducia* and *hypotheca*. *Fiducia* contracts effectively caused the debtor to part with his property, only retaining a right of repurchase. The debtor was certain to lose his repurchase right in the case of non-payment, and hence to lose his real estate for good. This system only provided security for the lender (or mortgagee); it did not entice property owners to put their property up as collateral for a loan. It is argued that although the *fiducia* existed throughout history, it was not conducive to the emergence or expansion of financial markets. On the other hand, and in contrast to the *fiducia*, the *hypotheca* allowed the debtor to remain the property owner and granted the creditor a right to execute a claim in case of non-payment. This construction was more to the benefit of the debtor, who retained his property, and less to the benefit of the creditor, who had to file a claim for execution with the court in case of non-payment. It is argued that the latter system was crucial for the emergence of mortgage markets, as it provided security to both mortgagors and mortgagees, and thus enticed both debtors and creditors to enter into a contract. How this worked in practice is demonstrated in the second part of the chapter, which shows how the *hypotheca* could be used to protect mortgagors who had run into financial difficulties in a village in Holland. Villagers who reneged on mortgage interest payments were protected from expropriation, as there were large differences between the legal rights that mortgagees held to pursue foreclosure, and their ability to execute these. This was due to two characteristics of mortgage contracts: first, judges at local law courts had to authorize foreclosure, and as a result the execution of mortgage law was at their discretion. Second, judges looking to apply leniency were helped by the fact that mortgage contracts usually combined special and general mortgages. This allowed judges to allow seizure of movables only, thus preventing large-scale expropriation of real estate. As a result, the number of foreclosures of real estate was rather modest and expropriation was mainly applied in exceptional circumstances, such as debtors fleeing their creditors. The case study demonstrates how mortgage contracts allowed for debtor protection and arguably helped increase demand for mortgage loans.

11.2 Borrowing on Collateral

That mortgagors who pledged their real estate entered into an unequal relationship, and ran the risk of expropriation, was already pointed out by Karl Marx (1818–1883), who 'recognized the importance of the mortgage in the development of capitalist democracy' and claimed it brought about 'an unequal relationship of dependence contributing to poverty and exploitation' (Krznaric 2001, p. 449). Indeed, in Marxist-inspired thought, mortgages are often regarded as an expression of power relations that caused a worsening in the position of peasants. Mao Zedong (1893–1976), in his 1930 essay *Report from Xunwu*, explained that 'rich peasants buy mortgages and not land... because the bankruptcy of peasants and landlords occurs gradually, not suddenly'. What Mao implies here is that peasants and landlords can be lured into mortgaging, even if they might have been unwilling to sell their property. This was only putting off the evil day, though. Mao apparently was of the opinion that most mortgagors would eventually renege on their obligations and lose the land to land-hungry mortgagees, and therefore concluded: 'buying a mortgage is almost the same as buying land' (Mao Zedong 1995, p. 387).

Historians have also connected mortgages to the expropriation of peasants: as a result of worsening conditions, self-sufficient smallholders lost their land to their creditors, causing the emergence of a class of landless labourers and large landowners that was necessary for agrarian capitalism. They identified smallholders putting up land as collateral for loans as a crucial element contributing to expropriation. According to H. J. Gilomen, 'the commercialized and transferable *rente* loosened the foundation of [seigneurial] dues in bonds of personal dependence and transformed them into nothing more than obligations on a piece of property', thus enabling expropriation (Gilomen 1998, p. 137). J. Bart suggested that creditors anticipated their debtors not being able to repurchase their land, writing that 'the rent charge had a dual goal: it was a credit instrument; it also was an instrument to conquer land'. Bart sees the rent charge as an instrument creditors wittingly used to remove peasants from their land: 'the rent charge was one of the most effective and formidable weapons used by the fifteenth- and sixteenth-century moneylenders to acquire property' (Bart 1962, p. 143). G. Corazzol's study of the Veneto also paints a rather bleak picture of the loan with land as collateral: in his review of this book, M. Aymard calls its use 'much more widespread and stubborn than in contemporary France' and states that, 'For the wealthy classes of the towns of Terme Ferme, as well as Venice itself, speculating on annuities in kind...was a powerful and effective instrument to expropriate peasant land' (Aymard 1983, p. 1148). A similar point is made by G. Maifreda (2002, p. 195), who claims that in the Veronese countryside often 'it was not difficult for the creditor to predict that the debtor would not be able to honour his obligations, and would lose his real estate'.

Whether loans on collateral in practice brought about expropriation and helped to transform rural property structures, or whether expropration was merely the theoretical and rather unlikely outcome of a debt-recovery process, appears to have varied across time and space. It was always true, however, that debtors ran the risk of losing their land when they took out a loan using their land as collateral. Such a loss was disastrous for several reasons. First of all, whereas smallholders could achieve at least some self-reliance by working their own land, landless labourers came to depend on the whims of the market, causing a great deal of uncertainty. Second, a loss of real estate severely undermined individuals' position in society: whereas smallholders often had political rights, landless labourers did not. Furthermore, the loss of real estate also had repercussions for the social position of individuals: whereas property owners used their immovables to acquire creditworthiness and accountability,[1] highly mobile landless labourers generally met with distrust. Third, expropriation was painful in terms of what has been called the family–land bond: the 'strong emotional ties between family members and between the family and a particular landholding'.[2]

In theory, all mortgagors ran the risk of expropriation: missing a single payment of the financial obligation could result in creditors seeking compensation through the collateral. Missing a single payment was far from unlikely in a largely agrarian economy lacking strong social security systems and private insurance. A range of events could jeopardize timely payments, such as the illness or death of a household member, harvest failures due to bad weather or declining prices for agricultural goods due to economic cycles and warfare. For smallholders it was difficult to rule out such risks, and as a result mortgaging was always hazardous. Exactly how hazardous was a matter of the type of contract used—*fiducia* or *hypotheca*—which in turn seems to have depended on the protection local authorities offered to defaulters, and also on local and regional socio-economic structures.[3]

Since classical antiquity, Roman law distinguished four contract types available for using land as collateral for loans, each providing differing degrees of security for the mortgagor—and as a consequence for the mortgagee as well. These four contract types are visually represented in the introduction to this volume (Briggs and Zuijderduijn, this volume). The construction that was most disadvantageous to the mortgagor was the *mancipatio cum fiducia* of Roman law, which required him to hand over ownership and possession of the collateral to the mortgagee. A second option was the *pignus*: the debtor retained ownership of collateral, which was held in possession by the creditor. Slightly better was the *in iure cessio cum fiducia* (or *fiducia*), which allowed the mortgagor to keep possession of the collateral, but still required him to transfer ownership to the mortgagee. Finally, the contract derived from the *hypotheca* of Roman law allowed the debtor to remain in possession of the collateral, and also to retain ownership; the *hypotheca* only provided the creditor with a right to acquire possession and ownership when certain conditions were met, such as default (Goebel 1961, p. 29).

Of these four contract types, the *hypotheca* vested possession and ownership in the mortgagor, putting him in a strong position, especially when compared to the *mancipatio cum fiducia*, which vested possession and ownership in the mortgagee. The risk debtors ran of losing their collateral varied accordingly, being relatively low in the case of *hypotheca* and high in the case of *mancipatio cum fiducia*. Although all four contract types were used throughout history, their use varied through time and space; as a result, the risk debtors and creditors ran differed too.

In pre-industrial Europe, *fiducia* and *hypotheca* were probably the commonest contracts for loans using land as collateral. The *fiducia* usually involved the transfer of title from the debtor to the creditor, whereby the former retained the right to regain the title by means of repurchase by repaying the principal (or the principal plus an extra sum that served as concealed interest); often the debtor then became the tenant of the property (Casper 2005, p. 26; de Blécourt and Fischer 1950, p. 247). The *fiducia* was often identified as a 'fictitious sale': although the ownership changed hands, the debtor remained in possession and held a right to repurchase. Such instances of a 'fictitious sale' already existed in classical antiquity and the early middle ages (Urbanik 2013, pp. 166–167; Von Reden 2000, p. 99) and continued to emerge throughout the Middle Ages and early modern period. These transactions go by names such as 'sale and resale' and 'rent charge' in Anglo-Saxon literature (Noonan 1957, p. 95; Clark 1988, p. 268), *réméré* in French, *Wiederkauf* in German (Casper 2005, pp. 25–28) and *livello* in Italian (Ferraro 1993, p. 129). The *fiducia* was still being used in the French and Mexican countryside as late as the nineteenth century.[4]

The popularity of the *fiducia* has often been attributed to medieval concerns about usury. Since the rent charge was a fictitious sale-and-resale transaction, with a 'buyer' of land (the creditor) and a 'seller' (the debtor) who received a 'purchase price' (the principal) and became a tenant paying 'rent', it was possible to craft loan constructions in such a way as to make commercial loans appear not usurious. That the *fiducia* was in fact a clever way to hide the taking of interest, was for instance the conviction of Pope Innocent III (1198–1216), who therefore 'forbade false repurchase as a disguise of interest' (Le Bras 1963, p. 567). It is of course impossible to determine exactly to what extent creditors and debtors opted for a rent charge as a way of avoiding being usurious or being accused of usury. However, it may be useful to add an economic explanation—the fact that this financial instrument provided the creditor with good security—to the sociocultural motivation for the use of the rent charge—the fact that this financial instrument was not usurious. Under certain circumstances, creditors required a *fiducia*; under other circumstances, they sufficed with a *hypotheca*. Of course, both motivations may have coexisted, and some individuals may have attached more weight to one or the other because of personal preferences.

Arguably, for creditors to agree to lending on security of *hypotheca* required considerable trust in the authorities that would have to execute their possessory interest should the debtor renege on his obligations. Only a solid institutional framework could have allowed for the widespread use of *hypotheca*: such a framework would need to provide a reliable foreclosure procedure that would allow the mortgagee to obtain inexpensive compensation should the mortgagor default. It would also have to enable the mortgagee to assess the value of the collateral and check the title held by the mortgagor (Van Bochove et al. 2015). However, as should be clear by now, for smallholders to put up their land as collateral using *hypotheca*, their risks of expropriation would also have to be mitigated; for the number of *hypotheca* to exceed a certain threshold and for mortgage markets to appear, authorities had to strike a fine balance between creditors' security and debtors' risks.

11.3 A Fine Balance: Debtor Protection in Holland

In a recent publication, Christiaan Van Bochove, Heidi Deneweth and Jaco Zuijderduijn (2015) argued that mortgage law in the Low Countries differed from that in England. In the Low Countries, mortgagors who were no longer able to pay mortgage interest were protected against expropriation: foreclosure was subject to a court ruling, which often resulted in judges forcing mortgagees to accept debt-recovery schemes rather than allowing them to go ahead with foreclosure. In England, mortgage law allowed the mortgagee to seize the mortgaged real estate as soon as the mortgagor reneged. The situation in England was very tough for the mortgagor, and it has been argued this scared potential borrowers away from using their real estate as collateral, and thus prevented the emergence of a mortgage market (Allen 1992, pp. 102–104, Briggs in this volume). In contrast, the situation in the Low Countries was less harsh on the mortgagor, and harsher on the mortgagee, who faced a debt-recovery procedure if the mortgagor reneged. To date, our knowledge of this debt-recovery procedure has been mainly theoretical: we know very little about how mortgagees in the Low Countries could force their mortgagors to pay in practice. To what degree did debt recovery depend on judges' discretion? How lengthy were these procedures? Such questions are important for understanding how the *other* fundamental problem of exchange could be solved and under what conditions mortgage markets could emerge. The remainder of this chapter considers debt recovery in a village in Holland to learn how local authorities struck a fine balance between the interests of creditors and debtors. Our case study focuses on the practice of foreclosure in the village of Mijnsheerenland in Holland and provides precise information about the extent of expropriation. Whenever possible, other rural areas will be included in the discussion.

In the county of Holland, in the west of the present-day Netherlands, mortgage markets emerged in the late middle ages in cities, towns and villages (Zuijderduijn and de Moor 2013; Van Zanden 2012). These markets were characterized by frequent transactions (Van Bochove et al. 2015, pp. 18–19) and transactions between locals and non-residents (Zuijderduijn 2014). To illustrate this point, Table 11.1 presents a sample of mortgages contracted in five villages in the sixteenth century; the villages were located in the far north of Holland (Heiloo and Oosdom), centre (Heemskerk, Leiderdorp) and south (Oost-IJsselmonde, Mijnsheerenland). The number of mortgages varied from four to ten per annum; when expressed in mortgages per 1000 inhabitants per annum, the volume of local capital markets varied between 6.7 and 22.2. The upper limit does not differ much from today's figure for the Netherlands (about 21.3 mortgages per 1000 inhabitants per annum).[5] This rather high market volume must be ascribed in part to an increasing number of townsmen gaining ownership of rural land, a process that already began in the fourteenth century[6] and probably accelerated during the sixteenth century (Van Bavel 2009; Hoppenbrouwers 2001).

These townsmen not only made their presence felt as landowners, letting their property to villagers, or as mortgagees, accepting rural land as security for loans, but also as mortgagors, using their rural land as collateral for loans. The percentage in the latter capacity is also given in Table 11.1: the proportion of urban mortgagors taking out a mortgage on their rural land ranged from 50.8% in Mijnsheerenland to 81.3% in Heemskerk. The participation of townsmen in rural mortgage markets could be quite large: in the village of Leiderdorp, where 22 out of 37 mortgages (59.5%) were given by an urban mortgagor to secure an urban mortgagee—both parties came almost exclusively from the nearby town of Leiden. The reason for this high involvement of Leiden citizens may be linked to legislation restricting the mortgaging of real estate

Table 11.1 Mortgages in five villages in Holland (sixteenth century)

	N	*N per annum*	*N per annum per 1000 inhabitants*	*% mortgagors who were urban inhabitants*	*Inhabitants 1514*
Heiloo and Oosdom 1560–1562	20	c. 7	10.9	60.0	c. 645
Heemskerk 1557–1564	80	c. 10	22.2	81.3	c. 450
Leiderdorp 1569–1574	37	c. 6	16.0	72.9	c. 375
Oost-IJsselmonde 1552–1575	45	c. 2	6.7	53.3	c. 300
Mijnsheerenland 1532–1567	132	c. 4	10.0	50.8	c. 375

Sources Mortgages: Heiloo en Oosdom: Gemeentearchief Alkmaar, oud-rechterlijk en weeskamerarchief Heiloo, inv. nr. 70; Heemskerk: Gemeentearchief Haarlem, Ambachts- en gemeentearchief van Heemskerk, inv. nr. 243; Oost-IJsselmonde: Stadsarchief Rotterdam, Archieven van de voormalige Gemeente Ijsselmonde, inv. nr. 183; Leiderdorp: Erfgoed Leiden en Omstreken, archief Leiderdorp, oud-rechterlijk archief, inv. nr. 2.; Mijnsheerenland: Helms Van Eis (1982–1985). Inhabitants 1514: Fruin (1866, pp. 37, 29, 286, 582, 596). This source records the number of people who received Holy Communion; infants younger than 13–14 years were excluded from this. To calculate population figures, Ad Van der Woude's approach was followed, who calculated that c. 33% of the population must have been younger than 13–14 years (Van der Woude 1972, pp. 77–85)

intra muros, which was in effect between 1430 and 1568.[7] Other towns had taken similar measures, allegedly in an attempt to prevent abuses such as having an item of real estate encumbered by too many mortgages (Brand 1996, p. 219). It seems that one of the results was for townsmen to invest in rural land—which they could still use as collateral, and which therefore may have become more attractive than urban land, or if they already owned such land, to use this to secure 'urban transactions'.

To investigate the degree to which mortgages can be said to have exposed villagers to expropriation by (urban) mortgagees, we investigate foreclosures in the village of Mijnsheerenland, or Mijnsheerenland van Moerkerken, as it was also called. Mijnsheerenland was located in the south of Holland, in the region of Hoekse Waard. In the sixteenth century, it was a relatively new settlement: it was rebuilt by the Flemish knight Lodewijk Praet van Moerkercken, after the 'St. Elizabeth' flood of 1421 had inundated the region and destroyed the existing villages.[8]

The village was situated on one of the many islands in the Meuse estuary in the south of Holland, right in the centre of the island of Hoekse Waard. A large government inquiry for the purpose of the reorganization of tax assessments, which took place in 1514, provides information about Mijnsheerenland in this period. At the time of the inquiry, Mijnsheerenland's sheriff and aldermen (who are referred to as *heemraden* in the sources) claimed that the village contained 63 houses and, according to the sexton, the parish had around 250 inhabitants who were more than 13 or 14 years old and who would therefore receive Holy Communion during Mass; the entire population, including young children, would probably have been numbered about 375 individuals (Van der Woude 1972, pp. 77–85). Mijnsheerenland was estimated to cover 1000 *morgen*, or approximately 2104 acres, of which only 15.5 *morgen*, or 38 acres, was owned by residents of the village[9]; the rest was owned by people who lived in nearby towns, such as Dordrecht, and further away, in towns such as Utrecht. It is doubtful that these figures are very accurate; the villagers may have understated their landownership in order to obtain a relatively low tax assessment (Hoppenbrouwers 2001, pp. 67–69). In addition, the 1514 inquiry tells us that most of the inhabitants of Mijnsheerenland earned their living in agriculture or fishing, by catching birds and by digging dikes (Fruin 1866, pp. 582–583). Mijnsheerenland was a rather large village, but not excessively wealthy, judging by the taxes per capita: 0.16 pounds (hereafter *lbs.*); the average for other villages in the region was 0.17 *lbs.*[10]

To study foreclosure in Mijnsheerenland, we begin with a case study. On 22 March 1562, Gerrit van Scharlaken Pietersz., a resident of the nearby city of Dordrecht, filed for the foreclosure of a *hypotheca* used to secure an annuity. The annuity had been issued by Joost Jorisz., a resident of Mijnsheerenland, to Gijsbert van Scharlaken Pietersz.—brother of the aforementioned Gerrit—on 4 February 1555.[11] The annuity was secured on a small piece of land of 400 *roe* (about 1.4 acres, an area that is less than a football pitch). Gerrit requested execution because Joost had missed his annuity payment for the year 1561.

This was not the first time Gerrit had filed for foreclosure of Joost Jorisz. (Table 11.2): he had also done so on 20 March 1560 and 5 December 1560,[12] for a debt of 28.65 *Karolusgulden* (Kg) in annuities—a sum equivalent to about 60–80 days' wages for a skilled

Table 11.2 Joost Jorisz. as defendant before the court of Mijnsheerenland

Date	*Plaintiff*	*Type*
20 March 1560	Gerrit Pietersz.	Execution mortgage
5 December 1560	Gerrit Pietersz.	Execution mortgage
27 November 1561	Gerrit Pietersz.	Execution mortgage
22 March 1562	Gerrit Pietersz.	Execution mortgage
25 November 1562	Gerrit Pietersz.	*Schatting*
24 January 1565	Gijsbrecht Pietersz.	Public auction of house of Joost

Sources Regionaal archief Dordrecht, Oud-rechterlijke archieven van Mijnsheerenland, inv. nr. 21, f. 22, 28, 94; Regionaal archief Dordrecht, Oud-rechterlijke archieven van Mijnsheerenland, inv. nr. 2, f. 163v

labourer.[13] As a mortgagee, Gerrit might have been confident about recovering his debt: annuity contracts explicitly stated that the collateral was there to insure the mortgagee against default. Mortgagees such as Gerrit were also preferential creditors, so they would be among the first to be allowed to seek compensation from their mortgagors. On top of this, mortgagees were also allowed summary justice, which should have made for a swift execution. To make sure this would be the case, contracts usually explicitly stated that the mortgagor was not allowed to delay the process leading up to foreclosure, for instance by appealing against sentences in the court of first instance (Zuijderduijn 2009, ch. 5).

Yet in practice execution did not go as swiftly as many mortgagees might have hoped. Expropriating a mortgagor was something law courts were very reluctant to do. The law court of Mijnsheerenland was no exception. In the case of Gerrit, the law court first asked to see the original contracts: three contracts recorded on parchment, two of them with a green wax seal. These were apparently presented on 27 November 1561 and were to be used on the next court day.[14] There is no record of what happened during this court day, which may indicate that Gerrit and Joris arrived at an out-of-court settlement, or that another type of agreement was ruled by the judges.

Joost continued to struggle with paying his dues: over the following years, he frequently faced seizure of his goods as an attachment for debt[15] on the initiative of his creditors. Eventually, on 24 January 1565, the apparently inevitable happened: the house of Joost Jorisz. was sold to the highest bidder at a public auction. The highest bidder was Gijsbert van Schaerlaken Pietersz., whom we already encountered as the creditor who transferred the annuity contract of 28.65 Kg to his brother Gerrit.

Gijsbrecht agreed to pay 130 Kg—money that would be used to pay Joost's creditors, including probably Gerrit. Joost agreed to vacate the house before the end of May.[16]

When we look at Joost Jorisz., it appears he was heavily indebted. Apart from the annuity he sold to Gijsbrecht Pietersz. in 1554, we also encounter him in 1550 selling an annuity worth 4 Kg to Neeltge Jansdr. van Slingeland in Dordrecht,[17] and in 1555 selling a redeemable annuity worth 12 Kg to Willem Jansz., a brewer from Dordrecht.[18] Combined, these annuities amounted to the obligation to pay out 44.65 Kg per annum—about 74–112 days' wages for a skilled labourer (de Vries 1998, pp. 610–611). Joost had probably expected to pay this from his revenues from agriculture: in 1557 he was listed as tenant, landowner and landlord. Joost leased 4 *morgen* from a Carthusian monastery, and in addition he owned 1.5 *morgen*, which he leased out to a group of tenants, and another 1.7 *morgen*, which he apparently used himself (Table 11.3). When we look at his landholdings—as a landlord and the land he used himself—Joost's two plots of land amounted to 3.17 *morgen*: less than 0.12% of all the land in Mijnsheerenland.[19] Furthermore, he was listed as a homeowner, presumably of the house he would eventually lose in 1565. In 1557, there were 57 houses in Mijnsheerenland, of which the average rental value was 2.4 guilders, which suggests that Joost was among the more prominent homeowners. In short, Joost was a typical smallholder with a house and a tiny bit of landed property, and furthermore he depended to a large degree on lease markets to let and lease land.

Table 11.3 Property of Joost Jorisz

Size	*Landlord/tenant*	*Rent (Kg/morgen)*
Tenant		
4 *morgen*	Kartuizers Geertruidenberg	5
Landlord		
1.5 *morgen*	Wouter Pietersz. cs	9.25
Landowner		
1.67 *morgen*	Joost Jorisz.	6
Home		
–	Joost Jorisz.	3.5

Source See text

Briefly turning to the plaintiff: Gerrit Pietersz. Schaerlaecken was a wealthy inhabitant of the town of Dordrecht. He was married to Grietken Jansdr., and the couple probably lived in the house named 'Zwartsenborch' in Dordrecht city centre.[20] Gerrit hailed from a wealthy and influential family, including his aforementioned brother Gijsbert Pietersz. Schaerlaecken, who was depicted as a proud citizen in a portrait of 1552. A copy of the portrait shows Gijsbert with his wife Adriana van Slingelandt, sitting at a desk looking after their business affairs (see Nobel 2012, p. 132). Gijsbert is depicted making calculations, using jetons; Adriana uses scales to check coins the couple kept in the large purse (a *stokbeurs*) shown to the right. Both Gijsbert and his brother Gerrit were quite active in Mijnsheerenland (which was located c. 15 km from Dordrecht), as landlords and mortgagees, and they would quite nicely fit the description of wealthy townsmen increasingly investing in the rural economy and accumulating an increasing proportion of land in the countryside. To what degree can it be said that mortgages accelerated this process?

To answer this question, we should first of all point out that although Joost already missed an annuity payment in 1560, there are no signs of him being expropriated to pay off his creditors before 1565, when his house was sold during a public auction. This was so even though he had put up a mortgage to secure his creditors. As explained, in theory this should have allowed creditors summary jurisdiction; in practice, things worked out differently. This is not only evident in the case of Joost, who was only expropriated many years after he missed his first annuity payment, but also in many law codes that reveal that debtors were not easily removed from their property. To discourage debtors from opposing the claims of their creditors, and thus stalling the legal process, many towns in the Low Countries came up with legislation to prevent the obstruction of foreclosure. Furthermore, almost all late-medieval annuity contracts contain clauses in which the debtor promises to refrain from opposing summary jurisdiction—these clauses are called *willige condemnatie* and they were designed to reduce debtors' possibilities for frustrating the course of justice (Zuijderduijn 2009, pp. 219–220). Thus, in an annuity contract sold in 1532 by the church fabric of Mijnsheerenland, the debtors literally promised not to use any 'legal tricks' to escape prosecution in the event that they defaulted: *alle dinc sonder arch ofte list*.[21]

Law courts obviously protected creditors, but at the same time also seemed to favour debtors. Law codes of towns and regions in Holland usually stipulated that debtors were to receive protection against losing their livelihood due to expropriation: the land they worked, the premises they used for their business and their tools should ideally be the last items to be expropriated. Perhaps as a result of this, law courts were often quite lenient towards debtors, listening to their explanations of why they had failed to meet an annuity payment (one can imagine that there could be several good reasons for this, such as poor harvests, floods and fires). It seems that rather than expropriating debtors, judges usually came up with instalment plans: in several towns in Holland, such plans were explicitly mentioned in law codes, allowing the debtor to take out another interest-bearing annuity to pay the arrears (Zuijderduijn 2009, p. 219). The case of Joost is therefore quite typical for the situation in Holland and possibly other regions in the Low Countries. As a debtor who had failed to make payments he was no doubt pressured by the law court to come to terms with his creditors, but local authorities also refrained from so harsh an instrument as summary jurisdiction. They were rather lenient when dealing with debtors, who after all may just have had a stroke of bad luck.

The fact that foreclosure was subject to judges' sentencing thus allowed local authorities to be lenient towards debtors. A second element contributing to leniency was the widespread use of the 'general mortgage' in annuity contracts. With a general mortgage, the debtor pledged all his present and future property (Herman 1914, pp. 15–18, 27–28; Zuijderduijn 2009, p. 217). This type of security differed from the 'special mortgage', which was linked to an item of real estate, and allowed the creditor only to attach this item of real estate. In contrast, with a general mortgage the creditor could attach any type of property belonging to the debtor. In sixteenth-century Holland, annuity contracts usually contained both a special and a general mortgage: a debtor mortgaged a clearly specified item of real estate, and additionally also pledged all his present and future property.[22] The latter provided judges with yet more options for exercising discretion because upon receiving a complaint from a creditor, the judges could decide whether they would allow the creditor to attach the special mortgage (real estate) or the general mortgage (cattle, harvest etc.) (Fockema Andreae 1915, p. 22). Such combinations of special and general mortgages appear in almost all late-medieval annuity contracts, in the Low Countries and also the north of France.[23] Although the general mortgage can be said to have provided creditors with extra security, at the same time it also allowed judges to protect debtors against expropriation.[24] This effect is clearly visible in the case between Joost Jorisz. and Gerrit Pietersz.; the latter constantly pressed for execution of the special mortgage he held, but apparently local authorities initially refused to go along with this. There is evidence that this was not only a matter of judges being lenient, but also a principle of law: several law codes indicate that in foreclosure movables were to be attached first, and real estate only after this had been done. In this respect, the legal historians de Blécourt and Fischer speak of 'the ubiquitous rule, that real estate could only be attached, if the movables did not suffice' (de Blécourt and Fischer 1950, p. 262).[25]

Table 11.4 gives foreclosures in Mijnsheerenland. Edicts issued by emperor Charles V forced local authorities to keep track of real estate transactions—including those that were the result of foreclosure—and therefore it is quite certain the table gives the names of all those that were expropriated (Zuijderduijn 2009, pp. 65–66). When we look at the trajectory leading up to expropriation, we see first that the law court of Mijnsheerenland tended to start by attaching movables rather than real estate. Pieter Aartsz., a mortgagor who lost his house on 19 June 1561, first faced attachment of his 'best bed', pewter and copperware.[26] Shortly after, his creditors began to press for expropriation of his house,[27] presumably because he was a fugitive (*landvluchtig*)—he had abandoned his property and left the village, probably to escape his debtors.

Table 11.4 Foreclosures in Mijnsheerenland 1560–1578

Date of foreclosure	*Debtor*	*First occasion pursued by a creditor*	*Months elapsed*	*Fugitive*
8-11-1560	Jacob Jacobsz and his wife Adriaantje	?	?	
26-10-1560	Cornelis Heijenz	21-6-1560	4	
19-6-1561	Pieter Aartsz	5-10-1560	8	x
8-11-1563	Jan Phazen	26-12-1561	35	
14-10-1563	Rijck Albertsz	18-2-1562	20	x
9-12-1563	Wouter Jansz and his wife	15-10-1562	14	x
22-9-1564	Cornelis Willemsz	11-2-1560	55	x
24-1-1564	Joost Jorisz	20-3-1560	46	
13-12-1565	Lambrecht Cornelisz	19-4-1561	56	x
6-6-1576	Crijn Jansz	4-3-1560	194	

Source Helms Van Eis (n.d.4, n.d.5, n.d.6)

In his absence, the judges apparently decided to auction publicly Pieter's house.[28] It should be mentioned that fleeing the jurisdiction led to foreclosure in several other cases. The house of the debtor Cornelis Willemsz. was put up for auction because he had suddenly left Mijnsheerenland,[29] and the same was true for Lambrecht Cornelisz.[30] Furthermore, we learn of Ryck Albrechtsz. that he was outside the region shortly before his house was put up for auction. According to the plaintiff, Ryck had failed to pay for a house 'and because Ryck is now living outside Hoekse Waard, he requests for this house to be publicly auctioned'.[31] Finally, Wouter Jansz. also lived outside Hoekse Waard when he faced foreclosure because he had failed to pay tithes.[32] Curiously, in two cases, our sources also indicate that in the case of flight, the right to summary execution fell to the sheriff: creditors filing against runaway debtors could therefore be as good as certain their demands would be met.[33]

Not every debtor fled though. Cornelis Heijenz., a resident of Mijnsheerenland, faced numerous plaints prior to his house being auctioned off in 1560, but he stayed in the village. In September 1560, the plaintiffs were a woman named Wilhelmina, who was trying to recover 182 Kg, and furthermore the aforementioned Pieter Aartsz., trying to recover a quantity of rye.[34] In October, Tielman Hugensz. filed a plaint because of an obligation (*schepenschuldbrief*) issued in Dordrecht, and on the same day (10 October 1560) the messenger of Mijnsheerenland came to Cornelis Heijenz. to tell him his bed had been seized on behalf of yet another plaintiff, Kors Reijersz. That same day, Cornelis' summer and winter rye were also attached.[35] Apparently this was all in vain: on October 23, Cornelis' property was assessed (*schatting*), and three days later his house was transferred to one of his creditors, Wilhelmina, the widow of Willem Jansz. Nuijssenburg, a resident of Dordrecht. Unlike the debtors discussed above, Cornelis did not flee the scene but continued to live in the village. In November 1560, he was again the subject of *panding* for 5.55 Kg worth of wages, and for 2.75 Kg because of an obligation. The same day, the aforementioned Tielman Hugensz. was allowed *panding* of Cornelis' summer and winter rye—on 15 December, Tielman received 'all winter rye of Cornelis Heijenz., whether pledged or not, found inside the house and haystack'.[36] A year later, Cornelis was still in dire straits with his rye being attached, and also his horses.[37] Shortly after he died.[38]

It is difficult to get an impression of the time that elapsed between the beginning of a dispute, and eventual foreclosure. A first problem concerns our sources for Mijnsheerenland (*dingboeken*), which only begin in February 1560, so we miss data on any actions creditors may have undertaken prior to this date. A second problem presents itself when we try to link foreclosure to a single creditor—and hence to pinpoint when the dispute that led to foreclosure began. Table 11.4 gives foreclosure dates and the dates of the first legal action undertaken against the debtor that we know of. The first creditor appearing in our sources as filing against the debtor may not have been behind the foreclosure that occurred at a later point in time. What these data capture is merely a suggestion of how long debtors could hold out in their attempts to prevent the loss of their real estate. Cornelis Heijenz. held out for four months, but others clearly held out much longer. They did so while frequently being summoned into court, having the value of their property estimated (*schatting*), and even having their property seized and put up for auction. This gave them time to recover from hardship, to restructure their debts or to arrive at a settlement with their creditors—all things that could prove crucial in preventing foreclosure.

In Mijnsheerenland, a large number of mortgages were contracted: between 1532 and 1567, on average four annuities were contracted per annum, in a village of about 375 inhabitants and with no more than around 100 households (Van Bochove et al. 2015).[39] Keeping in mind that these were long-term debts that usually ran for many decades, it follows that a large proportion of the real estate in Mijnsheerenland was put up as collateral, and many of the resident owners were at risk of being expropriated in the event of default.[40] That this risk was in fact very real, and non-payment happened quite often in Mijnsheerenland, can be deduced from the data provided in Table 11.5. This table gives a sample of one year of court activity, 1560, when the judges of the law court of Mijnsheerenland held court sessions on 63 days throughout the year, resulting in the recording of 135 legal actions for a variety of reasons.

Table 11.5 Legal actions in the law court of Mijnsheerenland, 1560

	N	*Real estate*	*Cattle*	*Corn*	*Other*	*Unknown*
Attachment	66	–	8	11	6	41
Schatting	20	–	9	4	1	6
Other	49	–	–	–	–	–

Source Helms Van Eis (n.d.4)

Most lawsuits were about debtors failing to pay on time (86 of the 135 legal actions, or 63.7%): creditors asked the court to prepare for attachment (*schatting*) or proceed with attachment itself (*beslag* or *panding*). It seems that cattle and corn were particularly popular; in this source, there is no evidence of attachment of land.[41] Debtors frequently failed to pay on time and faced legal action as a result. The underlying reasons are unknown, but they are likely to have been linked to the uncertainty of agricultural yields. It stands to reason that this uncertainty also had an effect on the many mortgagors of Mijnsheerenland, and caused difficulties in mortgage payments as well, as apparently happened to Joost Jorisz. and a few others.

Foreclosures were not absent in Mijnsheerenland: the mid-sixteenth century witnessed a transition of the rural economy, which would eventually cause many smallholders to lose their land (de Vries 1974). Can it be said that the mortgaging of land contributed to this? Table 11.6 presents a tentative comparison of mortgages and foreclosures in the sixteenth century and the present day. In Mijnsheerenland, 10 mortgages were contracted per 1000 inhabitants per annum, a figure not much lower than today's. In contrast, there were 1.3 foreclosures per 1000 inhabitants per annum, much more than the present-day figures for the same region, the province of Zuid-Holland (0.2), and the Netherlands (0.1), but less than those for the USA (5.7). Of course, the number of foreclosures depends in part on the number of mortgages that

Table 11.6 Mortgages and foreclosures

	Mortgages per 1000 inhabitants per annum (A)	*Foreclosures per 1000 inhabitants per annum (B)*	*B/A*
Mijnsheerenland (1532–1567)	10.0	1.3	0.130
Zuid-Holland (2004–2015)	20.0	0.2	0.010
The Netherlands (2004–2015)	21.4	0.1	0.005
USA(2005–2014)	25.7	5.7	0.220

Sources See text; also http://www.kadaster.nl/web/Zakelijk/Vastgoedcijfers/Downloads.htm; http://www.statisticbrain.com/home-foreclosure-statistics/; https://www.quora.com/How-many-mortgage-loan-applications-are-made-in-the-USA-annually

were contracted, and to take this into account, the fourth column of Table 11.6 gives the relative number of foreclosures divided by the relative number of mortgages. The average mortgagor in Mijnsheerenland was much more likely to face foreclosure than in the present-day Netherlands. However, it seems that he or she was still less likely to be expropriated than the average present-day mortgagor in the USA. So foreclosures were far from absent in the sixteenth-century countryside, and did in all likelihood contribute to the fundamental changes in property structures. By now it should be clear though that their incidence must not be ascribed to legal structures that allowed lenders to expropriate debtors, but rather due to such elements as population growth contributing to fragmentation of property, or external shocks in the absence of insurance that contributed to reduced income.[42]

11.4 Conclusion

Our case study reveals that even though Mijnsheerenland had many debtors who had put up their real estate as collateral, only a few of them ever lost their property because they failed to pay their creditors. Foreclosure was a right held by all mortgagees and explicated in all mortgage contracts; however, before they could execute this right, they had to convince the judges of the local law court that foreclosure was absolutely necessary. Our reading of the sources suggests that these judges carefully weighed the options available to them and tried to arrive at solutions that would not ruin debtors. Such leniency was possible because in the Low Countries the mortgage was a claim that was to be effectuated by judges, and also because mortgage contracts usually combined a special mortgage and a general mortgage. The latter exposed all possessions of the debtor to the debt-recovery process—and this provided judges with the ability to redirect claims from real estate to cattle, corn, furniture and other movables. Expropriation of real estate was a measure of last resort rather than the inevitable consequence of a default. The expropriation of peasants that Holland experienced in the sixteenth century, and that did indeed lead to a sharp increase in landholding among urban inhabitants, was not a matter of peasants being tricked into a mortgage market where they faced inevitable expropriation.

Many economic historians have focused on the position of the creditor, following Avner Greif's concept of the fundamental problem of exchange. This concept is indeed crucial for understanding the rise of market economies, but it also reveals only part of the story: not only do creditors have to be persuaded to enter into a transaction, but debtors have to be persuaded to do so as well. In a pre-industrial economy, where risks abounded and the means for insurance were very limited, anyone could miss a payment. If this were to have inevitably resulted in the loss of the collateral, few people would have been willing to conclude a mortgage contract, except perhaps if they were exceptionally hard pressed. In contrast, those looking to borrow money for productive investments, or for the arrangement of intergenerational transfers of property, would probably have deemed the risks involved too high.

For mortgage markets to emerge, mortgagors need to be confident that borrowing on collateral will not immediately jeopardize their position as property owners. If their risks are too high, only destitute smallholders will be willing to mortgage their land. This type of adverse selection will inevitably lead to defaults and expropriation in the way Marx and Mao described. Sustainable mortgage markets cannot emerge under such circumstances: such 'thick' markets require a sufficient number of creditors and debtors, who are willing and able to participate in exchange repeatedly. If the *other* fundamental problem of exchange is not solved, and authorities fail to strike a fine balance between creditors and debtors, only destitute borrowers are likely to engage in one-off transactions, after which they drop out of mortgage markets due to expropriation. Lacking debtor protection, the better-off, who have the potential to become a structural presence in mortgage markets, are unlikely to participate at all.

Notes

1. Hernando de Soto included creditworthiness and accountability among his 'property effects' associated with the offering of land as a security (de Soto 2000, pp. 47–68).
2. Also see the discussion of this land–family bond in Whittle (1998, pp. 26–27) and the literature cited there.
3. For changes in the protection for defaulters, see the contribution of Waddilove, this volume.
4. In the canton Vernon, *vente à réméré* still accounted for 0.25% of real estate transactions between 1807 and 1826 (Boudjaaba 2008, p. 191). The same instrument existed in nineteenth-century Mexico (Léonard 2008).

5. Between 2005 and 2009, the number of mortgages contracted per annum was about 340,000; this amounted to about 21.3 mortgages per 1000 inhabitants (http://www.woningmarktcijfers.nl/downloads/201008_HRA_studie.pdf).
6. Already in the fourteenth century, the inhabitants of the town of Leiden owned 32.3% of the land in the villages in the surrounding area (Van Kan 1988, pp. 282–288).
7. Erfgoed Leiden en omstreken, Archief der secretarie, *Stedeboek*, f. 296; Hamaker (1873, pp. 206, 270, 376, 383–384). Cf. Brand (1996, p. 219), who mentions 1459 as the year of introduction.
8. The 'St. Elizabeth' flood occurred around 19 November, the feast day of St Elizabeth, and caused large parts of the south of Holland to become inundated. A survey of Mijnsheerenland's earliest history is provided by Tresling (1937, pp. 149–155).
9. *Delflandse morgen* = 0.85 Ha; one *hont* = 1/6 *morgen*.
10. These pounds are a unit of account used by the government of Holland to distribute taxes among towns and villages. Taxation figures are available in Zuijderduijn (2014, p. 27).
11. Helms Van Eis (n.d.5, 52) (22 March 1562).
12. He did so by means of *schatting*: having the defendant's property assessed (Helms Van Eis n.d.5, 18) (5 December 1560).
13. Helms Van Eis (n.d.5, 21) (20 March 1561).
14. Helms Van Eis (n.d.5, 31). The contracts were dated 10 February 1554 *stilo curie Hollandie*, 10 November 1558 (*getransfixeert*) and 14 November 1559.
15. In our sources, this is called both *panding* and *beslag*—both words probably meant the same thing: attachment for debt.
16. Helms Van Eis (n.d.4, 35) (24 January 1565).
17. Helms Van Eis (n.d.3, 39) (10 June 1550).
18. Helms Van Eis (n.d.4, 7). This latter transaction may be linked to Joost buying land from Willem on 14 September 1553 (ORA Mijnsheerenland, inv.nr. 4, f. 24v; cf. Helms Van Eis (n.d.4, 47) dating this transaction 9 September 1553).
19. In 1557, the acreage was estimated at 2671 morgen (Helms Van Eis n.d.1).
20. http://www.uwstamboomonline.nl/passie/sites/index.php?mid=220496&kid=2147&pagina=tekstpagina.
21. Helms Van Eis (1982–1985, f. 2).
22. To give an example: in 1532 Evert Adriaensz., a resident of Mijnsheerenland, sold an annuity that was mortgaged on a piece of land of 14 morgen, as well as a general mortgage, so that 'in case of default Evert Adriaensz. was liable, both for the principal and the annuity, and arrears could be claimed [by the creditor] on his property, both present

and future' (Helms Van Eis 1982–1985, f. 2v: *voert of hier aen yet gebrake soe selt evert adriaensz voirs hem selven noch als waerborch alsoe wel voer dat hoetgelt als voer die rente te mogen verhalen op sijn gerechte guede gewonnen ende ongewonnen...*; see also another example: Helms Van Eis 1982–1985, f. 41).

23. Schnapper (1957, p. 55); Helms Van Eis (1982–1985, f. 4v, 6, 6v etc). Other examples from the region of Hoekse Waard are: Helms Van Eis (n.d.2, 6) (20 November 1545), 9 (13 March 1547), 14 (3 May 1554), 15 (26 May 1555), etc. Cf. other examples from the villages mentioned in Table 11.1: Leiderdorp: Erfgoed Leiden en omstreken, Archief Leiderdorp, oud-rechterlijk archief inv. nr. 2, f. 12v, 13v, 41v, 42 etc.; Heiloo en Oosdom: Gemeentearchief Alkmaar, oudrechterlijk en weeskamerarchief Heiloo, inv. nr. 70, f. 10v, 13v, 18v, 23v etc.
24. The practice in Mijnsheerenland differs from the assumptions of B. Schnapper, who regarded general mortgages as an additional clause, and the special mortgage as the 'proper' security (Schnapper 1957, p. 56).
25. The preference for movables over real estate was also formulated in the 1815 draft Napoleonic law code (art. 2464) (Hugenholtz 1937, p. 4). For further evidence for this practice (see: Van der Linden 1796, p. 333; de Blécourt 1937, pp. 99, 176; Van de Water 1729, pp. 1018–1019; Van Wassenaer 1729, p. 283; Pols 1885–1888, p. cxxxvi; Van Hasselt 1779, pp. 447–448; Racer 1866, p. 156).
26. Helms Van Eis (n.d.5, 23) (21 May 1561).
27. Helms Van Eis (n.d.5, 23) (26 May 1561), 23 (28 May 1561).
28. Helms Van Eis (n.d.5, 25) (19 June 1561).
29. Helms Van Eis (n.d.5, 71) (27 April 1564).
30. Helms Van Eis (n.d.5, 77) (28 September 1564).
31. Helms Van Eis (n.d.5, 61) (22 August 1563), 63 (14 October 1563).
32. Helms Van Eis (n.d.5, 64–65) (9 December 1563).
33. This was so because of 'ambachtsherenrecht': Helms Van Eis (n.d.5, 71) (27 April 1564).
34. Helms Van Eis (n.d.5, 12).
35. Helms Van Eis (n.d.5, 12).
36. Helms Van Eis (n.d.5, 18) (15 December 1560).
37. Helms Van Eis (n.d.5, 26) (25 June 1561), 29 (30 October 1561).
38. Helms Van Eis (n.d.5, 53) (25 March 1562).
39. In the 1557 real estate taxation, 63 homeowners were listed (Helms Van Eis n.d.1).
40. It was not at all unusual for a large proportion of the real estate to be mortgaged: reports from villages in the surrounding of Mijnsheerenland, in 1514, hint at many village inhabitants having used their real estate to secure loans, such as Lekkerkerk, Krimpen aan de Lek, Krimpen aan de

Ijssel, Stolwijk, Berkhou, Kijfhoek (Fruin 1866, pp. 571, 573, 574, 578, 579, 590). Participation of villagers in financial markets, using their real estate to secure loans, is also discussed in Van Zanden et al. (2012).

41. Since our sources are often silent about what was attached, in theory it is possible that in addition an unknown number of items of real estate were attached. However, considering the limited number of actual foreclosures in 1560 (only two) it seems legal actions were in fact directed at other unspecified goods.
42. Similarly, a decline in income due to losing a job is currently one of the main causes of missing mortgage payments and the start of a foreclosure procedure (Been et al. 2011).

Acknowledgement The author thanks participants in workshops in Cambridge and Vienna for helpful comments.

References

Primary Sources

de Blécourt, A.S. (ed.), 1937. *Bewijsstukken behorende bij het kort begrip van het oud- vaderlandsch burgerlijk recht*, 2nd edn. (Groningen: Wolters).

Helms Van Eis, L. (ed.), 1982–1985. 'Register en protocol van eijgen- ende rentebrieve van moerkerken, ingaende anno XVc XXXII ende eindigende metten jare 1552', *Ons Voorgeslacht: maandblad van de vereniging ter bevordering van het stamboomonderzoek voor Rotterdam en omstreken*, vol. 37 (1982), pp. 97–132 and vol. 40 (1985), pp. 143–155.

Helms Van Eis, L. (ed.), n.d.1. 'Kohier 10e penning van Mijnsheerenland 1557', www.hogenda.nl.

Helms Van Eis, L. (ed.), n.d.2. 'Heinenoord. Prothocol van eijgen brieven en renten beginnende in den jare dertich (1535–1579)', www.hogenda.nl.

Helms Van Eis, L. (ed.), n.d.3. 'Het register van Moerkercken resp. Mijnsheerenland (1532–1552), Oud-Rechterlijk Archief van Mijnsheerenland, inv. nr. 1', www.hogenda.nl.

Helms Van Eis, L. (ed.), n.d.4. 'Het register van Moerkercken resp. Mijnsheerenland (1553–1567), Oud-Rechterlijk Archief van Mijnsheerenland, inv. nr. 2', www.hogenda.nl.

Helms Van Eis, L. (ed.), n.d.5. 'Register van Moerkercken - Oud-Rechterlijk Archief van Mijnsheerenland, inv. nr. 21', www.hogenda.nl.

Helms Van Eis, L. (ed.), n.d.6. 'Register van Moerkercken - Oud-Rechterlijk Archief van Mijnsheerenland, inv. nr. 22', www.hogenda.nl.

Secondary Works

Allen, R.C., 1992. *Enclosure and the Yeoman. The Agricultural Development of the South Midlands 1450–1850* (Oxford: Oxford University Press).

Aymard, M., 1983. 'Review of G. Corazzol, *Fitti e livelli a grano. Un aspetto del credito rurale nel Veneto del '500*', *Annales. Économies, Sociétés, Civilisations*, vol. 38, pp. 1147–1149.

Bart, J., 1962. 'La vente à réméré en Mâconnais (1450–1560 env.)', *Mémoires de la Société pour l'Histoire du Droit et des Institutions des anciens pays bourguignons, comtois et romands*, vol. 23 (1962), pp. 137–161.

Been, V., S. Chan, I. Gould Ellen, and J.R. Madar, 2011. 'Decoding the foreclosure crisis: Causes, responses, and consequences', *Journal of Policy Analysis and Management*, vol. 30, pp. 388–396.

Boudjaaba, F., 2008. *Des paysans attachés à la terre? Familles, marchés et patrimoines dans la région de Vernon (1750–1830)* (Paris: Presses de l'université Paris-Sorbonne).

Brand, H., 1996. *Over macht en overwicht. Stedelijke elites in Leiden (1420–1510)* (Louvain and Apeldoorn: Garant).

Casper, M., 2005. *Der Optionsvertrag* (Tübingen: Mohr Siebeck).

Clark, G., 1988. 'The cost of capital and medieval agricultural technique', *Explorations in Economic History*, vol. 25, pp. 265–294.

de Blécourt, A.S., and H.F.W.D. Fischer, 1950. *Kort begrip van het oudvaderlands burgerlijk recht*, 6th edn. (Groningen: J.B. Wolters).

de Soto, H., 2000. *The Mystery of Capital. Why Capitalism Triumphs in the West and Fails Everywhere Else* (London: Black Swan).

de Vries, J., 1974. *The Dutch Rural Economy in the Golden Age, 1500–1700* (New Haven: Yale University Press).

de Vries, J., and A. Van der Woude, 1998. *The First Modern Economy. Success, Failure, and Perseverance of the Dutch Economy, 1500–1815* (Cambridge: Cambridge University Press).

Ferraro, J.M., 1993. *Family and Public Life in Brescia, 1580–1650: The Foundations of Power in the Venetian State* (Cambridge: Cambridge University Press).

Fockema Andreae, S.J., 1915. *Het richtsnoer van den rechter in vroeger dagen* (Amsterdam: Müller).

Fruin, R. (ed.), 1866. *Informacie op den staet, faculteyt ende gelegenheyt van de steden ende dorpen van Hollant ende Vrieslant...* (Leiden: Sijthoff).

Gilomen, H.-J., 1998. 'L'endettement paysan et la question du crédit dans les pays d'Empire au Moyen Âge', in M. Berthe (ed.), *Endettement paysan et credit rural dans L'Europe medievale et moderne* (Toulouse: Presses Universitaires du Mirail), pp. 99–137.

Goebel, R.J., 1961. 'Reconstructing the Roman Law of real security', *Tulane Law Review*, vol. 36, pp. 29–66.

Greif, A., 2000. 'The fundamental problem of exchange: A research agenda in historical institutional analysis', *European Review of Economic History*, vol. 4, pp. 251–284.

Hamaker, H.G. (ed.), 1873. *De middeneeuwsche keurboeken van de stad Leiden* (Leiden: Van Doesburgh).

Herman, A., 1914. *Het karakter van ons hypotheekrecht historisch beschouwd* (n.p.).

Hoppenbrouwers, P.C.M., 2001. 'Town and country in Holland, 1300–1550', in S.R. Epstein (ed.), *Town and Country in Europe, 1300–1800* (Cambridge: Cambridge University Press), pp. 54–79.

Hugenholtz, W., 1937. *Over reële executie* (Leiden: Brill).

Krznaric, R., 2001. 'Mortgaged democracy', in P. Barry Clarke and J. Foweraker (eds.), *Encyclopedia of Democratic Thought* (Abingdon: Routledge), pp. 449–452.

Le Bras, G., 1963. 'Conceptions of economy and society', in M.M. Postan, E.E. Rich and E.Miller (eds.), *The Cambridge Economic History of Europe*, vol. III (Cambridge: Cambridge University Press), pp. 554–575.

Léonard, E., 2008. 'Marché foncier, asymétries de pouvoir et exclusion. Incidences régionales des réformes libérales mexicaines à la fin du XIXe siècle', *Économie rurale*, vol. 303–305, pp. 136–153.

Maifreda, G., 2002. *Rappresentanze rurali e proprietà contadina: il caso veronese tra Sei e Settecento* (Milan: FrancoAngeli).

Mao Zedong, 1995. 'Report from Xunwu', in S.R. Schram (ed.), *Mao's Road to Power: Revolutionary Writings 1912–1949*, 8 vols. (New York and London: Routledge), iii, pp. 296–418.

Nobel, A., 2012. *Besturen op het Hollandse platteland. Cromstrijen 1550–1780* (Zutphen: Walburg Pers).

Noonan, J.T., 1957. *The Scholastic Analysis of Usury* (Cambridge, MA: Harvard University Press).

North, D.C., 1990. *Institutions, Institutional Change, and Economic Performance* (Cambridge: Cambridge University Press).

Pols, M.S. (ed.), 1885–1888. *Westfriese stadsrechten*, 2 vols. (The Hague: Nijhoff).

Racer, J.W., 1866. *Aanmerkingen omtrent de grondbeginselen der zes eerste titels van het landregt van Overijssel* (Deventer: J. de Lange).

Schnapper, B., 1957. *Les rentes au XVIe siècle. Histoire d'un instrument de crédit* (Paris: S.E.V.P.E.N).

Tresling, J.D., 1937. *Rondom de Binnenmaas* (Rotterdam: Stemerding).

Urbanik, J., 2013. 'Tapia's banquet hall and Eulogio's cell: Transfer of ownership as a security in some late Byzantine papyri', in P.J. du Plessis (ed.),

New Frontiers: Law and Society in the Roman World (Edinburgh: Edinburgh Uinversity Press), pp. 151–176.

Van Bavel, B.J.P., 2009. 'Rural development and landownership in Holland, c.1400–1650', in O. Gelderblom (ed.), *The Political Economy of the Dutch Republic* (Aldershot: Ashgate), pp. 167–196.

Van Bochove, C., H. Deneweth, and J. Zuijderduijn, 2015. 'Real estate and mortgage finance in England and the Low Countries, 1300–1800', *C&C*, vol. 30, pp. 9–38.

Van de Water, J., 1729. *Groot placaatboek*, 2 (Utrecht: Jacob van Poolsum).

Van der Linden, J. (ed.), 1796. *Groot placaet-boek*, 9 (Amsterdam: Joannes Allart).

Van der Woude, A.M., 1972. *Het Noorderkwartier. Een regionaal historisch onderzoek in de demografische en economische geschiedenis van westelijk Nederland van de late middeleeuwen tot het begin van de negentiende eeuw* (Wageningen: Afdeling Agrarische Geschiedenis, Landbouwhogeschool).

Van Hasselt, J.J., 1779. *Aantekeningen op de gereformeerde land-rechten ende gewoonten van het Ryk van Nymegen*, 2 (Nijmegen: Isaac van Kampen).

Van Kan, F.J.W., 1988. *Sleutels tot de macht. De ontwikkeling van het Leids patriciaat tot 1420* (Hilversum: Verloren).

Van Wassenaer, G., 1729. *Practyk judicieel*, 1 (Utrecht: Jacob van Poolsum).

Van Zanden, J.L., J. Zuijderduijn, and T. De Moor, 2012. 'Small is beautiful: The efficiency of credit markets in late medieval Holland', *European Review of Economic History*, vol. 16, pp. 3–22.

Von Reden, S., 2000. *Money in Classical Antiquity* (Cambridge: Cambridge University Press).

Whittle, J., 1998. 'Individualism and the family-land bond: A reassessment of land transfer patterns among the English peasantry *c.*1270–1580', *P&P*, vol. 160, pp. 25–63.

Zuijderduijn, C.J., 2009. *Medieval Capital Markets: Markets for Renten, State Formation and Private Investment in Holland (1300–1550)* (Leiden and Boston: Brill).

Zuijderduijn, J., and T. de Moor, 2013. 'Spending, saving, or investing? Risk management in sixteenth-century Dutch households', *EcHR*, vol. 66, pp. 38–56.

Zuijderduijn, J., 2014. 'On the home court advantage. Participation of locals and non-residents in a village law court in sixteenth-century Holland', *C&C*, vol. 29 (2014), pp. 19–48.

CHAPTER 12

Afterword: Mortgages as Mediation Between Kin and Capital

Craig Muldrew

In the UK in 2016, a report by the Office for National Statistics on the net worth of the country estimated that it stood at £8.8 trillion. Of this value, the report noted that 'dwellings remained the most valuable non-financial asset in the UK at £5.5 trillion, accounting for 62% of the UK's total net worth at the end of 2015'.[1] More remarkable is the fact that the same report also notes that the real value of corporations and government has actually declined since 1995; while the value of household wealth and dwellings increased from £2.84 to £10.2 trillion (insurance and pensions were worth £3.7 trillion), the assets of government and corporations have gone from being in balance with their liabilities to representing a debt of £1.38 trillion. In addition, in 2012, UK banks obtained 37% of their profits from mortgage lending—a much higher figure than for other leading European economies (Quarry et al. 2012). These figures show starkly how important the value of fixed property remains to the balance sheet of a modern industrial economy. Of course, almost all of this property is now urban, and the rapid increase

C. Muldrew (✉)
University of Cambridge, Cambridge, UK
e-mail: jcm11@cam.ac.uk

C. Briggs and J. Zuijderduijn (eds.), *Land and Credit*,
Palgrave Studies in the History of Finance,
https://doi.org/10.1007/978-3-319-66209-1_12

in its value is due to the pressure of demand where space is limited. Most readers of this book will live in an urban area and because of the very high value of property compared to annual earnings will need to borrow money from a bank to actually purchase a property. Thus, a modern mortgage is a loan to purchase property owned by someone else, based on the security of the resale value of the property.

The value of land measured by rent has always represented something of a problem for economists since Ricardo. Land has a productive value in terms of crops and whatever resources lie on or under it. But it also has a 'social' value in that people need shelter as a necessity and then also desire gardens and extra dwelling space in which to place consumer items and simply to enjoy the process of living with others in the household. Many people also desire a pleasurable view and quiet. At the same time, humans find many advantages to living in close proximity with one another. More importantly, towns have grown as nodes of communication around markets and sites of government, and especially around river and ocean ports. All this means that the competition for such things raises the value of land in urban areas and desirable rural retreats for urban dwellers far beyond its productive value. As this happens, property which is more expensive, thus also becomes an item of status competition. Wealth does not just purchase valuable housing in attractive areas, but living in such dwellings comes to define wealth in a much more graduated way than in the countryside. Even a little space, if very expensive, can give status, and whole areas can gain status if they become centres of attraction for people seeking status. Thus, the asset with by far the greatest value if measured as a proportion of national accounts does not directly obtain that value from economic growth. It only does so in a residual way because, of course, economic growth has led to increased urbanisation due to the cost saving in communication and transport that cities have traditionally provided.

However, in late medieval and early modern Europe, the period covered here, it was the case that the vast majority of the land was rural farmland, and its value was based mostly on its productive capacity measured in rental value per year and a sale price based on so many years of rental income. A very extensive literature exists across many national historiographies on the nature of medieval and early modern land tenure in terms of the status and social relations of the peasantry, and the essays here, of necessity, given the complexity of tenurial law, build upon that literature to show how mortgaging evolved. A great deal of work has also been done on the nature of the land market for England, but less for other areas (see below). Also, as urbanisation increased, property in larger centres such as London, Paris or Florence, for example, must have been greatly increasing in value as a result of the factors listed above (De Vries 1984; McKellar 1999; Baer 2002; Goldthwaite 2009). Surely one important development in the process of capitalism is to what degree urban properties were mortgaged as, after all, cities were where almost all the largest capitalists lived before the rise of capitalist farming in the eighteenth century. Although we have rates of urbanisation and measurements of the occupational structure by which we can measure the number of people engaged in agriculture as compared to other non-food-producing activities, it is more difficult to know the value of urban in comparison with rural land, but it would surely have been considerably greater. Most urban houses and tenements would have been built by speculators and rented at leasehold to subtenants, but how this building was financed still needs fuller investigation. The contributions to this collection present research on largely rural land, and they collectively achieve something very important in showing how important the nature of mortgaging is to understand both credit and capital markets in medieval and early modern Europe. They point the way to further work, which now needs to be done on the value of urban property for credit markets.

But whatever way land receives its value, it has a special status as a form of security because of its fixed nature. A debtor cannot take it and flee the country. However, the way in which different legal regimes negotiated between rights of inheritance and the freedom of the current proprietor to put up land as a security, or the degree to which the property in the land, as opposed to its yearly rental value, was placed at risk in the form of security for a loan is the subject of the essays in this book. Land provided, as now, simply the most value when providing security for substantial loans. But it was also bound up with the survival of families through time in a way that other forms of credit were not, and was subject to the legacy of varying degrees of feudal tenurial relations. From the point of view of mortgaging, the most important of these were customs of inheritance centred on the family. The strength of the rights of primogeniture or partible inheritance, or the widow's third, all needed to be balanced against a creditor's right to foreclose on an unpaid loan and claim either property or rent on land, which another member of a family might consider theirs by right in the future (Brooks 2013, pp. 185–186; Poos and Bonfield 1998, pp. clix–clxvii). There has been a vigorous debate about this concept for England sparked off by Alan Macfarlane's argument that medieval English peasants had the power to devise land freely through wills (Macfarlane 1978). The substance of this argument has centred around the nature of individualism versus community and kinship and the nature of 'peasant mentality', as well as the emotional tie to land. But all parties acknowledge that many manors retained rights such as primogeniture and protection for widows even if further kin were not included, and even without this assumption of an emotional tie to the land, the economic value of a right would certainly be something its recipient would have wanted to retain, all of which could pose a problem for the freedom to mortgage (Razi 1981; Hoyle 1995; Sreenivasan 1991; Whittle 1998). One outcome of this debate is that land sales and transfers have been counted in various studies, and these show that in general in the thirteenth and fourteenth centuries, some 50–60% of manorial land transactions were between members of the same family, whether as inheritances (around 40% of the total) or inter vivos transfers. This proportion declined in the fifteenth century, but studies of the sixteenth and seventeenth centuries then show a return to a similar level, which persisted into the eighteenth century.[2] However, over the course of the eighteenth century, as both Robert Allen and Richard Hoyle have argued, the rise of very large capitalist farms in the south of England must logically have meant that extra-familial transactions were becoming more common, at least in terms of acreages, in order for such a process of amalgamation to occur (Allen 1992, pp. 102–104; Hoyle 1995, pp. 172–173).

Thus, for the population which worked growing food, both inheritance and inter-familial land sales remained very important, even as the commercial market for land expanded. As in the examples cited above, in most areas, many studies have indicated that an active land market also existed together with inheritance transfers and sales to kin. Sales could take place for many reasons, including consolidation of small plots in areas of partible inheritance to maintain financially viable field sizes, or expansion on the part of financially successful farmers who were using saved profits to finance their purchases. Mortgages could be used to finance further purchases but, as will be discussed below, for many other things as well. Given this situation, if we are to think of mortgaging in the sense of being used to raise capital for 'economic' investment and growth, it would seem sensible to also try to trace how people thought about the difference between the value of the land for the family and the risk entailed in using it as security for investment.

What all of the authors in this volume show is that while the security of property was important for the creditor, what was much more important in freeing up the capital value of farmland was the protection of the borrower from losing the title to the land. In essence what allowed the mortgage market to work in these areas of Europe was not the security of property for the creditor, but for the debtor, which crucially allowed the mortgage to be taken out with much less pressure on the familial rights of inheritance or expectation of sale. The key to this happening was a myriad of different forms of achieving the same thing, which was the creation of interest-bearing long-term repayments, which were less than the rental value of the land. As long as these obligations could legally be passed on with an inheritance of the property, creditors were satisfied with their security and commercialisation could proceed. Land could thus remain as a primary element of hierarchical feudal tenure and familial continuity *and* release its 'capital' value.

This volume sets the way for future research into both how credit markets were related to land and how inheritance came to adapt to the need to use the land to provide security. The focus on rural land builds on both work which already exists on mortgages and, of course, the history of land tenure and inheritance. As noted above, further work on the urban property is still needed. The chapters here cover late medieval to eighteenth-century England, the late medieval and sixteenth-century Low Countries and Italy, late medieval Spain and eighteenth-century France. There is a great deal of valuable information on the various legal strategies employed, the nature of the land as well as the amount of land mortgaged over time in the various places studied. Probably one of the main themes, which comes through in all of the chapters for every period, is that the stereotypical avaricious lender hoping to acquire a piece of valuable land through forfeiture on an unpaid mortgage was very much a minority activity. All the legal systems and practices outlined here stress that both lenders and borrowers simply wanted to use the value of real estate to make capital markets and credit work. The lenders wanted to profit through an interest rate or rent on what was lent, and the borrower wanted access to capital. In most cases, it is difficult to know the purpose for which the loan was needed, or where the capital for lending came from, but in the case of Juliet Gayton's chapter, this has been investigated, and these results (discussed below) provide a rare window into the social world of a local mortgage market. The other theme which is directly raised by Zuijderduijn and Van Onacker, and is related to this, is that of the economic relationship between secure and well-defined property rights and economic growth. Both these authors cite the study of Hernando de Soto stressing the importance of such rights for the so-called long-term rise of the west, and it is a position which derives from the influential work of Douglass North on the importance of institutions in providing what he termed 'credible commitment' and in reducing transaction costs associated with providing security (De Soto 2000, pp. 6, 46ff; North 1990). The contribution by Schraer is the only one to deal directly with the question of religion and lending and concludes that before the fifteenth-century expulsion of the Jews from this region, they were actively involved in lending to landowners even though there were restrictions on the degree to which they could possess land, as they could rely on rent charges. All of the chapters also examine the question of where the lenders originated, and interestingly, in England and the Low Countries, most credit is found to have originated locally, usually from other farmers in the vicinity. In contrast, in Spain, and sixteenth-century northern Italy, urban centres such as Zaragoza and Milan are shown to have been important sources of capital. Dermineur also shows in her chapter that in late eighteenth-century France, there was a sudden shift from local mortgagees in the seigneurie of Delle to liberal professionals from towns.

12.1 England

Another situation, which clearly emerges from these studies, is that England's different path of legal development, in which the laws of property tenure and inheritance remained separate from the common law of contract, marked an important contrast with all the other various regimes described here, which were based more specifically on Roman law principles. As the editors note above in their Introduction, the variety of principles which *all* legal systems (including English customary law) used were variations on basic forms, but the different way in which the pattern of mortgaging developed in England has, I think, serious implications for the theory which links secure property rights with economic growth. For the early modern period, the separation of the law of real property from contract had quite profound implications for how credit markets developed in England. Elsewhere, the idea of a rent charge secured by both fixed and movable properties was used to avoid the Catholic Church's doctrine that a bare interest rate, simply designed to earn money from money, was a form of usury. In England, both lawsuits of debt (restitution of movable property) and contract (tort, a breach of trust) were covered by a different set of laws than the customs of each manor, which governed the nature of rent in relation to the rights of the lord of a manor. As a result, real (landed) property could not be attached (or distrained, i.e. lawfully seized) by a creditor to meet a court awarded judgment against a debtor in a case involving a debt or broken contract. A distraint could only be made upon movable goods. This was one of the reasons why England dealt with the problem of usury in a statutory fashion by providing a maximum state-sanctioned allowable interest rate in 1571 (Jones 1989). As a result, the mortgage was conceived of legally in a completely different jurisdictional and procedural framework, even while many concepts were shared, which was typical of English law at the time.

The picture presented in the chapter by Briggs is one of very little mortgaging in medieval England, except for a small number of isolated manors where it was common, and these worked in a similar way to contemporary mortgages on the continent. However, in general, Briggs concludes that this situation is likely to have been the result of the terms of mortgage law in England containing too much risk of forfeiture for the borrower, and not enough flexibility for the lender in terms of renegotiation. As Waddilove demonstrates, this changed in terms of legal doctrine in the sixteenth century with the development of the equity of redemption. Equity was an important principle, which worked alongside the common law and its objective was mitigation of the harshness of strict legal rules, especially concerning the penal conditions of sealed contractual bonds of the sort used by Shakespeare in *The Merchant of Venice*, in the case of a misfortune such as the loss of a ship in a storm. To achieve this, the Lord Chancellor, primarily in the Court of Chancery, developed a complex series of procedures to apply fair discretionary principles. But equity also guided the principles of the law of real property, which was based, similarly, on the discretionary interpretation of remembered customary rules of each manor in the country concerning land tenure. Thus, equity was not just the individual application of discretion but also operated as a guiding precedent, creating a national form of procedure as doctrine. As Waddilove demonstrates, the equity of redemption allowed the mortgagor to remain the true owner of the property despite lacking legal title, while the mortgagee's interest was mere security and forfeiture had to be declared by a court. What this meant in reality was that mortgages became a convenient way of creating a long-term, legal, interest-bearing debt, which provided an income for the lender and capital for the borrower. Waddilove stresses two important points. One is that the concept of ancient inheritance, which has also been termed 'the family land bond' (discussed below), was now not threatened by all but the most extensive over-borrowing. The second is flexibility, in that the law allowed the mortgagor and mortgagee a great deal of freedom to arrange their methods of repayment privately.

Waddilove shows how the doctrine developed through important test cases in Chancery within the much broader prevailing context of social credit in England at the time which, as noted above, was very flexible. Relatively little work has been done to assess the actual level of mortgaging in the sixteenth century, though a study of Devon found that most mortgages were made between the gentry, with around of five or six a year being enrolled (Kew 1967, pp. 168, 176–178). The chapters by both Gayton and Wedd focus on local case studies for the seventeenth century in order to examine change over time, the social context of the lenders and borrowers and the value of their transactions. However, Gayton's survey is based on an examination of conditional surrenders of title in a selection of manors from Hampshire, whereas Wedd has examined transactions from Kent, which was the only significant area of England to practice partible inheritance or 'gavelkind'. This also meant that most land here was freehold, which provided a great deal of freedom of disposition in contrast to the copyhold land examined by Gayton. Gayton further emphasizes that in the area of her study only 'copyhold of inheritance' could be mortgaged. Tenures held in so-called copyhold for lives often listed two or even three relatives with stated inheritance rights, and these were not mortgaged. In their study of copyhold mortgages in the manor of Slaidburn in Yorkshire, French and Hoyle do not distinguish between copyhold of inheritance and copyhold for lives (French and Hoyle 1999). Briggs suggests that mortgages of freehold land were no more common than those on customary land, and Brooks has also argued that by the seventeenth-century possessors of copyhold were increasingly being given more freedom to devise at will (Briggs, this volume; Brooks 2013, pp. 195ff.). However, since custom could vary between each manor, this contrast between the different forms of copyhold is something which will need further investigation, especially with regard to the ability of the equity of redemption to overcome problems of multiple interests in a property by distributing obligations and responsibilities privately as long as forfeiture was not a possibility.

The contributions of Gayton and Wedd, together with French and Hoyle's study of Slaidburn, show an impressive rise in the number of mortgages taken out over the course of the seventeenth century, especially during the Restoration period (French and Hoyle 1999, pp. 370–371). It is during this period, and especially during the chancellorship of Lord Nottingham in the 1680s, that the doctrine of the equity of redemption is usually said to have become fixed as an established legal norm (Sugarman and Warrington 1995). Curiously, Gayton shows a decline in the early eighteenth century (her end date is 1735). This was not the case in Slaidburn, and we certainly know from other sources that overall in England, the amount of mortgaging in England rose considerably in the eighteenth century (see below). All of these studies demonstrate important common features of mortgaging. Mortgaging was usual for all sizes of landholding, and the value borrowed per rental value per acre could also vary considerably, which indicates that the amount of security desired by the borrower was considered to be more than just a ratio of the annual rental value. Also, although there were always outside investors, only a few were from distant urban areas, and overall, the mortgage market was a local one where both farmers and tradesmen sought investment opportunities. Gayton has also provided a very valuable breakdown of the reasons why people borrowed. Interestingly, what Fig. 3.4 shows is that, while borrowing to deal with financial difficulties was high in the early seventeenth century, it declined after the 1680s, whereas borrowing for investment and to provide 'cash' legacies for children increased.

12.2 Civil Law Areas

The remaining contributions here range in period and geographical focus from fourteenth-century Zaragoza (Schraer) to eighteenth-century France (Dermineur), including three studies focusing on the Northern and Southern Low Countries before the revolt of the Netherlands: Zuijderduijn considers the province of Holland in the sixteenth century; Van Onacker, the Campine area to the north-east of Antwerp in the fifteenth and sixteenth centuries; and Limberger and de Vijlder cover fifteenth- and sixteenth-century Brabant. Finally, De Luca and Lorenzini consider the rise of mortgaging in seventeenth-century northern Italy. As noted, all of these studies have important things to say about how mortgages worked in the local context of each area, but all demonstrate a similar range of practices based on the Roman law principles outlined in the editors' Introduction. These practices were designed to provide capital for the borrower and income for the lender, as in England, but dealt with the need to deal legally with the Catholic Church's prohibition against usury by defining a mortgage as a type of rent or as an annuity, which was allowed under canon law. By the eighteenth century in France, other types of obligations bearing an interest rate of 5%, which could be secured with collateral had also become common (Dermineur, this volume). As this volume's geographical coverage suggests, the Low Countries has been a particularly intensively studied area, and what is striking is that in all the areas within that region studied here, as well as in thirteenth- and fourteenth-century Spain, both the range of formal procedures as well as the institutionalised practice of mortgaging was already common in the medieval period using remarkably similar legal forms derived from a common body of law and designed to confirm to universal canon law about usury, albeit adapted and developed through local legal institutions.

Both Van Onacker and Zuijderduijn make reference to Hernando de Soto's argument in exploring the proposition that there was a positive correlation between a reliable system of property rights and the precocious economic growth found in the late medieval Low Countries. This theory argues that the legal security of using property was the key in freeing up capital so that it could be invested with more confidence in agricultural improvement or industrial development. However, Van Onacker's study shows that while the institutional security and predictability of procedure for both mortgagors and mortgagees offered by local courts could certainly be used to provide capital for economic investment, the same legal system in a different area could be used to provide borrowing primarily used to meet cyclical demands such as marriage, death and land amalgamation, and for other reasons unrelated to growth. For northern Italy, De Luca and Lorenzini also find that mortgage borrowing could be used for cyclical as well as investment purposes, but they find that the latter was increasingly the case in the sixteenth century. In general, the contributions to the collection show that the security offered by law both to protect creditors and to allow debtors time for repayment before foreclosure was very similar, which begs the question why did some areas like northern Italy and the Low Countries see economic growth, while others did not?

An even more serious problem for this theory is presented by the case of England, as discussed above. Although the Low Countries were certainly much wealthier than England in the fifteenth and early sixteenth centuries when mortgaging was difficult in the latter country, England underwent very rapid economic growth from about 1550 on, until the end of the century, when mortgaging was still very uncommon (Muldrew 1998). There was clearly a great deal of economic growth in terms of profitable farming by yeomen, but even more in terms of the expansion of interurban trade and the massive surge in London's population. Further, most of this growth was achieved not through the security of lending on collateral defined by property rights but via credit secured only by word of mouth. Certainly, there was an extremely robust and reliable legal system, but it was based primarily on flexible contracts rather than collateralised security. It is true that this did lead to a depression in the 1590s and slower growth through to the 1630s, but as the work here shows, this was the period when English mortgaging began to grow beyond the level of gentry finance. Also, as noted below, land registration which had developed in the province of Holland, and was subsequently advocated by a number of post-1650 reformers in England, failed to become law, but this had little effect on the huge rise in mortgaging in the eighteenth century.

This then seems to contradict the New Institutional Economics (NIE) position that legal security of *property* and transparency of ownership or tenurial rights somehow has a positive correlation to economic growth. The extra security offered by mortgages was undoubtedly useful, but it does not seem to have been the key factor. The credit system in England relied much more heavily on personal trust rather than on securitised collateral. Certainly, lenders took notice of the property of borrowers, but the law was not organised in a way that provided legal security from the onset of the loan. It could only be obtained through the initiation of a lawsuit (Shepard 2015). As a result, the development of English mortgaging had to accommodate itself to this existing institutional and cultural set of practices. In continental civil law regimes, while informal credit certainly existed, notaries processed larger loans in most places, and as a number of authors here note, mortgaging was integrated into this market for secure credit. But in many places, the poor also needed to provide security for loans through the institutions of state-operated public pawn shops where material goods were deposited for loans at interest (Maegraith and Muldrew 2015, p. 379). As Waddilove argues here, the equity of redemption developed slowly to provide flexibility, and the legal historian Christopher Brooks has also argued that what landowners wanted from lawyers in the sixteenth century was not added security but to be able to 'use and enjoy, demise or alienate their lands with as much room for manoeuvre as possible' (Brooks 2013, p. 194). The

English continued to prefer the normative acceptance of the redemption and private negotiable nature of equity rather than the public negotiation that, say, the court officers in the Low Countries offered. It could also be argued with the same correlative logic of the NIE security/growth paradigm that the English system allowed mortgagors to borrow more freely because exposure was not made public and could even be hidden from family members (this is something which the scrivener John Cannon, mentioned below, did, eventually requiring his wealthy aunt to settle his debts so the land would not be lost from the family, even though it was only four acres; Money 2010, pp. 147, 156). Both positions are hard to prove by establishing a causal link, however. Yet what remains certain in both cases is that in order for mortgaging to take place both parties relied on a legal system in which provided rules, practices and penalties, which were satisfactory enough to make them willing participants. If it had been the case that other powerful forces had supported the absolute right of unencumbered primogeniture or the total prohibition of interest rate lending, the mortgage market could easily have been stymied.

Zuijderduijn, van Bochove and Deneweth have also given attention to de Soto's more specific assertion that the transparency of land registers was also beneficial to releasing more capital through mortgage lending. This, again, does not obviously hold true in a comparison with the province of Holland and England. By the mid-seventeenth century, Holland had well established and effective public land registers, which could be consulted with minimal effort and cost. Numerous English commentators, including law reformers during the Commonwealth period, argued that the creation of such registers in England would indeed free up credit and aid economic growth, which they termed improvement (Van Bochove et al. 2015, pp. 10–11).[3] However, registries were successfully created in just two counties—Yorkshire and Middlesex—out of 39. For most of the country, landowners preferred to keep their financial affairs private, but this did not stop the development of mortgaging in England in the late seventeenth century. Van Bochove, Deneweth and Zuijderduijn acknowledge that the crucial role of brokers to match mortgagors and mortgagees could develop with and without systems of registration in different institutional and cultural contexts (Van Bochove et al. 2015, pp. 28–31).

But this understates the case. Not only did mortgage lending occur in England, the late seventeenth and eighteenth centuries saw the firm acceptance of the equity of redemption and an explosion of mortgaging activity. Increasingly, local attorneys made most of their money from conveyancing. M. Miles's studies of two West Riding attorneys show that one made 47% of his profits from conveyancing, and the other 40%, in comparison with 25 and 13%, respectively, derived from litigation. Also, in an examination of the securities held by John Howarth on behalf of his clients from 1762–1796, the amounts of mortgages were consistently between two and ten times as valuable as those on bond. In addition to this, Henry Horwitz and Patrick Polden have found that in the court of Chancery between 1627 and 1735, lawsuits over debts and bonds dropped, while those concerning estate matters and other business contracts rose (Miles 1981, pp. 133–142, 1984; Horwitz and Polden 1996, p. 35).[4] The court books of the manor of Cheltenham (Gloucestershire) for the years 1692–1803 also reveal a steady rise over the eighteenth century in the number of copyhold mortgages recorded per annum, with a particularly sharp increase in the last decade of this period (Hodsdon 2010). In their article on Slaidburn, French and Hoyle also show that although in numerical terms there was not a great expansion in mortgage lending in the eighteenth century, in this period the ratio between the amounts borrowed and the sale value of land reached, in their words, 'absurd levels' (French and Hoyle 1999, p. 379). The number of local attorneys actually expanded in the eighteenth century to deal with the great amount of conveyancing involving mortgages. Landowners in England evidently preferred to trust the local knowledge of their neighbouring attorneys over the efficiency of public registers. This is more evidence that flexibility mattered more than transparency of security. Indeed, evidence for such attitudes can be found in the 'chronicles', or memoir, of the small Somerset scrivener John Cannon, who in the 1730s and 1740s recorded numerous occasions where he drew up local mortgages. In these examples, we can see people, like Cannon himself, who secretly mortgaged his land against the will of his aunt, or mortgages involving numerous family members, and also individuals who raised more capital by re-mortgaging for greater amounts. This certainly involved more risk: Cannon included a story involving one individual who had borrowed too much being pursued for foreclosure by the local attorney and barricading himself together with some of his friends in a local alehouse while firing shots at those who approached (Money 2010, p. 695)!

A close study of Cannon's chronicles reveals an aspect which I believe was crucial to the expansion of the mortgage market in England after 1700, which was a means of securing an expansion of the money supply to facilitate economic growth not by providing investment capital but by transforming informal credit into local paper money.[5] The obsession of modern economics literature in linking credit and micro-finance to investment-based growth has seriously neglected the equally important question of how macroeconomics can be used to understand the need to provide consumers, especially poorer consumers, with the purchasing power to maintain demand for any goods, which investment might be able to produce. In England, in the eighteenth century, mortgages were used to solve this problem by creating capital which local landowners could use to pay for goods and labour with paper notes of hand. Whether this was the case in the areas studied here for earlier periods in the economically advanced Low Countries is a difficult question. But it also freed up a vast amount of capital. Certainly, mortgaging could provide capital for agrarian improvement and later investment in canals and industry, but mostly it acted as a form of currency creation laid on top of the very different interpersonal credit system, which had developed based on personal trust.

But whatever the motives for mortgaging land, what this volume demonstrates above all was that what mattered most was not the absolute security of property, but the acceptance by all parties of legal rules and procedures that were both robust, if needed, but flexible for the most part. The early modern legal and economic world was one of continual negotiation rather than absolute standards, and the degree to which different legal rules and institutions helped or hindered economic growth is more complex than the simple ability to create capital from land, and protecting landed assets for one's spouse or children was the crucial point around which negotiation took place. As we saw at the outset of this Afterword, the current value of UK property completely dwarfs the value of corporate investment and debt. It could be argued that this sucks investment capital out of more risky business activity. As long as the population continues to grow faster than the housing supply, the returns on capital invested in buildings and land will remain very attractive. In the early modern period, there was much more relationship between the productive value of land expressed through rent and its capital value, but inheritance and the maintenance of familial social standing through time were just as vital. It also remains true that inheritance plays a vitally important role in property value for the middle class today. It is perhaps a salutary point, of which economists should take note, that if there is a direction which change over time has taken from the early modern period until today, it is that the value created through mortgages has become *more* the result of social than productive factors.

Notes

1. https://www.ons.gov.uk/economy/nationalaccounts/uksectoraccounts/bulletins/nationalbalancesheet/2016estimates.
2. Whittle (1998, p. 45, Table 4) shows that a significant share of land was transferred by inheritance at Hevingham (Norfolk) before the Black Death (e.g. 50% of acreage transferred in the period 1274–1299), but that this share declined in the fifteenth century. Razi found that at Halesowen (Worcestershire) between 1351 and 1430, 174 out of a total of 417 land transactions (42%) were post-mortem between kin (i.e. inheritances), and 57% of the total were between kin (Razi 1981, p. 17, Table 3). Mullan and Britnell found that on the bishopric of Winchester estate between 1269 and 1349, 46.5% of recorded land transfers were intra-familial, and most of these (34.5% of the total) were by inheritance; equivalent figures for 1350–1415 were 39.2 and 33.7%. Most of the large, standard holdings such as 'virgates' passed by inheritance; of 4340 transfers of virgates across the whole estate in the period 1320–1349, 60.0% were inheritances, though this declined to 37.4% in 1350–1379 and 37.7% in 1380–1415; Mullan and Britnell (2010, pp. 41, 103). For early modern evidence, see French and Hoyle (2007, pp. 184–190).
3. On the general subject of improvement, see Slack (2014).
4. This is discussed at greater length in Muldrew (2011, pp. 398–399).
5. This is discussed in my forthcoming study, 'The social acceptance of paper credit as currency in eighteenth-century England: A case study of Glastonbury *c.*1720–1742' in D. Coffman, M. Lorenzini and C. Lorandini (eds.), *Financing in Europe. Evolution, Coexistence and Complementarity of Lending Practices from the Middle Ages to Modern Times* (Palgrave, 2018).

References

Primary Sources

Hodsdon, J. (ed.), 2010. *The Court Books of the Manor of Cheltenham 1692–1803* (Gloucester Record Series, vol. 24).

Money, J. (ed.), 2010. *The Chronicles of John Cannon, Excise Officer and Writing Master* (Oxford: British Academy).

Poos, L.R. and L. Bonfield (eds.), 1998. *Select Cases in Manorial Courts 1250–1550. Property and Family Law* (London: Selden Society, vol. 114).

Secondary Works

Allen, R.C., 1992. *Enclosure and the Yeoman. The Agricultural Development of the South Midlands 1450–1850* (Oxford: Oxford University Press).

Baer, W.C., 2002. 'The institution of residential investment in seventeenth-century London', *Business History Review*, vol. 76, pp. 515–551.

Brooks, C., 2013. 'The agrarian problem in revolutionary England', in J. Whittle (ed.), *Landlords and Tenants in Britain, 1440–1660: Tawney's* Agrarian Problem *Revisited* (Woodbridge: Boydell).

De Soto, H., 2000. *The Mystery of Capital. Why Capitalism Triumphs in the West and Fails Everywhere Else* (London: Black Swan).

De Vries, J., 1984. *European Urbanization, 1500–1800* (London: Methuen).

French, H.R. and R.W. Hoyle, 1999. 'The land market of a Pennine manor: Slaidburn, 1650–1780', *C&C*, vol. 14, pp. 349–383.

French, H.R. and Hoyle, R.W., 2007. *The Character of English Rural Society. Earls Colne, 1550–1750* (Manchester: Manchester University Press).

Goldthwaite, R., 2009. *The Economy of Renaissance Florence* (Baltimore: Johns Hopkins University Press).

Horwitz, H. and P. Polden, 1996. 'Continuity or change in the Court of Chancery in the seventeenth and eighteenth centuries?,' *Journal of British Studies*, vol. 35, pp. 24–57.

Hoyle, R.W., 1995. 'Debate: The land-family bond in England', *P&P*, vol. 143, pp. 151–73.

Jones, N., 1989. *God and the Moneylenders: Usury and Law in Early Modern England* (Oxford: Basil Blackwell).

Kew, J.E., 1967. 'Mortgages in mid Tudor Devonshire', *Report and Transactions of the Devonshire Association*, vol. 99, pp. 165–179.

Macfarlane, A.D., 1978. *The Origins of English Individualism: The Family, Property and Social Transition* (Oxford: Basil Blackwell).

McKellar, E., 1999. *The Birth of Modern London: The Development and Design of the City, 1660–1720* (Manchester: Manchester University Press).

Maegraith, J. and C. Muldrew, 2015. 'Consumption and material life', in Hamish Scott (ed.), *Oxford Handbook of Early Modern European History*, 2 vols (Oxford: Oxford University Press), ii, pp. 369–397.

Miles, M., 1981. 'The money market in the early industrial revolution: The evidence from West Riding attorneys *c.*1750–1800,' *Business History*, vol. 23, pp. 127–146.

Miles, M., 1984. '"Eminent practitioners": The new visage of country attorneys *c.*1750–1800', in G.R. Rubin and D. Sugarman (eds.), *Law, Economy and Society, 1750–1914: Essays in the History of English Law* (Abingdon: Professional Books), pp. 470–503.

Muldrew, C., 1998. *The Economy of Obligation: The Culture of Credit and Social Relations in Early Modern England* (Basingstoke: Palgrave).

Muldrew, C., 2001. 'Hard food for midas: Cash and its social value in early modern England', *P&P*, vol. 170, pp. 78–120.

Mullan, J. and R. Britnell, 2010. *Land and Family: Trends and Local Variations in the Peasant Land Market on the Winchester Bishopric Estates, 1263–1415* (Hatfield: University of Hertfordshire Press).

North, D.C., 1990. *Institutions, Institutional Change, and Economic Performance* (Cambridge: Cambridge University Press).

Quarry, J., S. Low, G. Hill, and R. Baveja, 2012. *Perspectives on the UK Retail Banking Market* (New York: Oliver Wyman Financial Services), at: http://www.oliverwyman.com/content/dam/oliver-wyman/global/en/files/archive/2012/Perspectives_on_the_UK_retail_banking_market.pdf. Accessed July 2017.

Razi, Z., 1981. 'Family, land and the village community in later medieval England', *P&P*, vol. 93, pp. 3–36.

Shepard, A., 2015. *Accounting for Oneself: Worth, Status and the Social Order in Early Modern England* (Oxford: Oxford University Press).

Slack, P., 2014. *The Invention of Improvement: Information and Material Progress in Seventeenth-Century England* (Oxford: Oxford University Press).

Sreenivasan, G., 1991. 'The land-family bond at Earls Colne (Essex), 1550–1650', *P&P*, vol. 131, pp. 3–37.

Sugarman, D. and R.A. Warrington, 1995. 'Land law, citizenship, and the invention of "Englishness". The strange world of the equity of redemption', in J. Brewer and S. Staves (eds.), *Early Modern Conceptions of Property* (Abingdon: Routledge), pp. 111–143.

Van Bochove, C., H. Deneweth, and J. Zuijderduijn, 2015. 'Real estate and mortgage finance in England and the low countries, 1300–1800', *C&C*, vol. 30, pp. 9–38.

Whittle, J., 1998. 'Individualism and the family-land bond: A reassessment of land transfer patterns among the English peasantry *c.*1270–1580', *P&P*, vol. 160, pp. 25–63.

Index

C. Briggs and J. Zuijderduijn (eds.), *Land and Credit*,
Palgrave Studies in the History of Finance,
https://doi.org/10.1007/978-3-319-66209-1

R

S

Z

The manufacturer's authorised representative in the EU is Springer Nature Customer Service Centre GmbH, Europaplatz 3, 69115 Heidelberg, Germany. If you have any concerns regarding our products, please contact ProductSafety@springernature.com

Printed and bound by CPI Group (UK) Ltd, Croydon, CR0 4YY
05/10/2026
02228140-0012